# Professional Azure SQL Database Administration

## Second Edition

Equip yourself with the skills to manage and maintain data in the cloud

Ahmad Osama

## Professional Azure SQL Database Administration
*Second Edition*

Author: Ahmad Osama

Technical Reviewers: Aaditya Pokkunuri and Shashikant Shakya

Managing Editor: Aditya Datar

Acquisitions Editors: Aditya Date and Karan Wadekar

Production Editor: Shantanu Zagade

Editorial Board: David Barnes, Mayank Bhardwaj, Ewan Buckingham, Simon Cox, Mahesh Dhyani, Taabish Khan, Manasa Kumar, Alex Mazonowicz, Douglas Paterson, Dominic Pereira, Shiny Poojary, Erol Staveley, Ankita Thakur, and Jonathan Wray

First Published: May 2018

Second Edition: July 2019

Production Reference: 1100719

ISBN: 978-1-78980-254-2

Published by Packt Publishing Ltd.

Livery Place, 35 Livery Street

Birmingham B3 2PB, UK

# Table of Contents

# Migrating a SQL Server Database to an Azure SQL Database

# Preface

**About**

This section briefly introduces the author, the coverage of this course, the technical skills you'll need to get started, and the hardware and software required to complete all of the included activities and exercises.

# About the Book

Despite being the cloud version of SQL Server, Azure SQL Database differs in key ways when it comes to management, maintenance, and administration. This book shows you how to administer Azure SQL Database to fully benefit from its wide range of features and functionality.

*Professional Azure SQL Database Administration - Second Edition* begins by covering the architecture and explaining the difference between Azure SQL Database and the on-premise SQL Server to help you get comfortable with Azure SQL Database. You'll perform common tasks such as migrating, backing up, and restoring a SQL Server database to an Azure database. As you progress, you'll study how you can save costs and manage and scale multiple SQL databases using elastic pools. You'll also implement a disaster recovery solution using standard and active geo-replication. Whether through learning different techniques to monitor and tune an Azure SQL database or improving performance using in-memory technology, this book will enable you to make the most out of Azure SQL Database's features and functionality for data management solutions.

By the end of this book, you'll be well versed with key aspects of an Azure SQL Database instance, such as migration, backup restorations, performance optimization, high availability, and disaster recovery.

## About the Author

**Ahmad Osama** works for Pitney Bowes India Pvt Ltd as a technical architect and is a Microsoft Data Platform Reconnect MVP and MCSE: SQL Server 2016 data management and analytics. At Pitney Bowes, he works on developing and maintaining high-performance on-premise and cloud SQL Server OLTP environments, building CI/CD environments for databases and automation. Other than his day-to-day work, Ahmad blogs at DataPlatformLabs and has written over 100 blogs on various topics, including SQL Server administration/development, Azure SQL Database, and Azure Data Factory. He regularly speaks at user group events and webinars conducted by the DataPlatformLabs community. You can reach him on LinkedIn at `ahmadosama3` or follow his Twitter handle, `@_ahmadosama`.

## Objectives

- Understand Azure SQL Database configuration and pricing options.

- Provision a new SQL database or migrate an existing on-premise SQL Server database to Azure SQL Database.

- Back up and restore Azure SQL Database.

- Secure an Azure SQL database.

- Scale an Azure SQL database.

- Monitor and tune an Azure SQL database.

- Implement high availability and disaster recovery with Azure SQL Database.

- Automate common management tasks with PowerShell.

- Develop a scalable cloud solution with Azure SQL Database.

- Manage, maintain, and secure managed instances.

## Audience

If you're a database administrator, database developer, or an application developer interested in developing new applications or migrating existing ones with Azure SQL database, then this book is for you. Prior experience of working with an on-premise SQL Server or Azure SQL Database, along with a basic understanding of PowerShell scripts and C# code, is necessary to grasp the concepts covered in this book.

## Approach

Each section in this book has been explicitly designed to engage and stimulate you so that you can retain and apply what you learn in a practical context with maximum impact. You'll learn how to tackle intellectually stimulating programming challenges that will prepare you for real-world topics through test-driven development practices.

## Hardware Requirements

For an optimal student experience, we recommend the following hardware configuration:

- Processor: Pentium 4, 1.8 GHz or higher (or equivalent)

- Memory: 4 GB RAM

- Hard disk: 10 GB free space

- An internet connection

## Software Requirements

You'll also need the following software installed in advance:

- Windows 8 or above.

- The latest version of Google Chrome.

- An Azure subscription.

- The Azure Machine Learning service is in public preview at the time of writing this book and should be enabled by sending an email to `sqldbml@microsoft.com`.

- SQL Server Management Studio 17.2 or above.

- PowerShell 5.1 or above.

- Microsoft Azure PowerShell (the new Azure PowerShell Az module). To install the new Azure PowerShell Az module and enable backward compatibility with AzureRM, please visit https://dataplatformlabs.com/the-new-azure-powershell-module-az/.

- Microsoft RML Utilities.

- Visual Studio 2013 or above (Community Edition).

## Conventions

Code words in text, database table names, folder names, filenames, file extensions, pathnames, dummy URLs, user input, and GitHub handles are shown as follows: "The application defines a single connection using the `OpenConnectionForKey` method defined in the Elastic Database Client Library. The syntax for `OpenConnectionForKey` is given in the following snippet."

A block of code is set as follows:

```
SELECT COUNT(*) FROM Sales.Customers GO

INSERT INTO Warehouse.Colors

VALUES(100,'Light Green',1,getdate(),getdate()+10);
```

New terms and important words are shown in bold. Words that you see on the screen, for example, in menus or dialog boxes, appear in the text like this: "If you don't wish to delete the firewall rule and have accidentally clicked **Delete**, instead of clicking **Save** in the top menu, click **Discard** to undo the changes."

## Installation and Setup

The Azure SQL Database and the Azure SQL Server Database names should be unique across Microsoft Azure and should follow these naming rules and conventions at https://docs.microsoft.com/en-us/azure/architecture/best-practices/naming-conventions.

## Sign up for a Free Azure Account

1. Open the following link in a browser: https://azure.microsoft.com/en-us/free/.

2. Select **Start Free**. In the sign-up page, login using your Microsoft account and follow the steps to create a free Azure account.

3. If you don't have a Microsoft account, you can create a new one by selecting **Create one!**

4. An Azure account requires you to provide credit card details. However, no money is charged even if you have exhausted your free credit or free month. The resources you created will be stopped and can only be started once you sign-up for a paid account.

## Install SQL Server Management Studio

Follow the instructions to download the latest version of SQL Server Management studio provided here: https://docs.microsoft.com/en-us/sql/ssms/download-sql-server-management-studio-ssms?view=sql-server-2017.

## Installing Microsoft PowerShell 5.1

1. Open the following URL in the browser to get to open the download page: https://www.microsoft.com/en-us/download/details.aspx?id=54616.

2. Click on the **Download** button and select **Win8.1AndW2K12R2-KB3191564-x64. msu**. Click on **Next** to download and install the Windows Management Framework 5.1 to upgrade to PowerShell 5.1.

## Installing Microsoft Azure PowerShell

1. Open the following link in a browser https://www.microsoft.com/web/downloads/platform.aspx.

2. Scroll to the end and select x64 under Download WebPI 5.0 to download the web platform installer.

3. Double click the downloaded exe file and follow the steps to install Web PI 5.0

4. Open Web PI and type Microsoft Azure PowerShell in the search box. Follow the steps to download the latest version.

**Microsoft RML Utilities**

1.  Open the following link in a browser: https://www.microsoft.com/en-us/download/details.aspx?id=4511.

2.  Click **Download** to download the installer. Click the downloaded file and follow the instructions to install RML Utilities.

**Installing Visual Studio Community Edition**

1.  Visual Studio command prompt is required to generate self-signed certificates. As there's no easy way to install only the Visual Studio command prompt, it's advised to install the Visual Studio 2013 or above community edition.

2.  Open the following link in a browser: https://visualstudio.microsoft.com/downloads/.

3.  Download and install the Visual Studio 2017 community edition and follow the instructions to install it.

4.  You may get a different version to download. Download the latest one.

## Installing the Code Bundle

Download the code files from GitHub at https://github.com/TrainingByPackt/Professional-Azure-SQL-Database-Administration-Second-Edition and place them in a new folder called `C:\Code`. Refer to these code files for the complete code bundle.

## Additional Resources

We also have other code bundles from our rich catalog of books and videos available at https://github.com/PacktPublishing/. Check them out!

# Microsoft Azure SQL Database Primer

**Learning Objectives**

By the end of this lesson, you will be able to:

- Describe the architecture of Microsoft Azure SQL Database
- Identify the differences between the on-premises SQL Server and Azure SQL Database
- Provision a SQL managed instance
- Provision an Azure SQL database using the Azure portal and Windows PowerShell

This lesson introduces the Azure SQL Database architecture, the difference between Azure SQL Database and on-premises SQL Server, and Azure SQL Database managed instance (SQL managed instance).

# Introduction

There are very few relational database systems as established and widely used as Microsoft's SQL Server. Azure SQL Database, released on February 1, 2010, is a cloud database service that is based on Microsoft's SQL Server.

It is compatible with most SQL Server features and is optimized for **Software-as-a-Service** (**SaaS**) applications.

As organizations are adopting cloud computing and moving their applications into the cloud, Azure SQL Database offers everything that **Database-as-a-Service** (**DBaaS**) can offer. Azure SQL Database is a DBaaS option for any organization with applications built on SQL Server Database.

Azure SQL Database uses familiar Transact-SQL programming and a user interface that is well known and is also easy to adopt. It is therefore important for SQL Server Database administrators and developers to learn how to use Azure SQL Database.

> **Note**
>
> Azure SQL Database is also known as SQL Azure or SQL Database instance.

This lesson covers the Azure SQL Database architecture in detail. After familiarizing ourselves with the architecture, we'll learn how to provision Azure SQL Database through activities and explore pricing, settings, and its properties. We'll also identify the key differences between Azure SQL Database and SQL Server – mainly the SQL Server features that are not supported by Azure SQL Database.

# The Azure SQL Database Architecture

Azure SQL Database is a highly scalable multi-tenant and a highly available **Platform-as-a-Service** (**PaaS**) or Database-as-a-Service (DBaaS) offering from Microsoft.

Microsoft takes care of the operating system (OS), storage, networking, virtualization, servers, installation, upgrades, infrastructure management, and maintenance.

Azure SQL Database has the following deployment options:

- Single
- Elastic pool
- Managed instance

Azure SQL Database allows users to focus only on managing data, and is divided into four layers that work together to provide users with relational database functionality, as shown in the following diagram:

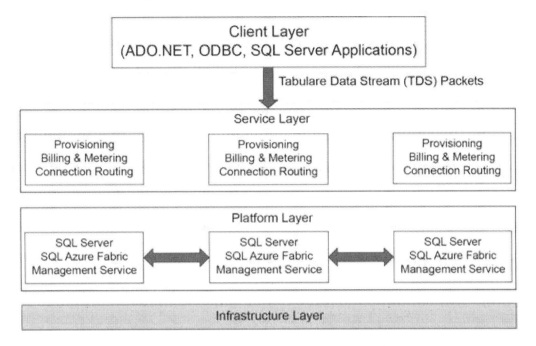

Figure 1.1: The four layers of Azure SQL Database

> **Note**
>
> If you were to compare it to the on-premise SQL Server architecture, other than the **Service Layer**, the rest of the architecture is pretty similar.

## Client Layer

The client layer acts as an interface for applications to access a SQL database. It can be either on-premises or on Microsoft Azure. The **Tabular Data Stream** (**TDS**) is used to transfer data between a SQL database and applications. SQL Server also uses TDS to communicate with applications. This allows applications such as .NET, ODBC, ADO.NET, and Java to easily connect to Azure SQL Database without any additional requirements.

### Service Layer

The service layer acts as a gateway between the client and platform layers. It is responsible for:

- Provisioning a SQL database

- User authentication and SQL database validation

- Enforcing security (firewall rules and denial-of-service attacks)

- Billing and metering for a SQL database

- Routing connections from the client layer to the physical server hosting the SQL database in the platform layer

### Platform Layer

The platform layer consists of physical servers hosting SQL databases in data centers. Each SQL database is stored on one physical server and is replicated across two different physical servers:

As shown in *Figure 1.1*, the **Platform Layer** has two other components: Azure Fabric and Management Services. **Azure Fabric** is responsible for load balancing, automatic failover, and the automatic replication of a SQL database between physical servers. **Management Services** takes care of an individual server's health monitoring and patch updates.

### Infrastructure Layer

This layer is responsible for the administration of the physical hardware and the OS.

> **Note**
>
> Dynamic routing allows us to move a SQL database to different physical servers in the event of any hardware failures or for load distribution.

## Azure SQL Database Request Flow

The following diagram shows the Platform layer:

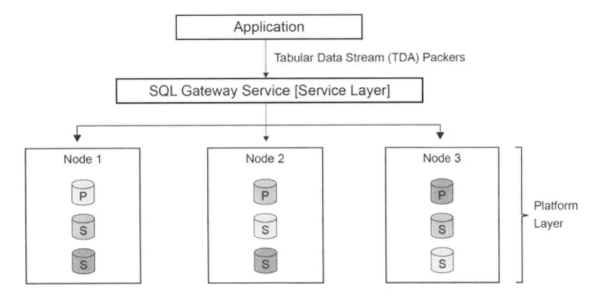

Figure 1.2: Platform layer – nodes

The application sends a TDS request (login, DML, or DDL queries) to the SQL database. The TDS request is not directly sent to the Platform layer. The request is first validated by the SQL Gateway Service at the Service layer.

The **Gateway Service** validates the login and firewall rules, and checks for denial-of-service attacks. It then dynamically determines the physical server on which the SQL database is hosted and routes the request to that physical server in the Platform layer. Dynamic routing allows the SQL database to be moved across physical servers or SQL instances in the event of hardware failures.

> **Note**
>
> Here, a node is a physical server. A single database is replicated across three physical servers internally by Microsoft to help the system recover from physical server failures. The Azure SQL Server user connects to just a logical name.
>
> Dynamic routing refers to routing the database request to the physical server that hosts an Azure SQL database. This routing is done internally and is transparent to the user. If one physical server hosting the database fails, dynamic routing will route the requests to the next available physical server hosting the Azure SQL database.
>
> The internals of dynamic routing are out of the scope of this book.

As shown in *Figure* 1.2, the Platform layer has three nodes: **Node 1**, **Node 2**, and **Node 3**. Each node has a primary replica of a SQL database and two secondary replicas of two different SQL databases from two different physical servers. The SQL database can fail over to the secondary replicas if the primary replica fails. This ensures the high availability of the SQL database.

## Provisioning an Azure SQL Database

Provisioning an Azure SQL database refers to creating a new and blank Azure SQL database.

In this section, we'll create a new SQL database in Azure using the Azure portal:

1. Open a browser and log in to the Azure portal using your Azure credentials: https://portal.azure.com.

2. On the left-hand navigation pane, select **Create a resource**:

Figure 1.3: Azure pane

3. On the **New** page, under **Databases**, select **SQL Database**:

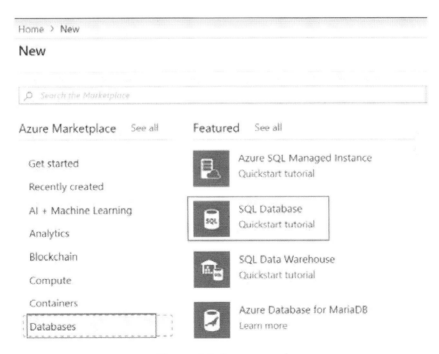

Figure 1.4: Azure panel

4. On the **SQL Database** page, under the **PROJECT DETAILS** heading, provide the **Subscription** and the **Resource group**. Click the **Create new** link under the **Resource group** textbox. In the pop-up box, set the **Resource group** name as `toystore`.

> **Note**
>
> A resource group is a logical container that is used to group Azure resources required to run an application.
>
> For example, the **toystore** retail web application uses different Azure resources such as Azure SQL Database, Azure VMs, and Azure Storage. All of these resources can be grouped in a single resource group, say, **toystore**.

The SQL database name should be unique across Microsoft Azure and should follow the following naming rules and conventions: https://docs.microsoft.com/en-us/azure/architecture/best-practices/naming-conventions.

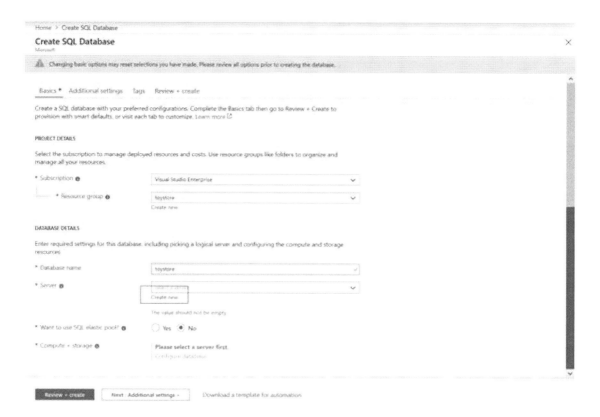

Figure 1.5: SQL database panel

5. Under the **DATABASE DETAILS** heading, enter the **Database name** and **Server**.

6. To create a new server, click on **Create new** under the **Server** textbox.

   On the **New server** page, provide the following details and click **Select** at the bottom of the page: **Server name**, **Server admin login**, **Password**, **Confirm password**, and **Location**.

   The server name should be unique across Microsoft Azure and should follow the following naming rules and conventions: https://docs.microsoft.com/en-us/azure/architecture/best-practices/naming-conventions.

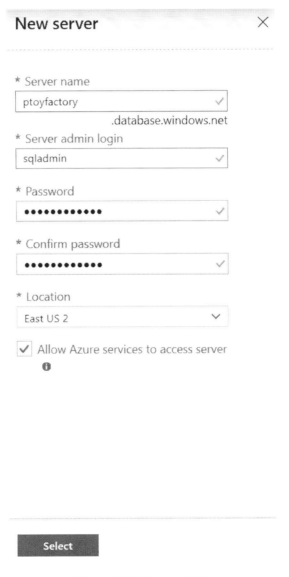

Figure 1.6: Server pane

7. Under the **Want to use SQL elastic pool?** option, select **No**.

8. In **Compute + storage**, click **Configure database** and then select **Standard**:

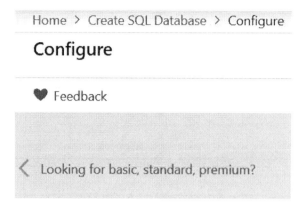

Figure 1.7: The Configure window

Note that you will have to click the **Looking for basic, standard, premium?** link for the standard option to be available:

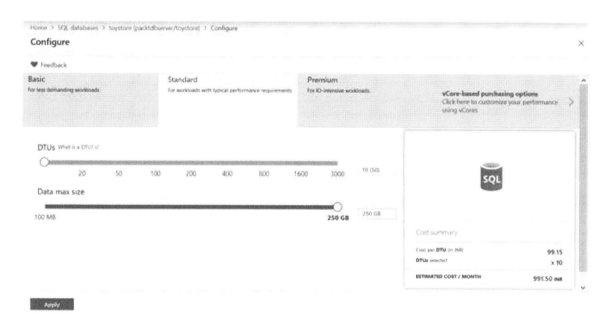

Figure 1.8: The Configure pane

9. Click **Review + create** to continue:

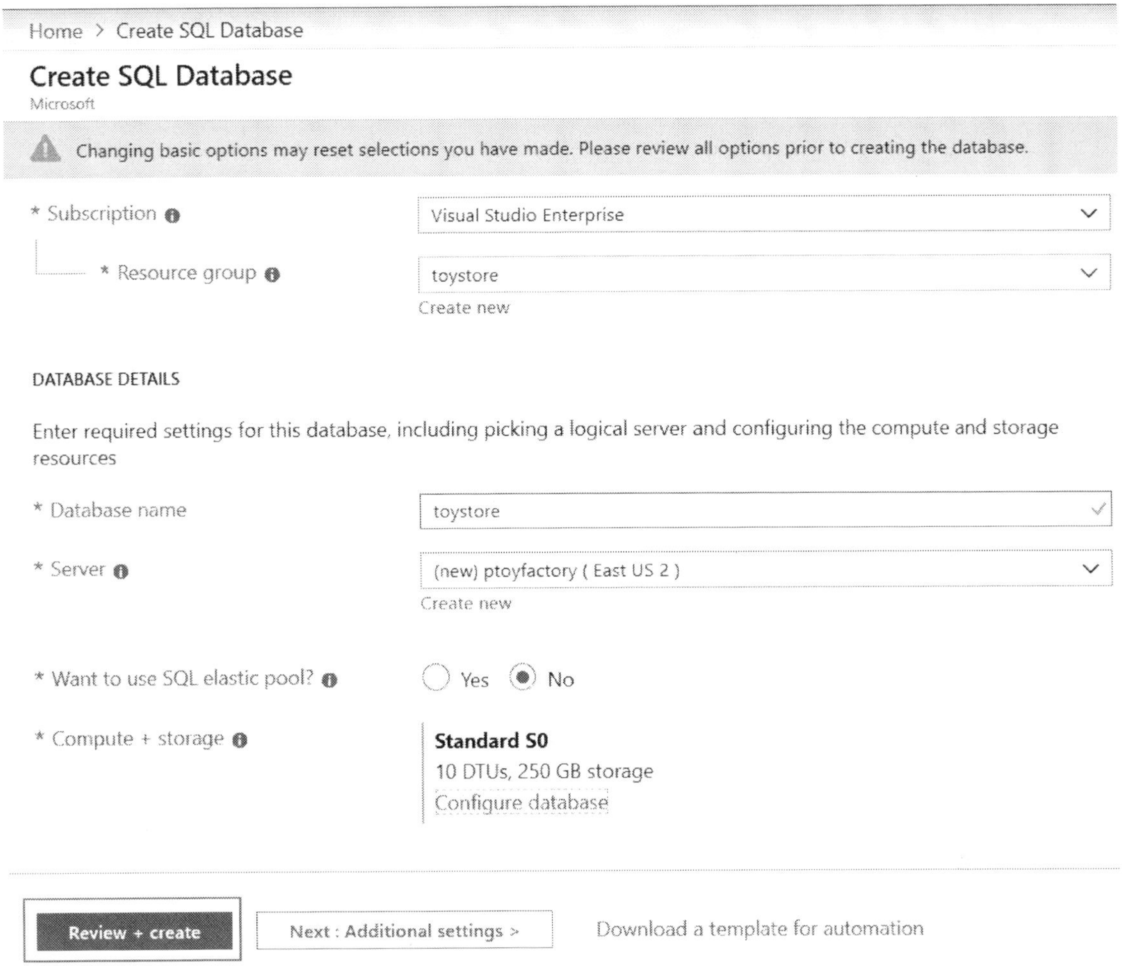

Home > Create SQL Database

## Create SQL Database
Microsoft

⚠ Changing basic options may reset selections you have made. Please review all options prior to creating the database.

\* Subscription ⓘ

| Visual Studio Enterprise | ∨ |

       \* Resource group ⓘ

| toystore | ∨ |

Create new

DATABASE DETAILS

Enter required settings for this database, including picking a logical server and configuring the compute and storage resources

\* Database name

| toystore | ✓ |

\* Server ⓘ

| (new) ptoyfactory ( East US 2 ) | ∨ |

Create new

\* Want to use SQL elastic pool? ⓘ    ◯ Yes   ⦿ No

\* Compute + storage ⓘ

**Standard S0**
10 DTUs, 250 GB storage
Configure database

[ Review + create ]    [ Next : Additional settings > ]    Download a template for automation

Figure 1.9: SQL pane provisioning panel

10. On the **TERMS** page, read through the terms and conditions and the configuration settings made so far:

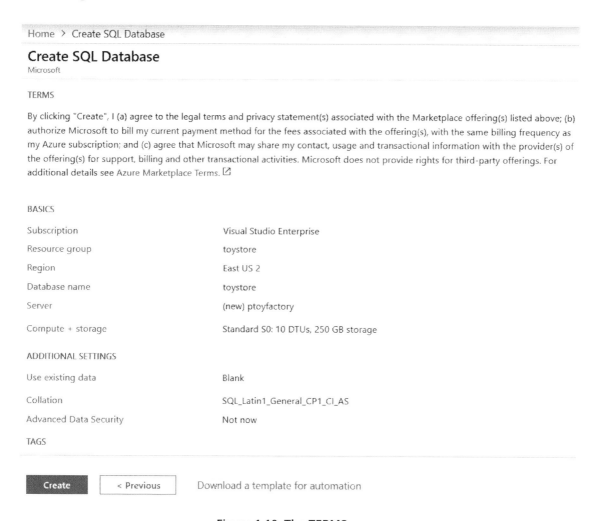

Figure 1.10: The TERMS page

11. Click **Create** to provision the SQL database.

Provisioning may take 2-5 minutes. Once the resources are provisioned, you'll get a notification, as shown in the following screenshot:

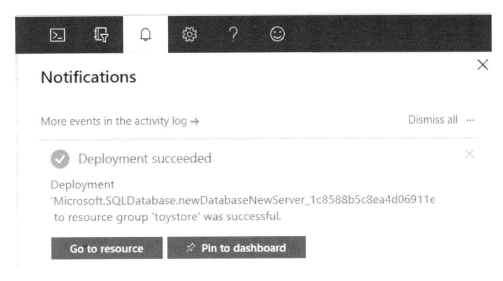

Figure 1.11: Notification after provision completion

12. Click **Go to resource** to go to the newly created SQL database.

## Connecting and Querying the SQL Database from the Azure Portal

In this section, we'll learn how to connect and query the SQL database from the Azure portal:

1. On the **toystore** pane, select **Query editor (preview)**:

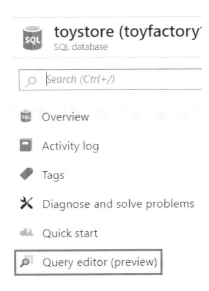

Figure 1.12: Toystore pane

2. On the **Query editor (preview)** pane, select **Login** and under **SQL server authentication**, provide the username and password:

Figure 1.13: The Query Editor pane

Select **OK** to authenticate and return to the **Query editor (preview)** pane:

3. Open **C:\Code\Lesson01\sqlquery.sql** in Notepad. Copy and paste the query from the notepad into the **Query 1** window in the **Query editor** on the Azure portal.

The query creates a new table (**orders**), populates it with sample data, and returns the top 10 rows from the **orders** table:

```
-- create a new orders table
CREATE TABLE orders
(
orderid INT IDENTITY(1, 1) PRIMARY KEY,
quantity INT, sales MONEY
);
--populate Orders table with sample data
;
WITH t1
     AS (SELECT 1 AS a
          UNION ALL
```

```
           SELECT 1),
    t2
    AS (SELECT 1 AS a
        FROM t1
              CROSS JOIN t1 AS b),
    t3
    AS (SELECT 1 AS a
        FROM t2
              CROSS JOIN t2 AS b),
    t4
    AS (SELECT 1 AS a
        FROM t3
              CROSS JOIN t3 AS b),
    t5
    AS (SELECT 1 AS a
        FROM t4
              CROSS JOIN t4 AS b),
    nums
    AS (SELECT Row_number()
                  OVER (
                   ORDER BY (SELECT NULL)) AS n
        FROM t5)
INSERT INTO orders SELECT n,
n * 10
FROM    nums;
GO
SELECT TOP 10 * from orders;
```

4. Select **Run** to execute the query. You should get the following output:

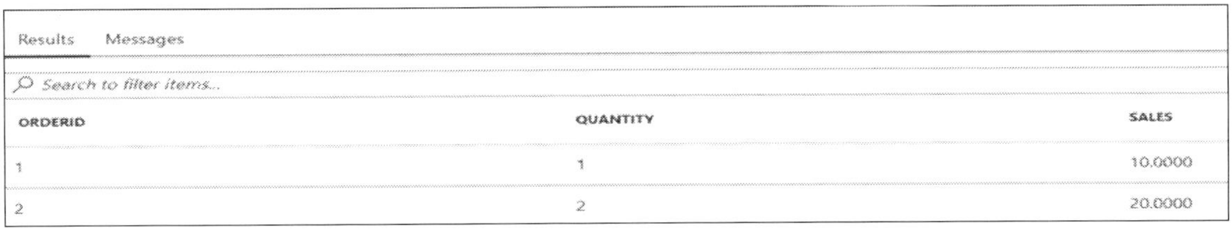

| Results | Messages |
| --- | --- |

*Search to filter items...*

| ORDERID | QUANTITY | SALES |
| --- | --- | --- |
| 1 | 1 | 10.0000 |
| 2 | 2 | 20.0000 |

Figure 1.14: Expected output

## Connecting to and Querying the SQL Database from SQL Server Management Studio

In this section, we'll connect to and query an Azure SQL database from **SQL Server Management Studio** (**SSMS**):

1.  Open SQL Server Management Studio. In the **Connect to Server** dialog box, set the **Server** type as **Database Engine**, if not already selected.

2.  Under the **Server name**, provide the Azure SQL server name. You can find the Azure SQL server in the **Overview** section of the **Azure SQL Database** pane on the Azure portal:

Figure 1.15: Overview pane of the toystore database

3.  Select **SQL Server Authentication** as the **Authentication** Type.

4.  Provide the login and password for Azure SQL Server and select **Connect**:

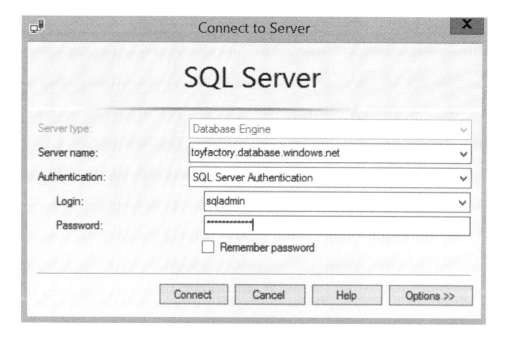

Figure 1.16: Login panel of SQL Server

You'll get an error saying **Your client IP address does not have access to the server**. To connect to Azure SQL Server, you must add the IP of the system you want to connect from under the firewall rule of Azure SQL Server. You can also provide a range of IP addresses to connect from:

Figure 1.17: New Firewall Rule pane

To add your machine's IP to the Azure SQL Server firewall rule, switch to the Azure portal.

Open the **toystore** SQL database **Overview** pane, if it's not already open.

From the **Overview** pane, select **Set server firewall**:

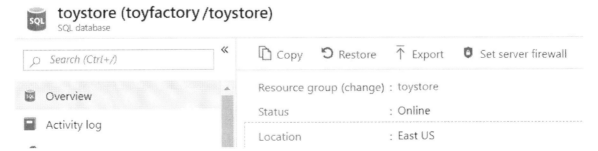

Figure 1.18: Set the server firewall in the Overview pane

5.  In the **Firewall settings** pane, select **Add client IP**:

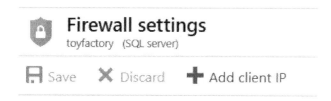

Figure 1.19: The Add client IP option on the Firewall settings pane

6.  The Azure portal will automatically detect the machine's IP and add it to the firewall rule.

    If you wish to rename the rule, you can do so by providing a meaningful name in the **RULE NAME** column.

    All machines with IPs between **START IP** and **END IP** are allowed to access all of the databases on the **toyfactory** server.

> **Note**
>
> The virtual network can be used to add a SQL database in Azure to a given network. A detailed explanation of virtual networks is out of the scope of this book.

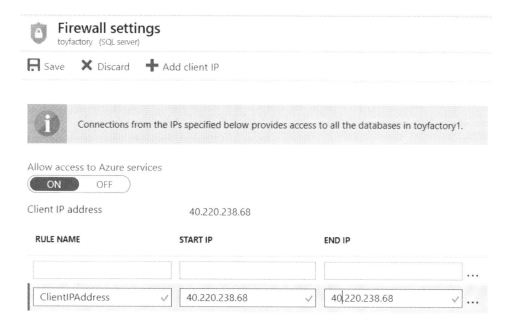

Figure 1.20: The Firewall settings pane

Click **Save** to save the firewall rule.

7.  Switch back to **SQL Server Management Studio (SSMS)** and click **Connect**. You should now be able to connect to Azure SQL Server. Press F8 to open **Object Explorer**, if it's not already open:

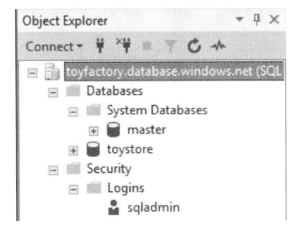

Figure 1.21: Object Explorer pane

8.  You can view and modify the firewall settings using T-SQL in the master database. Press *Ctrl* + N to open a new query window. Make sure that the database is set to `master`.

> **Note**
>
> To open a new query window in the master database context, in **Object Explorer**, expand **Databases**, then expand **System Databases**. Right-click the `master` database and select **New Query**.

9.  Enter the following query to view the existing firewall rules:

```
SELECT * FROM sys.firewall_rules
```

You should get the following output:

| | id | name | start_ip_address | end_ip_address | create_date | modify_date |
|---|---|---|---|---|---|---|
| 1 | 1 | AllowAllWindowsAzureIps | 0.0.0.0 | 0.0.0.0 | 2017-10-21 11:33:51.403 | 2017-10-21 11:33:51.403 |
| 2 | 3 | ClientIPAddress_2017-10-22_03:58:23 | 47.30.225.105 | 47.30.225.105 | 2017-10-22 03:58:25.873 | 2017-10-22 03:58:25.873 |
| 3 | 2 | Developer | 47.30.12.132 | 47.30.12.132 | 2017-10-22 03:55:16.713 | 2017-10-22 03:55:16.713 |

Figure 1.22: Existing firewall rules

The **AzureAllWindowsAzureIps** firewall is the default firewall, which allows resources within Microsoft to access Azure SQL Server.

The rest are user-defined firewall rules. The firewall rules for you will be different from what is shown here.

You can use **sp_set_firewall_rule** to add a new firewall rule and **sp_delete_firewall_rule** to delete an existing firewall rule.

10. To query the **toystore** SQL database, change the database context of the SSMS query window to **toystore**. You can do this by selecting the **toystore** database from the database dropdown in the menu:

Figure 1.23: Dropdown to select the toystore database

11. Copy and paste the following query into the query window:

```
SELECT COUNT(*) AS OrderCount FROM orders;
```

The query will return the total number of orders from the **orders** table. You should get the following output:

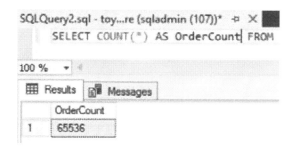

Figure 1.24: Total number of orders in the "orders" table

## Deleting Resources

To delete an Azure SQL database, an Azure SQL server, and Azure resource groups, perform the following steps:

> **Note**
>
> All resources must be deleted to successfully complete the activity at the end of this lesson.

1. Switch to the Azure portal and select **All resources** from the left-hand navigation pane.

2. From the **All resources** pane, select the checkbox next to **toyfactory** and the Azure SQL server that is to be deleted, and then select **Delete** from the top menu:

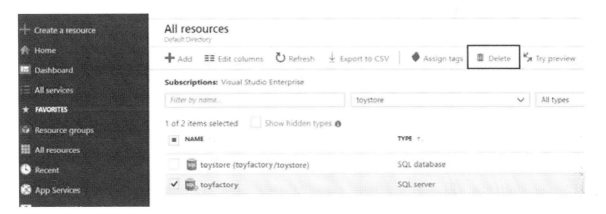

Figure 1.25: Deleting the toyfactory SQL Server

3.  In the **Delete Resources** window, type **yes** in the confirmation box and click the **Delete** button to delete the Azure SQL server and Azure SQL database:

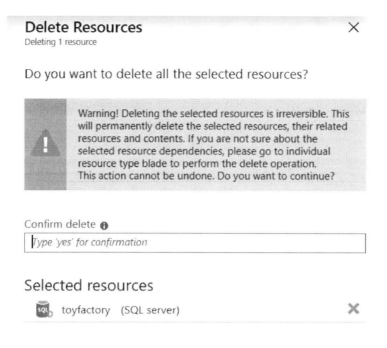

Figure 1.26: Confirming to delete the selected resource

**Note**

To only delete an Azure SQL database, check the Azure SQL database checkbox.

4. To delete the Azure resource group, select **Resource groups** from the left-hand navigation pane:

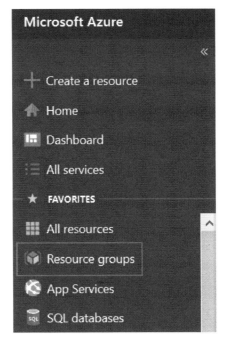

Figure 1.27: Resource groups

5. In the **Resource groups** pane, click the three dots next to the **toystore** resource group, and then select **Delete resource group** from the context menu:

Figure 1.28: Delete resource group option

6. In the delete confirmation pane, type the resource under the **TYPE THE RESOURCE GROUP NAME** section, and then click **Delete**.

## Differences between Azure SQL Database and SQL Server

Azure SQL Database is a PaaS offering and therefore some of its features differ from the on-premises SQL Server. Some of the important features that differ are as follows:

### Backup and Restore

Conventional database backup and restore statements aren't supported. Backups are automatically scheduled and start within a few minutes of the database provisioning. Backups are consistent, transaction-wise, which means that you can do a point-in-time restore.

There is no additional cost for backup storage until it goes beyond 200% of the provisioned database storage.

You can reduce the backup retention period to manage backup storage costs. You can also use the long-term retention period feature to store backups in the Azure vault for a much lower cost for a longer duration.

Apart from automatic backups, you can also export the Azure SQL Database **bacpac** or **dacpac** file to Azure storage.

### Recovery Model

The default recovery model of an Azure SQL database is FULL and it can't be modified to any other recovery model as in on-premises recovery models.

The recovery model is set when the master database is created, meaning when an Azure SQL server is provisioned, the recovery model can't be modified because the master database is read-only.

To view the recovery model of an Azure SQL database, execute the following query:

```
SELECT name, recovery_model_desc FROM sys.databases;
```

> **Note**
>
> You can use either of the two methods discussed earlier in the lesson to run the query – the Azure portal or SSMS.

You should get the following output:

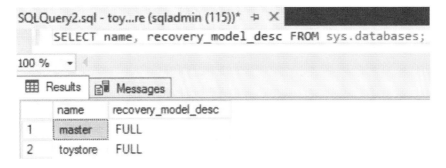

Figure 1.29: Recovery model of an SQL database

**SQL Server Agent**

Azure SQL Server doesn't have SQL Server Agent, which is used to schedule jobs and send success/failure notifications. However, you can use the following workarounds:

- Create a SQL Agent job on an on-premise SQL server or on an Azure SQL VM SQL Agent to connect and run on the Azure SQL database.

- Azure Automation allows users to schedule jobs in Microsoft Azure to automate manual tasks. This topic is covered in detail later in the book.

- Elastic Database Jobs is an Azure Cloud service that allows the scheduled execution of ad hoc tasks. This topic is covered in detail later in the book.

- Use PowerShell to automate a task and schedule PowerShell script execution with Windows Scheduler, on-premises, or Azure SQL VM SQL Agent.

**Change Data Capture**

**Change Data Capture** (**CDC**) allows you to capture data modifications to CDC-enabled databases and tables. The CDC feature is important in incremental load scenarios, such as incrementally inserting changed data to the data warehouse from an OLTP environment. The CDC requires SQL Server Agent, and therefore isn't available in Azure SQL Database. However, you can use the temporal table, SSIS, or Azure Data Factory to implement CDC.

## Auditing

The auditing features, such as C2 auditing, system health extended events, SQL default trace, and anything that writes alerts or issues into event logs or SQL error logs, aren't available. This is because it's a PaaS offering and we don't have access to or control of event logs or error logs.

However, there is an auditing and threat-detection feature available out of the box for Azure SQL Database.

## Mirroring

You can't enable mirroring between two Azure SQL databases, but you can configure Azure SQL Database as a mirror server. You can also set up a readable secondary for an Azure SQL database, which is better than mirroring.

## Table Partitioning

Table partitioning using a partition scheme and partition function is allowed in Azure SQL Database; however, because of the PaaS nature of the SQL database, all partitions should be created on a primary filegroup. You won't get a performance improvement by having partitions on different disks (spindles); however, you will get a performance improvement with partition elimination.

## Replication

Conventional replication techniques, such as snapshot, transactional, and merge replication, can't be done between two Azure SQL databases. However, an Azure SQL database can be a subscriber to an on-premise or Azure VM SQL Server.

However, this too has limitations. It supports one-way transactional replication, not peer-to-peer or bi-directional replication; it supports only push subscription.

Note that you should have SQL Server 2012 or above at on-premises. Replication and distribution agents can't be configured on Azure SQL Database.

## Multi-Part Names

Three-part names (`databasename.schemaname.tablename`) are only limited to `tempdb`, wherein you access a temp table as `tempdb.dbo.#temp`. For example, if there is a temporary table, say `#temp1`, then you can run the following query to select all the values from `#temp1`:

```
SELECT * FROM tempdb.dbo.#temp1
```

You can't access the tables in different SQL databases in Azure on the same Azure SQL server using three-part names. Four-part (`ServerName.DatabaseName.SchemaName.TableName`) names aren't allowed at all.

You can use an elastic query to access tables from different databases from an Azure SQL server. Elastic queries are covered in detail later in the book. You can access objects in different schemas in the same Azure SQL database using two-part (`Schemaname.Tablename`) names.

To explore other T-SQL differences, visit https://docs.microsoft.com/en-us/azure/sql-database/sql-database-transact-sql-information.

## Unsupported Features

Some features not supported by Azure SQL Database or Azure SQL Server are:

- **SQL Browser Service**: SQL Browser is a Windows service and provides instance and post information to incoming connection requests. This isn't required because Azure SQL Server listens to port **1433** only.

- **Filestream**: Azure SQL Database doesn't support `FileStream` or `filetable`, just because of the PaaS nature of the service. There is a workaround to use Azure Storage; however, that would require a re-work on the application and the database side.

- **Common Language Runtime (SQL CLR)**: SQL CLR allows users to write programmable database objects such as stored procedures, functions, and triggers in managed code. This provides a significant performance improvement in some scenarios. SQL CLR was initially supported and then the support was removed due to concerns about security issues.

- **Resource Governor**: Resource Governor allows you to throttle/limit resources (CPU, memory, and I/O) for different SQL Server workloads. This feature is not available in Azure SQL Database.

  Azure SQL Database comes with different service tiers, each suitable for different workloads. You should evaluate the performance tier your application workload will fit into and accordingly provision the database for that performance tier.

- **Global Temporary Tables**: Global temporary tables are defined by **##** and are accessible across all sessions. These are not supported in Azure SQL Database. Local temporary tables are allowed. Global temporary tables created with **##** are accessible across all sessions for a particular database. For example, a global temporary table created in database **DB1** will be accessible to all sessions connecting to database **DB1** only.

- **Log Shipping**: Log shipping is the process of taking log backups on a primary server and copying and restoring them on a secondary server. Log shipping is commonly used as a high-availability or disaster-recovery solution, or to migrate a database from one SQL instance to another. Log shipping isn't supported by Azure SQL Database.

- **SQL Trace and Profiler**: SQL Trace and Profiler can't be used to trace events on Azure SQL Server. As of now, there isn't any direct alternate other than using DMVs, monitoring using the Azure portal, and extended events.

- **Trace Flags**: Trace flags are special switches used to enable or disable a particular SQL Server functionality. These are not available in Azure SQL Server.

- **System Stored Procedures**: Azure SQL Database doesn't support all the system stored procedures supported in the on-premises SQL Server. System procedures such as `sp_addmessage`, `sp_helpuser`, and `sp_configure` aren't supported. In a nutshell, procedures related to features unsupported in Azure SQL Database aren't supported.

- **USE Statement**: The `USE` statement is used to switch from one database context to another. This isn't supported in Azure SQL Database.

## Introduction to Managed Instance

SQL managed instance is a fully managed SQL Server instance offering announced in May 2017 and made generally available from October 1, 2018.

SQL managed instance provides nearly 100% surface area compatibility with on-premises SQL Server instances and the DBaaS benefits available with Azure SQL Database, such as automatic backups, updates, automatic performance tuning, Intelligent Insights, and so on.

Note that SQL managed instance is not a replacement for Azure SQL Database, rather a new deployment option for Azure SQL Database with near 100% compatibility with on-premises SQL Server instances.

Managed instance supports most of the features of an on-premise deployment, which were earlier not available in Azure SQL Database. It therefore provides easy lift and shift migration from an on-premises environment to the cloud.

When you migrate to managed instance on Azure, you don't only migrate databases, you migrate licenses too.

> **Note**
>
> You can save up to 55% on managed instance, when migrating from SQL Server Enterprise or Standard edition with software assurance. For more details, please visit https://azure.microsoft.com/en-us/blog/migrate-your-databases-to-a-fully-managed-service-with-azure-sql-database-managed-instance/ or contact Azure Support.

Some of the important features supported by managed instance that are not available in Azure SQL Database are as follows:

- Native backup and restore
- Global temporary tables
- Cross-database queries and transactions
- Linked servers
- CLR modules
- SQL agent
- Database mail
- Transactional replication (Azure SQL Database can only be a subscriber)

DTC is not supported in managed instance.

These and other features of managed instance make it 100% compatible with an on-premise SQL Server.

## Purchasing Model

SQL Server managed instance follows a **vCore** based purchasing model. The vCore model gives you the flexibility to choose the compute, memory, and storage based on different workload requirements.

The vCore model supports two hardware generations, Gen4 and Gen5:

- Gen4 has Intel E5-2673 v3 (Haswell) 2.4 GHz processors (1 vCore is 1 Physical Core), 7 GB per vCore Memory with 3 GB per vCore In-Memory, and max storage size of 8 TB.

- Gen5 has intel E5-2673 v4 (Broadwell) 2.3 GHz processors, fast NVMe SSD, (1 vCore = 1 Logical Processor (hyper-thread), 5.1 GB memory per vCore, 2.6 GB per vCore In-Memory, and a max storage size of 8 TB.

The vCore model comes with two service tiers: General Purpose and Business Critical.

The General Purpose service tier is designed for SQL Server workloads with typical performance requirements and is suitable for the majority of applications.

The Business Critical service tier, as the name suggests, supports high-performance, low I/O latency environments. The Business Critical service tier provides 1-2 millisecond (approximately) I/O latency, 48 MB/s per instance of log throughput, and 24-48 MB/s of data throughput per vCore.

## Connecting to SQL Managed Instance

A SQL managed instance is a set of services hosted on one or more isolated virtual machines inside a virtual network subnet.

When we provision a managed instance, a virtual cluster is created. A virtual cluster can have one or more managed instances.

Applications connect to databases via an endpoint, `<mi_name>.<dns_zone>.database.windows.net`, and should be inside a virtual network, a peered virtual network, or an on-premise network connected via VPN or Azure ExpressRoute.

Unlike Azure SQL Database, SQL managed instance supports Azure **Virtual Network (VNet)**. An Azure Virtual Network is a logical boundary or isolation that groups resources within a specified Azure region and enables secure communication between resources, the internet, and on-premise networks.

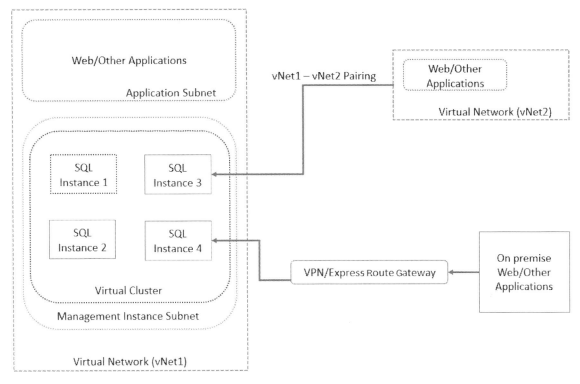

Figure 1.30: High-level connectivity architecture for SQL managed instances

The preceding diagram shows a high-level connectivity architecture for SQL managed instances. Let's go through it:

- All managed instances are part of a virtual cluster and are in a managed instance subnet in virtual network **vNet1**

- Web and other applications in vNet1 connect to the managed instance using an endpoint, for example, `sqlinstance3.dnszone.database.windows.net`.

- Applications in any other virtual network connect using the same endpoint; however, the two virtual networks are peered to allow connectivity between them.

- On-premise applications connect using the same endpoint via VPN or an ExpressRoute gateway.

## Exercise: Provisioning a SQL-Managed Instance Using the Azure Portal

In this exercise, we'll provision and connect to a managed instance. We'll also learn about VNet support in SQL-managed instances.

To provision a SQL-managed instance, perform the following steps:

1. Log in to https://portal.azure.com using your Azure credentials.

2. In the top search box, type SQL Managed Instance and select **SQL managed instances** from the dropdown:

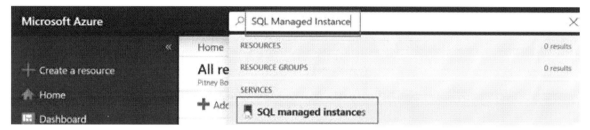

Figure 1.31: Searching for SQL Managed Instance.

3. In the **SQL managed instances** window, select **Add**:

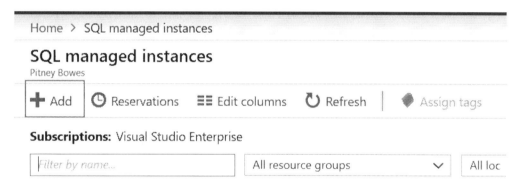

Figure 1.32: The SQL managed instances pane

4. In the **SQL managed instance** window, provide the information shown in the following screenshot:

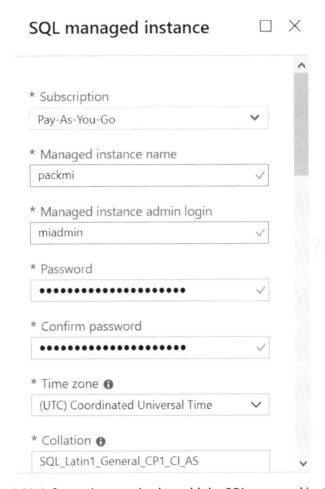

Figure 1.33: Information required to add the SQL managed instance

Note

Figure 1.31, Figure 1.32, and Figure 1.33 are all a part of one SQL managed instance window. The window is split into three images for clarity.

In the **Subscription** box, provide your Azure subscription type. SQL managed instances currently support the following subscription types: **Enterprise Agreement (EA)**, **Pay-As-You-Go**, **Cloud Service Provider (CSP)**, **Enterprise Dev/Test**, and **Pay-As-You-Go Dev/test**.

If you have a different subscription, you won't be able to create a SQL managed instance.

The **Managed instance name** box is for the name of the managed instance you plan to create. It can be any valid name, in accordance with the naming rules at https://docs.microsoft.com/en-us/azure/architecture/best-practices/naming-conventions.

The **Managed instance admin login box** is for any valid login name, as long as it fits the naming conventions at https://docs.microsoft.com/en-us/azure/architecture/best-practices/naming-conventions.

The password can be any valid password that follows these rules:

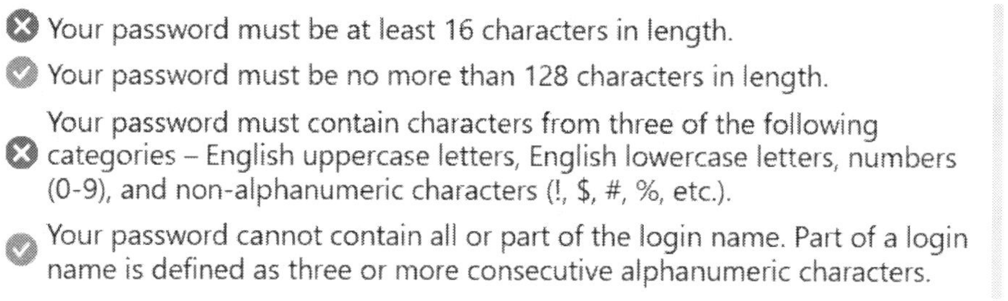

> ❌ Your password must be at least 16 characters in length.
>
> ✅ Your password must be no more than 128 characters in length.
>
> ❌ Your password must contain characters from three of the following categories – English uppercase letters, English lowercase letters, numbers (0-9), and non-alphanumeric characters (!, $, #, %, etc.).
>
> ✅ Your password cannot contain all or part of the login name. Part of a login name is defined as three or more consecutive alphanumeric characters.

Figure 1.34: Password requirements

The **Time zone** box denotes the time zone of the managed instance. The preferred time zone is **UTC**; however, this will differ from business to business.

**Collation** is the SQL Server collation that the managed instance will be in.

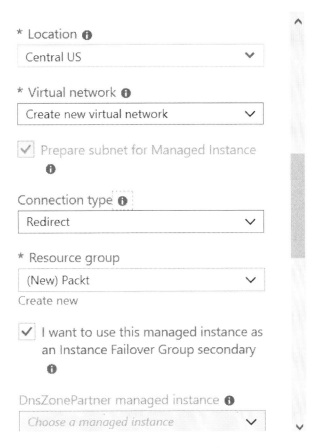

**Figure 1.35: Server collation information**

In the **Location** box, enter the Azure location the managed instance will be created in.

The **Virtual network** box is for setting the virtual network that the managed instance will be a part of. If no network is provided, a new virtual network is created.

> **Note**
>
> A detailed explanation of the networking requirements is beyond the scope of the book. For more details, please visit https://docs.microsoft.com/en-us/azure/sql-database/sql-database-managed-instance-connectivity-architecture.

For the **Connection type** box, SQL managed instances support two connection types, Redirect and Proxy. Redirect is the recommended connection type because the client directly connects to the node hosting the database, and therefore it offers low latency and high throughput.

In **Proxy connection type**, requests to the database are proxied through the Azure SQL Database gateways.

**Resource group** sets the resource group the SQL managed instance will be part of. It can be a new or existing one.

To use this managed instance as a secondary instance in a failover group, check **I want to use this managed instance as an Instance Failover Group secondary** and specify the managed instance to share an instance failover group within **DnsZonePartner managed instance**.

The **DnsZonePartner managed instance** box is left blank because we don't have any other managed instances.

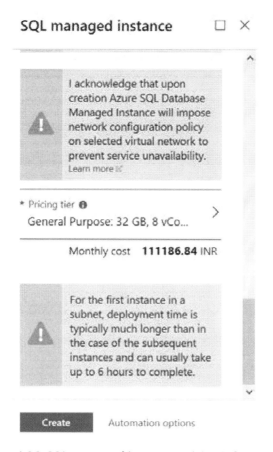

Figure 1.36: SQL managed instance pricing information

For **Pricing tier**, select the optimal pricing tier that suits your business needs. However, for demo purposes, select **General Purpose: 32 GB, 8 vCore** for a lower price.

The first managed instance in a subnet may take up 6 hours to complete and a warning pops up to inform you of this.

5. Click **Create** to validate and provision the SQL-managed instance.

   To monitor the progress, click the **Notifications** (bell) icon in the top-left corner:

Figure 1.37: Notification icon in the instance window

As we can see, the deployment is in progress:

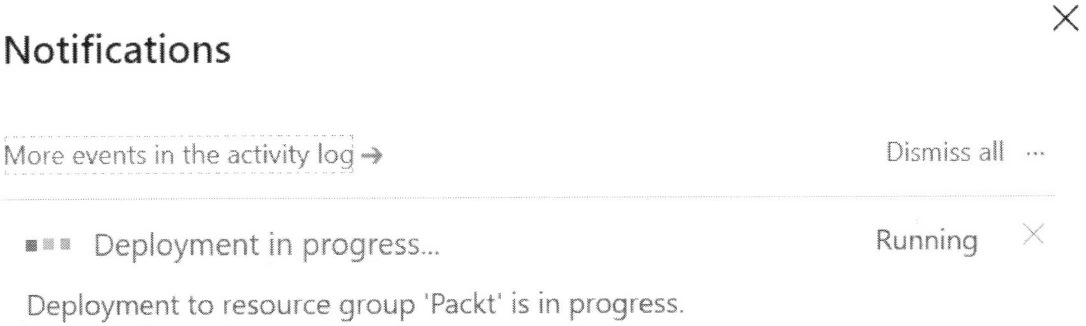

# Notifications     ✕

More events in the activity log →      Dismiss all  ...

■■■ Deployment in progress...    Running  ✕

Deployment to resource group 'Packt' is in progress.

Figure 1.38: The Notifications pane

After the deployment is complete, a deployment complete notification will come up in the notification window.

## Activity: Provisioning an Azure SQL Server and SQL Database Using PowerShell

This section discusses provisioning an Azure SQL server and SQL database using PowerShell. To understand the process, let's take the example of Mike, who is the newest member of the Data Administration team at ToyStore Ltd., a company that manufactures toys for children. ToyStore has an e-commerce web portal that allows customers to purchase toys online. ToyStore has migrated the online e-commerce portal to Microsoft Azure and is therefore moving to Azure SQL Database from the on-premises SQL Server. Mike is asked to provision the Azure SQL database and other required resources as his initial assignment. This can be achieved by following these steps:

> **Note**
>
> If you are short of time, you can refer to the `C:\code\Lesson01\` `ProvisionAzureSQLDatabase.ps1` file. You can run this file in the PowerShell console instead of typing the code as instructed in the following steps. Open a PowerShell console and enter the full path to execute the PowerShell script. You'll have to change the Azure Resource Group name, the Azure SQL server, and the Azure SQL database name in the script before executing it.

1. Save the Azure profile details into a file for future reference. Press *Windows* + *R* to open the **Run** command window.

2. In the **Run** command window, type **powershell** and then press *Enter*. This will open a new PowerShell console window:

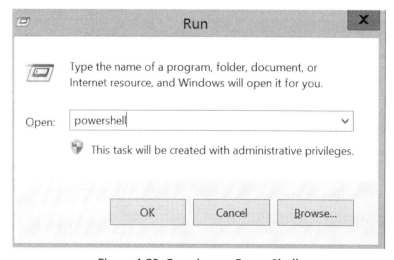

Figure 1.39: Opening up PowerShell

3.  In the PowerShell console, run the following command:

    ```
    Add-AzureRmAccount
    ```

    You'll have to enter your Azure credentials into the pop-up dialog box. After a successful login, the control will return to the **PowerShell** window.

4.  Run the following command to save the profile details to a file:

    ```
    Save-AzureRmProfile -Path C:\code\MyAzureProfile.json
    ```

    The Azure subscription details will be saved in the **MyAzureProfile.json** file in **JSON** format. If you wish to explore the JSON file, you can open it in any editor to review its content:

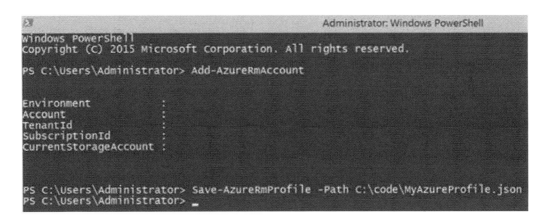

Figure 1.40: The PowerShell command window

> **Note**
>
> Saving the profile in a file allows you to use the file to log in to your Azure account from PowerShell instead of providing your credentials every time in the Azure authentication window.

5. Press *Window* + R to open the **Run** command window. Type `PowerShell_ISE.exe` in the **Run** command window and press *Enter*. This will open a new PowerShell ISE editor window. This is where you'll write the PowerShell commands:

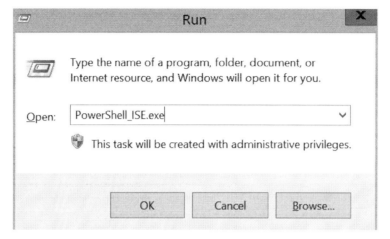

Figure 1.41: Run command window

6. In the PowerShell ISE, select **File** from the top menu, and then click **Save**. Alternatively, you can press *Ctrl* + S to save the file. In the **Save As** dialog box, browse to the `C:\Code\Lesson01\` directory. In the **File name** textbox, type `Provision-AzureSQLDatabase.ps1`, and then click **Save** to save the file:

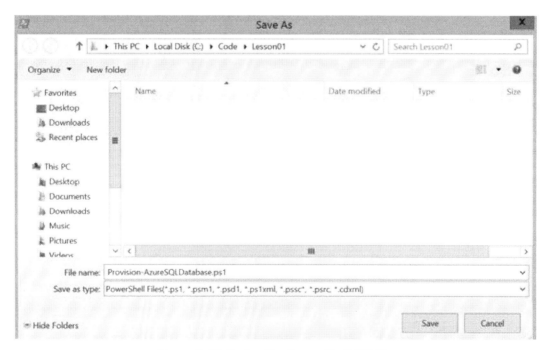

Figure 1.42: Saving the PowerShell ISE file

7. Copy and paste the following lines in the **Provision-AzureSQLDatabase.ps1** file one after another. The code explanation, wherever required, is given in the comments within the code snippet.

8. Copy and paste the following code to define the parameters:

```
param (
[parameter(Mandatory=$true)] [String] $ResourceGroup,
[parameter(Mandatory=$true)] [String] $Location,
[parameter(Mandatory=$true)] [String] $SQLServer,
[parameter(Mandatory=$true)] [String] $UserName,
[parameter(Mandatory=$true)] [String] $Password,

[parameter(Mandatory=$true)] [String] $SQLDatabase,
[parameter(Mandatory=$true)] [String] $Edition="Basic",
[parameter(Mandatory=$false)] [String] $AzureProfileFilePath
)
```

The preceding code defines the parameters required by the scripts:

**ResourceGroup**: The resource group that will host the logical Azure SQL server and Azure SQL database.

**Location**: The resource group location. The default is **East US 2**.

**SQLServer**: The logical Azure SQL server name that will host the Azure SQL database.

**UserName**: The Azure SQL Server admin username. The default username is **sqladmin**. Don't change the username; keep it as the default.

**Password**: The Azure SQL Server admin password. The default password is **Packt@ pub2**. Don't change the password; keep it as the default.

**SQLDatabase**: The Azure SQL database to create.

**Edition**: The Azure SQL Database edition. This is discussed in detail in *Lesson 2, Migrating a SQL Server Database to an Azure SQL Database*.

**AzureProfileFilePath**: The full path of the file that contains your Azure profile details. You created this earlier under the *Saving Azure Profile Details to a File* section.

9. Copy and paste the following code to log in to your Azure account from PowerShell:

```
Start-Transcript -Path .\log\ProvisionAzureSQLDatabase.txt -Append
if([string]::IsNullOrEmpty($AzureProfileFilePath))
{
$AzureProfileFilePath="..\..\MyAzureProfile.json"
}
if((Test-Path -Path $AzureProfileFilePath))
{
$profile = Import-AzureRmContext-Path $AzureProfileFilePath
$SubscriptionID = $profile.Context.Subscription.SubscriptionId
}
else
{

Write-Host "File Not Found $AzureProfileFilePath"
-ForegroundColor Red
$profile = Login-AzureRmAccount
$SubscriptionID = $profile.Context.Subscription.
SubscriptionId
}
Set-AzureRmContext -SubscriptionId $SubscriptionID | Out-Null
```

The preceding code first checks for the profile details in the Azure profile file. If found, it retrieves the subscription ID of the profile; otherwise, it uses the **Login-AzureRmAccount** command to pop up the Azure login dialog box. You have to provide your Azure credentials in the login dialog box. After a successful login, it retrieves and stores the subscription ID of the profile in the **$SubscriptionID** variable.

It then sets the current Azure subscription to yours for the PowerShell cmdlets to use in the current session.

10. Copy and paste the following code to create the resource group if it doesn't already exist:

```
# Check if resource group exists
# An error is returned and stored in the notexists variable if the
resource group exists
Get-AzureRmResourceGroup -Name $ResourceGroup -Location $Location
-ErrorVariable notexists -ErrorAction SilentlyContinue
```

```
#Provision Azure Resource Group
if($notexists)
{

Write-Host "Provisioning Azure Resource Group $ResourceGroup"
-ForegroundColor Green
$_ResourceGroup = @{
  Name = $ResourceGroup;
  Location = $Location;

}
New-AzureRmResourceGroup @_ResourceGroup;
}
else
{

Write-Host $notexists -ForegroundColor Yellow
}
```

The **Get-AzureRmResourceGroup** cmdlet fetches the given resource group. If the given resource group doesn't exist, an error is returned. The error returned is stored in the **notexists** variable.

The **New-AzureRmResourceGroup** cmdlet provisions the new resource group if the **notexists** variable isn't empty.

11. Copy and paste the following code to create a new Azure SQL server if one doesn't exist:

```
Get-AzureRmSqlServer -ServerName $SQLServer -ResourceGroupName
$ResourceGroup -ErrorVariable notexists -ErrorAction SilentlyContinue
if($notexists)
{
Write-Host "Provisioning Azure SQL Server $SQLServer"
-ForegroundColor Green
$credentials = New-Object -TypeName System.Management.Automation.
PSCredential -ArgumentList $UserName, $(ConvertTo-SecureString
-String $Password -AsPlainText -Force)
$_SqlServer = @{
ResourceGroupName = $ResourceGroup; ServerName = $SQLServer;
Location = $Location; SqlAdministratorCredentials = $credentials;
ServerVersion = '12.0';
}
```

```
New-AzureRmSqlServer @_SqlServer;
}
else
{
Write-Host $notexists -ForegroundColor Yellow
}
```

The **Get-AzureRmSqlServer** cmdlet gets the given Azure SQL server. If the given Azure SQL server doesn't exist, an error is returned. The error returned is stored in the **notexists** variable.

The **New-AzureRmSqlServer** cmdlet provisions the new Azure SQL server if the **notexists** variable isn't empty.

12. Copy and paste the following code to create the Azure SQL database if it doesn't already exist:

```
# Check if Azure SQL Database Exists
# An error is returned and stored in the notexists variable if the
resource group exists
Get-AzureRmSqlDatabase -DatabaseName $SQLDatabase -ServerName
$SQLServer -ResourceGroupName $ResourceGroup -ErrorVariable notexits
-ErrorAction SilentlyContinue
if($notexists)
{
# Provision Azure SQL Database
Write-Host "Provisioning Azure SQL Database $SQLDatabase"
-ForegroundColor Green
$_SqlDatabase = @{
ResourceGroupName = $ResourceGroup; ServerName = $SQLServer; DatabaseName
= $SQLDatabase; Edition = $Edition;
};
New-AzureRmSqlDatabase @_SqlDatabase;
}
else
{
Write-Host $notexists -ForegroundColor Yellow
}
```

**Get-AzureRmSqlDatabase** gets the given Azure SQL database. If the given Azure SQL database doesn't exist, an error is returned. The error returned is stored in the **notexists** variable.

**New-AzureRmSqlDatabase** provisions the new Azure SQL database if the **notexists** variable isn't empty.

13. Copy and paste the following code to add the system's public IP address to the Azure SQL Server firewall rule:

```
$startip = (Invoke-WebRequest http://myexternalip.com/ raw
--UseBasicParsing -ErrorVariable err -ErrorAction SilentlyContinue).
Content.trim()
$endip=$startip
Write-host "Creating firewall rule for $azuresqlservername with StartIP:
$startip and EndIP: $endip " -ForegroundColor Green
$NewFirewallRule = @{ ResourceGroupName = $ResourceGroup; ServerName =
$SQLServer; FirewallRuleName = 'PacktPub'; StartIpAddress = $startip;
EndIpAddress=$endip;
};
New-AzureRmSqlServerFirewallRule @NewFirewallRule;
```

The preceding code first gets the public IP of the system (running this PowerShell script) by calling the **http://myexternalip.com/raw** website using the **Invoke-WebRequest** command. The link returns the public IP in text format, which is stored in the **$startip** variable.

The IP is then used to create the firewall rule by the name of **PacktPub** using the **New-AzureRmSqlServerFirewallRule** cmdlet.

14. To run the PowerShell script, perform the following steps: Press *Window* + *R* to open the **Run** command window. Type PowerShell and hit *Enter* to open a new PowerShell console window.

15. Change the directory to the folder that has the **shard-toystore.ps1** script. For example, if the script is in the **C:\Code\Lesson01\** directory, then run the following command to switch to this directory:

```
cd C:\Code\Lesson01
```

16. In the following command, change the parameter values. Copy the command to the PowerShell console and hit *Enter*:

```
.\ProvisionAzureSQLDatabase.ps1 -ResourceGroup toystore -SQLServer
toyfactory -UserName sqladmin -Password Packt@pub2 -SQLDatabase toystore
-AzureProfileFilePath C:\Code\MyAzureProfile.json
```

The preceding command will create the **toystore** resource group, the **toyfactory** Azure SQL server, and the **toystore** Azure SQL database. It'll also create a firewall rule by the name of PacktPub with the machine's public IP address.

## Exercise: Provisioning a Managed Instance

To provision a managed instance using a PowerShell script, perform the following steps:

1. Create a file called **ProvisionSQLMI.ps1** and add the following code:

```
<#
Managed Instance is not supported in Visual Studio Enterprise
subscription.
If you are using Pay-as-you-go subscription, do check the managed instance
cost
#>
param(
[string]$ResourceGroup="Packt-1",
[string]$Location="centralus",
[string]$vNet="PackvNet-$(Get-Random)",
[string]$misubnet="PackSubnet-$(Get-Random)",
[string]$miname="Packt-$(Get-Random)",
[string]$miadmin="miadmin",
[string]$miadminpassword,
[string]$miedition="General Purpose",
[string]$mivcores=8,
[string]$mistorage=32,
[string]$migeneration = "Gen4",
[string]$milicense="LicenseIncluded",
[string]$subscriptionid="f0193880-5aca-4fbd-adf4-953954e4fdd7"
)
```

2. Add the following code to log in to Azure:

```
# login to azure

$Account = Connect-AzAccount

if([string]::IsNullOrEmpty($subscriptionid))
{
    $subscriptionid=$Account.Context.Subscription.Id
}

Set-AzContext $subscriptionid
```

3. Add the following code snippet to verify that the resource group exists:

```
# Check if resource group exists
# An error is returned and stored in notexists variable if resource group
exists
Get-AzResourceGroup -Name $ResourceGroup -Location $location
-ErrorVariable notexists -ErrorAction SilentlyContinue
```

4. Provision a resource group:

```
#Provision Azure Resource Group
if(![string]::IsNullOrEmpty($notexists))
{

Write-Host "Provisioning Azure Resource Group $ResourceGroup"
-ForegroundColor Green
$_ResourceGroup = @{
  Name = $ResourceGroup;
  Location = $Location;
  }
New-AzResourceGroup @_ResourceGroup;
}
else
{

Write-Host $notexists -ForegroundColor Yellow
}


Write-Host "Provisioning Azure Virtual Network $vNet" -ForegroundColor
Green
$obvnet = New-AzVirtualNetwork -Name $vNet -ResourceGroupName
$ResourceGroup -Location $Location -AddressPrefix "10.0.0.0/16"

Write-Host "Provisioning Managed instance subnet $misubnet"
-ForegroundColor Green

$obmisubnet = Add-AzVirtualNetworkSubnetConfig -Name $misubnet
-VirtualNetwork $obvnet -AddressPrefix "10.0.0.0/24"
$misubnetid = $obmisubnet.Id
$_nsg = "mi-nsg"
$_rt = "mi-rt"
```

```
Write-Host "Provisioning Network Security Group" -ForegroundColor Green
$nsg = New-AzNetworkSecurityGroup -Name $_nsg -ResourceGroupName
$ResourceGroup -Location $Location -Force

<#
Routing table is required for a managed instance to connect with
Azure Management Service.
#>
Write-Host "Provisioning Routing table" -ForegroundColor Green
$routetable = New-AzRouteTable -Name $_rt -ResourceGroupName
$ResourceGroup -Location $Location -Force
```

5. Assign a network security group to the managed instance subnet:

```
#Assign network security group to managed instance subnet
Set-AzVirtualNetworkSubnetConfig '
-VirtualNetwork $obvnet -Name $misubnet '
-AddressPrefix "10.0.0.0/24" -NetworkSecurityGroup $nsg '
-RouteTable $routetable | Set-AzVirtualNetwork
```

6. Configure the network rules in the network security group by adding the following code:

```
#Configure network rules in network security group
Get-AzNetworkSecurityGroup -ResourceGroupName $ResourceGroup -Name $_nsg '
  | Add-AzNetworkSecurityRuleConfig '
                      -Priority 100 '
                      -Name "allow_management_inbound" '
                      -Access Allow '
                      -Protocol Tcp '
                      -Direction Inbound '
                      -SourcePortRange * '
                      -SourceAddressPrefix * '
                      -DestinationPortRange 9000,9003,1438,1440,1452 '
                      -DestinationAddressPrefix * '
  | Add-AzNetworkSecurityRuleConfig '
                      -Priority 200 '
                      -Name "allow_misubnet_inbound" '
                      -Access Allow '
                      -Protocol * '
                      -Direction Inbound '
                      -SourcePortRange * '
                      -SourceAddressPrefix "10.0.0.0/24" '
                      -DestinationPortRange * '
```

```
                              -DestinationAddressPrefix * '
| Add-AzNetworkSecurityRuleConfig '
                              -Priority 300 '
                              -Name "allow_health_probe_inbound" '
                              -Access Allow '
                              -Protocol * '
                              -Direction Inbound '
                              -SourcePortRange * '
                              -SourceAddressPrefix AzureLoadBalancer '
                              -DestinationPortRange * '
                              -DestinationAddressPrefix * '
| Add-AzNetworkSecurityRuleConfig '
                              -Priority 1000 '
                              -Name "allow_tds_inbound" '
                              -Access Allow '
                              -Protocol Tcp '
                              -Direction Inbound '
                              -SourcePortRange * '
                              -SourceAddressPrefix VirtualNetwork '
                              -DestinationPortRange 1433 '
                              -DestinationAddressPrefix * '
| Add-AzNetworkSecurityRuleConfig '
                              -Priority 1100 '
                              -Name "allow_redirect_inbound" '
                              -Access Allow '
                              -Protocol Tcp '
                              -Direction Inbound '
                              -SourcePortRange * '
                              -SourceAddressPrefix VirtualNetwork '
                              -DestinationPortRange 11000-11999 '
                              -DestinationAddressPrefix * '
| Add-AzNetworkSecurityRuleConfig '
                              -Priority 4096 '
                              -Name "deny_all_inbound" '
                              -Access Deny '
                              -Protocol * '
                              -Direction Inbound '
                              -SourcePortRange * '
                              -SourceAddressPrefix * '
                              -DestinationPortRange * '
                              -DestinationAddressPrefix * '
| Add-AzNetworkSecurityRuleConfig '
```

```
                          -Priority 100 '
                          -Name "allow_management_outbound" '
                          -Access Allow '
                          -Protocol Tcp '
                          -Direction Outbound '
                          -SourcePortRange * '
                          -SourceAddressPrefix * '
                          -DestinationPortRange 80,443,12000 '
                          -DestinationAddressPrefix * '
    | Add-AzNetworkSecurityRuleConfig '
                          -Priority 200 '
                          -Name "allow_misubnet_outbound" '
                          -Access Allow '
                          -Protocol * '
                          -Direction Outbound '
                          -SourcePortRange * '
                          -SourceAddressPrefix * '
                          -DestinationPortRange * '
                          -DestinationAddressPrefix "10.0.0.0/24" '
    | Add-AzNetworkSecurityRuleConfig '
                          -Priority 4096 '
                          -Name "deny_all_outbound" '
                          -Access Deny '
                          -Protocol * '
                          -Direction Outbound '
                          -SourcePortRange * '
                          -SourceAddressPrefix * '
                          -DestinationPortRange * '
                          -DestinationAddressPrefix * '
    | Set-AzNetworkSecurityGroup
```

7. Update the routing table configuration:

```
#update the routing table configuration.
Get-AzRouteTable '
    -ResourceGroupName $ResourceGroup '
    -Name $_rt '
    | Add-AzRouteConfig '
    -Name "ToManagedInstanceManagementService" '
    -AddressPrefix 0.0.0.0/0 '
    -NextHopType Internet '
```

```
  | Add-AzRouteConfig '
  -Name "ToLocalClusterNode" '
  -AddressPrefix "10.0.0.0/24" '
  -NextHopType VnetLocal '
  | Set-AzRouteTable
```

8. Add the following code to provision a managed instance:

```
# Provision managed instance
 $creds = New-Object -TypeName System.Management.Automation.PSCredential
-ArgumentList $miadmin, (ConvertTo-SecureString -String $miadminpassword
-AsPlainText -Force)

New-AzSqlInstance -Name $miname -ResourceGroupName $ResourceGroup
-Location $Location -SubnetId $misubnetid '
                    -AdministratorCredential $creds '
                    -StorageSizeInGB $mistorage -VCore $mivcores
-Edition $miedition '
                    -ComputeGeneration $migeneration -LicenseType
$milicense


<#
Clean-Up : Remove managed instance
Remove-AzSqlInstance -Name $miadmin -ResourceGroupName $ResourceGroup
-Force

#>
```

> **Note**
>
> The PowerShell script is self-explanatory. Review the comments in the script to understand what each command is used for.

9. Open a new PowerShell console window. Set the directory to the one containing the `ProvisionSQLMI.ps1` file.

10. Copy and paste the following command in the PowerShell window:

```
.\ProvisionSQLMI.ps1 -ResourceGroup Packt1 -Location westus2 -vNet mi-vnet
-misubnet mi-subnet -miname packtmi -miadmin miadmin -miadminpassword
Thisismypassword$12345 -miedition "General Purpose" -mivcores 8 -mistorage
32 -migeneration Gen4 -milicense LicenseIncluded
```

You may change the parameter values if you wish to.

> **Note**
>
> If you have more than one subscription, specify the subscription ID in the
> preceding command for the parameter subscription ID.

This will create a new SQL managed instance with all the required network
specifications.

> **Note**
>
> It may take more than 3 hours to provision the first SQL managed instance.

11. Once you are done with the managed instance, execute the following command to
delete it:

```
Remove-AzSqlInstance -Name $miadmin -ResourceGroupName $ResourceGroup
-Force
```

This command expects the managed instance name and the resource group to
delete that managed instance.

## Summary

This lesson was an introduction to the SQL DBaaS offering from Microsoft. We learned about the Azure SQL Database architecture and the different layers that make up the Azure SQL Database infrastructure.

We also learned about the request flow through the different layers when a user connects to and queries an Azure SQL database. We learned how to connect to and query a database from SQL Server Management Studio and the Azure portal.

We learned about the latest Azure SQL Database offering, Azure managed instance, and also learned how to provision a managed instance using PowerShell.

Most importantly, the lesson covered the differences between an on-premises SQL database and an Azure SQL database, along with the unsupported features on an Azure SQL database.

In the next lesson, we will discuss how to migrate data from an on-premises system to an Azure SQL database.

# Migrating a SQL Server Database to an Azure SQL Database

**Learning Objectives**

By the end of this lesson, you will be able to:

- Select a service tier for your migrated Azure SQL Database based on your needs

- Explain Database Transaction Units (DTUs)

- Identify and fix SQL Server-to-Azure SQL Database compatibility issues

- Migrate from an on-premises database to Azure SQL Database using different tools

In this lesson, you'll learn how to find and fix compatibility issues, determine an appropriate service tier, figure out a migration strategy and tool and migrate to the cloud.

## Introduction

Migrating an on-premises SQL Server database is an important task and should be planned to perfection. An ideal migration methodology should be like the one shown in the following diagram:

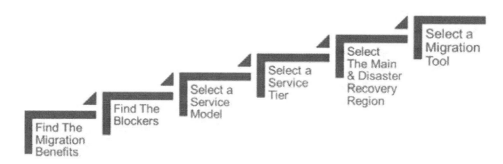

Figure 2.1: Migration methodology

### Finding the Migration Benefits

You should first analyze and find out the benefits of migrating an on-premises SQL database to an Azure SQL database. Migration involves a lot of time, effort, and cost, and it shouldn't be done just for the sake of having a cloud database.

### Finding the Blockers

The next step is to find out the compatibility issues that may stop you from migrating to Azure SQL Database.

### Selecting a Service Model

The next step is to find out whether the database will be deployed individually, in an elastic pool, or as a SQL managed database instance. This is important as the service model will affect the overall pricing, service tier, performance, and management of the Azure SQL Database.

### Selecting a Service Tier

The next step is to find an appropriate service tier and performance level for Azure SQL Database. This is important as it will directly affect the performance of an Azure SQL Database. A too-low service tier will result in bad performance, and a too-high service tier will result in unnecessary cost.

## Selecting the Main Region and Disaster Recovery Region

The next step is to find the main region and the disaster recovery region for your Azure SQL Database. It's advisable to have the database in a region that would provide fast connectivity to your users.

## Selecting a Migration Tool

Microsoft provides various tools to automate database migration. You can also write PowerShell or C# scripts to automate the database migration process. Tool selection largely depends on the database's size and the downtime SLA.

## Choosing Between Azure SQL Database and SQL Database Managed Instance

Azure SQL Database and SQL Database managed instance both offer the benefits of the **Software-as-a-Service (SaaS)** model, in which the user doesn't manage the underlying hardware, software upgrades, and operating system configuration. The user therefore saves on the administrative cost of managing the platform.

These two deployments (Azure SQL Database and SQL managed instance) provide additional services such as automated backups, Query Performance Insight, advanced data security, high availability, and disaster recovery. Each of the two deployments, therefore, provides a ready-to-use database for new or existing applications.

The two deployment options have common performance tiers, with Azure SQL Database now supporting the vCore pricing tiers.

With the two options each having similar sets of features, consider the following aspects when choosing between an Azure SQL database and a SQL managed database instance.

## Features

As mentioned earlier in *Lesson 1, Microsoft Azure SQL Database Primer*, in the *Introduction to Managed Instance* section, SQL database managed instances provide near 100% surface area compatibility and support almost all of the on-premises SQL Server features.

On the other hand, Azure SQL Database doesn't support some of important on-premises features, such as Common Language Runtime (SQL CLR), global temporary tables, SQL Server Agent, cross-database queries, and log shipping (for a complete list, see the *Unsupported Features* section in *Lesson 1, Microsoft Azure SQL Database Primer*).

Therefore, if you are looking to use any of the features not supported in Azure SQL Database, you can opt for a SQL database managed instance.

An especially important feature to consider is cross-database queries. If you have an application with two or more databases that performs cross-database queries, it's better to opt for a SQL database managed instance.

> **Note**
>
> For a list of features not supported by SQL managed instance, please visit https://feedback.azure.com/forums/915676-sql-managed-instance.

## Migration

A SQL database managed instance provides speedy migration with little to no downtime, as it's almost 100% compatible with on-premises SQL Server features.

As you prepare to migrate and work finding the migration issues, with a SQL database managed instance, there will be zero or minimal migration constraints compared to migration constraints with an Azure SQL Database.

## Time to Develop and Market

Azure SQL Database provides fast database deployment for a team with limited database expertise and development and deployment time constraints. With DTU-based pricing, a team can easily provision an Azure SQL Database and start the application development. As the application takes shape and the database and scalability requirements become clearer, the Azure SQL Database can be easily scaled to a higher DTU-based pricing tier or a vCore pricing tier.

On the other hand, if a team migrates an existing application from on-premises SQL Server, a SQL database managed instance provides fast and easy cloud migration with minimal application changes being required.

When opting for a SQL database managed instance for new applications, you need to choose the compute and storage resources in the vCore pricing tier. If a team doesn't have database expertise or clear compute and storage requirements, a DTU-based pricing model proves to be the best fit.

## Azure SQL Database Service Tiers

Azure SQL Database has two types of pricing models: DTU-based pricing tiers and the new vCore-based pricing tiers. A pricing model defines the size, performance, features, and most importantly, the cost of your solution.

# DTU Pricing Models

## Database Transaction Units

The amount of resources (CPUs, I/O, and RAM) to be assigned to an Azure SQL Database in a particular service tier is calculated in **Database Transaction Units** (**DTUs**).

DTUs guarantee that an Azure SQL Database will always have a certain amount of resources and a certain level of performance (offered under a particular DTU model) at any given point of time, independent of other SQL databases on the same Azure SQL server or across Microsoft Azure.

The ratio for the aforementioned resources was calculated by Microsoft by running an **Online Transaction Processing** (**OLTP**) benchmark.

The DTU amount signifies how powerful an Azure SQL Database is. For example, if a workload of, say, 5 queries takes 80 seconds on the Basic tier with 5 DTUs, then it'll take around 4 seconds on the Standard S3 tier with 100 DTUs.

There are four pricing tiers available in the DTU-based pricing model:

> **Note**
>
> The DTU is the measure of Azure SQL Database performance. This is discussed later in the lesson.

Figure 2.2: The DTU-based pricing model

- Basic service tier: The Basic tier is the lowest tier available and is applicable to small, infrequently used applications, usually supporting one single active transaction at any given point in time.

  The Basic tier has a size limit of 2 GB, a performance limit of 5 DTUs, and costs $5/month:

| PERFORMANCE LEVEL | BASIC |
|---|---|
| Max DTUs | 5 |
| Max database size* | 2 GB |
| Max in-memory OLTP storage | N/A |
| Max concurrent workers (requests) | 30 |
| Max concurrent logins | 30 |
| Max concurrent sessions | 300 |

Figure 2.3: Performance statistics of the Basic tier

- Standard service tier: This is the most commonly used service tier and is best for web applications or workgroups with low to medium I/O performance requirements. Unlike the Basic service tier, it has four different performance levels: S0, S1, S2, and S3. Each performance level offers the same size (250 GB); however, they differ in terms of DTUs and cost. S0, S1, S2, and S3 offer 10, 20, 50, and 100 DTUs, and cost $15, $30, $75, and $150 per month, respectively:

### Standard service tier

| PERFORMANCE LEVEL | S0 | S1 | S2 | S3 |
| --- | --- | --- | --- | --- |
| Max DTUs | 10 | 20 | 50 | 100 |
| Max database size* | 250 GB | 250 GB | 250 GB | 250 GB |
| Max in-memory OLTP storage | N/A | N/A | N/A | N/A |
| Max concurrent workers (requests) | 60 | 90 | 120 | 200 |
| Max concurrent logins | 60 | 90 | 120 | 200 |
| Max concurrent sessions | 600 | 900 | 1200 | 2400 |

Figure 2.4: Standard service tier

- Premium service tier: The Premium service tier is used for mission-critical, high-transaction-volume applications. It supports a large number of concurrent users and has a high I/O performance compared to the Basic and Standard service tiers.

  It has six different performance levels: P1, P2, P4, P6, P11, and P15. Each performance level offers different sizes and DTUs. P1, P2, P4, P6, P11, and P15 are priced at $465, $930, $1,860, $3,720, $7,001, and $16,003 per month, respectively:

| PERFORMANCE LEVEL | P1 | P2 | P4 | P6 | P11 | P15 |
|---|---|---|---|---|---|---|
| Max DTUs | 125 | 250 | 500 | 1000 | 1750 | 4000 |
| Max database size* | 500 GB | 500 GB | 500 GB | 500 GB | 4 TB | 4 TB |
| Max in-memory OLTP storage | 1 GB | 2 GB | 4 GB | 8 GB | 14 GB | 32 GB |
| Max concurrent workers (requests) | 200 | 400 | 800 | 1600 | 2400 | 6400 |
| Max concurrent logins | 200 | 400 | 800 | 1600 | 2400 | 6400 |
| Max concurrent sessions | 30000 | 30000 | 30000 | 30000 | 30000 | 30000 |

Figure 2.5: Premium service tier

- Premium RS service tier: The Premium RS service tier is used for low-availability, I/O-intensive workloads such as analytical workloads. It has four different performance levels: PRS1, PRS2, PRS3, and PRS4, which are priced at $116, $232, $465, and $930 per month, respectively:

| PERFORMANCE LEVEL | PRS1 | PRS2 | PRS4 | PRS6 |
| --- | --- | --- | --- | --- |
| Max DTUs | 125 | 250 | 500 | 1000 |
| Max database size* | 500 GB | 500 GB | 500 GB | 500 GB |
| Max in-memory OLTP storage | 1 GB | 2 GB | 4 GB | 8 GB |
| Max concurrent workers (requests) | 200 | 400 | 800 | 1600 |
| Max concurrent logins | 200 | 400 | 800 | 1600 |
| Max concurrent sessions | 30000 | 30000 | 30000 | 30000 |

Figure 2.6: Premium RS service tier

> **Note**
>
> The prices listed here are for a single database and not for an elastic pool.

The Premium service tier supports read scale-out and zone redundancy.

Read scale-out, when enabled, routes read queries to a read-only secondary replica. The read-only secondary is of the same compute and storage capacity as the primary replica.

An Availability Zone in an Azure region is an isolated datacenter building. There can be more than one Availability Zone in an Azure region. When opting for the Premium service tier, you can choose the Azure SQL Database to be zone-redundant. This will ensure that a copy of the database is available in another zone within the same region to facilitate high availability.

The zone-redundancy feature is available for databases up to 1 TB in size.

### vCore Pricing Model

Unlike DTU-based pricing models, where compute and storage are governed by the DTU size, the vCore (virtual core) pricing tiers allow you to independently define and control the compute and storage based on the workload of your on-premises SQL Server infrastructure.

> **Note**
>
> Compute = vCore + Memory

As mentioned earlier in *Lesson 1, Microsoft Azure SQL Database Primer*, in the *Introduction to Managed Instance* section, the vCore pricing model supports two hardware generations.

### Hardware Generations

**Gen4** offers up 24 logical CPUs, based on Intel E5-2673 v3 (Haswell) and 2.4 GHz processors, with 7 GB memory per core and attached SSD. Gen4 offers more memory per core.

**Gen5** offers up to 80 logical CPUs, based on Intel E5-2573 v4 (Broadwell) and 2.3 GHz processors, with 5.1 GB per core and fast eNVM SSD. Gen5 offers more compute scalability with 80 logical CPUs.

## vCore Service Tiers

There are three service tiers available with the vCore pricing model: General Purpose, Business Critical, and Hyperscale (in preview):

| Service Tier | Best For | Storage | IOPS | In-Memory | Availability |
|---|---|---|---|---|---|
| General Purpose | Cost-effective service tier suitable for most of the workloads with typical performance requirement | Remote storage up to 4 TB | 500 IOPS per vCore with maximum of 7000 IOPS and 5-10 millisecond latency | Not supported | Read-scale out and Zone redundant not supported. 1 Replica |
| Business Critical | IO intensive workloads with high business continuity requiredment[sm1] | Local SSD up to 4TB | 5000 IOPS per core with maximum of 200,000 and 1-2 millisecond latency | Supported | 1 Read-Scale out replica, 3 Replicas and Zone redundant supported for Gen5 hardware generation |
| Hyperscale (In-Preview) | Workloads with highly scalable and read-scale requirements | Scalable storage up to 100 TB. | Maximum of 200,000 IOPS for data file with 1-2 millisecond latency. Maximum of 7000 IOPS for log file with 5-10 millisecond latency. | Not Supported | Maximum of 4 secondary replicas for read-scale out and high availability and disaster recovery with automatic failover. |

Figure 2.7: Service tier feature table

> **Note**
>
> To find out more about the vCore resource limits for a single database, visit https://docs.microsoft.com/en-us/azure/sql-database/sql-database-vcore-resource-limits-single-databases.

## Azure Hybrid Benefit

Azure Hybrid Benefit for SQL Server allows you to use existing on-premises SQL Server Standard or Enterprise licenses with software assurance for discounted rates when migrating to Azure SQL Database with a vCore-based pricing tier.

Azure Hybrid Benefit provides an up to 30% cost saving for an existing on-premises license with software assurance.

When configuring a vCore-based service tier, there are two license types available:

- **BasePrice**, which provides discounted rates of existing on-premises SQL Server licenses. You only pay for the underlying Azure infrastructure. This is best to opt for when migrating an on-premises database to Azure SQL Database.

- **LicenseIncluded**, which includes the cost of the SQL Server license and Azure infrastructure.

## Hyperscale Service Tier

Hyperscale decouples the compute, storage, and log into microservices to provide a highly scalable and highly available service tier.

A traditional database server, as shown in the following diagram, consists of compute (CPU and memory) and storage (data files and log files):

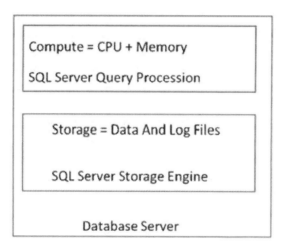

Figure 2.8: Database server architecture

A SQL Server engine is run by three main components: the query processor, the storage engine, and the SQL operating system.

The query processor does query parsing, optimization, and execution.

The storage engine serves the data required by the queries and manages the data and log files.

The SQL operating system is an abstraction over the Windows/Linux operating system that is mainly responsible for task scheduling and memory management.

Hyperscale takes out the storage engine from the database server and splits it into independent scale-out sets of components, page servers, and a log service, as shown in the following diagram.

Comparing it with the traditional database server, observe that the data and log files are no longer part of the database server.

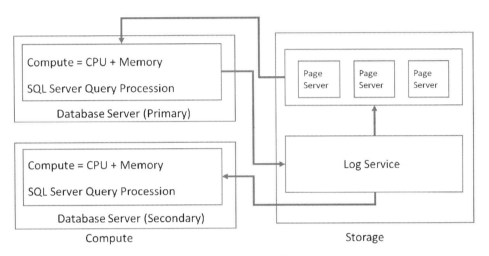

Figure 2.9: Architecture of Hyperscale

A detailed architecture diagram for Hyperscale is shown here:

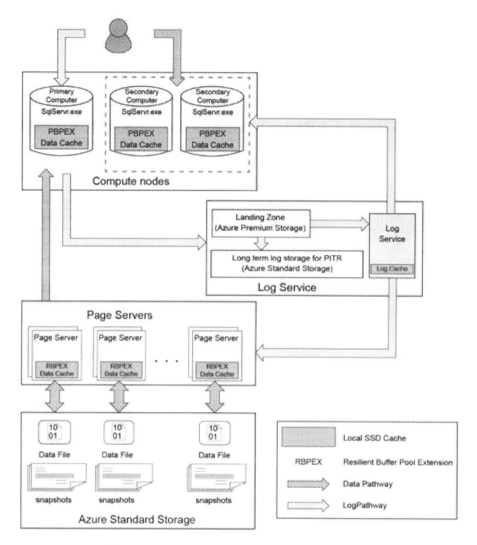

Figure 2.10: Detailed architecture of Hyperscale

The different Hyperscale components are explained here:

- **Compute nodes**: A compute node is a SQL server without the data files and the log files. Compute nodes are similar to the SQL Server query processor, responsible for query parsing, optimization, and execution. Users and applications connect and interact with the compute nodes.

Each compute node has a local data cache, a **Resilient Buffer Pool Extension (RBPEX)**.

> **Note**
>
> The RBPEX is a SQL Server feature that allows SSDs to be used as an extension to the buffer pool (server memory, or RAM). With an RBPEX, data can be cached to extended buffers (SSDs), thereby decreasing physical disk reads and increasing I/O throughput.

The primary compute node takes user and application transactions and writes them to the log service landing zone. If the data requested by a query isn't available in the primary node's **RBPEX**, it gets the missing data from the page servers.

The secondary compute nodes are used to offload reads from the primary compute node. The Hyperscale tier offers four secondary replicas for read scale-out, high availability, and disaster recovery. Each replica has the same vCore model as the primary replica and is charged separately.

You connect to a secondary replica by specifying **ApplicationIntent** as **ReadOnly** in the connection string.

Each secondary replica, similar to the case with the primary node, has a local cache (RBPEX). When a read request is received by a secondary replica, it first checks for the data in the local cache. If the data is not found in the local cache, the secondary replica gets the data from the page servers.

When the primary compute node goes down, a failover happens to a secondary node, and one of the secondary nodes promotes itself to a primary node and starts accepting read-write transactions.

A replacement secondary node is provisioned and warms up. It is cached in the background without affecting the performance of any of the other compute nodes.

No action needs to be taken at the storage level as the compute nodes are separated from the storage. This is contrary to the case in the regular SQL Server architecture, where a database serves hosts the SQL Server engine and the storage (as explained earlier in this section). If the database server goes down, the storage (that is, the data files and the log files) also goes down.

- **Page server node**: The page server node is where the database data files are. Each page server node manages 1 TB of data and represents one data file. The data from each page server node is persisted on Azure standard storage. This makes it possible to rebuild a page server from the data in the Azure standard storage in case of a failure. Therefore, there's no loss of data. The page servers get the data modifications from the log service and apply them to the data files. Each page server node has its own local cache (RPBEX). The data is fully cached in the page server local cache to avoid any data requests being forwarded to the Azure standard storage. A database can have one or more pages of server nodes depending on its size. As the database grows in size, a new page server is automatically added if the existing page server is 80% full. Hyperscale, for now, supports databases up to 100 TB in size.

- **Log service node**: The log service node is the new transaction log and is again separated from the compute nodes. The log service node gets the log records from the primary node, in the landing zone, which is Azure premium storage. Azure premium storage has built-in high availability, which prevents the loss of any log records. It persists the log records from the landing zone to a durable log cache. It also forwards the log records to the secondary compute nodes and the page server nodes. It writes the log records to long-term log storage, which is Azure standard storage. The long-term log storage is used for point-in-time recovery. When the log records are written to long-term storage, they are deleted from the landing zone to free up space.

  The log records are kept in long-term log storage for the duration of the backup retention period that has been configured for the database. No transaction log backups are needed.

  There's no hot standby for a log service node because it's not required. The log records are persisted first in Azure premium storage, which has its own high availability provision, and then in Azure standard storage.

Hyperscale, with this improved architecture, offers the following benefits:

- Nearly instantaneous backups. A backup is taken by taking a snapshot of the file in Azure standard storage. The snapshot process is fast and takes less than 10 minutes to back up a 50 TB database.

- Similar to database backups, database restores are also based on file snapshots and are a lot faster than in any other performance tier.

- Higher log throughput and faster transaction commits regardless of data volumes.

- The primary replica does not need to wait for an acknowledgement-of-transaction commit from the secondary replica. This is because the transaction log is managed by a log service.

- Supports up to 100 TB of database size.

- Rapid read scale-out by creating read replicas.

### Exercise: Provisioning a Hyperscale SQL Database Using PowerShell

1. Open a new PowerShell console window, change the working directory to **C:\Code\Lesson1**. Enter and execute the following PowerShell command:

   ```
   .\ProvisionAzureSQLDatabase.ps1 -ResourceGroup RGPackt -Location "East US
   2" -SQLServer sshsserver -SQLDatabase toystore -Edition Hyperscale
   ```

   The preceding command calls the **ProvisionAzureSQLDatabase.ps1** script to provision a new Hyperscale SQL database, **toystore**.

   > **Note**
   >
   > Change the SQLServer and SQLDatabase parameter values to avoid getting a
   > **Server/Database already exists** error.

2. Once the script completes, log in to the Azure portal and click **All resources** in the left navigation pane.

3. Click **toystore** to open the details window:

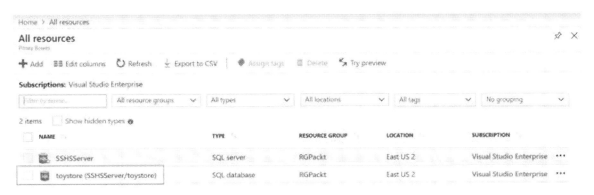

Figure 2.11: The All resources panel

The pricing tier is Hyperscale, Gen4, 1 vCore:

Figure 2.12: Configure pane in the toystore SQL database

## Scaling up the Azure SQL Database Service Tier

In this section, we'll learn how to scale up the Azure SQL Database service tier for better performance. Let's go back to our previous example of Mike, who observes that there is an increase in the load on the Azure SQL database. To overcome this problem, he plans to change the service tier for the database so that it can handle the overload. This can be achieved via the following steps:

1. Open a new PowerShell console. In the PowerShell console, execute the following command to create a new Azure SQL Database from a **bacpac** file:

   ```
   C:\Code\Lesson02\ImportAzureSQLDB.ps1
   ```

2. Provide the Azure SQL server name, SQL database name, Azure SQL Server administrator user and password, **bacpac** file path, and **sqlpackage.exe** path, as shown in the following screenshot:

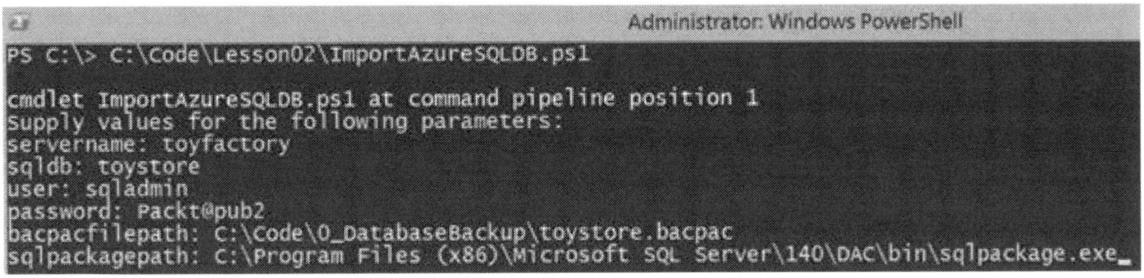

Figure 2.13: The Windows PowerShell window

The script will use **sqlpackage.exe** to import the **bacpac** file as a new SQL Database on the given Azure SQL Server. The database is created in the Basic service tier, as specified in the PowerShell script.

It may take 10–15 minutes to import the SQL database.

3. Open **C:\Code\Lesson02\ExecuteQuery.bat** in Notepad. It contains the following commands:

```
ostress -Sazuresqlservername.database.windows.net -Uuser
-Ppassword -dazuresqldatabase -Q"SELECT * FROM Warehouse. StockItems si
join Warehouse.StockItemholdings sh on si.StockItemId=sh.StockItemID join
Sales.OrderLines ol on ol.StockItemID = si.StockItemID" -n25 -r20 -1
```

4. Replace **azuresqlservername**, **user**, **password**, and **azuresqldatabase** with the appropriate values. For example, if you are running the preceding command against Azure SQL Database with **toystore** hosted on the **toyfactory** Azure SQL server with the username **sqladmin** and the password **Packt@pub2**, then the command will be as follows:

```
ostress -Stoyfactory.database.windows.net -Usqladmin -PPackt@ pub2
-dtoystore -Q"SELECT * FROM Warehouse.StockItems si join Warehouse.
StockItemholdings sh on si.StockItemId=sh.StockItemID join Sales.
OrderLines ol on ol.StockItemID = si.StockItemID" -n25
-r20 -q
```

The command will run 25 (specified by the **-n25** parameter) concurrent sessions, and each session will execute the query (specified by the **-Q** parameter) 20 times.

5.  Open the RML command prompt, enter the following command, and press *Enter*:

    ```
    C:\Code\Lesson02\ExecuteQuery.bat
    ```

    This will run the **ostress** command. Wait for the command to finish execution. Record the execution time:

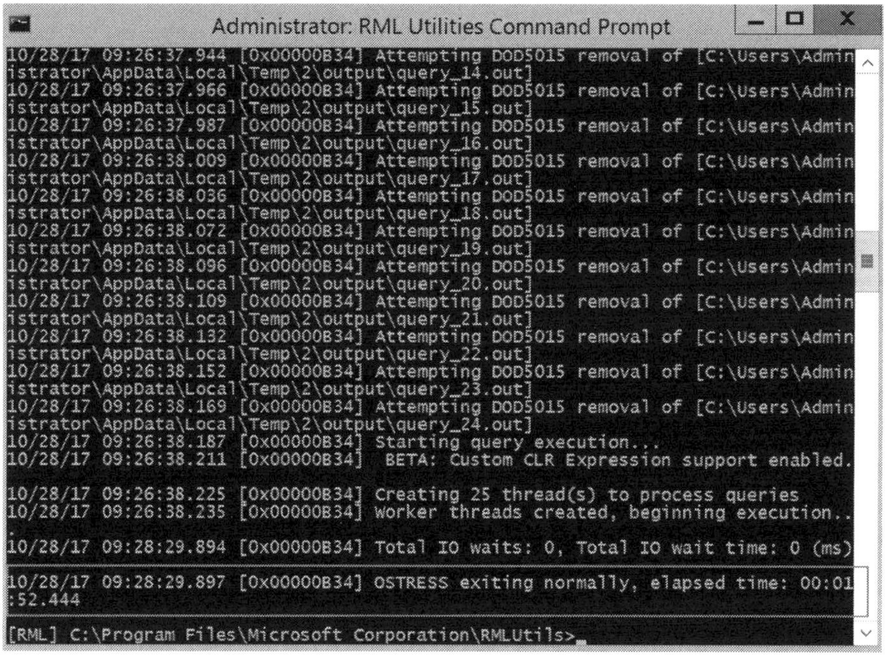

Figure 2.14: RML command prompt

It took around 1 minute and 52 seconds to run 25 concurrent connections against the Basic service tier.

6.  The next step is to scale up the service tier from Basic to Standard S3. In the PowerShell console, execute the following command:

    ```
    C:\Code\Lesson02\ScaleUpAzureSQLDB.ps1
    ```

Provide the parameters as shown in the following screenshot:

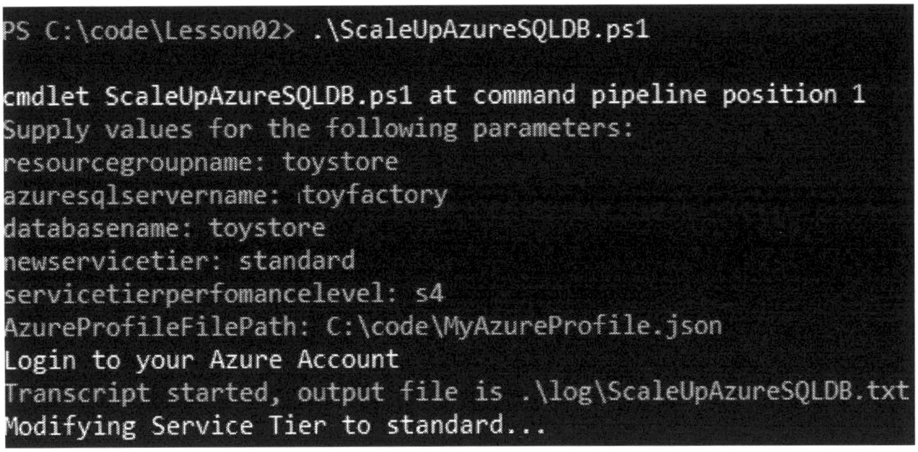

```
PS C:\code\Lesson02> .\ScaleUpAzureSQLDB.ps1

cmdlet ScaleUpAzureSQLDB.ps1 at command pipeline position 1
Supply values for the following parameters:
resourcegroupname: toystore
azuresqlservername: toyfactory
databasename: toystore
newservicetier: standard
servicetierperfomancelevel: s4
AzureProfileFilePath: C:\code\MyAzureProfile.json
Login to your Azure Account
Transcript started, output file is .\log\ScaleUpAzureSQLDB.txt
Modifying Service Tier to standard...
```

Figure 2.15: Scaling up the service tier

Observe that the database **Edition** has been changed to **Standard**.

7. Open a new RML command prompt and run the same **ostress** command as in step 4. You should see faster query execution time in the Standard S3 tier than in the Basic tier.

Here's the output from the **ExecuteQuery.bat** command:

```
Administrator: RML Utilities Command Prompt
10/28/17 09:39:13.328 [0x000002EC] Attempting DOD5015 removal of [C:\Users\Admin
istrator\AppData\Local\Temp\2\output\query_14.out]
10/28/17 09:39:13.345 [0x000002EC] Attempting DOD5015 removal of [C:\Users\Admin
istrator\AppData\Local\Temp\2\output\query_15.out]
10/28/17 09:39:13.358 [0x000002EC] Attempting DOD5015 removal of [C:\Users\Admin
istrator\AppData\Local\Temp\2\output\query_16.out]
10/28/17 09:39:13.373 [0x000002EC] Attempting DOD5015 removal of [C:\Users\Admin
istrator\AppData\Local\Temp\2\output\query_17.out]
10/28/17 09:39:13.392 [0x000002EC] Attempting DOD5015 removal of [C:\Users\Admin
istrator\AppData\Local\Temp\2\output\query_18.out]
10/28/17 09:39:13.406 [0x000002EC] Attempting DOD5015 removal of [C:\Users\Admin
istrator\AppData\Local\Temp\2\output\query_19.out]
10/28/17 09:39:13.416 [0x000002EC] Attempting DOD5015 removal of [C:\Users\Admin
istrator\AppData\Local\Temp\2\output\query_20.out]
10/28/17 09:39:13.434 [0x000002EC] Attempting DOD5015 removal of [C:\Users\Admin
istrator\AppData\Local\Temp\2\output\query_21.out]
10/28/17 09:39:13.457 [0x000002EC] Attempting DOD5015 removal of [C:\Users\Admin
istrator\AppData\Local\Temp\2\output\query_22.out]
10/28/17 09:39:13.468 [0x000002EC] Attempting DOD5015 removal of [C:\Users\Admin
istrator\AppData\Local\Temp\2\output\query_23.out]
10/28/17 09:39:13.485 [0x000002EC] Attempting DOD5015 removal of [C:\Users\Admin
istrator\AppData\Local\Temp\2\output\query_24.out]
10/28/17 09:39:13.499 [0x000002EC] Starting query execution...
10/28/17 09:39:13.523 [0x000002EC]  BETA: Custom CLR Expression support enabled.

10/28/17 09:39:13.526 [0x000002EC] Creating 25 thread(s) to process queries
10/28/17 09:39:13.532 [0x000002EC] Worker threads created, beginning execution..
.
10/28/17 09:39:54.751 [0x000002EC] Total IO waits: 0. Total IO wait time: 0 (ms)

10/28/17 09:39:54.754 [0x000002EC] OSTRESS exiting normally, elapsed time: 00:00
:41.807

[RML] C:\Program Files\Microsoft Corporation\RMLUtils>
```

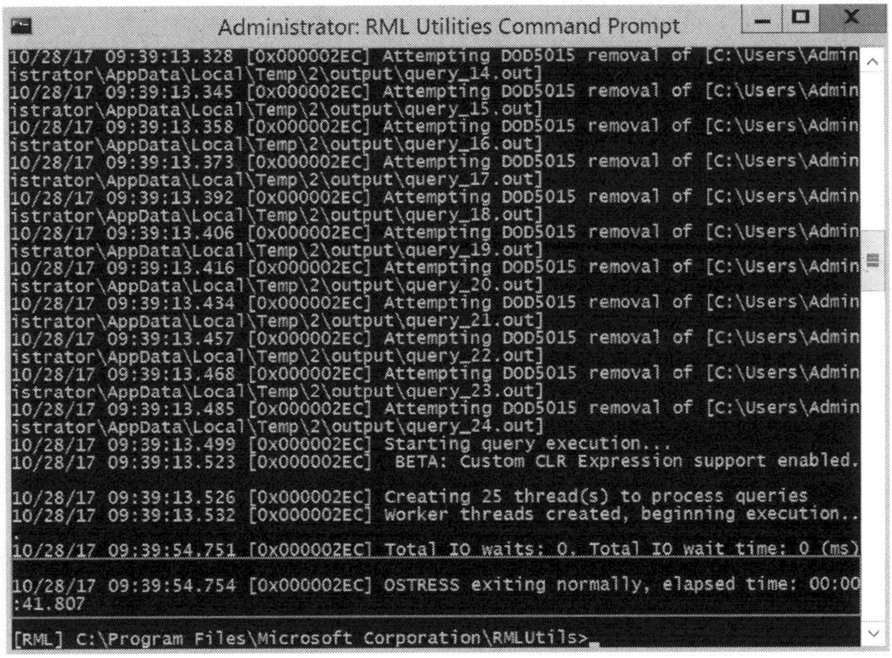

Figure 2.16: Output from the ExecuteQuery.bat command

It took around 42 seconds to run 25 concurrent connections against the Standard S3 service tier. This is almost 60% faster than the Basic tier. You get the performance improvement just by scaling up the service tier, without any query or database optimization.

## Changing a Service Tier

You can scale up or scale down an Azure SQL Database at any point in time. This gives the flexibility to save money by scaling down to a lower service tier in off-peak hours and scaling up to a higher service tier for better performance in peak hours.

You can change a service tier either manually or automatically. Service tier change is performed by creating a replica of the original database at the new service tier performance level. The time taken to change service tier depends on the size as well as the service tier of the database before and after the change.

Once the replica is ready, the connections are switched over to the replica. This ensures that the original database is available for applications during the service tier change. This also causes all in-flight transactions to be rolled back during the brief period when the switch to the replica is made. The average switchover time is four seconds, and it may increase if there are a large number of in-flight transactions.

You may have to add retry logic in the application to manage the connection disconnect issues when changing a service tier.

# Choosing Between a vCore Pricing Model and DTU-based Service Tiers

When choosing between vCore and DTU-based pricing tiers, consider the following.

## Licensing

A vCore pricing model provides up to 30% cost savings by using existing on-premises SQL Server Standard or Enterprise licenses with software assurance. Therefore, if you are migrating an existing on-premises SQL Server infrastructure, consider opting for a vCore pricing model.

## Flexibility

A DTU-based model bundles up the compute, IOPs, and storage under DTUs and provides a pre-configured range of varying DTU amounts for different types of workloads. It's therefore best suited for when you need a simple pre-configured option.

A vCore model provides flexibility when selecting compute and storage options and is therefore best when you want more transparency with control and over the compute and storage options.

Consider a scenario where you have a database with high compute requirements and low storage requirements; say, 125 DTUs with a database size of 200 GB. You'll have to opt for the Premium service tier and pay for the unused storage (300 GB):

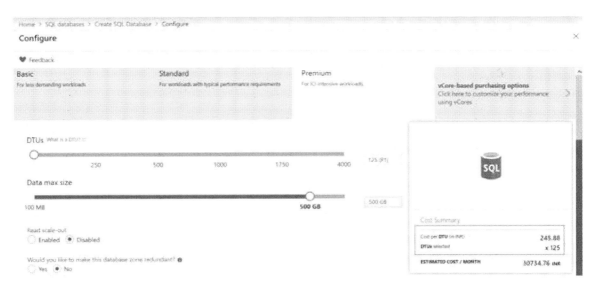

Figure 2.17: Azure portal pricing feature

The preceding screenshot is from the Azure portal and shows the pricing options for a Premium DTU-based tier. Observe that the pricing is calculated per DTU. The storage cost is inclusive of the DTUs. Therefore, in this instance, you will pay for all 500 GB of storage, even if it's not used.

In a vCore model, the compute and storage cost are calculated independently. Therefore, you only pay for the storage you use, which is 200 GB and the vCore used.

> **Note**
>
> The Premium service tier includes 500 GB of free storage. An additional cost of approximately $0.16 is applied on additional storage (beyond 500 GB) up to 1 TB.

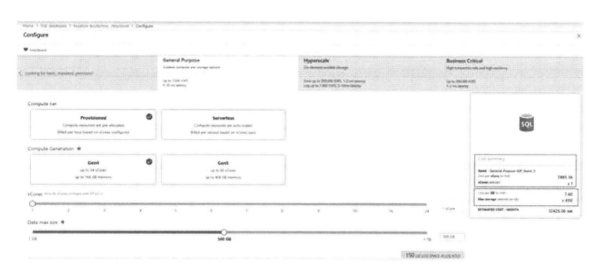

Figure 2.18: General Purpose vCore pricing model

The preceding screenshot is from the Azure portal and shows the pricing options for the General Purpose vCore pricing model. Observe that the pricing is calculated per vCore and per GB of storage used. Therefore, you pay for the storage you use. You can, however, scale the storage up or down at any time, as per your requirements.

Consider another scenario, where a team is just starting up with a product and is looking for a SQL database pricing tier; a Standard S2 or S3 tier with 50 to 100 DTUs and a maximum of 250 GB would be a good option to go for. As the product matures and the scalability requirements become clear, the team can scale up accordingly.

You can scale between vCore-based and DTU-based service tiers. When scaling from DTU- to vCore-based pricing tiers, consider the following rule of thumb for choosing the correct compute size:

- 100 Standard tier DTU = 1 vCore General Purpose tier

- 125 Premium tier DTU = 1 vCore Business Critical tier

> **Note**
>
> Once you move to the Hyperscale service tier, you can't move to any other service tier.

## Determining an Appropriate DTU Based Service Tier

As a SQL Server DBA, when migrating to an Azure SQL Database, you will need to have an initial estimate of DTUs so as to assign an appropriate service tier to an Azure SQL Database. An appropriate service tier will ensure that you meet most of your application performance goals. Estimating a lower or a higher service tier will result in decreased performance or increased cost, respectively.

This lesson teaches you how to use the DTU calculator to make an appropriate initial estimate of the service tier. You can, at any time, change your service tier by monitoring the Azure SQL Database's performance once it's up and running.

## Azure SQL Database DTU Calculator

Developed by Justin Henriksen, an Azure Solution Architect at Microsoft, the DTU Calculator can be used to find out the initial service tier for an Azure SQL Database. The calculator is available at https://dtucalculator.azurewebsites.net.

## DTU Calculator Work Flow

The DTU Calculator works as shown in the following diagram:

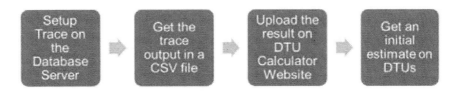

**Figure 2.19: DTU Calculator workflow**

First, you have to set up a trace to record the following counters for at least an hour:

- **Processor**: % processor time
- **Logical Disk**: Disk reads/sec
- **Logical Disk**: Disk writes/sec
- **Database**: Log bytes flushed/sec

You can run a trace by using either the command-line utility or the PowerShell script provided on the DTU Calculator website.

Capture the counters on a workload similar to that of the production environment. The trace generates a CSV report.

> **Note**
>
> These utilities capture the counters at the server level and not at the database level. To capture at the database level, use SQL Server **Dynamic Management Views** (**DMVs**).

The DTU Calculator uses this report to analyze and suggest an initial service tier.

### Finding an Initial Service Tier for the Database to be Migrated Using the DTU Calculator

Let's get back to Mike. Mike is unsure about the service tier that he has to select while migrating to Azure SQL Database. Hence, he wants to make use of the DTU Calculator to select the service tier to migrate to. The following steps describe how he can use the DTU Calculator to determine the initial service tier for his database:

Open https://dtucalculator.azurewebsites.net and download the command-line utility to capture the performance counters.

> **Note**
>
> You can also open the file saved at `C:\Code\Lesson02\ DTUCalculator\sql-perfmon-cl`.

The **sql-performance-cl** folder has two files, **SqlDtuPerfmon.exe** and **SqlDtuPerfmon.exe.config**. The first one is an executable that, when run, will capture the counter in a **CSV** file, and the second file is a configuration file that specifies the counters to be captured.

1. Open **SqlDtuPerfmon.exe.config** in Notepad and make changes, as suggested in the following points.

   Change the SQL instance name to be monitored:

   ```
   <!-- SQL COUNTER -->
   <!-- Change the SQL Server instance below if you are usin
   <!-- <add key="SqlCategory" value="SQLServer:Databases"/>
   <add key="SqlCategory" value="MSSQL$SQL2016:Databases"/>
   <add key="SqlInstance" value="_Total"/>
   ```

   Figure 2.20: Change in the config file

   Under the **SQL COUNTER** comment, modify the value of **SqlCategory** as per the instance name of your SQL server.

   If you are running on a default instance, then replace **MSSQL$SQL2016:Databases** with **SQLServer:Databases**.

   If you are running on a named instance, say, **Packtpub**, then replace **MSSQL$SQL2016:Databases** with **MSSQL$Packtpub:Databases**.

   Set the output file path:

   ```
   <!-- DISK LOCATION OF THE OUTPUT FILE -->
   <add key="CsvPath" value="C:\Code\Lesson02\DTUCalculator\sql-perfmon-log.csv"/
   /appSettings>
   ```

   Figure 2.21: Output file path

   If you wish to change the output file, modify the value for the **CsvPath** key shown in the preceding screenshot.

   You are now ready to capture the performance trace.

2.  Double-click the `C:\Code\Lesson02\DTUCalculator\sql-perfmon-cl\SqlDtuPerfmon.exe` file to run the performance trace.

    A new command prompt will appear and will display the counters as they are being monitored and saved into the CSV file.

    You should get a command-line window similar to the one shown in the following screenshot:

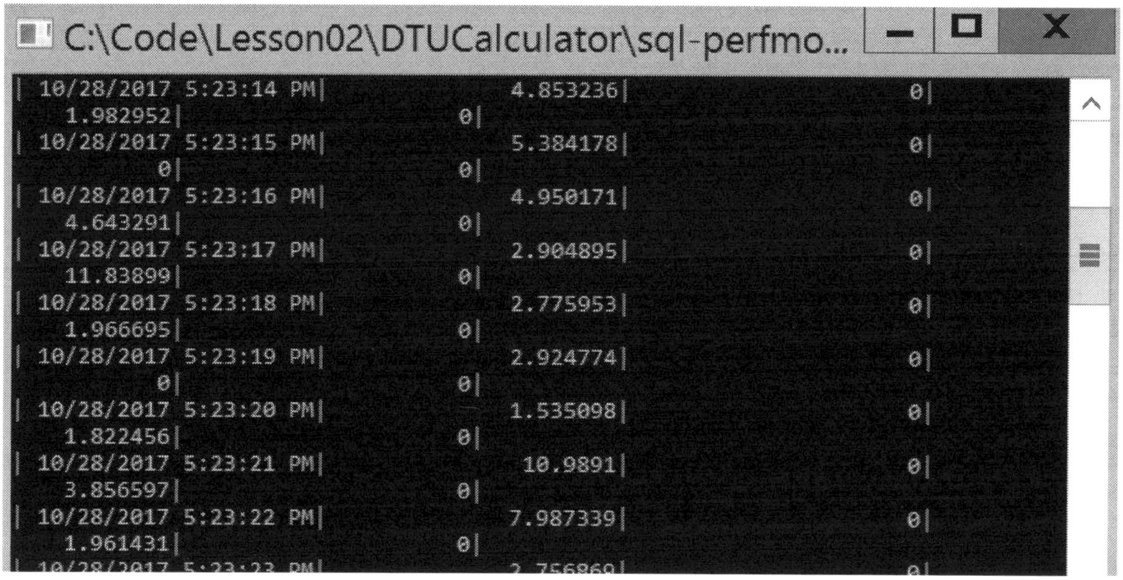

Figure 2.22: Command Prompt window with counters

3.  The next step is to upload the output file on the DTU Calculator website and analyze the results. To do this, open https://dtucalculator.azurewebsites.net/ and scroll down to the *Upload the CSV file and Calculate* section.

    In the **Cores** text box, enter the number of cores on the machine you ran `SqlDtuPerfmon.exe` on to capture the performance counters.

    Click **Choose file** and in the **File Open Dialog box**, select the `C:\Code\Lesson02\DTUCalculator\sql-perfmon-log.csv` file.

Click the **Calculate** button to upload and analyze the performance trace:

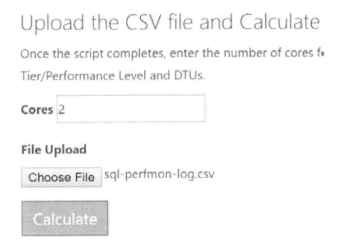

**Figure 2.23: Panel to upload the CSV file**

4. The DTU Calculator will analyze and then suggest the service tier you should migrate your database to. It gives an overall recommendation and further breaks down the recommendation based on only CPU, I/O, and logs utilization.

## Overall Recommendation

The DTU Calculator suggests migrating to the Premium – P2 tier, as it will cover approximately 100% of the workload.

You can hover your mouse over different areas of the chart to check what percentage of the workload each tier covers:

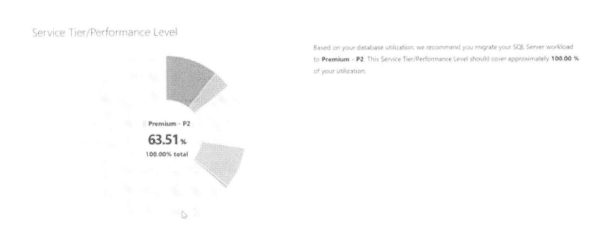

**Figure 2.24: Service tier recommendation window**

## Recommendation Based on CPU Utilization

The calculator recommends the Premium – P2 tier based on CPU utilization:

Service Tier/Performance Level for CPU

Based solely on **CPU** utilization, we recommend you migrate your SQL Server workload to **Premium - P2**. This Service Tier/Performance Level should cover approximately **100.00 %** of your CPU utilization.

Figure 2.25: Recommendation based on CPU utilization

## Recommendation Based on IOPs Utilization

Based solely on IOPs utilization, the DTU Calculator suggests going for a Standard – S2 tier, which covers approximately 90% of the workload. However, it also mentions that approximately 10% of the workload will require a higher service tier. Therefore, the decision lies with you. The Premium – P2 service tier is costlier, but it covers 100% of the workload. If you are okay with 10% of the workload performing slowly, you can choose the Standard – S2 service tier.

Remember, this is an estimation of the service tier and you can at any time scale up to a higher service tier for improved performance:

Service Tier/Performance Level for Iops

Based solely on **Iops** utilization, we recommend you migrate your SQL Server workload to **Standard - S2**. This Service Tier/Performance Level should cover approximately **89.81 %** of your Iops utilization.

NOTE: There is approximately **10.19 %** of your workload that falls into a higher Service Tier/Performance Level. After migrating your database to Azure, you should evaluate your database's performance using the guidance mentioned in the ❶ information section above.

Figure 2.26: Recommendation based on IOPs utilization

## Recommendation Based on Log Utilization

Based solely on log utilization, the DTA Calculator recommends the Basic service tier. However, it is also mentioned that approximately 11% of the workload requires a higher service tier.

At this point, you may decide to start with the Basic service tier and then scale up as and when required. This will certainly save money. However, you should consider that the Basic service tier allows only 30 concurrent connections and has a maximum database size limit of 2 GB:

Figure 2.27: Recommendation based on log utilization

## Determining Compatibility Issues

Once you have finalized the service tier, the next step is to migrate both schema and data from the on-premises SQL database to the Azure SQL Database. As we learned in *Lesson 1, Microsoft Azure SQL Database Primer*, not all features are the same and supported on Azure SQL Server. Therefore, you will first have to do a compatibility test or assessment to find and fix the compatibility issues.

The following are the tools available to detect compatibility issues with. Although these tools can be used to migrate the database, in this section, we'll specifically talk about using them to assess compatibility.

## Data Migration Assistant

**Data Migration Assistant (DMA)** is a standalone tool for detecting compatibility issues and migrating on-premises SQL Server databases to Azure SQL Databases. It provides a wizard-type, easy-to-use graphical user interface for compatibility assessment and migration.

It detects and highlights compatibility issues. Once all compatibility issues are identified and fixed, you can migrate the database.

### SQL Server Data Tools (SSDT) for Visual Studio

SSDT is the best tool for Azure SQL Database (V12) to find and fix incompatibility issues. It has the most recent compatibility rules. The compatibility issues can be fixed from SSDT itself, after which we can migrate the database.

### SQL Server Management Studio (SSMS)

SSMS has two options to detect and migrate:

- Export Data Tier Application: This exports the data and schema in a **bacpac** file, and while doing so, lists out any of the incompatibilities found.

- Deploy Database to Microsoft Azure SQL Database: This deploys the database to Azure SQL Database, first by exporting the database in a **bacpac** file and then importing the **bacpac** file into an Azure SQL Database. It lists incompatibilities when generating the **bacpac** file.

### SQLPackage.exe

This is a command-line tool that helps to automate database development tasks such as importing, exporting, and extracting **bacpac** or **dacpac** files. Its actual use is to help automate database life cycle management; however, it can be used to detect and get a report of the incompatibilities found.

It is included in SSDT. You can download a different version of SSDT from here: https://docs.microsoft.com/en-us/sql/ssdt/download-sql-server-data-tools-ssdt?view=sql-server-2017.

### SQL Azure Migration Wizard

This is a community-supported tool that provides a wizard-driven graphical user interface to detect compatibility issues and migrate the database. The tool isn't updated fully to work with the later Azure SQL Database V12 version.

You can download it from here: https://github.com/adragoset/SQLAzureMigration.

## Azure Database Migration Services

Azure Database Migration Services, or DMS, is a fully managed Azure service that enables seamless migrations from multiple data sources to Azure databases.

Here are some examples of migrations that DMS can do:

- Migrate on-premises SQL Server to Azure SQL Database or SQL managed instance. Supports both online and offline migrations.

- Migrate Azure SQL Database to SQL database managed instances.

- Migrate an AWS SQL Server RDS instance to Azure SQL Database or SQL managed instance.

- Migrate MySQL to Azure Database for MySQL.

- Migrate PostgreSQL to Azure Database for PostgreSQL.

- Migrate MongoDB to Azure Cosmos DB Mongo API.

> **Note**
>
> Online migration is a migration with zero downtime or near-zero downtime during the cut-over to the migrated database.

## Exercise: Migrating a SQL Server Database to Azure SQL Database Using Azure DMS

> **Note**
>
> In the exercise, the source database is on a SQL server on Azure VM. To migrate an on-premises database, site-to-site connectivity is required via VPN or Azure Express route. To find out more about it, please visit the following sites: https://docs.microsoft.com/en-us/azure/expressroute/expressroute-introduction
>
> https://docs.microsoft.com/en-us/azure/vpn-gateway/vpn-gateway-about-vpngateways
>
> The rest of the steps for the migration are similar to those of the exercise.

Follow these steps to migrate a SQL Server database on Azure VM to an Azure SQL Database:

1.  Use Database Migration Assistant to find the compatibility issues in the source database and migrate the source schema to an Azure SQL Database. Before migrating the schema, make sure you have a blank Azure SQL Database already provisioned.

    The steps to assess and migrate schema are given in *Activity: Using Database Migration Assistant*.

2.  The next step is to register the `Microsoft.DataMigration` resource provider. To do this, type `Subscriptions` in the search box and then select **Subscriptions**:

Figure 2.28: Registering the Microsoft.DataMigration resource provider

In the **Subscriptions** window, select the subscription in which you wish to create the Azure DMS instance:

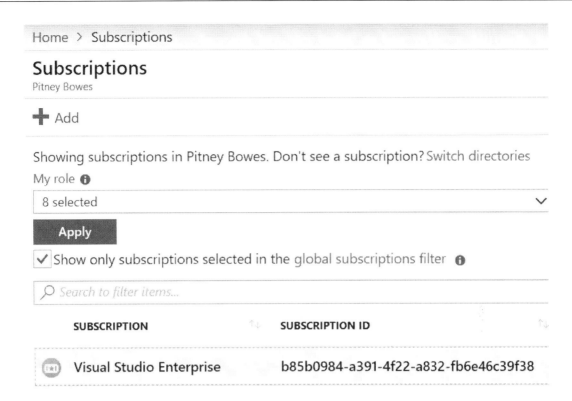

Figure 2.29: Subscription window

In the selected **Subscription** window, type `Resource Providers` in the search box:

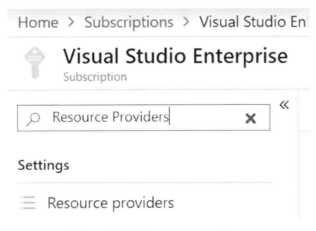

Figure 2.30: Resource providers

Click **Resource providers** to open the **Resource providers** window. Click **Register** against **Microsoft.DataMigration** if it's not already registered:

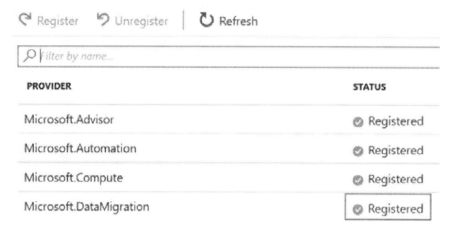

Figure 2.31: Registering Microsoft.DataMigration

3. Log in to the Azure portal and type **Azure Database Migration Services** in the search box:

Figure 2.32: Searching for Azure Database Migration services

Click the **Azure Database Migration Services** link under **Services**. In the **Azure Database Migration Services** window, click **Add**.

4. In the **Create Migration Service** window, provide the details as shown here:

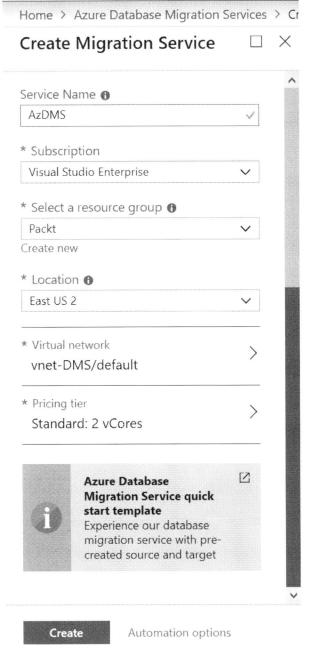

Figure 2.33: Create Migration Service window

Other than the name, subscription, location, and resource group, DMS requires a virtual network and a pricing tier.

A virtual network allows DMS to connect to the target and source. For example, if your source is an on-premises SQL Server database, the DMS virtual network should be connected to the on-premises network either through a VPN or an Azure Express route.

For the sake of the demonstration, the source is a SQL Server database on Azure VM. Azure VM and DMS are on the same virtual network in order to facilitate connectivity between them.

DMS has two performance tiers, Standard and Premium. The Standard tier is free and is for one-time or offline migrations. The Standard tier comes with one, two, or four vCores.

The Premium tier can be used for offline and online migrations. The Premium tier comes with four vCores.

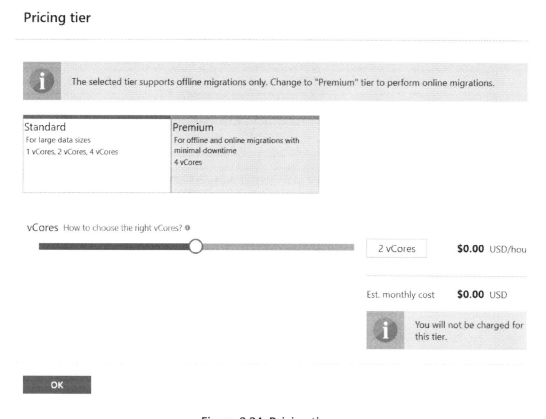

Figure 2.34: Pricing tiers

Click **Create** to provision a DMS instance.

5.  The next step is to create a new database migration project. To do that, open the AzDMS resource and click **New Migration Project**:

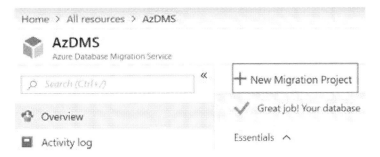

Figure 2.35: New Migration Project

In the **New Migration Project** window, provide the **Project name**, select **SQL Server** as the **Source server type**, and select Azure SQL Database as the **Target server type**.

Click **Create and run activity** to continue:

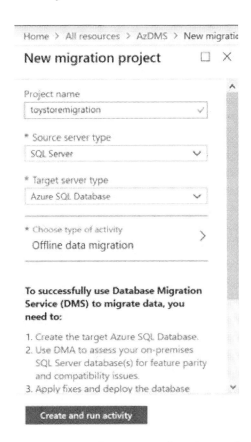

Figure 2.36: Creating a new migration project

6. In the next step, provide the source server details. The **Source SQL Server instance name** is the name or the IP of the source SQL server. The source server here is an Azure VM. The private IP of the VM is therefore used to connect to it:

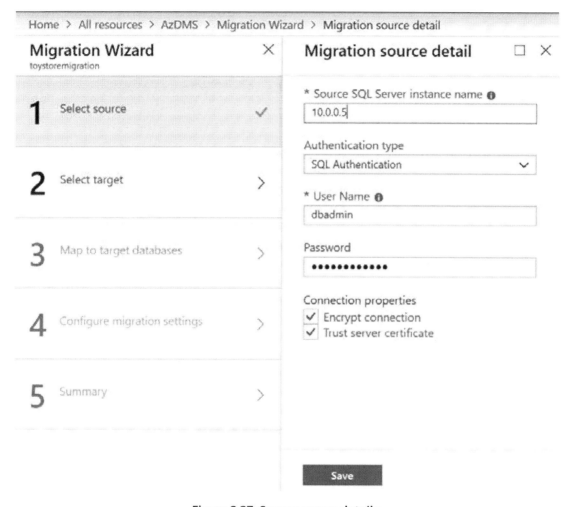

Figure 2.37: Source server details

7. Click **Save**. DMS will connect and verify that DMS can connect to the specified source server. Upon successful connection, the wizard will move to the next step.

8. In the **Select target** window, specify the Azure SQL Database server and username and password. Make sure that the target Azure SQL Database contains the tables and the other objects from the source database:

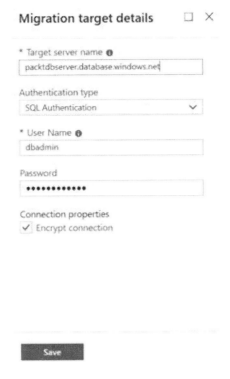

Figure 2.38: Migration target details

9. Click **Save** to verify and save the target server configuration.

10. In the next window, **Map to target databases**, map the source and the target database:

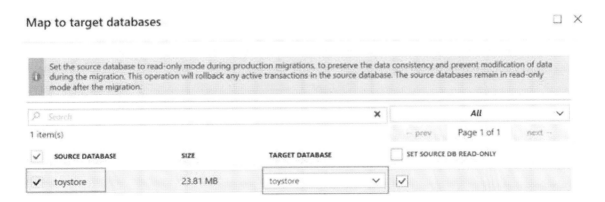

Figure 2.39: Map to target databases

11. In the next step, select the tables to migrate. The default is **All tables**.

Click **Save** to move to the **Summary** page.

On the **Summary** page, verify the configuration settings, name the activity, and select the validation option:

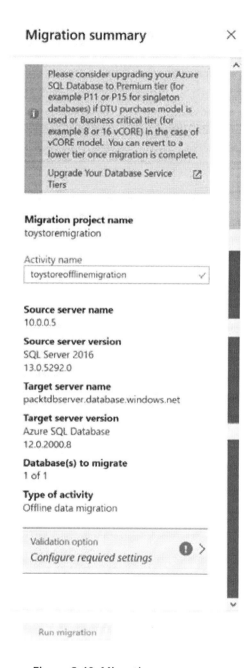

Figure 2.40: Migration summary

The validation option allows you to validate the data after the database migration is done. Now select **Do not validate my database(s)**:

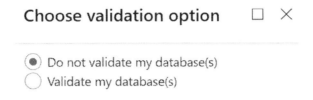

Figure 2.41: Validation option

12. Click **Run migration** to start the database migration.

As the migration starts, you'll be redirected to the migration project status page.

When the migration completes, the status is updated, as can be seen here:

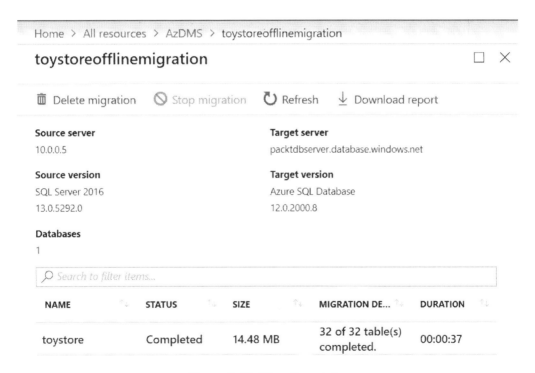

Figure 2.42: Migration status

## Determining the Migration Method

Once you have found and fixed compatibility issues, the next step is to select a migration tool or method and perform the actual migration. There are different methods available for various scenarios. The selection largely depends on downtime, database size, and network speed/quality.

Here's a comparison of various migration methods to help you correctly choose a migration method:

| Migration Method | Description | Downtime | Database Size |
|---|---|---|---|
| SQL Server Management Studio – Deploy Database to Azure SQL Database | Wizard-based GUI to export on-premises database to `bacpac` and import the `bacpac` onto Azure SQL Database. | Yes (depends on database size) | Small to Medium databases |
| Sqlpackage.exe | Command-line utility to export on-premises databases to `bacpac` and import the `bacpac` on to Azure SQL Database. | Yes (Depends on database size) | Small to Medium databases |
| Manual (Dacpac and BCP) | Use sqlpackage.exe to export dacpac (only schema) and bcp out data in a folder. Import the dacpac (only schema) followed by parallel bcp in. | Yes (Depends on database size) | Large to Very Large databases (improved performance from parallel bcp in) |
| SQL Azure Migration Wizard | Free Codeplex wizard- based GUI utility. It scripts out schema in a T-SQL file and then uses bcp, as mentioned in the previous method. | Yes (Depends on database size) | Large to Very Large |
| Data Migration Assistant | Wizard-based GUI standalone migration software. Uses T-SQL script to migrate schema and bcp to migrate data. Allows you to choose which objects and table to migrate. Detects and lists out compatibility issues as well. | Yes (Depends on database size) | Large to Very Large databases |
| Transactional Replication | Azure SQL Database as a subscriber to on- premises SQL Server Database publisher. Higher complexity, cost, and resources. Supports SQL Server 2012+ as the publisher and Azure SQL Database as the subscriber. | Short | Large to Very Large databases |

Figure 2.43: Determining the migration method

## Migrating an On-Premises SQL Server Database to Azure SQL Database

Let's consider our example of Toystore Ltd. from the previous lesson. Mike has performed all the steps that he had to complete before he could migrate the SQL Server database to Azure. Now all he has to do is perform the migration using the tool of his choice. He selects SSMS. In this section, we'll see how to use SSMS to migrate a database to Azure:

1.  Open SSMS. Press F8 to open **Object Explorer**. Connect to your SQL instance.

> **Note**
>
> A backup of **toystore** is available at `C:\Code\Lesson02\toystore.bak`.

2.  In Object Explorer, right-click **toystore database** and go to **Tasks | Deploy Database to Microsoft Azure SQL Database**:

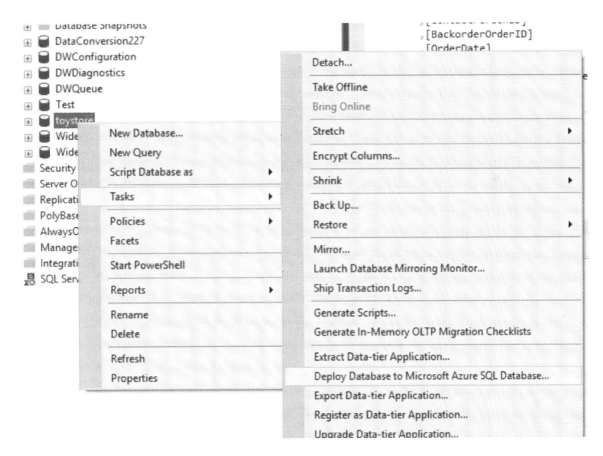

Figure 2.44: Deploy database to Microsoft Azure SQL Database

3.  In the **Deploy Database** wizard, click **Next** to continue:

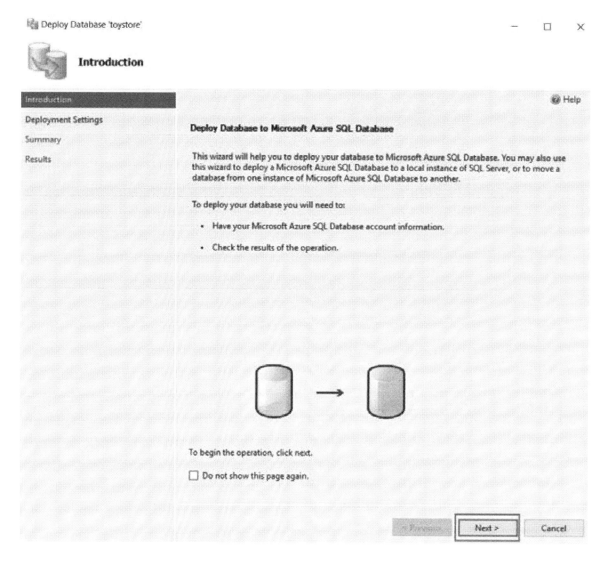

Figure 2.45: Deploy Database wizard

4. In the **Connect to Server** dialog box, provide your Azure SQL Server name, administrator login name, and password. Click **Connect** to connect to the Azure SQL server:

Figure 2.46: Connecting to the Azure SQL server

5. In the **Deployment Settings** window, under **New database name**, provide the name of the Azure SQL Database to which you wish to migrate as an on-premises database. The Azure SQL Database edition and the **Service Objective** are automatically detected by SSMS.

6. Under **Other settings**, under the **Temporary file name**, SSMS displays the path of the exported **bacpac** file. You can change it if you wish to, or you can leave it as default. Click **Next** to continue:

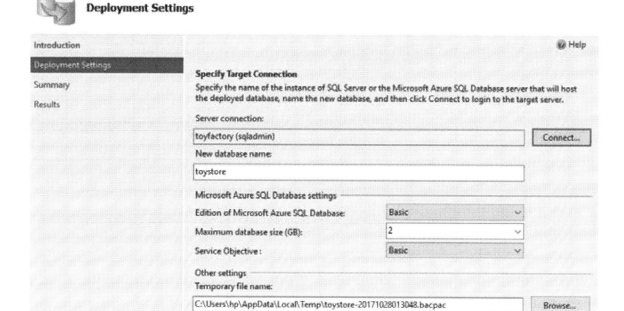

Figure 2.47: The Deployment Settings window

7. In the **Verify Specified Settings** window, review the **Source** and **Target** settings, and then click **Finish** to start the migration process:

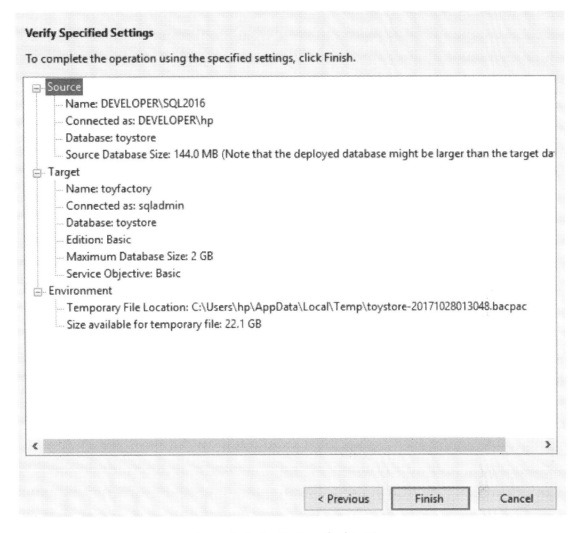

**Verify Specified Settings**

To complete the operation using the specified settings, click Finish.

- Source
  - Name: DEVELOPER\SQL2016
  - Connected as: DEVELOPER\hp
  - Database: toystore
  - Source Database Size: 144.0 MB (Note that the deployed database might be larger than the target da
- Target
  - Name: toyfactory
  - Connected as: sqladmin
  - Database: toystore
  - Edition: Basic
  - Maximum Database Size: 2 GB
  - Service Objective: Basic
- Environment
  - Temporary File Location: C:\Users\hp\AppData\Local\Temp\toystore-20171028013048.bacpac
  - Size available for temporary file: 22.1 GB

< Previous    Finish    Cancel

Figure 2.48: Verify Specified Settings

SSMS checks for compatibility issues, and the migration process terminates because there are compatibility issues. Click **Error**, next to **Exporting database**, to view the error's details:

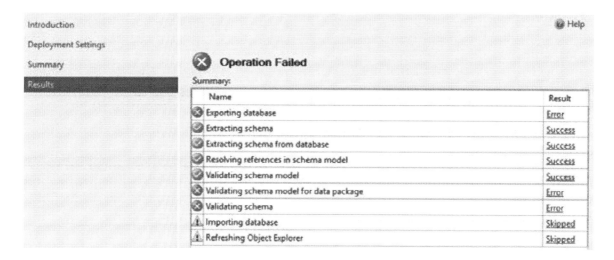

Figure 2.49: View error details

Here is the output showing a detailed description of the error:

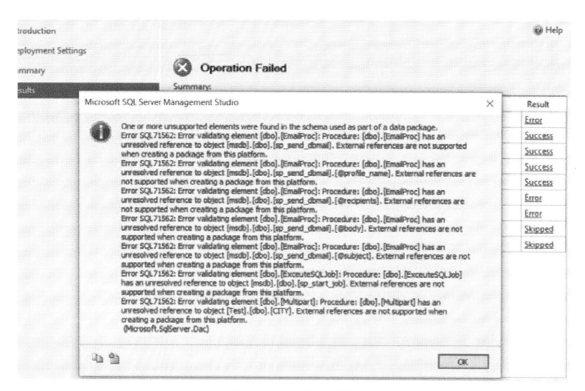

Figure 2.50: Description of the error

8. In the **Error Details** window, we can see that the migration was terminated because of unsupported objects found in the **bacpac** package. Click **OK** to close the **Error Details** window. The next step is to fix the errors.

9. Open **C:\code\Lesson02\FixCompatibilityIssues.sql** in SSMS. The script fixes the compatibility issues by commenting/correcting out the unsupported code within the stored procedures:

```
USE [toystore] GO
ALTER proc [dbo].[BackUpDatabase] As
-- Backup command isn't supported on Azure SQL Database
--backup database toystore to disk = 'C:\torystore.bak'
--with init, stats=10 GO
ALTER proc [dbo].[EmailProc] As
-- Database mail isn't supported on Azure SQL Database
--EXEC msdb.dbo.sp_send_dbmail
--      @profile_name = 'toystore Administrator',
--      @recipients = 'yourfriend@toystore.com',
@body = 'The stored procedure finished successfully.',
--      @subject = 'Automated Success Message' ;

select * from city
```

10. Press F5 to execute the script. Repeat *steps 1-10* to successfully migrate the database:

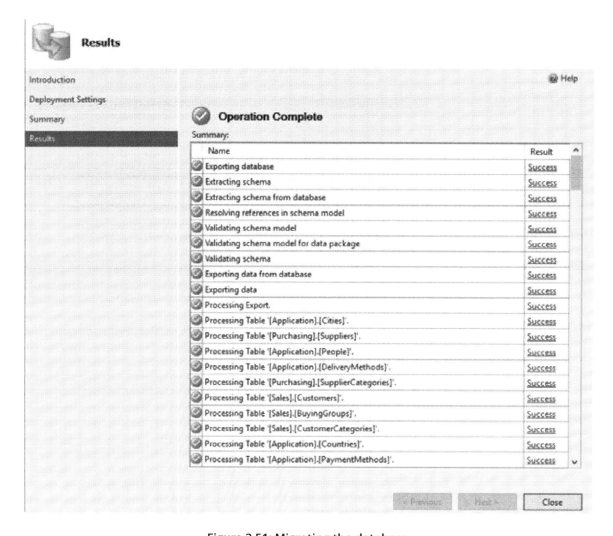

Figure 2.51: Migrating the database

11. To verify the migration, connect to Azure SQL Database using SSMS and run the following query:

```
SELECT TOP (1000) [OrderID]
      ,[CustomerID]
      ,[SalespersonPersonID]
      ,[PickedByPersonID]
      ,[ContactPersonID]
      ,[BackorderOrderID]
      ,[OrderDate]
```

```
        ,[ExpectedDeliveryDate]
        ,[CustomerPurchaseOrderNumber]
        ,[IsUndersupplyBackordered]
        ,[Comments]
        ,[DeliveryInstructions]
        ,[InternalComments]
        ,[PickingCompletedWhen]
        ,[LastEditedBy]
        ,[LastEditedWhen]
    FROM [toystore].[Sales].[Orders]
```

The following screenshot shows the output of the preceding code:

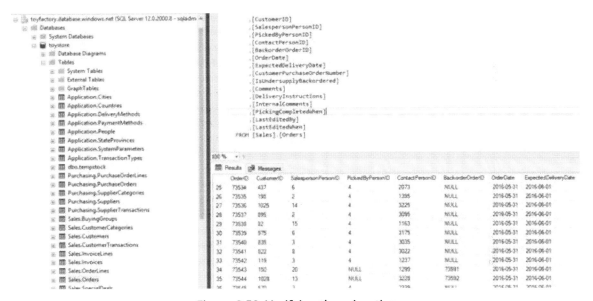

Figure 2.52: Verifying the migration

Congratulations! You have successfully migrated your SQL Server database to an Azure SQL database.

## Activity: Using DMA

This section describes how to migrate a SQL Server database, such as the **toystore** database, to an Azure SQL database using DMA:

1. Open Microsoft Data Migration Assistant on your computer. From the left ribbon, click the **+** sign, as shown in the following screenshot:

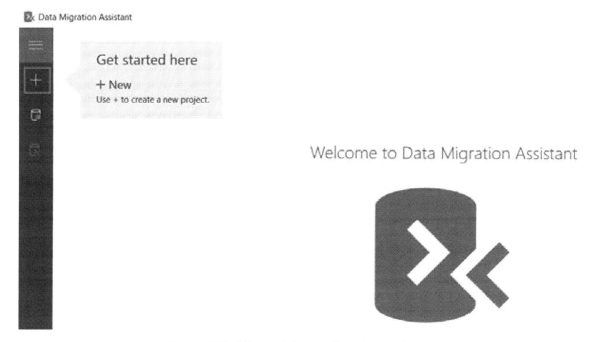

Figure 2.53: Microsoft Data Migration Assistant

2. In the resultant window, you will need to set these fields:

   For **Project type**, select **Assessment**.

   For **Project name**, type **toystore**.

   For **Source server type**, select **SQL Server**.

   For **Target server type**, select **Azure SQL Server**.

3. Click **Create** to create a new assessment project:

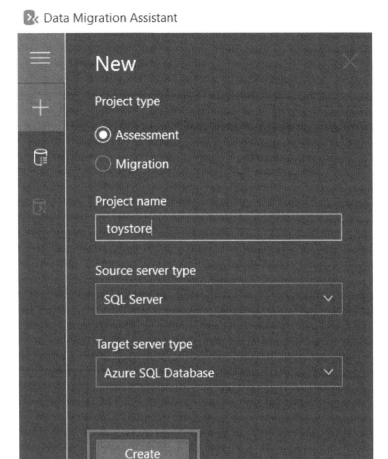

Figure 2.54: Creating new assessment project

4. In the resulting **Select report type** window, select the **Check database compatibility** and **Check feature parity** checkboxes. Click **Next** to continue:

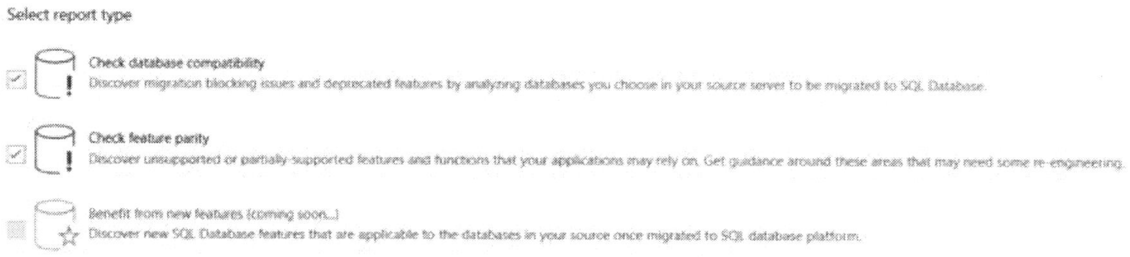

Select report type
Check database compatibility
Discover migration blocking issues and deprecated features by analyzing databases you choose in your source server to be migrated to SQL Database.
Check feature parity
Discover unsupported or partially-supported features and functions that your applications may rely on. Get guidance around these areas that may need some re-engineering.
Benefit from new features (coming soon...)
Discover new SQL Database features that are applicable to the databases in your source once migrated to SQL database platform.

Figure 2.55: Checking feature parity

5. In the **Connect to a server** window, do the following:

   For **Server name**, provide the SQL server name.

   For **Authentication type**, select **Windows Authentication**.

   Click **Connect** to continue:

Connect to a server
Connect to a server and select sources
Server name
developer\sql2016
Authentication type
Windows Authentication
Connection properties
Encrypt connection
Trust server certificate
SQL Server permissions
To run the selected advisor(s), credentials used to connect to a source SQL Server instance must be a member of the sysadmin server role.
Connect

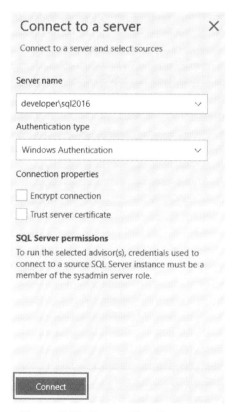

Figure 2.56: Connecting the server

6. In **Add Sources**, select `toystore` and click **Add** to continue.

7. Click **Start Assessment** to find compatibility issues.

8. DMA will apply the compatibility rules to find and list the compatibility issues. It tells you the features that aren't supported in the **SQL Server feature parity** section:

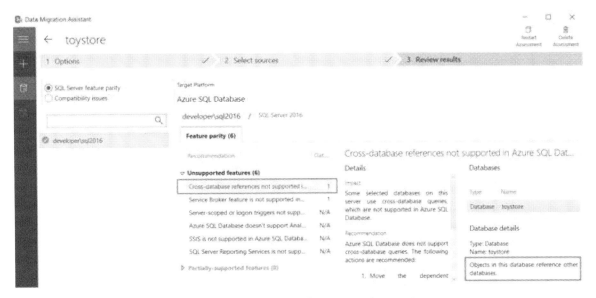

Figure 2.57: SQL Server feature parity section

According to DMA, you have one cross-database reference and one Service Broker instance, which aren't supported in Azure SQL Database.

9.  Under **Options**, select the **Compatibility issues** radio button:

Figure 2.58: Selecting compatibility issues

DMA lists out the stored procedures that failed the compatibility test. To fix the errors, open `C:\code\Lesson02\FixCompatibilityIssues.sql` in SSMS and execute it against the **toystore** database.

10. In the top-right corner, click **Restart Assessment**:

Restart
Assessment

Figure 2.59: Restart assessment

DMA will re-assess and notify you that there are no compatibility issues:

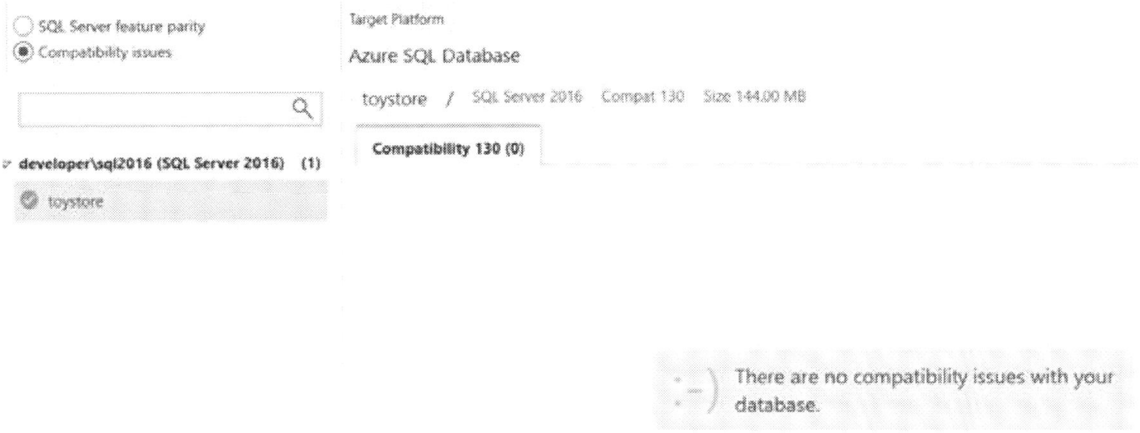

Figure 2.60: DMA ascertains that there are no compatibility issues

11. To migrate the database, in the left-hand navigation bar, click the **+** sign.

12. In the resulting window, do the following:

For **Project type**, select **Migration**.

For **Project name**, type **toystoremigration**.

For **Source server type**, select **SQL Server**.

For **Target server type**, select **Azure SQL Server**.

For **Migration scope**, select **Schema and Data**.

Click **Create** to create a new assessment project:

 Data Migration Assistant

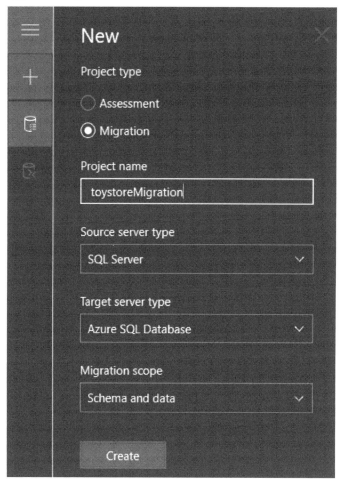

Figure 2.61: Creating a new assessment project

13. In the **Connect to server** window, do the following:

For **Server name**, provide the **SQL Server name**.

For **Authentication type**, select **Windows Authentication**.

Click **Connect** to continue:

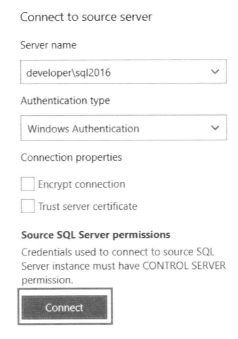

Figure 2.62: Connecting to the source server

14. Select **toystore** from the list of available databases and click **Next**:

Figure 2.63: Select toystore database

15. In the **Connect to target server** window, do the following:

    For **Server name**, provide the Azure SQL Server name.

    For **Authentication type**, select SQL Server Authentication.

    For **Username**, provide the Azure SQL Server admin user.

    For **Password**, provide the password.

Clear the **Encrypted connection** checkbox.

Click **Connect** to continue:

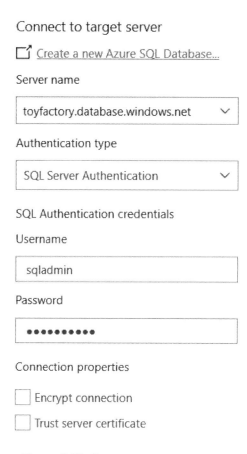

Figure 2.64: Connect to target server

16. In the resulting window, select the **toystore** database, and then click **Next** to continue:

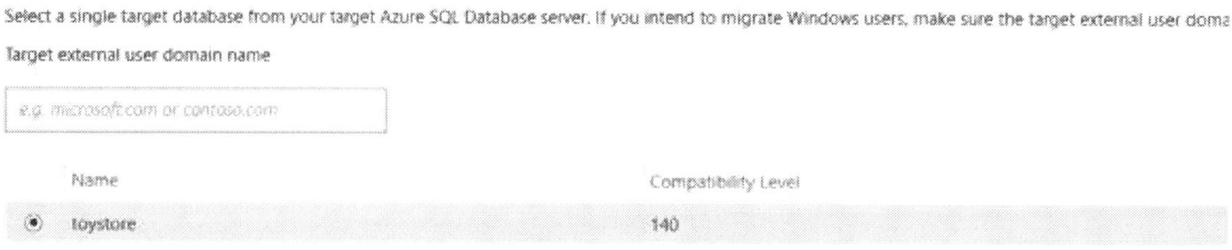

Select a single target database from your target Azure SQL Database server. If you intend to migrate Windows users, make sure the target external user doma

Target external user domain name

e.g. microsoft.com or contoso.com

| Name | Compatibility Level |
| --- | --- |
| ⦿ toystore | 140 |

Figure 2.65: Selecting the toystore database

17. In the resulting **Select objects** window, you can select which objects to move to Azure SQL Database. Select all and click **Generate SQL Scripts** at the bottom of the window to continue:

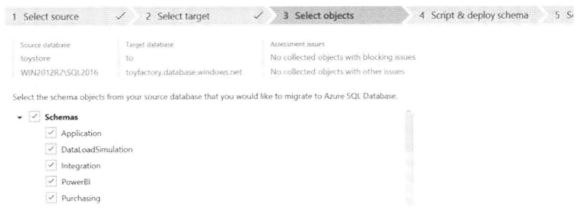

Figure 2.66: Generate SQL scripts

18. DMA will generate a T-SQL script to deploy the database schema. If you wish to save the T-SQL script, you can do so by clicking on the **Save** option in the **Generated script** section:

Figure 2.67: Generating a T-SQL script to deploy the database schema

19. In the **Script** and **Deploy** schema window, click the **Deploy schema** button to deploy the schema to the Azure server. DMA will execute the T-SQL script against the Azure SQL Database to create the selected database objects:

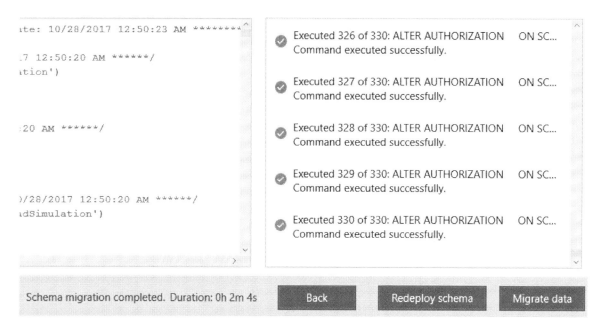

Figure 2.68: Creating database objects

20. Once schema migration is successful, click **Migrate data**.

21. In the resulting **Selected tables** window, you can choose what table data to migrate. Leave it as default, for this example, selecting all tables, and then click **Start data migration**:

Figure 2.69: Starting data migration

This migrates data from the selected tables in parallel and therefore can be used for large to very large databases:

▽ Tables (31)

| Status | Table name | Migration details |
|--------|-----------|-------------------|
| ✓ | [Application].[Cities] | Migration successful. Duration: 0 hrs 0 mins 14 secs |
| ✓ | [Application].[Countries] | Migration successful. Duration: 0 hrs 0 mins 14 secs |
| ✓ | [Application].[DeliveryMethods] | Migration successful. Duration: 0 hrs 0 mins 6 secs |
| ✓ | [Application].[PaymentMethods] | Migration successful. Duration: 0 hrs 0 mins 14 secs |
| ✓ | [Application].[People] | Migration successful. Duration: 0 hrs 0 mins 8 secs |
| ✓ | [Application].[StateProvinces] | Migration successful. Duration: 0 hrs 0 mins 8 secs |
| ✓ | [Application].[SystemParameters] | Migration successful. Duration: 0 hrs 0 mins 8 secs |
| ✓ | [Application].[TransactionTypes] | Migration successful. Duration: 0 hrs 0 mins 9 secs |
| ✓ | [Purchasing].[PurchaseOrderLines] | Migration successful. Duration: 0 hrs 0 mins 10 secs |
| ✓ | [Purchasing].[PurchaseOrders] | Migration successful. Duration: 0 hrs 0 mins 13 secs |

Figure 2.70: Migrate the data from selected tables

## Activity: Performing Transactional Replication

In this section, we will make use of the toy manufacturing company introduced in an earlier lesson as an example to understand how to migrate an SQL Server database to an Azure SQL database using transactional replication:

1. Open **SSMS**. Press F7 to open **Object Explorer**. In Object Explorer, click **Connect** to connect to your SQL server.

2. In **Object Explorer**, right-click the **Replication** node and click **New Publication...**:

Figure 2.71: Creating a new publication

3. In the **New Publication Wizard** welcome screen, click **Next** to continue.

4. In the **Publication Database** window, select **toystore** as the database to be published. Click **Next** to continue:

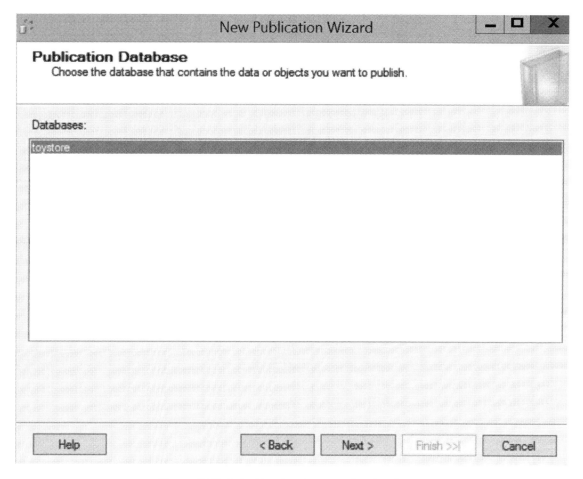

Figure 2.72: Selecting toystore as the database

5. In the **New Publication Wizard**, select **Transactional publication**. There are only two publication types allowed with Azure SQL Database as a subscriber. Click **Next** to continue:

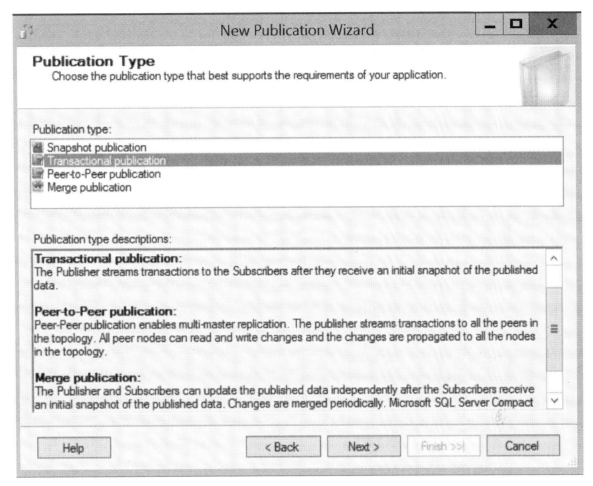

Figure 2.73: Publication and transactional window

6. In the **Articles** page, select all the objects to publish. Click **Next** to continue. If required, you can filter out objects that you don't want to migrate to an Azure SQL database here:

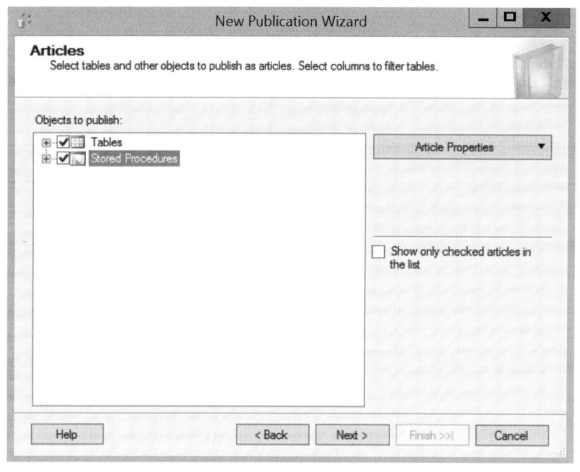

Figure 2.74: Selecting all the objects in the Articles page

7. The **Article Issues** page alerts you that you should migrate all tables that are referenced by views, stored procedures, functions, and triggers. As we are migrating all the tables, we don't have anything to do here. Click **Next** to continue:

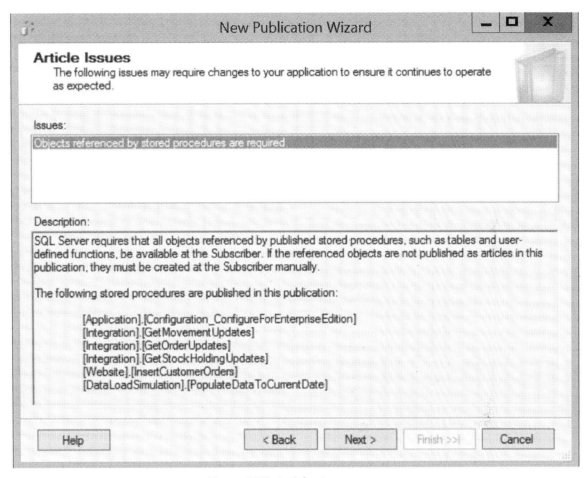

Figure 2.75: Articles Issues page

8. **Filter Table Rows** lets you filter unwanted rows that you don't want to publish. As you are publishing all rows, leave it as default and click **Next** to continue:

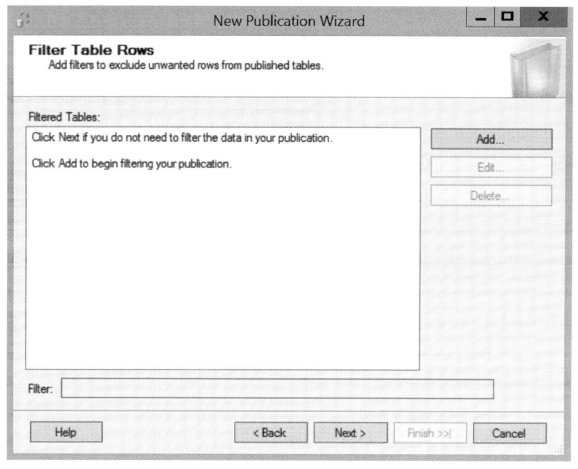

Figure 2.76: Filter Table Rows window

9.  In the **Snapshot Agent** page, select the **Create a snapshot immediately and keep the snapshot available to initialize subscriptions** option. You can also schedule the Snapshot Agent to run at specific times:

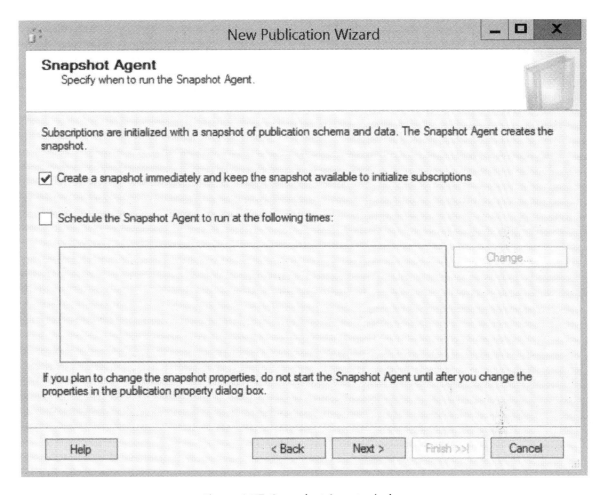

Figure 2.77: Snapshot Agent window

10. In the **Agent Security** page, select the **Security Settings** button:

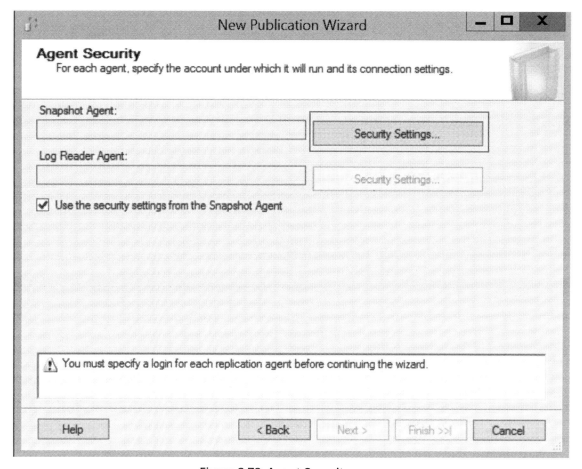

Figure 2.78: Agent Security page

11. In the **Snapshot Agent Security** page, specify the account for the Snapshot Agent to run on. You can either give the domain account that has permission to access the SQL Server instance and the database or you can choose it to run under the SQL Server agent service account, which isn't the recommended option.

Under the **Connect to the publisher** section, select **By impersonating the process account**. The process account must have read and write access to the publisher database:

Figure 2.79: Snapshot Agent Security window

12. Click **OK** to continue. You'll be taken back to the **Agent Security** page. Check the **Use the security settings from the Snapshot Agent** box, under the **Log Reader Agent** text box. The Log Reader Agent will run under the same account as the Snapshot Agent. You can choose different security settings for the Log Reader Agent if you wish to:

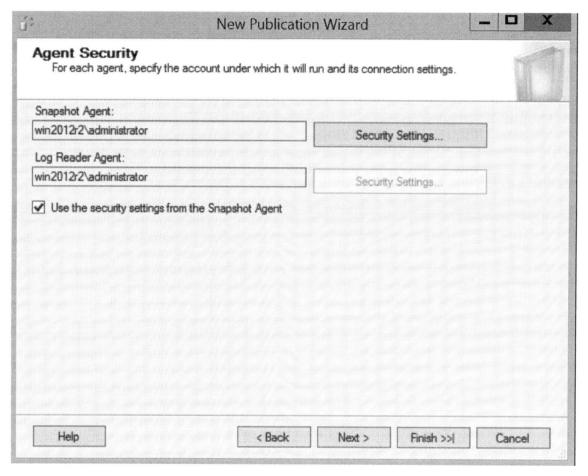

Figure 2.80: Agent Security window

Click **Finish** to continue.

13. On the **Complete the Wizard** page, under **Publication name**, provide a name for your publication. You can review the objects that are being published in this window.

Click **Finish** to create the publication:

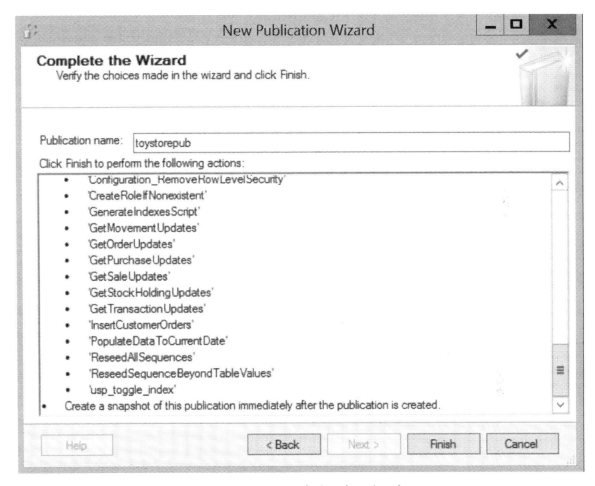

Figure 2.81: Completing the wizard

14. The **New Publication Wizard** will now create the publication. Add the selected articles to the publication and it will start the Snapshot Agent:

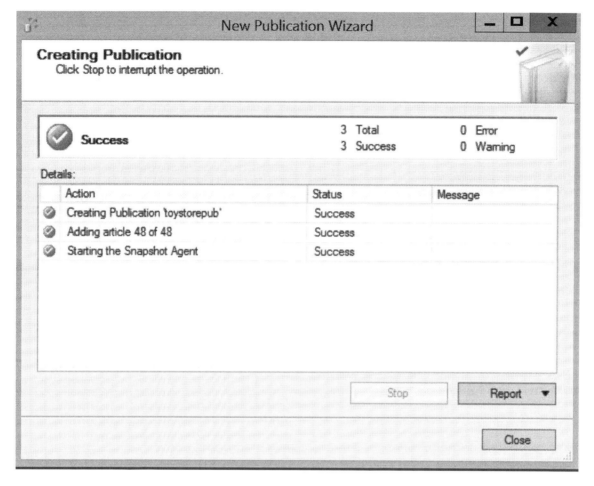

Figure 2.82: New Publication Wizard window

Click **+** to complete the **New Publication Wizard**.

In **Object Explorer**, expand the **Replication** node, and then expand **Local Publications**; the **toystorepub** publication has been added to the publication list:

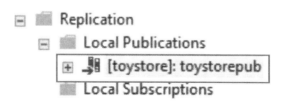

Figure 2.83: Check that toystore is added to the publication list

15. The next step is to create a subscription for the Azure SQL Database. Open **Object Explorer**, expand the **Replication** node, and right-click the **Local Subscription** option. Select **New Subscriptions** to continue. Azure SQL Database only supports push subscriptions:

Figure 2.84: Creating a subscription for the Azure SQL database

16. In **New Subscription Wizard**, select **Next** to continue:

Figure 2.85: New Subscription Wizard

17. In the **Publication** page, select the publication for which you wish to create the subscription. The **toystorepub** publication is listed under the **toystore** database. If it's the only publication, it'll be selected by default. Click **Next** to continue:

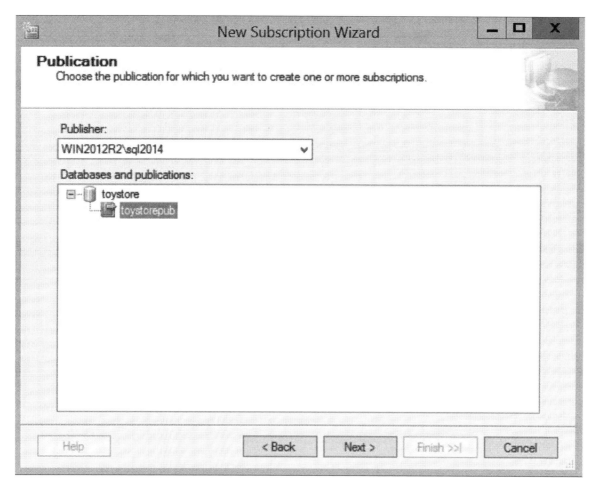

Figure 2.86: Selecting the toystore publication

18. In the **Distribution Agent Location** page, select **Run all agents at the Distributor**, which in our case is the push subscription. Pull subscriptions aren't allowed with Azure SQL Database as a subscriber. Click **Next** to continue:

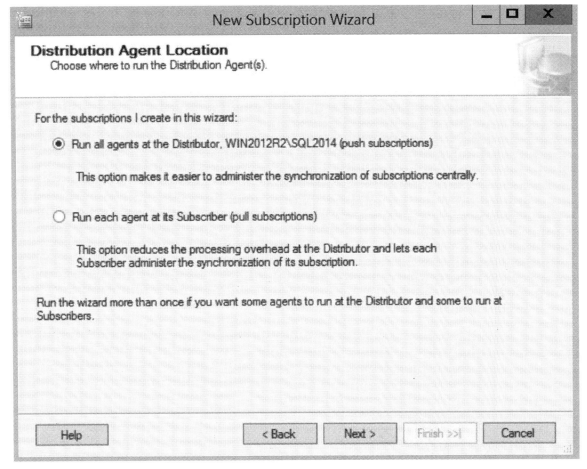

Figure 2.87: Distribution Agent Location

19. On the **Subscribers** page, click the **Add Subscriber** button at the bottom of the window and select **Add SQL Server Subscriber**:

Figure 2.88: Creating a subscription for the Azure SQL Database

On the **Connect to Server** dialog box, provide the Azure SQL Server name and SQL authentication login credentials to connect to the Azure SQL server. Click **Connect** to continue:

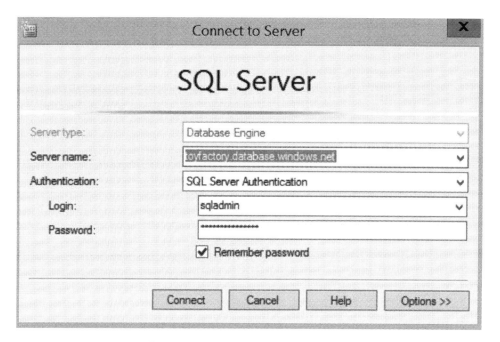

Figure 2.89: Connecting to the server

The **Subscribers** page will now list the Azure SQL server in the **Subscriber** column and the **toystore** database in the **Subscription Database** column. Select the Azure SQL server if it's not already selected and click **Next** to continue.

20. In the **Distribution Agent Security** window, click (**Options menu**) to set the security option:

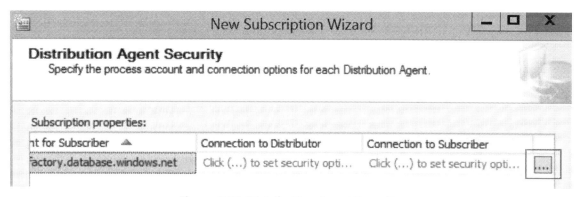

Figure 2.90: Distribution Agent Security

The distribution agent can run under the context of the domain account or the SQL Server Agent Service account (not recommended) for the agent. Provide a domain account that has appropriate access to the **Distribution Server**, which in our case is the same as the **Publication Server**.

In the **Connect to the Distributor** section, select the default option (by impersonating the process account). You can also use a SQL Server login if you wish to.

In the **Connect to the Subscriber** section, provide the Azure SQL server, SQL Server login, and password.

Click **OK** to go back to the **Distribution Agent Security** page. It'll now show the selected security options:

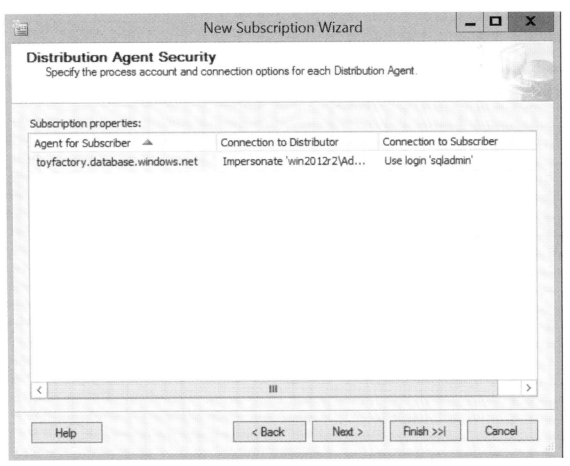

Figure 2.91: Connecting to the server

Click **Next** to continue.

21. On the **Synchronization Schedule** page, in the **Agent Schedule** section, select **Run Continuously** and click **Next** to continue:

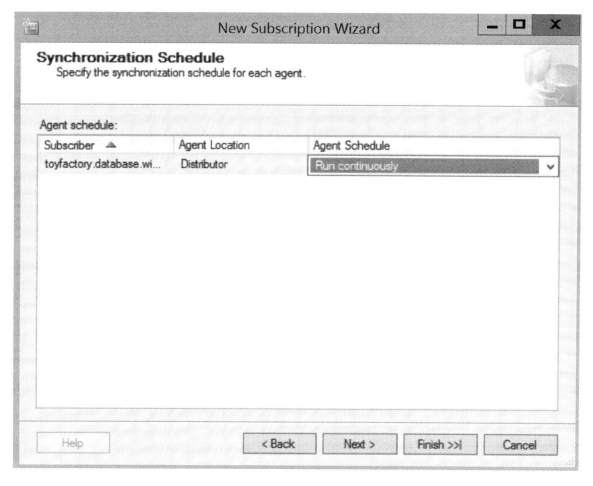

Figure 2.92: Synchronization schedule

22. On the **Initialize Subscriptions** page, under the **Initialize When** option, select **Immediately**, and then click **Next** to continue:

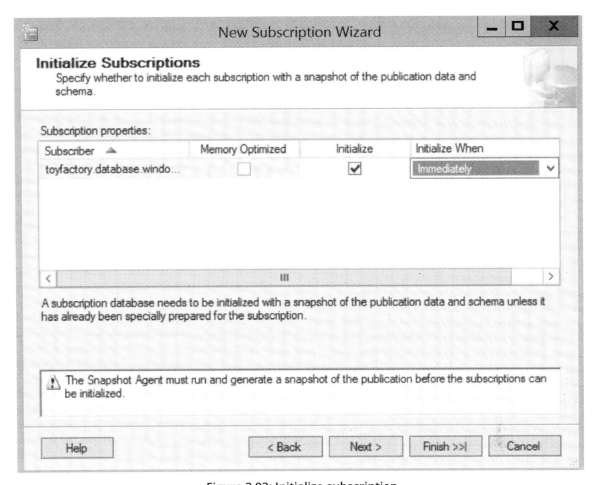

Figure 2.93: Initialize subscription

23. On the **Wizard Actions** window, select the **Create the subscription(s)** option and click **Next** to continue:

Figure 2.94: Wizard Actions

24. In the **Complete the Wizard** window, review the subscription settings and click **Finish** to create the subscription. The wizard will create the subscription and will initiate the Snapshot Agent to apply the initial snapshot on the subscriber.

Once the initial snapshot is applied, all of the transactions on the publisher will be sent to the subscriber.

Click **Close** to end the wizard.

25. To verify the replication, in **Object Explorer**, right-click the **Replication** node and select **Launch Replication Monitor**:

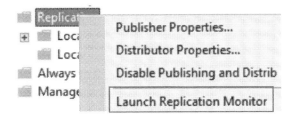

Figure 2.95: Launch Replication Monitor

In the replication monitor, expand the **My Publishers** node, then expand the SQL Server instance name node. The `toystorepub` publication will be listed there. Select the `toystorepub` publication to check the synchronization health:

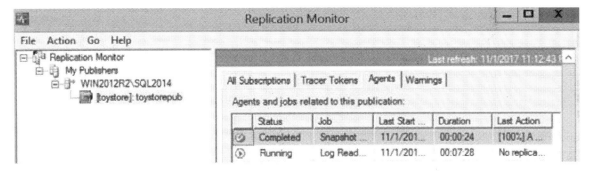

Figure 2.96: Replication Monitor

It may take time to generate and apply the initial snapshot depending on the database's size.

To further verify that the objects are migrated to Azure SQL Database, switch to SSMS and open Object Explorer if it's not already open.

Connect to your Azure SQL Database and expand the **Tables** node. Observe that all of the tables are listed under the **Tables** node:

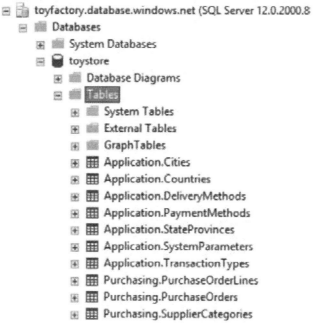

**Figure 2.93: Observing the Table nodes**

## Summary

Migrating to an Azure SQL database is an important task and should be planned to perfection. This lesson talked about a migration strategy that you should follow when migrating from an on-premises database to an Azure SQL database:

1. Find the migration benefits.

2. Find the blockers.

3. Select a service model.

4. Select a service tier.

5. Select the main region and the disaster recovery region.

6. Select a migration tool.

This lesson also talked about how to choose a service tier and covered different migration tools to migrate the data and the schema from an on-premises SQL Server database to an Azure SQL database. In the next lesson, we will learn how to perform manual and automatic backups that are unique to Azure SQL databases.

# 3

# Backing Up an Azure SQL Database

**Learning Objectives**

By the end of this lesson, you will be able to:

- Perform manual and automatic backups

- Export an Azure SQL Database using the Azure portal

- Export an Azure SQL Database using PowerShell

This lesson explores different backup and restore options such as automated backups, transactional consistent backups and manual backups.

## Introduction

Database backups are one of the most important things a database administrator has to perform. A good database backup strategy can help recover from system outages, unwanted deletes or updates, database corruption issues, and other related issues.

This lesson teaches you how to back up an Azure SQL Database. You'll learn about automated and manual backups, explore automated backup features, and perform the manual backup of an Azure SQL Database.

## Automatic Backups

Microsoft provides automated backups for Azure SQL databases. Automatic backup consists of full, differential, and log backups. The first automatic full backup is performed immediately after the database is provisioned. The differential backup is scheduled to occur every hour, and transaction log backups are scheduled for every 5-10 minutes. The full backup is scheduled for once a week:

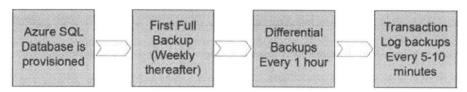

Figure 3.1: Automatic backups

> **Note**
>
> Automatic backups are inaccessible. You can't download or do a manual restore from an automatic backup.
>
> However, you can use an automatic backup to restore the database using the Azure portal, Azure CLI, PowerShell, and .NET SDKs.

## Backup Storage

Microsoft gives you free backup storage that is double the size of your maximum provisioned database storage. For example, if you have a 100 GB standard Azure SQL database, you get 200 GB of free backup storage. You can control the free backup storage size by limiting the retention period of the backups.

## Backup Retention Period

The backup retention period varies as per the different service tiers. The retention period for the Basic service tier is seven days, and for the Standard and Premium tiers, it's 35 days. You can extend the retention period through the long-term retention feature, which stores the backup in the Azure Backup Service Vault for as long as 10 years.

A Recovery Service vault is a storage service that's used to store backups of various Azure services such as VMs, Azure SQL databases, and even on-premises database backups.

## Configuring Long-Term Backup Retention for Azure SQL Database

Consider the **toystore** SQL database created in *Lesson 2, Migrating a SQL Server Database to an Azure SQL Database*. Mike has now been tasked with securing and backing up the data at ToyStore Ltd. In this section, we'll learn how to create and configure long-term backup retention for the **toystore** database:

1.  Log in to the Azure portal and find and open the Azure SQL Server resource the **toystore** SQL database is part of.

2.  In the SQL Server detail window, find and select **Manage Backups**:

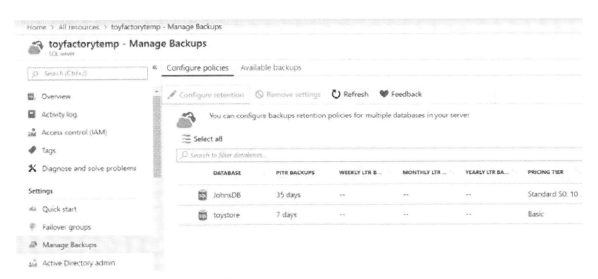

Figure 3.2: Manage Backups

3. Select the **toystore** database and then select the **Configure retention** option in the top menu:

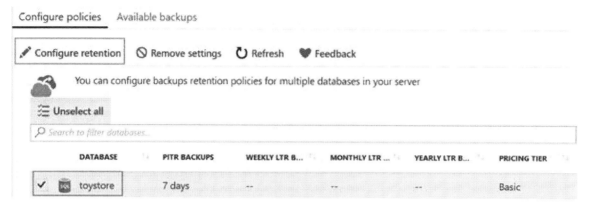

Figure 3.3: Select the database on which to configure long-term backup retention

4. In the **Configure policies** window, you can specify the retention period for the weekly, monthly, and yearly retention period:

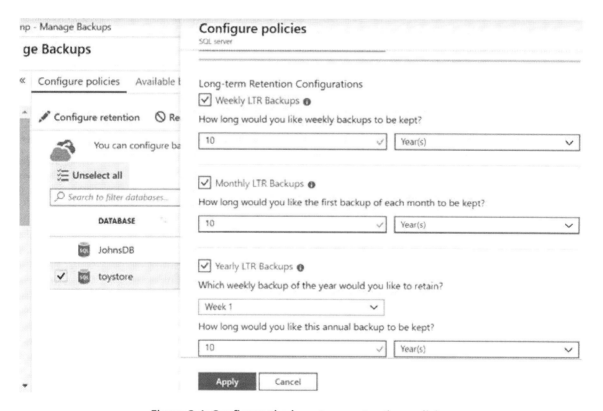

Figure 3.4: Configure the long-term retention policies

The configuration in the preceding screenshot states the following:

**Weekly LTR Backups**: Every backup will be retained for 10 years.

**Monthly LTR Backups**: The first backup of each month will be retained for 10 years.

**Yearly LTR Backups**: The Week 1 backup is retained for 10 years.

5. Click **Apply** to save the long-term retention configuration.

> **Note**
>
> Azure SQL Database long-term backups are copied and saved to Azure Blob storage. It may take up to 7 days for the long-term backups to be available and visible for restore.

## Manual Backups

Conventional database backup statements don't work in Azure SQL Database. Manual backup consists of exporting the database as a DACPAC (data and schema) or BACPAC (schema) and **bcp** out the data into **csv** files.

Manual backups can be performed in the following ways:

- Export BACPAC to your Azure storage account using the Azure portal
- Export BACPAC to your Azure storage account using PowerShell
- Export BACPAC using SQL Server Management Studio
- Export BACPAC or DACPAC to an on-premises system using `sqlpackage.exe`

## Backing up an Azure SQL Database Using SQL Server Management Studio (SSMS)

In this section, we will back up the Azure SQL **toystore** database using SSMS:

1. Open SSMS and press *F8* to open Object Explorer if it's not already open.

2. From Object Explorer, connect to Azure SQL Server. Once done, this is what you will see:

**Figure 3.5: The toystore database in the Object Explorer pane**

3. Right-click the **toystore** database, select **tasks**, then select **Export Data-Tier Application**. In the **Export Data-tier Application** introduction window, click **Next** to continue.

   **Upgrade Data-tier Application** is used to upgrade an existing database to a new DAC version. For example, upgrading the database schema of the production environment to that of a staging environment is commonly used in continuous integration and deployment scenarios.

> **Note**
>
> The Register Data-tier Application and Upgrade Data-tier Application options aren't relevant to this lesson and are used for database deployment. To find out more about them, follow these links:
>
> Register Data-tier Application: https://docs.microsoft.com/en-us/sql/relational-databases/data-tier-applications/register-a-database-as-a-dac
>
> Upgrade Data-tier Application: https://docs.microsoft.com/en-us/sql/relational-databases/data-tier-applications/upgrade-a-data-tier-application

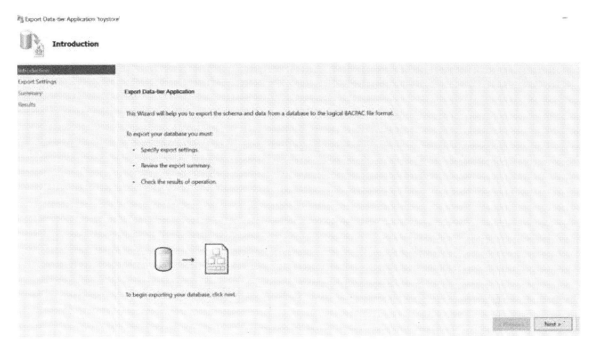

Figure 3.6: The Export Data-tier Application window

4.  In the **Export Settings** window, on the **Settings** tab, select **Save to local disk** and provide a local path to save the **bacpac** file. Alternatively, you can also save the **bacpac** file on Azure Storage. Click **Next** to continue:

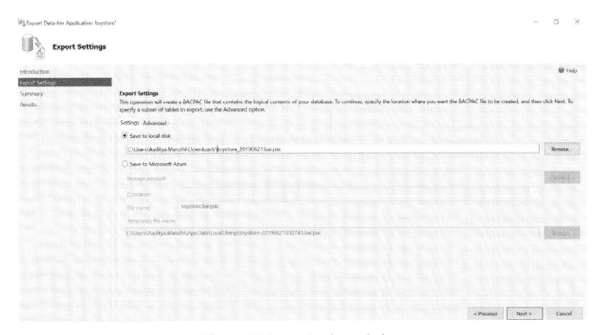

Figure 3.7: Export Settings window

5.  In the **Summary** window, verify the source and target settings and click **Finish** to continue:

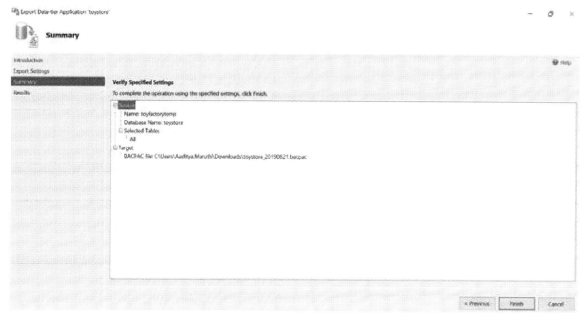

Figure 3.8: Export Data-tier Application toystore summary

6.  SSMS first extracts the schema and then the data into a **bacpac** package:

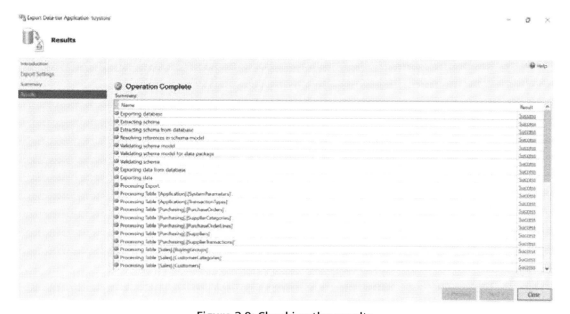

Figure 3.9: Checking the results

Click **Close** to close the wizard.

The BACPAC isn't transactionally consistent data. The BACPAC exports the table individually and data may change in the time between the first and last table export. A workaround for this is to create a transactionally consistent database copy and then export it as a BACPAC.

## DACPAC and BACPAC

**DACPAC** stands for **Data-Tier Application Package** and contains the database schema in `.xml` format. A BACPAC is a DACPAC with data.

DAC is a database life cycle management tool that simplifies the development, deployment, and management of data tier elements supporting an application.

A BACPAC is generally used to move a database from one server to another or for migrating a database, as shown in *Lesson 2, Migrating a SQL Server Database to an Azure SQL Database*.

> **Note**
>
> To find out more about DACPACs and BACPACs, visit this link: https://docs.
> microsoft.com/en-us/sql/relational-databases/data-tier-applications/data-tier-
> applications?view=sql-server-2017.

A BACPAC's or a DACPAC's contents can be viewed by changing the file extension to `.zip` and extracting the ZIP folder.

Navigate to the `C:\Code\Lesson03` folder (or to the folder to which you exported the BACPAC in the previous section) and change the extension of the **toystore.bacpac** file to `.zip`.

Extract the **toystore.zip** file to the **toystore** folder. Observe that it has the following files:

Figure 3.10: Details of the toystore zip file

- **model.xml**: This contains the database objects in .xml format.

- **Origin.xml**: This contains the count of each database object, database size, export start date, and other statistics about the BACPAC and the database.

- **DacMetadata.xml**: This contains the DAC version and the database name.

- **Data**: This folder contains a subfolder for each of the tables in the database. These subfolders contain the table data in BCP format:

| sson03 ▸ toystore ▸ Data ▸ Application.Cities | |
| --- | --- |
| Jame | Date |
| TableData-000-00000.BCP | 11/9/ |
| TableData-001-00000.BCP | 11/9/ |
| TableData-002-00000.BCP | 11/9/ |
| TableData-003-00000.BCP | 11/9/ |
| TableData-004-00000.BCP | 11/9/ |
| TableData-005-00000.BCP | 11/9/ |
| TableData-006-00000.BCP | 11/9/ |
| TableData-007-00000.BCP | 11/9/ |
| TableData-008-00000.BCP | 11/9/ |

Figure 3.11: Table data in BCP format

## Manual versus Automated Backups

Here is a comparison between manual and automated backups based on usability factors.

| Backup Type | Designed for Disaster Recovery | Point-In-Time Restore | Operational Overhead | Transactional Consistent | Additional Cost | On-Premise Restore |
| --- | --- | --- | --- | --- | --- | --- |
| Manual (Export) | No | No | Yes, Export needs to be taken manually | No (Create a database copy and export it for a transactional consistent backup) | Storage & additional DB cost | Yes |
| Built-In Automated Backups | Yes | Yes | No | Yes | No | No |

Figure 3.12: Features of manual versus built-in automated backups

## Activity: Performing Backups

Let's get back to our example of ToyStore Ltd. Mike has been tasked with ensuring that all the data of ToyStore Ltd. is backed up for crises such as system outages, unwanted deletes or updates, database corruption issues, and other related issues. In order to automate this process, he wants to make use of PowerShell scripts. In this activity, we'll learn how to back up an Azure SQL database using PowerShell scripts:

1. Press *Window* + R to open the **Run** dialog box. In the **Run** dialog box, type `powershell ise` to open a new PowerShell editor window.

2.  In the PowerShell ISE, click **File** in the top menu and then select **New** to create a new PowerShell script file:

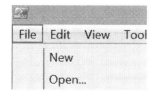

Figure 3.13: Creating a new PowerShell script file

> **Note**
>
> If you are running short of time, modify and run the **BackupAzureSQLDBToAzureStorage.ps1** PowerShell script, which is kept at **C:\Code\Lesson03**.

3.  In the new PowerShell script file, copy the code as instructed in the following steps.

4.  Define the PowerShell script parameters. The parameters are self- explanatory:

```
param(
[string]$storageaccountname,
[string]$resourcegroupname,
[string]$sqlserver,
[string]$container,
[string]$database,
[string]$sqluser,
[string]$sqlpassword
)
```

5.  Copy the following code. This will open a login window for a user to enter Azure credentials:

```
#Login to Azure account
Login-AzureRmAccount
```

6. Copy the following code to validate the parameters. The PowerShell script will terminate with an error message if the user doesn't provide an Azure storage account name (**$storageaccountname**) or a valid Azure Resource Group:

```
($resourcegroupname), and Azure Storage container ($container):
if([string]::IsNullOrEmpty($storageaccountname) -eq $true)
{
Write-Host "Provide a valid Storage Account Name"
-ForegroundColor Red return
}
if([string]::IsNullOrEmpty($resourcegroupname) -eq $true)
{
Write-Host "Provide a valid resource group" -ForegroundColor
Red

return
}
if([string]::IsNullOrEmpty($container) -eq $true)
{
Write-Host "Provide a valid Storage Container Name"
-ForegroundColor Red return
}
```

7. Copy the following code to initialize the **bacpac** filename. The **bacpac** file is created as the database name plus the current timestamp:

```
# create bacpac file name
$bacpacFilename = $database + "_"+(Get-Date). ToString("ddMMyyyymm") +
".bacpac"
```

8. Copy the following code to get the storage account key and set the default storage account for the PowerShell script. The **bacpac** file will be created in a container in the default Azure storage account. The storage account key is later used in the **export** cmdlet:

```
# set the current storage account
$storageaccountkey = Get-AzureRmStorageAccountKey
-ResourceGroupName $resourcegroupname -Name $storageaccountname
# set the default storage account
Set-AzureRmCurrentStorageAccount -StorageAccountName
$storageaccountname -ResourceGroupName $resourcegroupname | Out- Null
```

9. Copy the following code to set the storage URL. A storage URL defines the full path of the **bacpac** file on the Azure storage account:

```
# set the bacpac location
$bloblocation = "https://$storageaccountname.blob.core.windows.
net/$container/$bacpacFilename"
```

10. Copy the following code to create a credential object. This allows you to pass the password in an encrypted format when calling the **export** cmdlet:

```
#set the credential
$securesqlpassword = ConvertTo-SecureString -String $sqlpassword
-AsPlainText -Force
$credentials = New-Object -TypeName System.Management.Automation.
PSCredential -ArgumentList $sqluser, $securesqlpassword
```

11. Copy the following code to export the bacpac file to the given storage location. The **New-AzureRmSqlDatabaseExport** cmdlet takes the specified parameters and exports a bacpac file to the storage account:

```
Write-Host "Exporting $database to $bloblocation" -ForegroundColor Green


$export = New-AzureRmSqlDatabaseExport -ResourceGroupName
$resourcegroupname -ServerName $sqlserver.Split('.')[0] -DatabaseName
$database -StorageUri $bloblocation -AdministratorLogin $credentials.
UserName -AdministratorLoginPassword $credentials.Password -StorageKeyType
StorageAccessKey -StorageKey $storageaccountkey.Value[0].Tostring()



#Write-Host $export -ForegroundColor Green
```

12. Copy the following code to check and output the export progress:

```
While(1 -eq 1)
{
        $exportstatus = Get-AzureRmSqlDatabaseImportExportStatus
-OperationStatusLink $export.OperationStatusLink
        if($exportstatus.Status -eq "Succeeded")
        {
                Write-Host $exportstatus.StatusMessage -ForegroundColor
Green

                return
        }
        If($exportstatus.Status -eq "InProgress")
        {
```

```
                Write-Host $exportstatus.StatusMessage -ForegroundColor
    Green
                Start-Sleep -Seconds 5
        }
    }
```

13. Save the file as **ManualExport.ps1** to **C:\Code\Lesson03**, or to a location of your choice.

14. Open a PowerShell console and change the default directory to **C:\Code\Lesson03**, or to the directory where you have saved the PowerShell script.

    Type the following code and press *Enter* to start the export. You may have to change the parameter values as per your Azure environment:

    ```
    .\BackupAzureSQLDBToAzureStorage.ps1 -storageaccountname
    "toyfactorystorage" -resourcegroupname "toystore" -container "backups" -
    sqlserver toyfactory -database "toystore" -sqluser "sqladmin" -sqlpassword
    "Packt@pub2"
    ```

15. The PowerShell script will ask you to log in to your Azure account through a login pop-up window. Once you log in, the export will start. You should get a similar output to this:

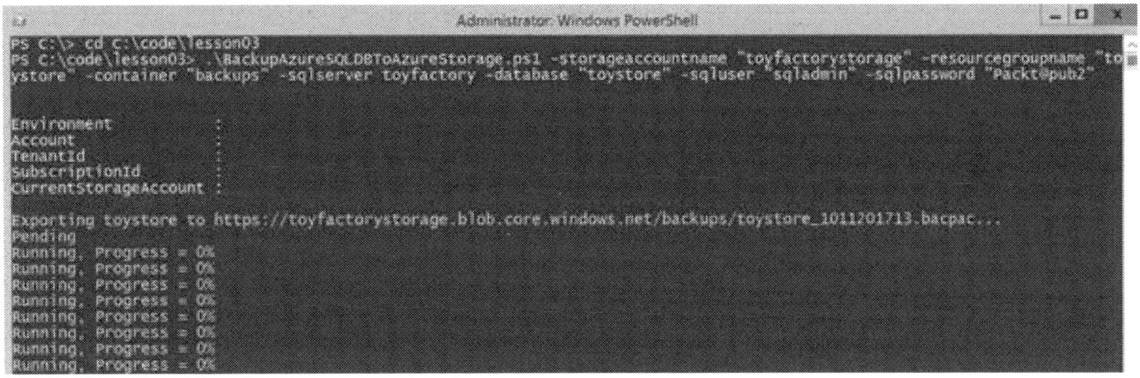

Figure 3.14: Export in progress

16. To verify the export, log in to the Azure portal with your credentials.

17. Open the storage account provided in the preceding script. You should see the **bacpac** file in the specified container:

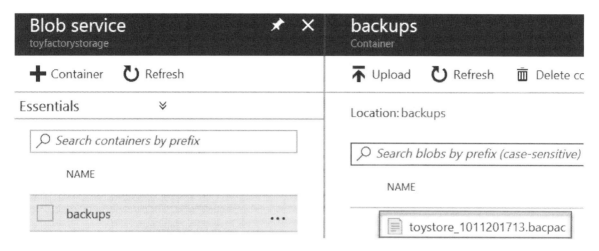

Figure 3.15: The backup bacpac file of the toystore database

## Summary

Azure SQL Database backups are different to on-premises database backups. The regular **backup** database command isn't supported in Azure SQL Database. In this lesson, we have learned about the automatic backups that are unique to Azure SQL Database and that aren't available in an on-premises database.

We also learned how to take manual backups of an Azure SQL database using SSMS and PowerShell. A manual backup is just an export of the schema, or the data and schema, stored in DACPAC or BACPAC format, respectively.

In the next lesson, we will look at the restore options available in Azure.

# Restoring an Azure SQL Database

**Learning Objectives**

By the end of this lesson, you will be able to:

- Use point-in-time restore to recover from unexpected data modifications.

- Restore a deleted database using the Azure portal.

- Learn about using geo-restore on a database.

- Restore an Azure SQL database by importing BACPAC.

This lesson explores different restore options such as Point-In-time restore, restore deleted database, geo-restore a database. You'll also learn to automate the restore task using PowerShell.

## Introduction

Azure SQL Database has the following restore options:

- Point-in-time Restore

- Restore a deleted database

- Geo-Restore a database

- Restore a database from Azure Vault

- Import a BACPAC

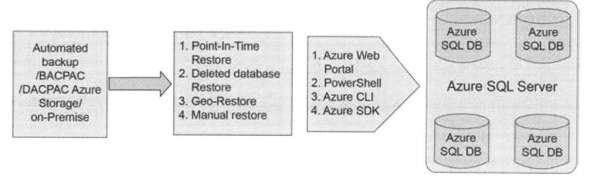

Figure 4.1: Types of restore

A restore can be performed using the Azure portal, PowerShell, Azure CLI, or Azure SDK. This lesson teaches you the differences between the restore types and how to perform a restore.

## Restore Types

This section discusses the different types of restore available in Azure SQL Database.

### Point-In-Time Restore

**Point-In-Time Restore** (**PITR**) isn't new in the world of SQL Server. On-premises SQL servers allow you to restore a database to a particular point in time by specifying the point-in-time option when restoring the database using the **restore** command.

As you know, the **restore** command isn't supported in Azure SQL Database, but the PITR can be performed using the Azure portal, PowerShell, Azure CLI, or Azure SDK. The PITR uses the automatic **Full** and **Log** backup.

The backup retention period depends on service types. For DTU(Database Throughput Unit)-based pricing models, the retention period is:

- 7 days for the Basic service tier

- 35 days for Standard and Premium service tiers

For vCore-based pricing models, the default retention period is 7 days for the General and Business service tiers. However, the retention period can be changed to up to 35 days. To learn how to change the default retention period, please visit https://docs. microsoft.com/en-us/azure/sql-database/sql-database-automated-backups#how-tochange-the-pitr-backup-retention-period.

A database can only be restored on the same Azure SQL server as the original database with a different name. If you are restoring a database using PITR to recover from a corruption issue and wish to use the restored database as the production database, you will have to rename the database accordingly.

PITR is useful for recovering from unexpected data modifications, corrupted databases, or for getting a database state from a previous state for application testing or debugging an issue.

Let's perform a PITR on an Azure SQL database using the Azure portal:

1. Open **SQL Server Management Studio (SSMS)** and connect to the Azure SQL server hosting the Azure SQL database you wish to perform a PITR on.

2. Open the **C:\Code\Lesson04\InsertNewColor.sql** file in SSMS. Make sure that the database's context is set to the **toystore** database.

3. Press F5 or click **Execute** in the top menu to run the query. The query adds a new row in the **Warehouse.Color** table with **ColorID=37**:

```
-- Insert a new color
INSERT INTO [Warehouse].[Colors]
SELECT
    37 AS ColorID
    ,'Dark Yellow' AS ColorName
    ,1 AS LastEditedBy
```

```
        ,GETUTCDATE() AS ValidFrom
        ,'9999-12-31 23:59:59.9999999' As Validto
GO
-- Verify the insert
SELECT [ColorID]
     ,[ColorName]
     ,[LastEditedBy]
     ,[ValidFrom]
     ,[ValidTo]
FROM [Warehouse].[Colors] WHERE ColorID=37
```

You should get an output similar to the following screenshot:

Figure 4.2: A new row added in the Warehouse.Color table

4.  Log in to the Azure portal with your Azure credentials. From the left-hand
    navigation pane, select **All Resources** and click the Azure SQL database you wish
    to perform a PITR on:

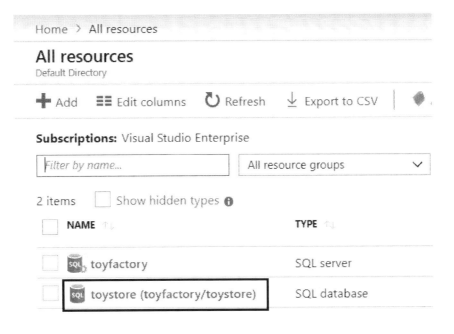

Figure 4.3: Selecting an Azure SQL database to perform PITR

5. From the **toystore** SQL database overview section, click **Restore**:

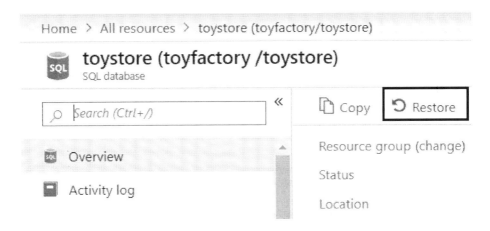

Figure 4.4: Restoring the database

6. You will now see the **Restore** pane:

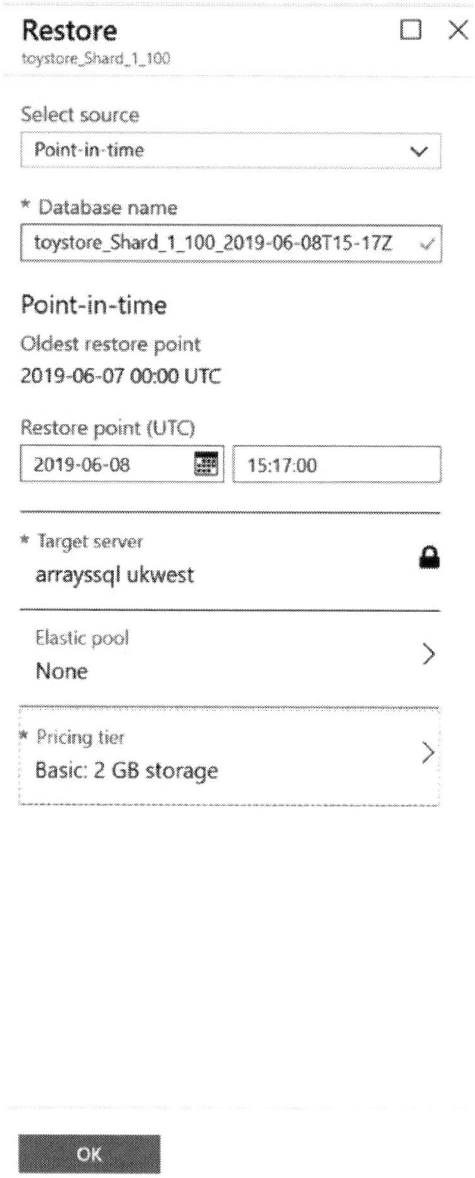


Figure 4.5: PITR restore

Observe the oldest restore point available – this might be different in your case.

Under the **Restore point**, specify the date when you want to perform the PITR. Observe that the **Database Name** changes as you change the restore time.

The database name is `toystore_PITRDate`. For example, if we are restoring the database to 11 November 2017, 12:41 PM, then the database name will be `toystore_2017-11-12T12-41Z`.

You can change the database if you wish to.

Observe that the option to select **Azure SQL Server** is locked. Therefore, the PITR can be only done on the same server as the original database.

Click **OK** to start the database restore. The restore time depends on the size of the database being restored.

Wait for the restore to be completed. You can look at the **Notifications** section on the Azure portal to see the progress of the restore:

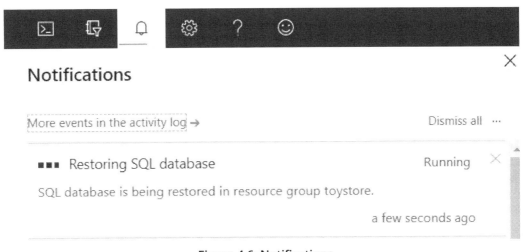

Figure 4.6: Notifications

7.  Once the restore is complete, open the **All Resource** pane and verify that the database is listed there:

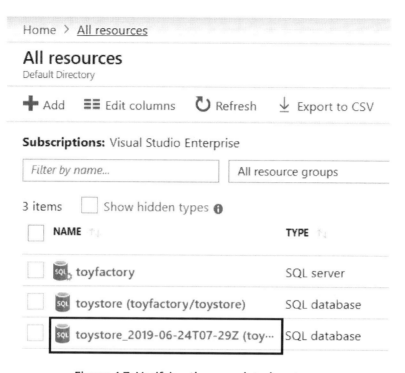

Figure 4.7: Verifying the completed restore

8.  Since the database has been restored and has the same data and schema that it had on 11th November 2017, this database shouldn't contain `ColorID 37`, which we added in *step* 1.

    Switch to SSMS and open `C:\Code\Lesson04\InsertNewColor.sql`, if it's not already open.

    Change the database context to `toystore_2017-11-11T12-41Z`. This will be different in your case.

9. Select and execute the following query in SSMS:

```
-- Verify the insert SELECT [ColorID]
    ,[ColorName]
    ,[LastEditedBy]
    ,[ValidFrom]
    ,[ValidTo]
FROM [Warehouse].[Colors] WHERE ColorID=37
```

You should get an output similar to the following:

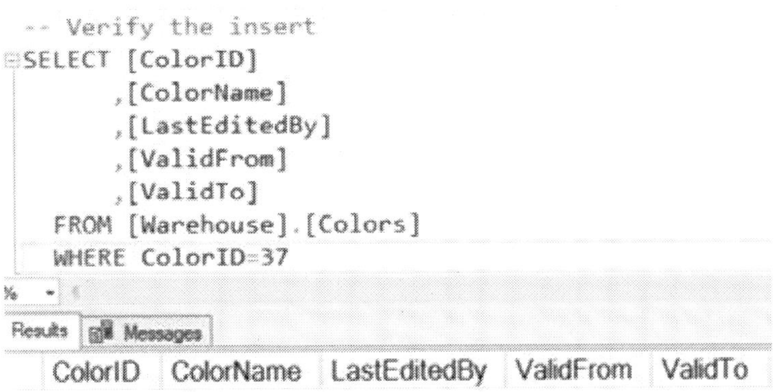

Figure 4.8: Output of the SELECT query

Observe that none of the rows contain **ColorID 37** in the **Warehouse.Colors** table.

## Long-Term Database Restore

The **Long-Term Database Restore** (**LTDR**) allows you to restore a database configured for long-term database backups. The backups are kept in the Azure Recovery Services vault.

The LTDR uses the same technique as PITR to restore the database; however, here, you can restore a database from the last 10 years.

Let's perform a long-term restore on an Azure SQL database using the Azure portal:

1. Log in to the Azure portal with your Azure credentials. From the left-hand navigation pane, select **All Resources** and click the Azure SQL database you wish to perform an LTDR on:

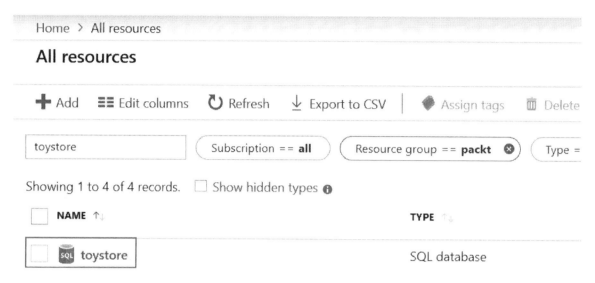

Figure 4.9: Selecting the Azure SQL database to perform LTDR

2. From the **toystore** SQL database overview section, click **Restore**:

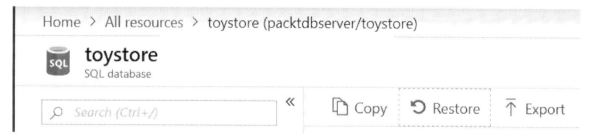

Figure 4.10: Restoring the database

3. In the **Restore** pane, from the **Select source** drop-down menu, select **Long-term backup retention**:

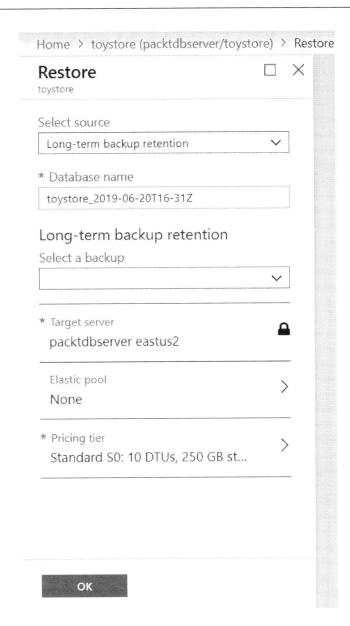

Figure 4.11: Selecting Long-term backup retention

Click **Select a backup** under the **Long-term backup retention** setting.

This setting will list all the backups from the vault. Choose a backup date from the resulting pane and click **Select**.

Observe that the **Target Server** option is locked and can't be set to any server other than the original database server.

Change the database name to `toystore_2019-06-20T16-31Z`. Click **OK** to start the restoration process.

4. The restore time depends on the size of the database being restored.

   Wait for the restore to be completed. You can look at the **Notifications** section on the Azure portal to see the progress of the restore:

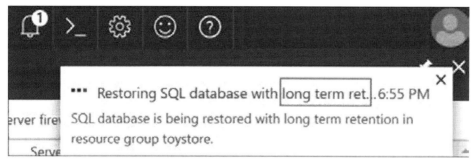

Figure 4.12: Checking restore notifications

Observe that the notification says that long-term retention is in progress.

5. Once the restore is complete, open the **All Resources** pane and verify that the database is listed there:

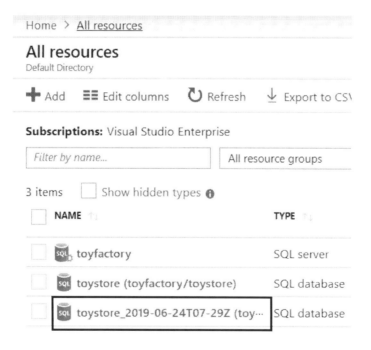

Figure 4.13: Verifying the completed restore

To verify the restore, follow *steps 8-9* under the *Point-In-Time Restore* section. The database shouldn't have a row `ColorID 37` in the `Warehouse.Colors` table.

## Restoring Deleted Databases

Microsoft Azure allows you to restore a deleted database to the time it was deleted, or to any time within the retention period. You can select the deleted database you wish to restore from the pool of deleted databases. You are able to restore a deleted database because the automatic backups are saved for a given retention period. The retention period depends on the service tier.

Let's restore a deleted database using the Azure portal:

1.  Log in to the Azure portal using your Azure credentials. Open **All resources** from the left-hand navigation pane.

2.  From the **All resources** pane, open the Azure SQL server that hosts the deleted database you wish to restore.

3.  In the Azure SQL Server pane, from the **Settings** section, select **Deleted databases**:

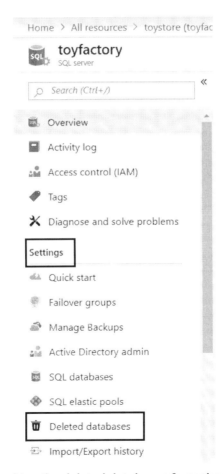

Figure 4.14: Checking the deleted databases from the settings section

4.  The **Deleted databases** pane lists out the databases and their deletion times. Select the **toystore** database for any deletion date you want to restore it to:

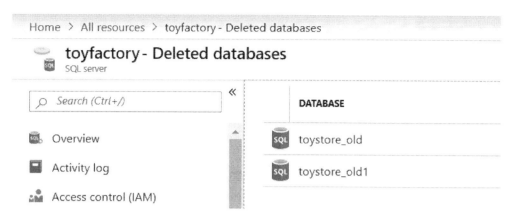

Figure 4.15: List of deleted databases

5.  In the **Restore** pane, provide the database name.

Observe that the **Target server** option is locked. Therefore, the deleted database can only be restored to the same server as that of the original database.

Observe that the **Restore point** option is set to the deletion date that you opted to restore the database to.

Click **OK** to restore the database:

Home > All resources > toyfactory- Deleted databases > Restore

**Restore**
toystore_old

\* Database name

toystore_old_2019-06-24T07 -35Z

Target server

toyfactory

Restore point (UTC)

2019-06-24 07:35 UTC

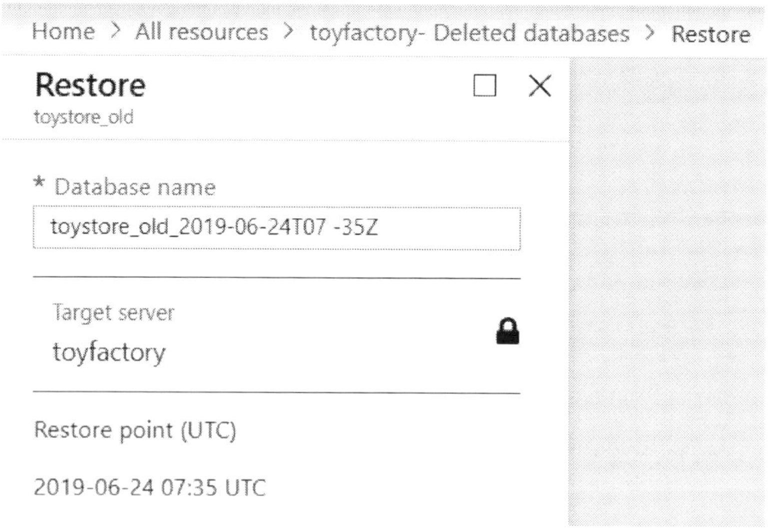

Figure 4.16: Providing database name for restore

Monitor the database's restoration progress in the **Notification** pane, as mentioned in the previous section.

6. Once the database is restored, navigate to the **All resources** section from the left-hand navigation pane. Observe that the database is now listed here:

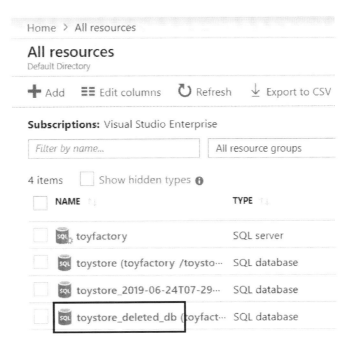

Figure 4.17: Verifying the restored database

You can use *steps 8-9* under the *Point-In-Time Restore* section to verify the restored database.

## Geo-Restore Database

Geo-restore allows you to restore a database from a geo-redundant backup to any of the available Azure SQL servers, irrespective of the region.

An Azure SQL database's automatic backups are copied to a different region as and when they are taken. There is a maximum delay of one hour when copying the database to a different geographical location. Therefore, in the case of a disaster, there can be up to an hour of data loss:

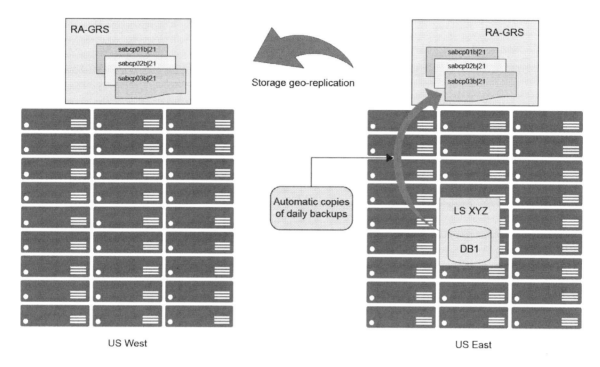

Figure 4.18: Geo-replication to a different geographical location

Geo-restore can be used to recover a database if an entire region is unavailable because of a disaster:

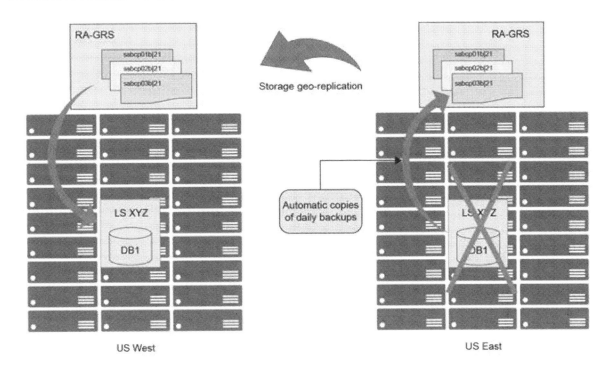

**Figure 4.19: Use of geo-restore in the case of unavailability of an entire region**

The most recent full and differential backups are used to perform a geo-restore.

Geo-restore doesn't support PITR. Geo-restore is the most basic disaster recovery solution with the longest recovery time, which can be up to 12 hours. This may be a reasonable recovery solution for databases using the Basic service tier; however, for the Standard and Premium service tiers, active geo-replication is recommended.

## Importing a Database

You can import a database into an Azure SQL server from a **BACPAC** or a **DACPAC** file kept in Azure Storage. The import operation will create a new Azure SQL database from the **BACPAC** file.

The **BACPAC** file can be imported to any of the available Azure SQL servers in any given region. This can be useful for quickly creating new test environments.

The import can be done through the Azure portal, PowerShell, Azure CLI, or Azure SDK.

Let's learn how to import a database from a **BACPAC** file kept in Azure Storage. Open the Azure portal, go to https://portal.azure.com, and log in with your Azure credentials:

1.  From the left-hand navigation pane, open the **All resources** section. Select the Azure SQL server you wish to import the database to.

2.  In the **Azure SQL Server overview** pane, select **Import database**:

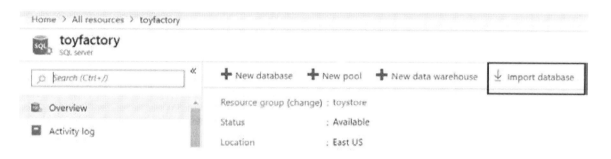

Figure 4.20: Selecting the Import database option

3.  In the **Import database** pane, under **Subscription**, select your Azure subscription:

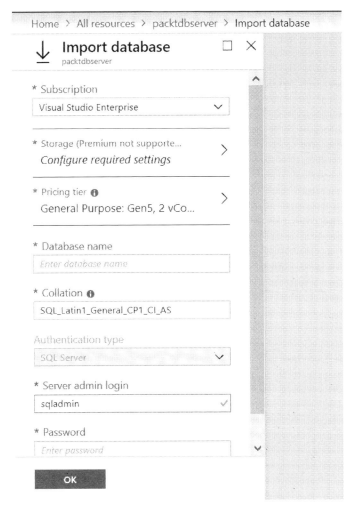

Figure 4.21: The Import database pane

Select **Storage**. In the **Storage accounts** pane, select the **Storage account** where your file is located:

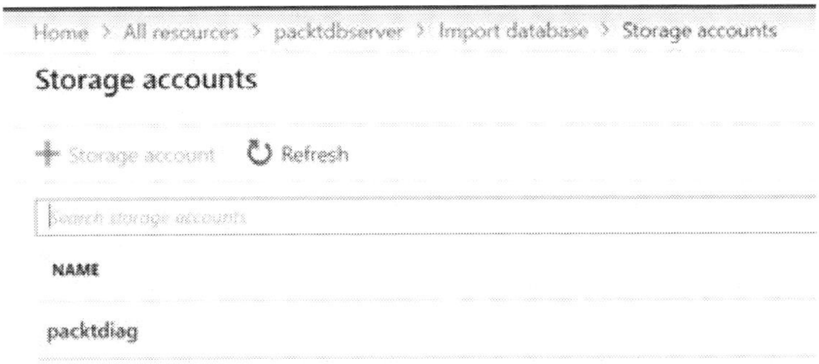

Figure 4.22: Selecting the container

Select the container, and then select the **BACPAC** file you wish to import by clicking on **Select**:

Figure 4.23: Selecting the BACPAC file for import

Under the **Pricing tier** option, choose your pricing tier.

Under the **Database Name** option, provide the database name.

Leave the **Collation** option as default.

Provide the username and password for the Azure SQL server.

4.  Select **OK** to import the database:

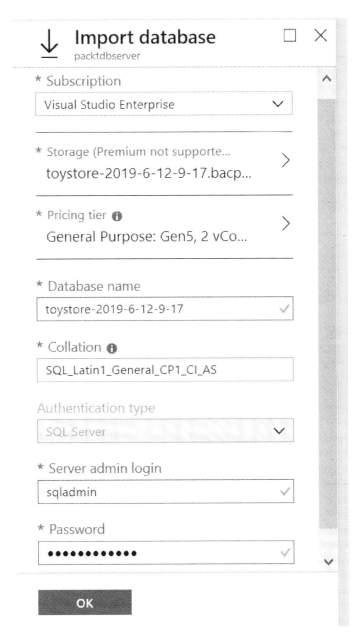

Figure 4.24: Importing the database

## Activity: Performing PITR

Consider the following scenario: Mike is a new DBA, so his trainer is aware that there might be some misses at his end. Therefore, his trainer wants to configure PITR on the databases that Mike is working on. In this section, we will perform a PITR using PowerShell by following these steps:

1.  Press *Window* + R to open the **Run** dialog box. In the **Run** dialog box, type **powershell ise** to open a new PowerShell editor window.

2.  In PowerShell ISE, click **File** from the top menu and then select **New** to create a new PowerShell script file:

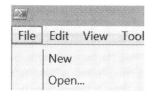

Figure 4.25: Creating a new PowerShell script

3.  In the new PowerShell script file, copy the code from the following step.

4.  Define the PowerShell script parameters. The parameters are self- explanatory:

```
param(
    [Parameter(Mandatory=$true)]
    [string]$sqlserver,
    [Parameter(Mandatory=$true)]
    [string]$database,
    [Parameter(Mandatory=$true)]
    [string]$sqluser,
    [Parameter(Mandatory=$true)]
    [string]$sqlpassword,
    [Parameter(Mandatory=$true)]
    [string]$resourcegroupname,
    [string]$newdatabasename
)
```

5. Copy the following code to let the users log in to their Azure subscription by providing Azure credentials in a login window:

```
#Login to Azure account
Login-AzureRmAccount
```

6. Copy the following code to output the earliest restore point available and let the users provide a point in time to restore the database to:

```
While (1)
  {
      #Retrieve the distinct restore points from which a SQL Database can
be restored
      $restoredetails = Get-AzureRmSqlDatabaseRestorePoints -ServerName
$sqlserver -DatabaseName $database -ResourceGroupName $resourcegroupname
      #get the earliest restore date
      $erd=$restoredetails.EarliestRestoreDate.
ToString();
      #ask for the point in time the database is to be restored
      $restoretime = Read-Host "The earliest restore time is $erd.`n Enter
a restore time between Earliest restore time and current time."
      #convert the input to datatime data type
      $restoretime = $restoretime -as [DateTime]
      #if restore time isn't a valid data, prompt for a valid date
            if(!$restoretime)
        {
          Write-Host "Enter a valid date" -ForegroundColor Red
        }else
        {
      #end the while loop if restore date is a valid date
          break;
        }
  }
```

Read through the comments to understand what the code does.

7. Copy the following code to set the new database name if it hasn't already been provided by the user, and perform the PITR:

```
#set the new database name
    if([string]::IsNullOrEmpty($newdatabasename))
    {
        $newdatabasename = $database + (Get-Date).
ToString("MMddyyyymm")
    }
```

```
...
#restore the database to point in time
    $restore = Restore-AzureRmSqlDatabase
-FromPointInTimeBackup -PointInTime $restoretime -ResourceId
$db.ResourceId -ServerName $db.ServerName -TargetDatabaseName
$newdatabasename -Edition $db.Edition -ServiceObjectiveName
$db.CurrentServiceObjectiveName -ResourceGroupName $db. ResourceGroupName

# restore deleted database
    if($rerror -ne $null)
    {
        Write-Host $rerror -ForegroundColor red;
    }
    if($restore -ne $null)
    {
        Write-Host "Database $newdatabasename restored Successfully";
    }
```

Read through the comments to understand what the code does.

8. Save the file as **PITRAzureSQLDB.ps1** to **C:\Code\Lesson04**, or a location of your choice.

9. Open a PowerShell console and change the default directory to **C:\Code\Lesson04** or to the directory where you have saved the PowerShell script.

10. Copy the following code and press *Enter* to start the export. You may have to change the parameter values to match your Azure environment:

```
.\PITRAzureSQLDB.ps1 -sqlserver toyfactory -database toystore
-sqluser sqladmin -sqlpassword Packt@pub2 -resourcegroupname toystore
-newdatabasename toystorepitr
```

The preceding command will restore the **toystore** database to a specified point in time on the **toyfactory** SQL server in the **toystore** resource group. The database will be restored as **toystorepitr**.

Once the script finishes, you should get a similar output to the following screenshot:

```
PS C:\Code\Lesson04> .\PITRAzureSQLDB.ps1 -sqlserver toyfactory -database toystore -sqluser sqla

Environment            : AzureCloud
Account                :
TenantId               :
SubscriptionId         :
CurrentStorageAccount  :

The earliest restore time is 11/8/2017 7:20:19 AM.
 Enter a restore time between Earlist restore time and current time.: 11/10/2017 2:00:00 AM
Restoring Database toystore as of toystorepitr to the time 11/10/2017 02:00:00
Database toystorepitr restored Successfully
```

Figure 4.26: A successful PITR on the toystorepitr database

You can also verify whether or not the available restore is visible in the Azure portal.

## Activity: Performing Geo-Restore

Let's once again consider our example of ToyStore Ltd. Mike is aware that, although on the cloud, his data is still physically stored on servers. Hence, there is a possibility of data loss due to natural disasters. Therefore, he has to perform a geo-restore operation to take care of this bit. This section makes use of PowerShell to perform a geo-restore:

1. Press *Window* + R to open the **Run** dialog box. In the **Run** dialog box, type **powershell ise** to open a new PowerShell editor window.

2. In PowerShell ISE, click **File** from the top menu, and then select **New** to create a new PowerShell script file:

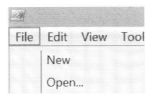

Figure 4.27: Creating a new PowerShell script

3. In the new PowerShell script file, copy the code as instructed in the following steps.

   Define the PowerShell script parameters. The parameters are self- explanatory:

   ```
   param(
        [Parameter(Mandatory=$true)]
        [string]$sqlserver,
        [Parameter(Mandatory=$true)]
        [string]$database,
        [Parameter(Mandatory=$true)]
        [string]$sqluser,
        [Parameter(Mandatory=$true)]
        [string]$sqlpassword,
        [Parameter(Mandatory=$true)]
        [string]$resourcegroupname,
        [string]$newdatabasename
   )
   ```

   Copy the following code to open a login dialog box to log in to Microsoft Azure:

   ```
   #Login to Azure subscription
   Login-AzureRmAccount
   ```

   Copy the following code to get the details of the database that is to be geo-restored in a PowerShell object and display the details on the console:

   ```
   # get the geo database backup to restore

   $geodb = Get-AzureRmSqlDatabaseGeoBackup -ServerName
   $sqlserver -DatabaseName $database -ResourceGroupName
   $resourcegroupname

   #Display Geo-Database properties
   $geodb | Out-Host
   ```

   Copy the following code to retrieve the name of the database that is to be restored:

   ```
   #get the database name from the geodb object
   $geodtabasename = $geodb.DatabaseName.ToString()
   ```

Copy the following code to set the new database name if it hasn't already been provided by the user:

```
#set the new database name if([string]::IsNullOrEmpty($newdatabasename))
{
    $newdatabasename = $database + (Get-Date).
ToString("MMddyyyymm")
}
```

Copy the following code to perform the geo-    restore:

```
Write-Host "Restoring database $geodtabasename from geo backup"
-ForegroundColor Green

# perform the geo restore
$restore = Restore-AzureRmSqlDatabase -FromGeoBackup
-ResourceId $geodb.ResourceID -ServerName $sqlserver
-TargetDatabaseName $newdatabasename -Edition $geodb.Edition
-ResourceGroupName $resourcegroupname -ServiceObjectiveName
$serviceobjectivename

if($rerror -ne $null)
{
    Write-Host $rerror -ForegroundColor red;
}

if($restore -ne $null)
{
    $restoredb = $restore.DatabaseName.ToString()
    Write-Host "Database $database restored from Geo Backup as database
$restoredb" -ForegroundColor Green
}
```

The new database has the same edition and performance level as the original database. You can change this by specifying different values in the **Restore-AzureRmSqlDatabase** cmdlet.

4.  Save the file as **GeoRestoreAzureSQLDB.ps1** to **C:\Code\Lesson04** or a location of your choice.

5. Open a PowerShell console and change the default directory to `C:\Code\Lesson04` or to the directory where you have saved the PowerShell script.

6. Copy the following code and press *Enter* to start the export. You may have to change the parameter values as per your Azure environment:

```
.\GeoRestoreAzureSQLDB.ps1 -sqlserver toyfactory -database toystore
-sqluser sqladmin -sqlpassword Packt@pub2
-resourcegroupname toystore -newdatabasename toystorepitr
```

The preceding command will restore the **toystore** database to a specified point in time on the **toyfactory** SQL server in the **toystore** resource group. The database will be restored as **toystorepitr**.

Once the script finishes, you should get an output similar to what is shown in the following screenshot:

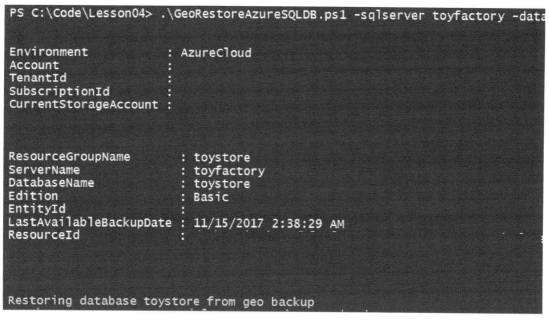

```
PS C:\Code\Lesson04> .\GeoRestoreAzureSQLDB.ps1 -sqlserver toyfactory -data

Environment           : AzureCloud
Account               :
TenantId              :
SubscriptionId        :
CurrentStorageAccount :


ResourceGroupName     : toystore
ServerName            : toyfactory
DatabaseName          : toystore
Edition               : Basic
EntityId              :
LastAvailableBackupDate : 11/15/2017 2:38:29 AM
ResourceId            :



Restoring database toystore from geo backup
```

Figure 4.28: Successful completion of geo-restore

Your **toystore** database has been successfully restored.

## Summary

Restoring an Azure SQL database is different from restoring an on-premises SQL Server database. In this lesson, you learned about the following restore options:

- PITR
- Restoring a deleted database
- Geo-restoring a database
- Restoring a database from Azure Vault
- Importing a BACPAC file

Each of these options can be leveraged in different scenarios. For example, a PITR will help you recover from a corrupt database or accidental deletion, whereas importing a **BACPAC** file helps you set up a development environment with the same schema and data across development, testing, and integration.

In the next lesson, we will look at the security mechanisms available to secure an Azure SQL database.

# 5

# Securing an Azure SQL Database

**Learning Objectives**

By the end of this lesson, you will be able to:

- Configure firewall settings for Azure SQL Server and SQL Database
- Implement audit and threat detection
- Implement encryption, dynamic data masking, and row-level security
- Implement AD authentication for an Azure SQL database

In this lesson, you'll learn to add firewall rules, create and manage logins, configure data masking, row-level security, auditing to secure your Azure SQL Database implementation.

# Introduction

Security is a major concern for organizations when migrating to the cloud, and so organizations are hesitant to do so. Microsoft provides strong security protection at the physical, logical, and data layers of Azure services. Microsoft data centers are among the most secure data centers in the world.

Azure SQL Database provides multiple layers of security to control access to databases using SQL Server or **Active Directory** (**AD**) authentication as well as firewall rules, which limits access to data through role-based permissions and row-level security.

Azure SQL Database provides proactive security using dynamic data masking, automated auditing, and threat detection.

It also provides transparent data encryption to encrypt data at rest, and Always Encrypted to encrypt data at rest or in motion.

This lesson covers all of these security mechanisms and how to implement and use them to secure an Azure SQL database.

# Access Control

Azure SQL Database limits access to databases through firewall rules, which are authentication techniques that require users to log in to a database with a valid username and password. Azure SQL Database further controls access to the underlying data through role-based permissions and row-level security. We'll now look at different access control methods in detail.

## Firewall Rules

Azure SQL Database uses firewall rules to limit access to authorized IPs and block access to unauthorized IPs. This is the first level of access control provided by Azure SQL Database. Firewall rules can be created at the server level and the database level.

When an SQL database is provisioned, it's inaccessible to everyone. To make it accessible, you first need to add a server-level firewall rule. A firewall allows an IP or a range of IP addresses to connect to an Azure SQL database. You can then create database firewall rules to enable certain clients to access individual secure databases.

Connection requests to an Azure SQL database are first validated against the firewall rules and the computers with the IPs specified in the firewall rules are allowed to connect to the database:

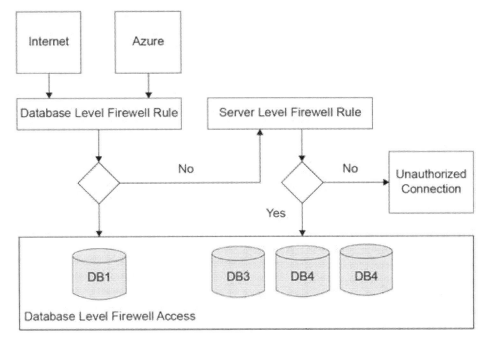

**Figure 5.1: Firewall rules**

If a computer attempts to connect to an Azure SQL database over the internet, then:

- The computer's IP address is validated against the database-level firewall rules. If the IP address is in the IP range specified in the database firewall rules, the connection is made.

- If the computer's IP address doesn't fall within the database-level firewall rules, then server-level firewall rules are checked. If the computer's IP address is in the server-level firewall rules, the connection is made.

- If the computer's IP address doesn't fall within the database-level or server-level firewall rules, the connection is terminated with an error.

**Note**

To create a server-level firewall rule, you should be a subscription owner or subscription contributor. The subscription used here is a Microsoft Azure subscription, which you get when you sign up for a Microsoft Azure account.

To allow Azure applications to connect to an Azure SQL database, you need to add the IP **0.0.0.0** as the start and end IP address to the server-level firewall rules:

| Server-Level Firewall Rule | Database-Level Firewall Rule |
|---|---|
| Allows clients to access all SQL databases in a given logical Azure SQL Server | Allows clients to access particular SQL databases within the logical Azure SQL Server |
| Rules are stored in the master database | Rules are stored within individual Azure SQL Databases |
| Can be configured using the Azure portal, PowerShell, and T-SQL | Can only be configured using T-SQL after configuring the first server-level firewall rule |

Figure 5.2: Firewall rule comparison

## Managing Server-Level Firewall Rules Using the Azure Portal

In this section, you will learn how to create, delete, and update server-level firewall rules from the Azure portal:

1. Log in to the Azure portal (https://portal.azure.com) using your Azure credentials.

2. Find and open the Azure SQL server you wish to manage the firewall for.

3. From the Azure SQL Server overview page, select the **Set server firewall** option:

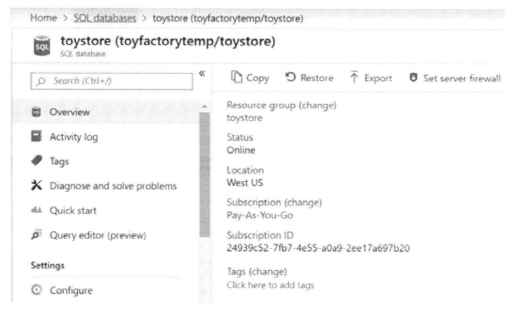

Figure 5.3: Setting the firewall

4.  On the **Firewall settings** pane, notice that no firewall rules have been configured:

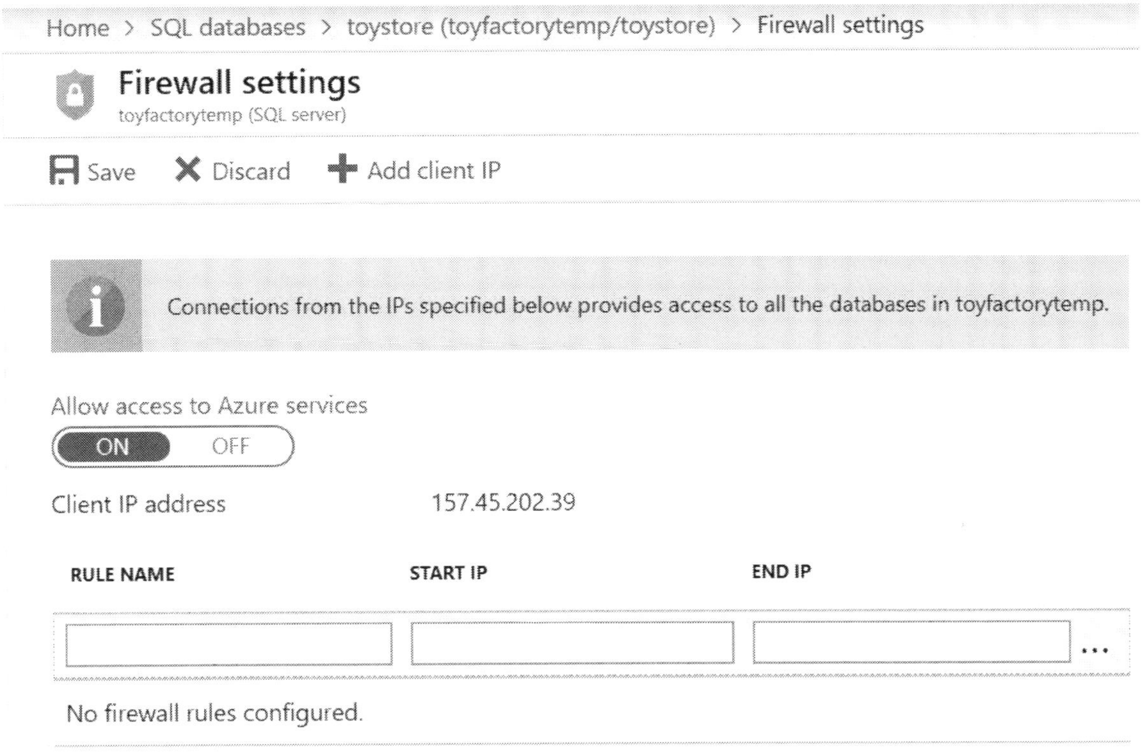

Home > SQL databases > toystore (toyfactorytemp/toystore) > Firewall settings

## Firewall settings
toyfactorytemp (SQL server)

🖫 Save   ✕ Discard   ➕ Add client IP

ℹ️  Connections from the IPs specified below provides access to all the databases in toyfactorytemp.

Allow access to Azure services

( **ON**    OFF )

Client IP address                157.45.202.39

| RULE NAME | START IP | END IP | |
|-----------|----------|--------|---|
|           |          |        | ... |

No firewall rules configured.

**Figure 5.4: The Firewall settings page**

Also, notice that it automatically detects and displays the public IP address of the computer from which the portal has been opened.

5. To add the client IP address, select **Add client IP** from the top menu:

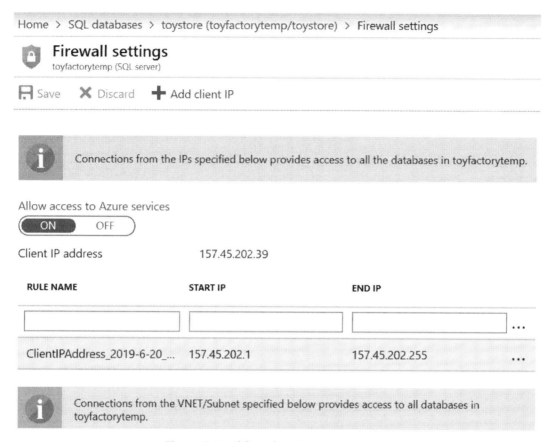

Home > SQL databases > toystore (toyfactorytemp/toystore) > Firewall settings

**Firewall settings**
toyfactorytemp (SQL server)

Save    X Discard    + Add client IP

Connections from the IPs specified below provides access to all the databases in toyfactorytemp.

Allow access to Azure services

ON    OFF

Client IP address          157.45.202.39

| RULE NAME | START IP | END IP | |
|---|---|---|---|
| | | | ... |
| ClientIPAddress_2019-6-20_... | 157.45.202.1 | 157.45.202.255 | ... |

Connections from the VNET/Subnet specified below provides access to all databases in toyfactorytemp.

Figure 5.5: Adding the client IP address

A firewall rule with the same start and end IP as the client IP address is added. You can change the rule name if you wish to. Click **Save** in the top menu to save the firewall rule.

You can provide access to all systems within a specified IP range by specifying the start and end IP accordingly.

6. You can update a firewall by clicking anywhere on the firewall rule row you wish to update.

7. To delete a firewall rule, click on the three dots to the right of the firewall rule row and select **Delete**. Click **Save** to save the changes:

**Figure 5.6: Deleting a firewall**

If you don't wish to delete a firewall rule and have accidentally clicked **Delete** instead of clicking **Save** in the top menu, click **Discard** to undo the changes.

8. To make an Azure SQL database accessible to Azure applications, toggle **Allow access to Azure services** to **ON** and click **Save** to save the configuration:

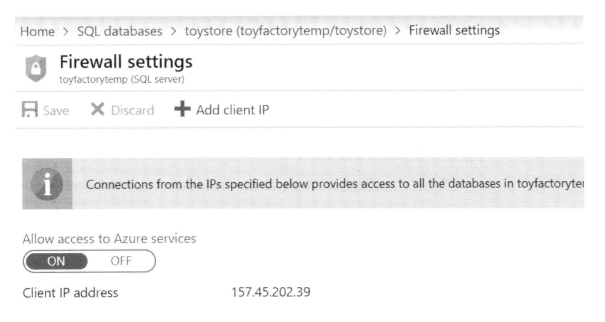

**Figure 5.7: Firewall settings page**

## Managing Server-Level Firewall Rules Using Transact-SQL

You can also make use of Transact-SQL instead of the Azure portal to manage server-level firewall rules. In this section, you will learn how to create, delete, and update server-level firewall rules using Transact-SQL:

1.  Open **SQL Server Management Studio (SSMS)** and connect to your Azure SQL server. You should be able to connect now, since you have added a server-level firewall rule.

2.  In the master database context, run the following query to list all of the existing server-level firewall rules:

    ```
    Select * from sys.firewall_rules
    ```

    The IP address will be different in your case. You should get an output like the one shown in the following screenshot:

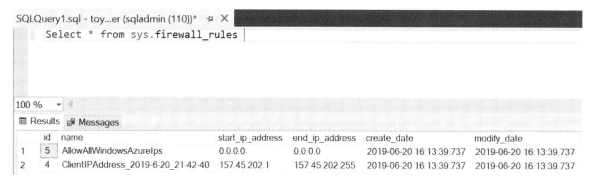

Figure 5.8: Listing the server-level firewall rules

3.  Execute the following command to add a new server-level firewall rule:

    ```
    Execute sp_set_firewall_rule @name = N'Work',
    @start_ip_address = '115.118.1.0',
    @end_ip_address = '115.118.16.255'
    ```

    Notice the **N** before **'Work'** in the preceding query. The query will fail if you don't add **N**. This is because the firewall rule is of the NVARCHAR data type, and **N** specifies that the string preceding it is a Unicode or NVARCHAR data type.

    A new firewall rule, **Work**, is when the start IP, 115.118.0.0, and the end IP, 115.118.16.255, is added to the firewall.

4. Execute the following command to verify whether or not the rule has been added:

```
Select * from sys.firewall_rules
```

You should get an output like the one shown the following screenshot:

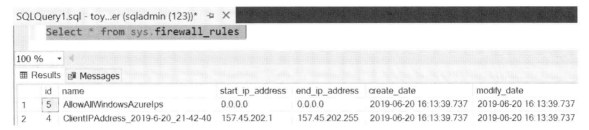

Figure 5.9: Verifying the added firewall

5. Firewall rule names are unique. If you wish to update a firewall rule, call the **sp_set_firewall_rule** procedure with the rule name you wish to update, as well as the updated IP addresses.

The following query updates the **Work** firewall rule with new IP addresses:

```
Execute sp_set_firewall_rule @name = N'Work',
@start_ip_address = '115.118.10.0',
@end_ip_address = '115.118.16.255'
```

6. Execute the following command to verify that the rule has been added:

```
Select * from sys.firewall_rules
```

You should get an output like the one shown in the following screenshot:

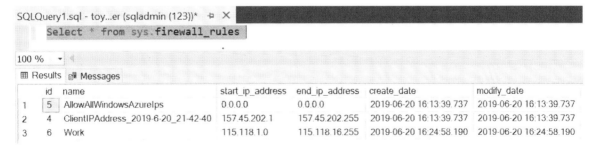

Figure 5.10: Verifying the added rule

Notice that the IP address for the **Work** firewall rule has been updated.

7.  To delete a firewall rule, run the following query:

    ```
    Execute sp_delete_firewall_rule @name= N'Work'
    ```

8.  Execute the following command to verify that the rule has been deleted:

    ```
    Select * from sys.firewall_rules
    ```

    You should get an output like the one shown in the following screenshot:

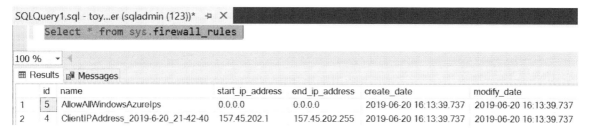

Figure 5.11: Verifying the firewall rule has been deleted

The **Work** firewall rule has been deleted from the firewall.

## Managing Database-level Firewall Rules Using Transact-SQL

Like server-level firewall rules, database-level firewall rules can also be managed with Transact-SQL. In this section, you will learn how to create, delete, and update a database-level firewall rule with Transact-SQL:

1.  Execute the following query to list the current database-level firewall rules:

    > **Note**
    >
    > You can do this within the master database context or any user SQL database context.

```
SELECT * FROM sys.database_firewall_rules
```

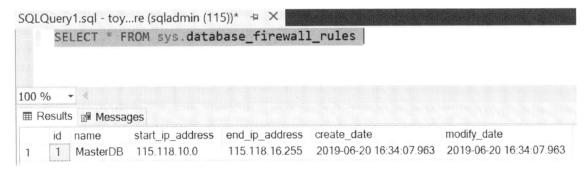

Figure 5.12: Listing the current firewall rules

Notice that no database-level firewall rules exist.

2. Execute the following query to create a new database-level firewall rule:

```
Exec sp_set_database_firewall_rule @name=N'MasterDB', @start_ip_
address='115.118.10.0', @end_ip_address='115.118.16.255'
```

3. Execute the following command to verify that the rule has been added:

```
Select * from sys.database_firewall_rules
```

You should get an output like the one shown in the following screenshot:

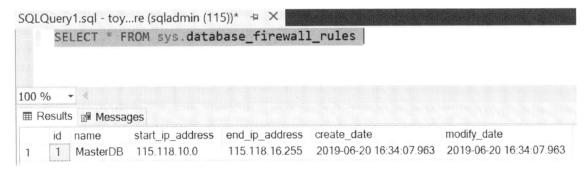

Figure 5.13: Verifying the added firewall rule

A new database-level firewall rule, **MasterDB**, has been added to the firewall.

4. To update a firewall rule, call the **sp_set_database_firewall_rule** procedure with the firewall rule you wish to update and the new start and end IP addresses. Execute the following query to update the **MasterDB** firewall rule created in the previous step:

```
Exec sp_set_database_firewall_rule @name=N'MasterDB', @start_ip_
address='115.118.1.0', @end_ip_address='115.118.16.255'
```

5. Execute the following command to verify that the rule has been updated:

```
Select * from sys.database_firewall_rules
```

You should get an output like the one shown in the following screenshot:

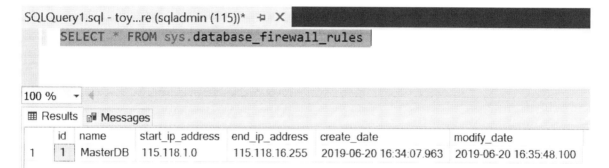

Figure 5.14: Verifying the updated firewall rule

Notice that the firewall rule has been updated.

6. To delete an existing database-level firewall rule, execute the following query:

```
Exec sp_delete_database_firewall_rule @name=N'MasterDB'
```

Execute the following command to verify whether or not the rule has been deleted:

```
Select * from sys.database_firewall_rules
```

You should get an output like the one shown in the following screenshot:

SQLQuery1.sql - toy...re (sqladmin (115))*    ⫩  X

SELECT * FROM sys.database_firewall_rules

100 %    ▼  ◀

⊞ Results   ⊒▪ Messages

| id | name | start_ip_address | end_ip_address | create_date | modify_date |
|----|------|------------------|----------------|-------------|-------------|

Figure 5.15: Deleting the firewall rule

The database-level firewall rule has been successfully deleted.

> **Note**
>
> Login details and server-level firewall rules are cached in each SQL database. The cache is periodically refreshed; however, you can run **DBCC FLUSHAUTHCACHE** to manually flush the authentication cache. This statement does not apply to the logical master database, because the master database contains the physical storage for the information about logins and firewall rules. The user executing the statement and other currently connected users remain connected.

# Authentication

Authentication refers to how a user identifies themselves when connecting to a database. There are two types of authentication mechanism: **SQL Server authentication** and **Azure Active Directory authentication**.

## SQL Authentication

This is similar to what we have in on-premise SQL servers; that is, it requires a username and password. When provisioning an Azure SQL database, you have to provide a server admin login with a username and password. This user has admin access to the Azure SQL server and **dbowner** access on all databases in a particular Azure SQL server.

There can be only one server admin account in an Azure SQL database.

## Azure Active Directory Authentication

Azure Active Directory authentication allows users to connect to an Azure SQL database by using the identities stored in **Azure Active Directory** (**Azure AD**).

**Azure AD**

When you create an Azure account, it creates a default directory for your account. This is where you can add users and give them permissions to access different Azure services as appropriate.

You can add custom domains to the default directory, or you can create directories from here.

You can also integrate your on-premise Windows AD to Azure AD using Azure AD Connect.

There are three different ways to authenticate – **Active Directory – Universal with MFA support**, **Active Directory – Password**, and **Active Directory – Integrated**, as shown in the following screenshot:

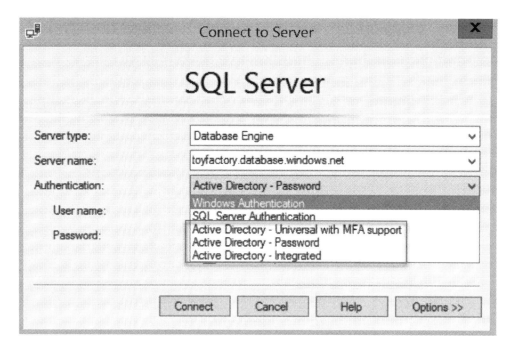

Figure 5.16: Authentication options

## Active Directory – Password

This is the easiest way to get started with Azure AD authentication. It works with Azure AD managed domains and federated domains.

The user authenticating to an Azure SQL database has to provide the Azure AD identity and the password for successful authentication:

Figure 5.17: Active Directory – Password option

## Azure Directory – Integrated

This is similar to conventional Windows authentication in on-premises SQL servers. To authenticate using this method, a user has to provide the domain account that has access to an Azure SQL database. The user doesn't have to provide the password – it's validated against Azure AD.

To get this method working, the on-premises AD should be integrated into Azure AD. This can be done using the free tool, Azure AD Connect.

When using SSMS to authenticate using the Azure Directory – Integrated method, it automatically takes the username as the logged-in username, similar to on-premises Windows authentication:

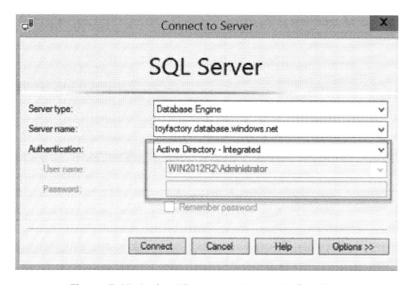

Figure 5.18: Active Directory – Integrated option

**Active Directory – Universal with MFA support**

MFA stands for multi-factor authentication. MFA allows you to provide a code received by a call, SMS, or by any other means. This further secures the authentication process, as the code received is only accessible by the person who has initiated the authentication process:

Figure 5.19: Multi-factor authentication

MFA requires you to provide a username, which is pre-populated after you configure MFA.

> **Note**
>
> Azure Active Directory authentication isn't supported when connecting to an Azure SQL database from an SQL server on Azure VM; you should use a domain Active Directory account.

### Using Active Directory – Password to Authenticate to an Azure SQL Database

This section covers how to authenticate to an Azure SQL database using Active Directory – Password. Let's consider the toy manufacturing company introduced previously. Mike needs to ensure that, if any of his networking workplaces expect access to a database, he gives them access by utilizing Active Directory – Password to authenticate to an Azure SQL database. He can achieve this by following these steps:

1. Log in to the Azure portal (https://portal.azure.com). From the left-hand navigation pane, find and open **Azure Active Directory**.

2. From the **Overview** pane, find and click **Add a user** (in the **Quick tasks** section):

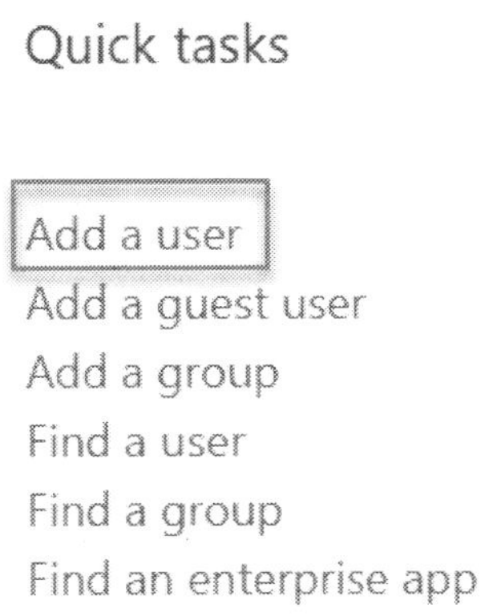

Quick tasks

Add a user
Add a guest user
Add a group
Find a user
Find a group
Find an enterprise app

**Figure 5.20: Quick tasks section**

3. In the **User** pane: provide a name and provide a username (the email is the username in this case). The email should belong to an existing verified domain in Azure AD.

> **Note**
>
> You can use the default domain when providing a user email. For example, if your Microsoft account email ID is **ahmad.osama1984@gmail.com**, then the default directory would be **ahmadosama1984.onmicrosoft.com**. Therefore, you can provide the username chris@ahmadosama1984.onmicrosoft.com.

4. You can find your default domain in the top-right corner of the Azure portal:

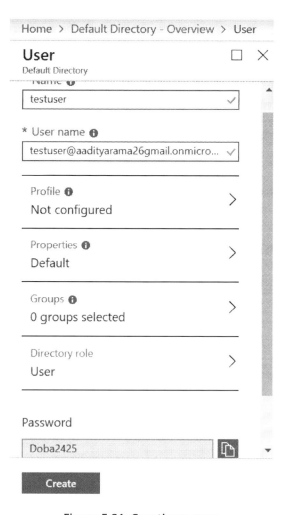

Figure 5.21: Creating a user

Check the **Show Password** checkbox and copy the password. You are not allowed to change the password.

Leave all the other options as the default values and click **Create** to create the user:

> **Note**
>
> Log out of the Azure portal and log in again using the new user credentials. You'll be asked to change the password. Once your password is changed, log out and log in with your Azure admin credentials.

5.  Once you have created a user, the next step is to make the user an Azure SQL Server Active Directory admin. In the Azure portal, find and click the **toyfactorytemp** Azure SQL server. In **toyfactorytemp**, find and select the **Active Directory admin** option in the **Settings** section:

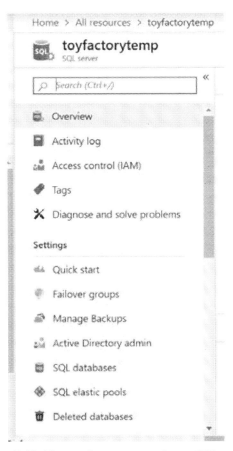

Figure 5.22: The toyfactorytemp Azure SQL server

6. In the **Active Directory admin** pane, select **Set admin** from the top menu:

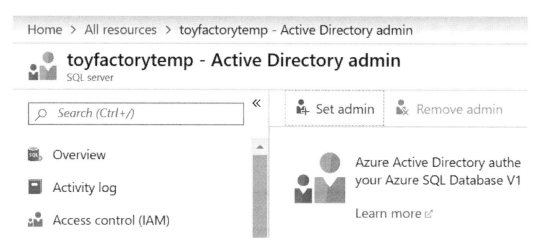

Figure 5.23: Active Directory admin pane

7. In the **Add admin** pane, type the username in the **Select** user and select the user you created in *step 3* as the **Active Directory** admin:

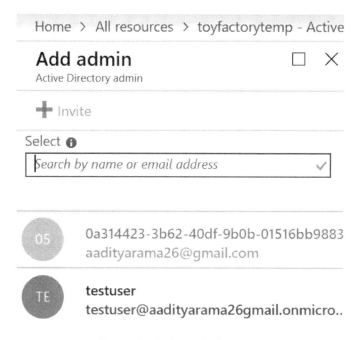

Figure 5.24: Add admin pane

You'll be taken back to the **Add admin** pane. Click **Save** to set the selected user as the Active Directory admin:

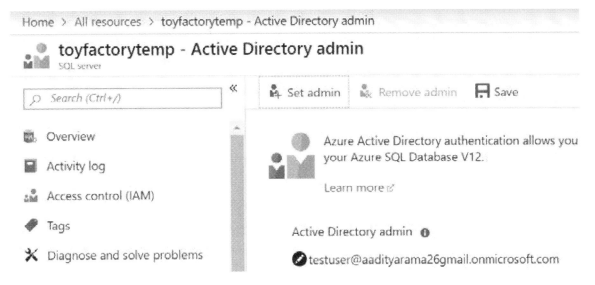

Figure 5.25: Active Directory admin pane

8. You now have an Active Directory admin defined for the **toyfactorytemp** SQL server. The AD admin has **dbowner** access to all of the databases in the **toyfactory** server.

   In the next step, you'll connect to the **toyfactory** server with the AD admin account using SSMS.

9. Open SSMS, and in the **Connect to Server** dialog box:

   Under **Server Type**, select **Database Engine**.

   Under **Server name**, enter the **toyfactorytemp** server name.

   Under **Authentication**, select **Active Directory – Password**.

   Under **Username**, enter the username (email) of the user created in *step* 3.

   Under **Password**, enter the user's password.

   Click **Connect**.

If you get the following error, you will have to change the password by logging in to the Azure portal as this user. You'll be asked to update the password on the login screen. Change the password and then try to connect to SQL Server from SSMS:

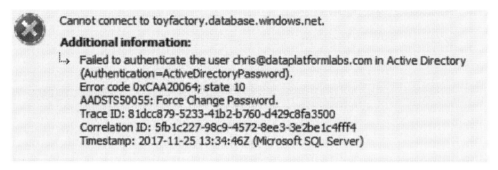

Figure 5.26: Cannot connect to database error

Notice that Object Explorer displays the username as **testuser@ aadityarama26gmail.onmicrosoft.com**:

toyfactorytemp.database.windows.net (SQL Server 12.0.2000.8 - testuser@aadityarama26gmail.onmicrosoft.com)
  Databases
    System Databases
    toystore

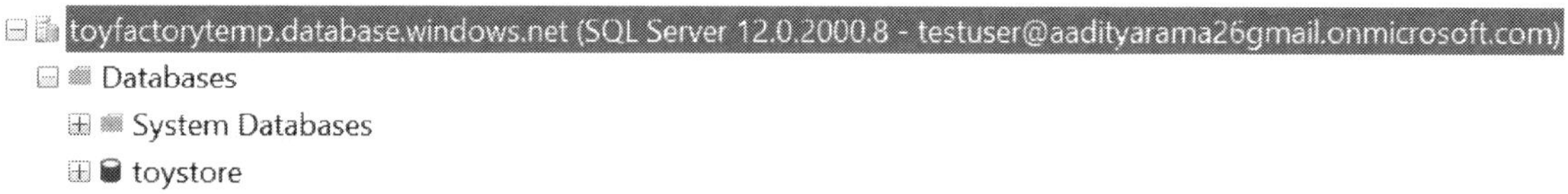

Figure 5.27: Object Explorer

**Note**

If you wish to explore Active Directory – Integrated and Active Directory – Universal with MFA, start here: https://docs.microsoft.com/en-us/azure/active-directory/hybrid/whatis-hybrid-identity.

## Azure SQL Database Authentication Structure

Azure SQL Database will always have two different administrators if Azure AD authentication is used: the original SQL Server administrator (SQL authentication) and the Azure AD admin. The Azure AD administrator login can be a user or a group. All users in the Azure AD admin group will have administrative access to an Azure SQL server:

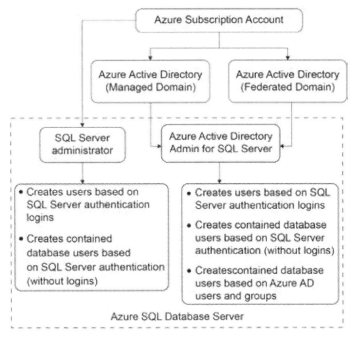

Figure 5.28: Azure SQL Database Authentication Structure

> **Note**
>
> An Azure administrator can either be a single user or a group. A user and a group administrator can't coexist.

## Azure SQL Database Authentication Considerations

You must consider the following factors for Azure SQL Database authentication:

- Create a dedicated Azure AD group as the Azure SQL Server administrator instead of creating an individual user administrator.

- You can configure either an Azure AD group or a user as an Azure SQL Server admin.

- **bcp.exe** can't connect to an Azure SQL database using Azure Active Directory authentication as it uses an old ODBC driver.

- SQLCMD versions 13.1 and above support Azure Active Directory authentication.

- To use Azure AD authentication with SSMS, you need to have .NET Framework 4.6 or above installed on your system.

# Authorization

Authorization refers to the object-level permission a user has within a SQL database. For example, a user may have access to read one set of tables and to read-write on another set of tables.

The admin accounts, SQL authentication accounts, and Azure AD accounts have **db_owner** access to all databases and are allowed to do anything within a database.

### Server-Level Administrative Roles

There are two additional server-level administrative roles: database creators and login managers.

### Database Creators

Members of database creators (**dbmanager**) are allowed to create new SQL databases. To create a new user with the database creator role:

1. Log in to SSMS with either Azure AD admin or SQL Server admin.

2. Create a new login in the master database using the following query:

   ```
   CREATE LOGIN John WITH PASSWORD = 'Very$Stro9gPa$$w0rd';
   ```

3. Create a new user in the master database mapped to log in John using the following query:

   ```
   CREATE USER John FROM LOGIN John
   ```

4. Add the user John to the **dbmanager** role using the following query:

   ```
   ALTER ROLE dbmanager ADD MEMBER John;
   ```

5. Open a new query window in SSMS and log in as John.

6. Execute the following query to create a new SQL database:

   ```
   CREATE DATABASE JohnsDB
   ```

   John will have **db_owner** access to all the databases he creates.

### Login Manager

Members of this role can create new logins in the master database. To create a new user with the `loginmanager` role, follow the preceding steps to create a user and add them to the `loginmanager` role.

## Non-Administrative Users

Non-administrative users don't have access to the master database and have limited access to the required databases and objects.

An example of a non-administrative user is an application user. An application user is one that is used by an application to connect to a database and perform DML operations.

A non-administrative user can either be an Azure AD user or an SQL Server authentication user.

# Creating Contained Database Users for Azure AD Authentication

In this section, you will learn how to create contained database users for Azure AD authentication for firms such as ToyStore Ltd., where there are many roles that require access to the database:

1. Open SSMS. From the top menu, select **File**, select **New**, and then select **Database Engine Query** to open a new query window:

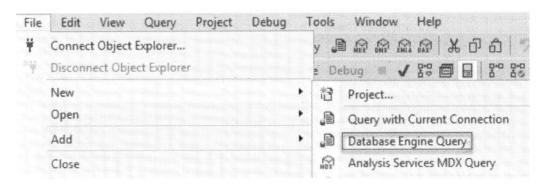

Figure 5.29: SSMS

2. Connect to the Azure SQL Server with Active Directory – Password authentication.

3. Execute the following query to create a contained database user (SQL authentication) and add it to the **db_owner** role:

```
--Create a contained database user (SQL Authentication) CREATE USER Mike
WITH PASSWORD='John@pwd'
GO
-- Make Mike toystore database owner ALTER ROLE db_owner ADD MEMBER Mike
```

4. Execute the following query to create a contained database user (Azure AD authentication) and add it to the **db_datareader** role:

```
--Create a contained database user (Azure AD Authentication)
CREATE USER [John@aadityarama26gmail.onmicrosoft.com] FROM EXTERNAL
PROVIDER
-- Give read access to John on all tables
ALTER ROLE db_datareader ADD Member [John@dataplatformlabs.com]
```

> **Note**
>
> You need to create an Azure AD user before you add them to the SQL database.
> You can use the steps in the previous section to create a new Azure AD user.

5. Press F8 to open Object Explorer. In Object Explorer, connect to your Azure SQL Server if you're not already connected.

Expand the **Databases** node. In the **Databases** node, expand the **toystore** database node. In the **toystore** database, expand the **Security** node and then expand the **Users** node.

You should see the users Mike and John listed in the **Users** section:

**Figure 5.30: Users section**

Notice that Mike and John are not mapped to a server login. This is because they are contained database users.

6. Press *Ctrl* + N to open a new query window. Click the change connection icon in the top menu, next to the database drop-down list:

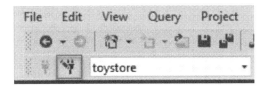

Figure 5.31: The Change connection icon

7. In the **Connect to Server** dialog box:

Under **Server name**, provide the Azure SQL server name.

Under **Authentication**, select **Active Directory – Password**.

Enter the username as `john@aadityarama26gmail.onmicrosoft.com`

Enter the password for the aforementioned user.

Click **Connect**:

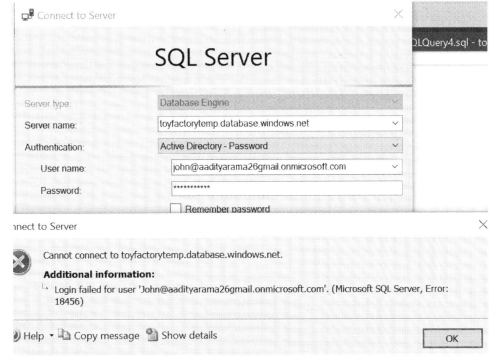

Figure 5.32: Connect to Server dialog box

8.  You will get an error like the one shown in the preceding screenshot. This is because SSMS tries to connect to the default database, which, in this case, is the **master** database. The database master doesn't contain the user `john@aadityarama26gmail.onmicrosoft.com` and therefore the connection fails.

9.  Click **OK** in the error dialog box. In the **Connect to Database Engine** dialog box, select **Options** from the lower-left corner of the dialog box window.

    Under **Options**, select the **Connection Properties** tab, and in the **Connect to database** setting, set the database to **toystore**.

    Click **Connect** to continue:

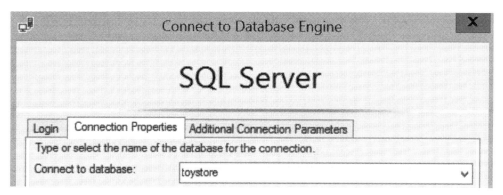

Figure 5.33: Setting the database to toystore

You should now be able to connect to the **toystore** database.

You can add users to different roles and test out the security. For example, you can add a user in the **db_dbwriter** role and then log in using the user and verify that they're only able to write to tables and can't do any other database operations, such as creating tables, databases, and so on.

## Groups and Roles

Additionally, you can group users with similar sets of permissions in an Azure AD group or an SQL database role. You can then assign the permissions to the group and add users to it. If a new user with the same permissions arrives, add the user to the group or role.

## Row-level Security

Authorization controls whether or not a user can read or write one or more tables. **Row-level security** (**RLS**) further controls what data in a table the user has access to:

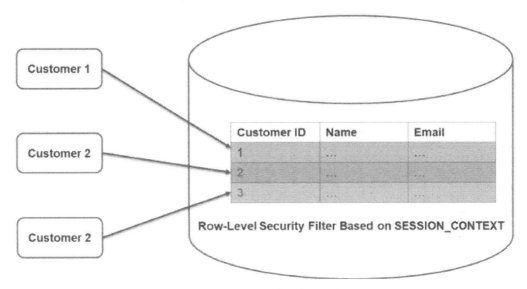

Figure 5.34: Row-level security

Let's say you have a customer table in a database and you want users to access only those rows in a table that belong to them; for example, customer 1 should only have access to rows with customer ID 1, and customer 2 should only access rows with customer ID 2, and so on and so forth.

RLS allows you to enable this at the database level and not the application level. Prior to RLS, such security was only possible by implementing access logic at the application level.

RLS is implemented by writing the row access logic or the security predicates in an inline table-valued function and then creating a security policy on top of the security predicate.

The security predicate defines the criteria to determine whether or not a user has read or write access to a given set of rows in a particular table.

RLS supports two types of security predicates:

- **Filter predicates**: Filter predicates apply to **SELECT**, **UPDATE**, and **DELETE**, and silently filter out unqualified rows.

- **Block predicates**: Block predicates apply to **AFTER INSERT**, **AFTER UPDATE**, **BEFORE UPDATE**, and **BEFORE DELETE**, and block unqualified rows being written to the table.

## Dynamic Data Masking

**Dynamic data masking** or **DDM** works on top of row-level security and further restricts the exposure of sensitive data by masking it to non-privileged users:

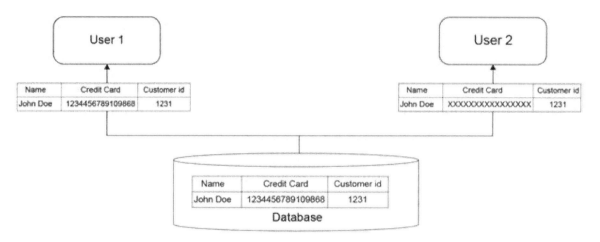

Figure 5.35: Dynamic data masking

For example, say users John and Chris can read and write data that belongs to customer 1. Row-level security ensures that they can only read and write data for customer 1 in the customer table. However, DDM will ensure that John can see the Social Security number of the customer and Chris can't, as he's not authorized to. Chris will see masked data in the SSN column, though he will be able to see data in the rest of the columns.

DDM is implemented by defining masks and applying them to columns as and when required. There aren't any changes required at the application level or the query level, as the masks are applied at the column level.

DDM can be used for full, partial, or random masking. For example, call-support people need the last four characters of a user's password to identify them. This can be done by masking all characters except the last four.

DDM has the following four types of masks to obfuscate data:

- **Default**: Implements full masking depending on the data type of the column being masked.

- **Email**: Partial masking, which masks all characters except the first letter and the `.com` suffix of an email address. For example, `john1984@ dataplatformlabs.com` would be masked as jxxx@xxxx.com.

- **Random**: Masks a column with a numeric data type with a random value within a specified range.

- **Custom String**: Partial masking, which masks all characters with a custom string, excluding the first and last letters.

DDM has the following limitations:

- Encrypted columns, filestreams, column sets, and sparse columns that are part of a column set can't be masked.

- Computed columns can't be masked; however, if a computed column depends on a masked column, the computed column will return masked values.

- A masked column can't be used as a fulltext index key.

- A mask can't be applied to a column with dependencies. For example, if an index depends on a column, it can only be masked by dropping the index, applying the mask, and then creating the index.

## Advanced Data Security

Advanced data security is a set of advanced SQL security features that provides vulnerability assessment, threat detection, and data discovery and classification.

It's a paid service, is priced independently of Azure SQL Database, and is free for the first 30 days.

Advanced data security for a database can be enabled when the database is created or at a later time.

> **Note**
>
> Threat detection was available earlier, along with the auditing feature. However, it's now available as part of advanced data security as advanced threat detection.

The following screenshot is from an older version of the Azure portal, showing the threat detection and auditing features:

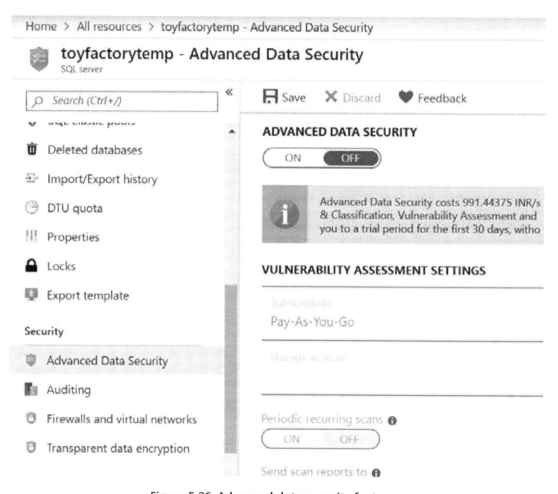

Figure 5.36: Advanced data security features

The three security features under **Advanced Data Security** are as follows:

- **<u>Vulnerability assessment</u>**: A vulnerability assessment, as the name suggests, checks an SQL database for any possible security vulnerabilities, database misconfigurations, extra permissions, unsecured data, firewall rules, and server-level permissions. The vulnerability assessment can help to meet data compliance and data privacy requirements. Database configurations are checked against the best practices defined by Microsoft.

- **<u>Advanced threat detection</u>**: Threat detection detects and alerts users about potential threats and suspicious activity. Alerts are integrated with Azure Security Center, which provides details about and possible solutions to alerts. Threat detection alerts against the following threats:

  **SQL injection**: An alert is triggered when an SQL injection attack happens or if there's bad code that could result in an SQL injection attack.

  **Access from an unusual location**: An alert is triggered when a user logs into an SQL database from a location that is different than the user's usual location.

  **Access from an unusual Azure data center**: An alert is triggered when someone logs into an SQL database from a data center other than the usual or the regular data center used to log in.

  **Access from an unfamiliar principal**: An alert is triggered when someone logs into an SQL database using an unfamiliar or unusual SQL login.

  **Access from a potentially harmful application**: An alert is triggered when a connection is made from a potentially harmful application; for example, common attack tools.

  **Brute-force SQL credentials**: An alert is triggered when there's an abnormally high number of failed login attempts with different credentials.

- **<u>Data Discovery and Classification</u>**: The Data Discovery and Classification feature (in preview) can be used to discover, classify, label, and protect sensitive data in an Azure SQL database. Data Discovery and Classification can help you achieve data privacy and regulatory compliance requirements, control and secure databases with highly sensitive data such as credit card numbers and confidential financial or other business information, and monitor and alert you to unusual access to sensitive data.

  Data Discovery and Classification consists of the following:

  **Discovery and recommendations**: The classification engine scans and identifies the column with sensitive data in an SQL database. It also provides possible resolutions and ways to apply the resolutions.

**Labeling**: This allows the tagging of columns with sensitive data using the new classification metadata attributes available in the SQL engine.

There are two attributes used to classify the sensitivity of data – a label, which specifies the level of the data sensitivity in a given column, and information types, which provide additional details on the type of data stored in the column.

This information can then be used in advanced sensitivity-based auditing and protection scenarios.

The classification details are available on a dashboard on the Azure portal and can also be downloaded for offline analysis.

## Exercise: Exploring Advanced Data Security Features

In this exercise, we'll enable advanced data security on the **toystore** database and we'll perform a vulnerability assessment and classify the sensitive data using Data Discovery and Classification:

1.  Enable **Advanced Data Security (ADS)** for the **toystore** database.

    To enable ADS, log in to the Azure portal. From the left-hand menu, select **All resources** and click the **toystore** database to open the database overview page.

    In the search box, type **Advanced Data Security**:

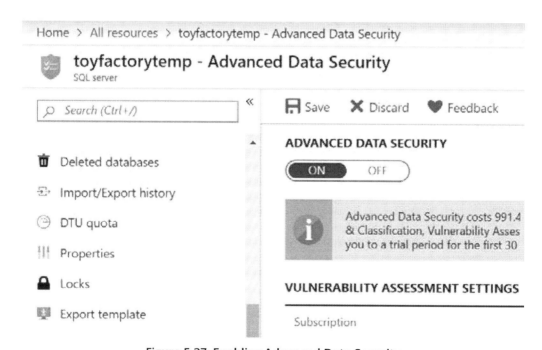

Figure 5.37: Enabling Advanced Data Security

2.  Select the **Advanced Data Security** option and then click the **Enable Advanced Data Security on the server** button.

    As Advanced Data Security is enabled, it automatically does a vulnerability scan, data discovery and classification, and threat detection:

Figure 5.38: Vulnerability scan

Notice that **Data Discovery and Classification**, **Vulnerability Assessment**, and **Advanced Threat Protection** reports are available.

3.  Click the **Vulnerability Assessment** tile to get the details:

Figure 5.39: Vulnerability Assessment details

Notice that there are 43 passed checks and 4 failed checks – 2 high-risk and 2 medium-risk.

The failed and passed checks are given in the result grid. Click the **Server-level firewall rules should be tracked and maintained at a strict minimum** failed check:

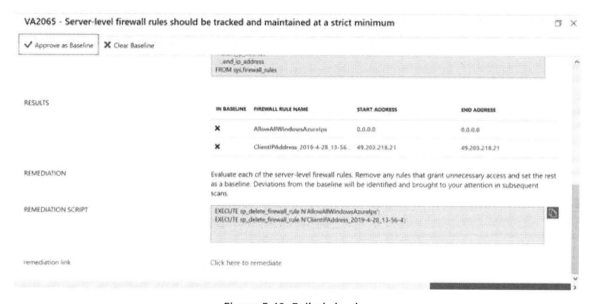

Figure 5.40: Failed checks

**VA2065 - Server-level firewall rules should be tracked and maintained at a strict minimum** keeps track of the server-level firewall rules.

It allows you to specify the firewall rules you need as the baseline firewall rules. An alert is generated for any deviation from the baseline, that is, when any new firewall is added to the server.

To specify the baseline, click **Approve as Baseline** in the top menu and click yes in the confirmation box.

Once the baseline is set as notified in the notification center, click the **Scan** link on the **Vulnerability Assessment** page to re-scan the database:

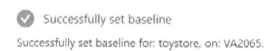

Successfully set baseline

Successfully set baseline for: toystore, on: VA2065.

Figure 5.41: Baseline set

Figure 5.42: Rescanning the database

When the scan completes, observe that the VA20165 risk has been mitigated as we added the existing firewall rules to the baseline:

Figure 5.43: VA20165 risk mitigated

Add a new server firewall rule and re-run vulnerability assessment. The VA2065 risk should appear again.

Other than adding a firewall rule to the baseline, you can also delete a firewall rule if it's not required.

To delete a firewall rule, either click **Click here to remediate** or delete the firewall using the queries specified on the VA2065 details page.

Similar to risk VA2065, every other risk allows you to specify a baseline, and an alert is raised if the baseline is changed.

Data Discovery and Classification: On the **toystore – Advanced Data Security** page, click the **Data Discovery & Classification (preview)** tile:

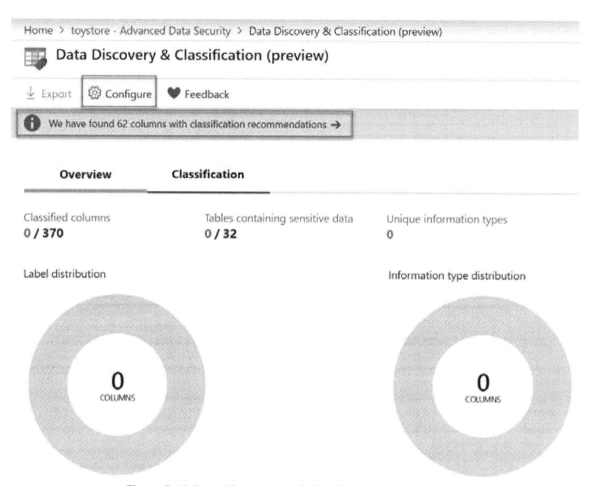

Figure 5.44: Data Discovery and Classification (preview) tile

Notice that there are 62 columns with classification recommendations; however, none of the columns are classified yet.

Click the **Configure** option to manage the sensitivity labels. A label defines the level of data sensitivity:

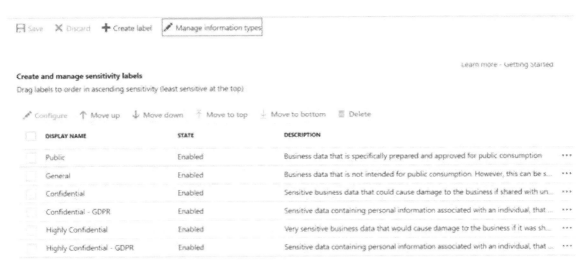

Figure 5.45: Managing information types

You can add, delete, and prioritize labels by moving them up or down the hierarchy.

4. Click **Manage information types** to add or delete information types:

✚ Create information type

**Create and manage information types**
Drag information types to order in ascending discovering ranking

🖊 Configure    ↑ Move up    ↓ Move down    ↑ Move to top    ↓ Move to bottom    🗑 Delete

| | INFORMATION TYPE | STATE | ASSOCIATED LABEL | TYPE | |
|---|---|---|---|---|---|
| ☐ | Networking | Enabled | Confidential | Built-in | ... |
| ☐ | Contact Info | Enabled | Confidential | Built-in | ... |
| ☐ | Credentials | Enabled | Confidential | Built-in | ... |
| ☐ | Name | Enabled | Confidential - GDPR | Built-in | ... |
| ☐ | National ID | Enabled | Confidential - GDPR | Built-in | ... |
| ☐ | SSN | Enabled | Confidential - GDPR | Built-in | ... |
| ☐ | Credit Card | Enabled | Confidential | Built-in | ... |
| ☐ | Banking | Enabled | Confidential | Built-in | ... |

Figure 5.46: Deleting information types

An information type details the type of data in a column; for example, the **Contact Info** information type is for the name, phone number, and address details of a person or business.

Each information type is associated with a label. This can be changed as per the business standard. For example, if **Contact Info** is allowed to be shared for a particular business, the label can be changed to **Public** from **Confidential**.

5. Let's now return to the Data Discovery & Classification page and look at the recommendations. To do this, click the **We have found 62 columns with classifications recommendations** link:

Figure 5.47: Recommendations

All of the classifications are listed under the **Classification** tab on the **Data Discovery & Classification** page.

You can filter the recommendations based on schema, table, column, information type, and label.

6. Let's look at the recommendations for the `Application.People` table:

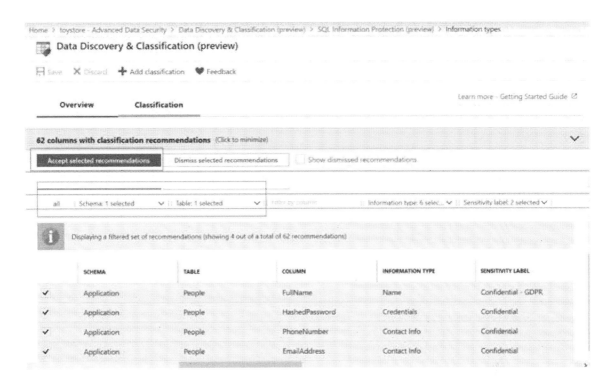

Figure 5.48: Recommendations for the Application.People table

Notice that the information type and sensitivity labels are correctly applied to the four columns.

7.  Click **Accept selected recommendations** to apply the data classification:

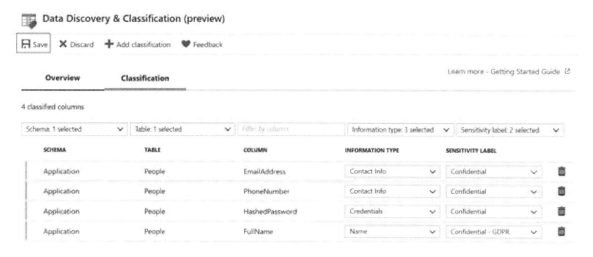

Figure 5.49: Applying data classification

8.  Click **Save** and then select the **Overview** tab:

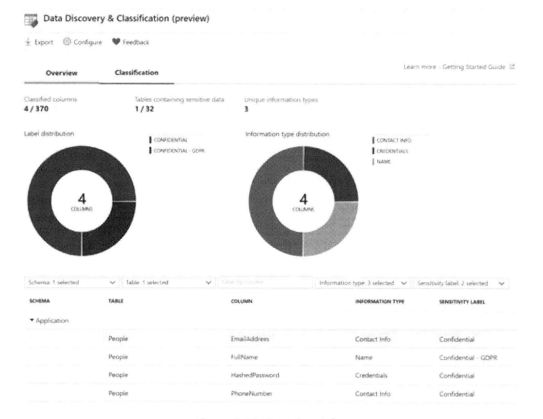

Figure 5.50: Overview tab

The **Overview** tab now shows the summary of the label and information type distribution and lists the data classification.

Any access to the classified columns is captured in the audit logs when SQL database auditing is on. An example of an audit report is shown in the next section *Auditing*.

## Auditing

Auditing tracks and records database events to an audit log and can help you to:

- Maintain regulatory compliance
- Understand database activity
- Catch discrepancies or anomalies indicating a security violation

Auditing allows you to:

- Define what database actions are to be audited
- Find unusual activities or trends by using preconfigured reports and dashboards to understand and analyze the audit log

Auditing can be configured at the server level and database level. If auditing is configured at the server level, it'll automatically apply to all of the databases in the server. Auditing configured at the database level will only apply to a particular database.

It's recommended to audit the server instead of auditing individual databases.

## Exercise: Configuring SQL Database Auditing

To configure SQL database auditing using the Azure portal, follow these steps:

1. Open the **toystore** database overview page and search for **Auditing** in the search box:

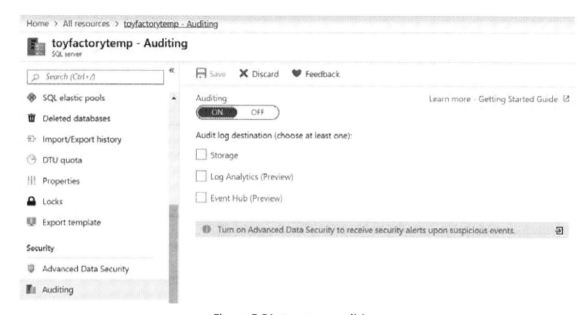

Figure 5.51: toystore auditing

Click **Auditing** to open the **toystore – Auditing** page.

2. On the **Auditing** page, click the **Auditing** toggle button to switch on auditing.

   There are three options to save the audit log: **Storage**, **Log Analytics (Preview)**, and **Event Hub (Preview)**.

   The storage account allows you to save the audit logs; however, it provides no native ways to perform analytics on saved logs.

   Log analytics saves the log data in the log analytics workspace and uses Azure Monitor to provide analysis and actions on the logged data.

   Azure Event Hubs is a big data streaming and event ingestion service. Audit logs are streamed to an event hub as events. Events from an event hub can be used to perform real-time analysis and can be saved into another database (CSV, Cosmos DB, or another SQL database) for further analytics.

3.  Check the **Storage and Log Analytics** options and configure them as follows.

    **Configuring storage**: To configure storage, click **Storage settings**. You can either select an existing storage account or create a new storage account:

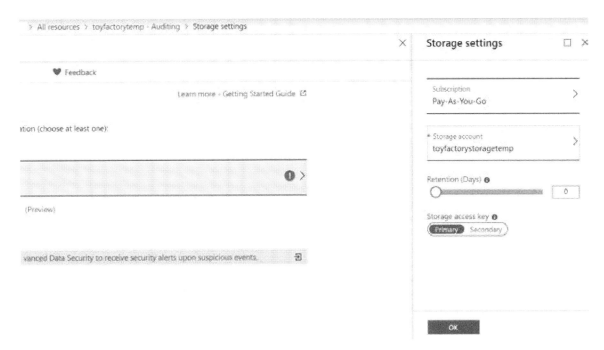

Figure 5.52: Storage settings page

To create a new storage account, click **Create new** and fill out the details as shown in the preceding screenshot.

---

**Note**

You can opt for premium storage for faster performance if required. Standard blob storage is preferred for demo purposes.

---

Click the **OK** button to create and link the storage account to SQL database auditing.

4. **Configuring log analytics**: To configure log analytics, click **Log Analytics**. You can use an existing Log Analytics workspace or create a new one:

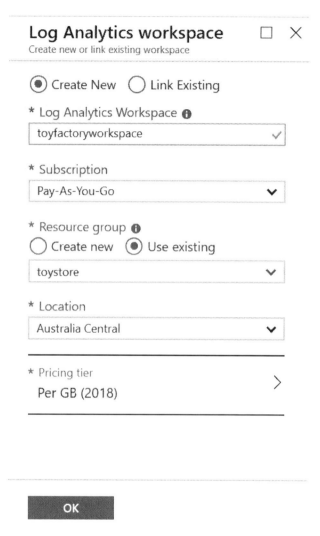

Figure 5.53: Log Analytics workspace page

To create a new workspace, click on the **Create New** option and fill out the details as shown in the preceding screenshot.

There's only one pricing tier, **Per GB (2018)**, currently available with Log Analytics.

Click **OK** to create and link the **Log Analytics** account with SQL database auditing.

After the storage account and log analytics workspace have been configured, click **Save** to save the configuration:

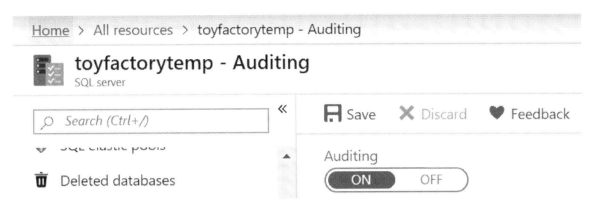

Figure 5.54: Creating a new workspace

This completes the auditing configuration. To view the audit logs, click on **View audit logs** in **toystoretemp – Auditing**:

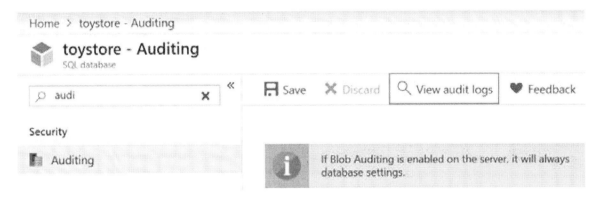

Figure 5.55: Viewing audit logs

5.  Let's execute queries against the **toystore** database and monitor the audit logs.

> **Note**
>
> To execute a query, you can connect to the **toystore** database from SSMS or you can use the query editor provided in the Azure portal.

To execute the query from SSMS, make sure the IP address of your machine has been added to the SQL database firewall rule. For more on how to connect and execute a query against an SQL database, refer to *Lesson 1, Microsoft Azure SQL Database Primer*.

```
SELECT
        EmailAddress,
        PhoneNumber
FROM Application.People
WHERE Fullname LIKE '%Edg%'
GO
SELECT
        *
FROM Purchasing.Suppliers
WHERE BankAccountName LIKE '%a%'
```

Here's what you should get when running queries from SSMS:

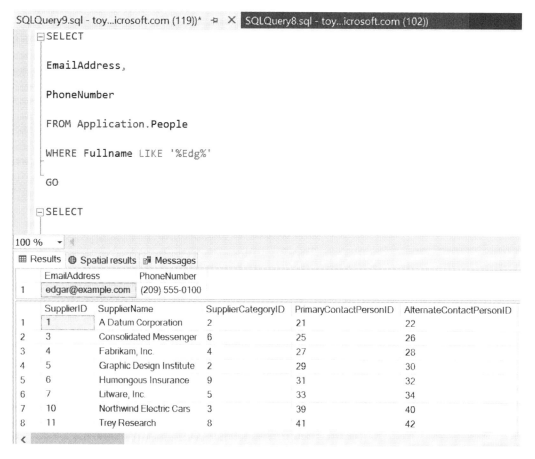

Figure 5.56: Running queries from SSMS

Let's switch to the Azure portal and open the **toystore – Auditing** page. On the **toystore – Auditing** page, click on **View audit logs**:

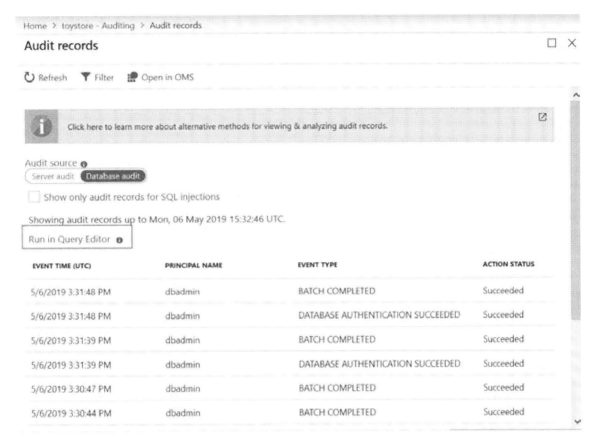

Figure 5.57: Query log files by clicking on Run in Query Editor

The **Audit records** page lists the stored audit logs. Click **Run in Query Editor** to query the log files using a Transact-SQL query:

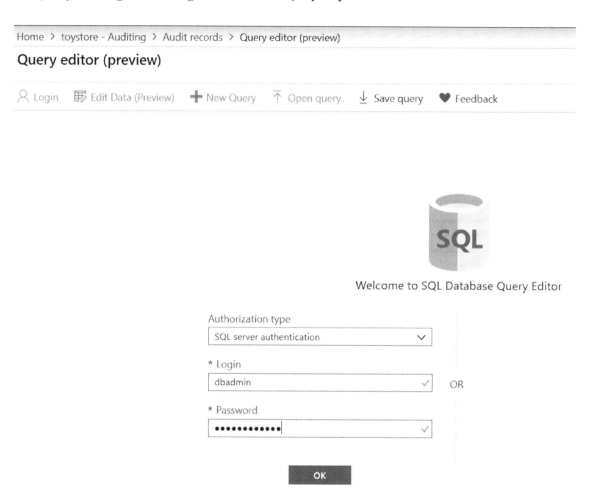

Figure 5.58: The Login page of the query editor

Log in to the **Query editor** using SQL authentication, as shown in the preceding screenshot.

A new query window opens up with the audit query. Replace the audit query with the following one:

```
SELECT TOP 100 event_time, server_instance_name, database_name, server_
principal_name, client_ip, statement, succeeded, action_id, class_type,
additional_information
FROM sys.fn_get_audit_file('https://toyfactorystoragetemp.blob.core.
windows.net/sqldbauditlogs/toyfactorytemp/toystore/SqlDbAuditing_Audit_
NoRetention/2019-06-20/18_57_50_932_0.xel', default, default)
WHERE (event_time <= '2019-06-20T19:03:22.910Z')
/* additional WHERE clause conditions/filters can be added here */
ORDER BY event_time DESC
```

> **Note**
>
> You can execute the preceding query either in the query editor on the Azure portal or in SSMS.

The query uses the **sys.fn_get_audit_file** function to read the audit log file stored in the Azure storage. You'll have to replace the path of the audit log file with the one you got in the query editor in the previous step.

Here's the output from the query:

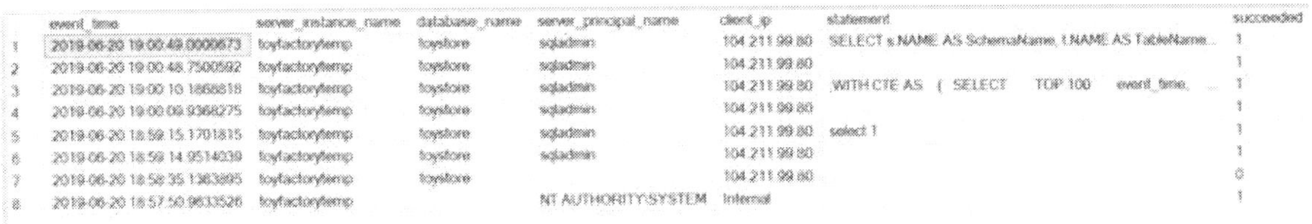

| | event_time | server_instance_name | database_name | server_principal_name | client_ip | statement | succeeded |
|---|---|---|---|---|---|---|---|
| 1 | 2019-06-20 19:00:49.0000673 | toyfactorytemp | toystore | sqladmin | 104.211.99.80 | SELECT s.NAME AS SchemaName, t.NAME AS TableName... | 1 |
| 2 | 2019-06-20 19:00:48.7500592 | toyfactorytemp | toystore | sqladmin | 104.211.99.80 | | 1 |
| 3 | 2019-06-20 19:00:10.1868818 | toyfactorytemp | toystore | sqladmin | 104.211.99.80 | ;WITH CTE AS ( SELECT TOP 100 event_time, ... | 1 |
| 4 | 2019-06-20 19:00:09.9368275 | toyfactorytemp | toystore | sqladmin | 104.211.99.80 | | 1 |
| 5 | 2019-06-20 18:59:15.1701815 | toyfactorytemp | toystore | sqladmin | 104.211.99.80 | select 1 | 1 |
| 6 | 2019-06-20 18:59:14.9514039 | toyfactorytemp | toystore | sqladmin | 104.211.99.80 | | 1 |
| 7 | 2019-06-20 18:58:35.1363895 | toyfactorytemp | toystore | | 104.211.99.80 | | 0 |
| 8 | 2019-06-20 18:57:50.9633526 | toyfactorytemp | | NT AUTHORITY\SYSTEM | Internal | | 1 |

Figure 5.59: Output of the previous query

Notice that the output has the label and the information type we assigned when configuring **Data Discovery and Classification**.

This information can be used to find out how often confidential information is accessed and who has access to it.

## Activity: Implementing Row-level Security

In this section, we will look at how to implement row-level security using our example of ToyStore Ltd. Mike has been asked to implement row-level security so that every customer is able to view and edit only their records. The **CustomerAdmin** user, however, should be allowed to view and edit all customer records. Follow these steps to complete the activity:

1.  Execute the following query to create the **dbo.Customers** table and populate it with sample records:

    ```
    CREATE TABLE Customers (
    CustomerID int identity, Name sysname,
    CreditCardNumber varchar(100), Phone varchar(100),
    Email varchar(100)
    )
    Go
    INSERT INTO Customers VALUES('Mike',0987654312345678,9876543210,'mike@
    outlook.com'), ('Mike',0987654356784567,9876549870,'mike1@outlook.
    com'), ('Mike',0984567431234567,9876567210,'mike2@outlook.com'), (' john@
    aadityarama26gmail.onmicrosoft.com ',0987654312345678,9876246210,'jo
    hn@outlook.com'),
    (' john@aadityarama26gmail.onmicrosoft.com ',0987654123784567,9876656870,'
    jo hn2@outlook.com'),
    (' john@aadityarama26gmail.onmicrosoft.com ',09856787431234567,9876467210,
    'jo hn3@outlook.com'),
    ('CustomerAdmin',0987654312235578,9873456210,'john@outlook. com'),
    ('CustomerAdmin',0984564123784567,9872436870,'mike2@outlook. com'),
    ('CustomerAdmin',0945677874312367,9872427210,'chris3@outlook. com')
    ```

2.  Execute the following query to create a new user, **CustomerAdmin**:

    ```
    CREATE USER CustomerAdmin WITHOUT LOGIN
    ```

3.  Execute the following query to grant read access to **Mike**, **John**, and **CustomerAdmin** on the **dbo.Customers** table:

    ```
    GRANT SELECT ON dbo.Customers TO Mike
    GO
    GRANT SELECT ON dbo.Customers TO [john@aadityarama26gmail.onmicrosoft.com]
    GO
    GRANT SELECT ON dbo.Customers TO CustomerAdmin
    ```

4. Create a security predicate to filter out the rows based on the logged-in username:

```
CREATE SCHEMA Security; GO
CREATE FUNCTION Security.fn_securitypredicate(@Customer AS sysname)
RETURNS TABLE WITH SCHEMABINDING AS
RETURN SELECT 1 AS predicateresult
WHERE @Customer = USER_NAME() OR USER_NAME() = 'CustomerAdmin';
```

The preceding query first creates a schema, **Security**. It then creates an inline table-valued function, **fn_securitypredicate**, which will return 1 (True) when the logged-in username is equal to the **@Customer** parameter, or when the logged-in user is **CustomerAdmin**.

5. Create a security policy for the preceding security predicate:

```
CREATE SECURITY POLICY CustomerFilter
ADD FILTER PREDICATE Security.fn_securitypredicate(Name) ON dbo.Customers,
ADD BLOCK PREDICATE Security.fn_securitypredicate(Name) ON dbo.Customers
AFTER INSERT
WITH (STATE = ON);
```

The preceding query adds the filter predicate created in step 4 to the security policy and sets the status to **ON**.

The policy also implements an **AFTER INSERT** block predicate. Afterward, the **INSERT** predicate will stop inserts that don't comply with the security policy and will show an error message for them.

The inline table-valued functions will take the customer name (the Name column) as the parameter and will return true if the passed parameter value is equal to the value returned by the **USER_NAME()** function.

6. Let's test the policy by executing the following query to switch the user context to **Mike** and return all the data from the **dbo.Customers** table:

```
EXECUTE AS USER='Mike' GO
SELECT USER_NAME() GO
SELECT * FROM dbo.Customers
```

You should get the following output:

Figure 5.60: Output of the preceding code

The query returns the records where the customer name is **Mike**. This is because the query is executed in the context of **Mike**.

7. Execute the following query to update John's record from Mike's security context:

```
EXECUTE AS USER='Mike' GO SELECT USER_NAME()
GO
-- CustomerID 11 belongs to John
UPDATE dbo.Customers SET Email='MikeBlue@outlook.com' WHERE CustomerID=11
GO

-- Switch User context to John
EXECUTE AS USER='john@aadityarama26gmail.onmicrosoft.com '

GO
SELECT USER_NAME()

GO
-- Verify if email is updated or not

SELECT * FROM dbo.Customers WHERE CustomerID=11
```

Mike can't update **CustomerID 11** as it belongs to John. You won't get an error; however, the value isn't updated.

You should get the following output:

```
EXECUTE AS USER='Mike'
GO

SELECT USER_NAME()
GO

-- CustomerID 4 belongs to John

UPDATE dbo.Customers SET Email='MikeBlue@outlook.com' WHERE CustomerID=11

GO

-- Switch User context to John
```

100 %

Results | Messages

| (No column name) |
|---|
| 1 | Mike |

| (No column name) |
|---|
| 1 | John@aadityarama26gmail.onmicrosoft.com |

| | CustomerID | Name | CreditCardNumber | Phone | Email |
|---|---|---|---|---|---|
| 1 | 11 | john@aadityarama26gmail.onmicrosoft.com | 987654123784567 | 9876656870 | jo hn2@outlook.com |

Figure 5.61: Updating John's record from Mike's security context

8. Execute the following query under Mike's security context to insert a record with a customer name of **john@aadityarama26gmail.onmicrosoft.com**:

```
EXECUTE AS USER='Mike'
GO
SELECT USER_NAME()
GO
INSERT INTO dbo.Customers VALUES('john@aadityarama26gmail.onmicrosoft.com'
,9876543445345678,65412396852,'Mike@dataplatformlabs.com')
```

The **AFTER INSERT BLOCK** predicate will block the insert, as defined by the security policy, and will show the following error:

Figure 5.62: Inserting a record in Mike's security context

9. Execute the following query in the **CustomerAdmin** security context to return all of the rows from the **dbo.Customers** table:

```
REVERT;
GO
EXECUTE AS USER='CustomerAdmin' GO
SELECT USER_NAME() GO
SELECT * FROM dbo.Customers
```

You'll get all of the rows defined in the security predicate:

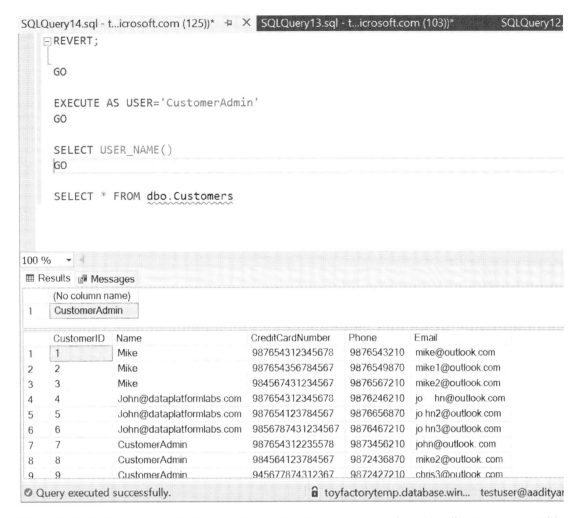

Figure 5.63: Adding a query in the security context to return rows from the dbo.Customers table

10. Execute the following query to switch off the security policy:

```
ALTER SECURITY POLICY CustomerFilter WITH (STATE = OFF);
```

## Activity: Implementing Dynamic Data Masking

With row-level security implemented in the previous activity, Mike has ensured that the customer can only view his own data; however, to take data security to the next level, he wants to mask some of the sensitive data that is shared by the customer. In order to do this, he has to implement dynamic data masking. In this activity, we'll implement dynamic data masking to mask the credit card number, phone number, and email ID of a customer:

1. Execute the following query to create a new user and grant select access to the user on the **dbo.Customers** table:

```
CREATE USER TestUser WITHOUT LOGIN; GO
GRANT SELECT ON dbo.Customers TO TestUser
```

2. Execute the following query to mask the **CreditCardNumber**, **Phone**, and **Email** column using different masking functions:

```
ALTER TABLE dbo.Customers ALTER COLUMN Phone VARCHAR(100) MASKED WITH
(FUNCTION = 'default()') GO
ALTER TABLE dbo.Customers ALTER COLUMN Email VARCHAR(100) MASKED WITH
(FUNCTION = 'email()')
GO
ALTER TABLE dbo.Customers ALTER COLUMN CreditCardNumber VARCHAR(100)
MASKED WITH (FUNCTION = 'partial(0,"XXX-XX-",4)')
```

The preceding query masks the phone number using the default masking function, the email with the email masking function, and the **CreditCardNumber** with the partial masking function, which masks all characters excluding the last four.

3. Execute the following query in the context of **TestUser** to return all of the rows from the **dbo.Customers** table:

```
EXECUTE AS USER='TestUser' GO
SELECT * FROM dbo.Customers;
```

Notice that the phone number, email, and credit card number columns are masked:

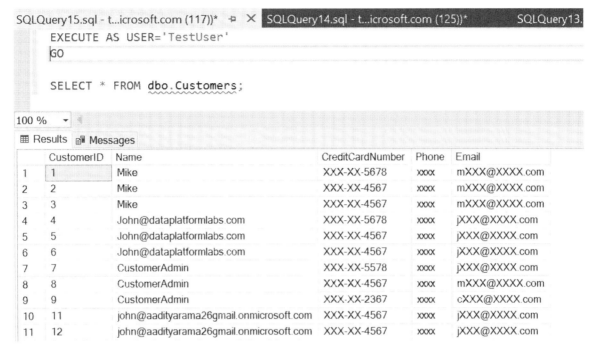

Figure 5.64: Execute a query in TestUser to return rows from the dbo.Customers table

4.  Execute the following query to list the masked columns and the functions for the **Customer** table:

```
REVERT;
GO
SELECT mc.name, t.name as table_name,mc.masking_function FROM sys.masked_
columns AS mc
JOIN sys.tables AS t
ON mc.[object_id] = t.[object_id]
WHERE is_masked = 1 and t.name='Customers'
```

The **sys.masked_columns** table stores the masked columns metadata. The **is_masked** column tells you whether a column is masked or not.

You should get the following output:

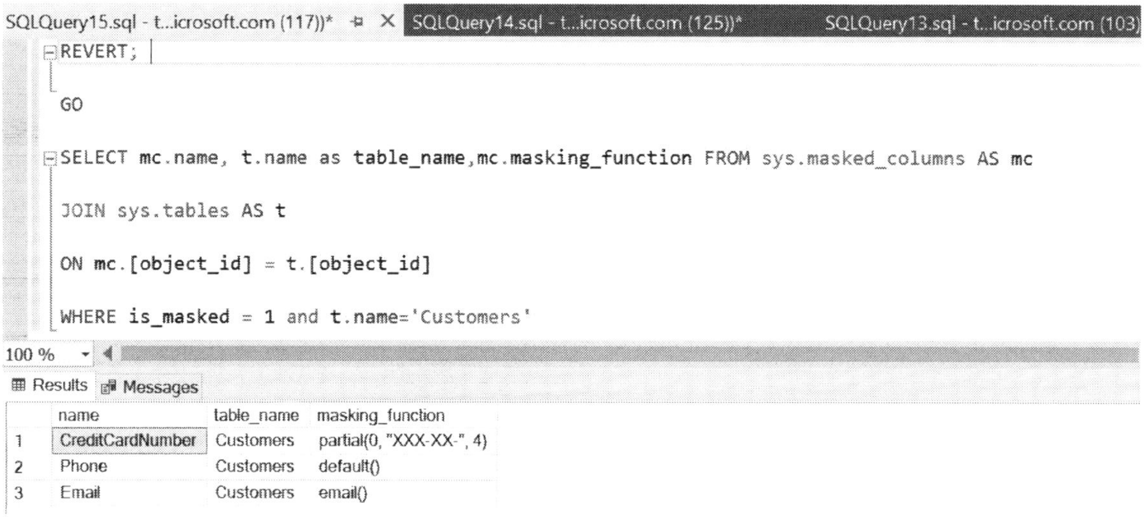

Figure 5.65: List of masked columns and functions for the Customer table

5. Execute the following query to allow the **TestUser** to see the masked data:

```
GRANT UNMASK TO TestUser; GO
EXECUTE AS USER='TestUser' GO
SELECT * FROM dbo.Customers; GO
```

The **UNMASK** permission allows the **TestUser** to see the masked data.

You should get the following output:

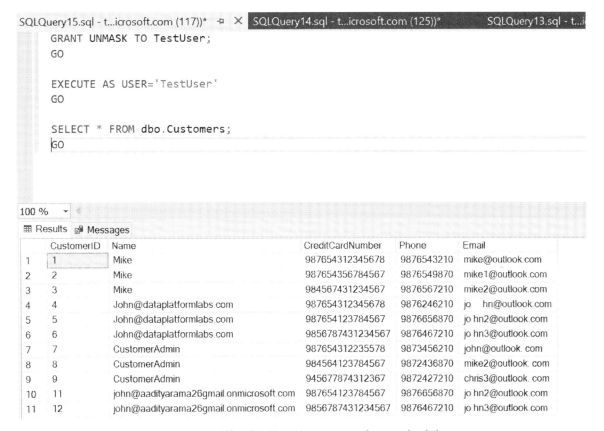

Figure 5.66: Allowing TestUser to see the masked data

6. To mask the data again, run the following query:

```
REVERT;
REVOKE UNMASK TO TestUSER
```

## Activity: Implementing Advanced Data Security to Detect SQL Injection

Earlier in the lesson, we learned that advanced threat protection automatically detects and alerts you about security issues such as SQL injection, brute force attacks, and anomalous access.

In this activity, we'll simulate SQL injection and a brute force attack and will study the email alerts raised by advanced threat detection.

To configure email alerts for advanced threat protection, open the Azure portal and then open the Azure SQL server you want to configure alerts for.

Search for and open the **Advanced Data Security** page. Provide the email address to get the notifications, under the **ADVANCED THREAT PROTECTION SETTINGS** heading, as shown here:

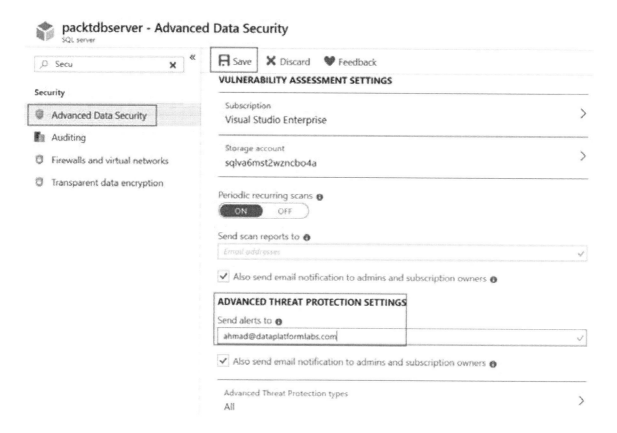

Figure 5.67: Advanced Data Security page

Click **Save** to save the settings.

**Simulating SQL Injection**

To simulate an SQL injection attack, perform the following steps:

1. Connect to the **toystore** database in SSMS and execute the following query:

```
CREATE TABLE users (userid INT, username VARCHAR(100),usersecret
VARCHAR(100))
GO
INSERT INTO users VALUES(1,'Ahmad','MyPassword'),(2,'John','Doe')
```

2. Navigate to **C:\Code\Lesson5\AdvancedThreatProtection\SQLInjection** and open the
**SQLInjection.exe.config** file:

```xml
<?xml version="1.0" encoding="utf-8" ?>
<configuration>
    <startup>
        <supportedRuntime version="v4.0" sku=".
NETFramework,Version=v4.5.2" />
    </startup>
  <appSettings>
    <add key="server" value="packtdbserver"/>
    <add key="user" value="dbadmin"/>
    <add key="database" value="toystore"/>
    <add key="password" value="Awesome@1234"/>
  </appSettings>
</configuration>
```

Under **appSettings**, replace the values for **server** (Azure SQL server), **user** (SQL
user), **database** (Azure SQL database), and **password** (Azure SQL user password)
with yours and save the file.

3. Double-click **SQLInjection.exe** in the **C:\Code\Lesson5\AdvancedThreatProtection\
SQLInjection** folder to run it:

Figure 5.68: Run SQLInjection.exe

**SQLInjection.exe** is a simple windows form application. It accepts a username and password as input and if the input matches the username and password in the database, the result is shown in the grid.

Enter the details as shown in the preceding screenshot and then click the **Search** button. The result is shown in the grid.

Let's now try hacking the database using SQL injection.

4. Enter the following in the **User Name** textbox and click the **Search** button:

```
' OR 1=1  union all select 1,name,name from sys.objects --'
```

Figure 5.69: Searching for the username in textbox

Notice that we are able to hack in and get the list of all the objects in the database.

5.  Let's now insert a new user in the **users** table. Enter the following in the **User Name** textbox and click the **Search** button:

    ```
    ' OR 1=1  insert into users values(100,'hacked','hacked') --'
    ```

    The preceding query inserts a new row in the **users** table:

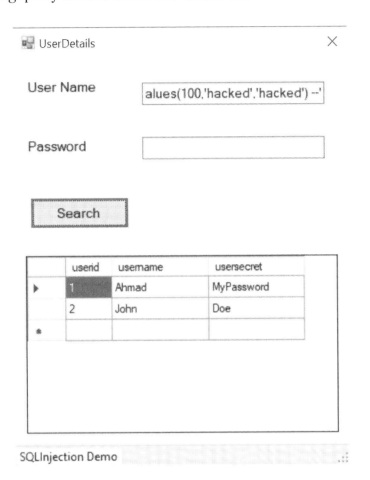

Figure 5.70: Adding a new row in the users table

Though we get the list of users, however, the insert query worked. Let's search for the **hacked** user that we inserted:

Figure 5.71: Searching for the inserted user

The **hacked** user was successfully inserted into the **users** table.

## Brute force attack

To simulate a brute force attack, follow these steps:

1. Navigate to **C:\Code\Lesson5\AdvancedThreatProtection\BruteForceAttack** and open **BruteForceAttack.exe.config** in a notepad:

```
<?xml version="1.0" encoding="utf-8" ?>
<configuration>
    <startup>
        <supportedRuntime version="v4.0" sku=".
NETFramework,Version=v4.5.2" />
```

```
        </startup>
    <appSettings>
        <add key="Server" value="packtdbserver"/>
        <add key="database" value="toystore"/>

    </appSettings>
  </configuration>
```

Under **appSettings**, change **Server** to the name of your Azure SQL server and change **database** to your Azure SQL database's name.

**Save** the file.

2.  In the **C:\Code\Lesson5\AdvancedThreatProtection\BruteForceAttack** folder, double-click **BruteForceAttack.exe** to start the attack. **BruteForceAttack.exe** is a windows console application. It attempts to connect to the Azure SQL server with a random username and password.

    You should get the following output:

Figure 5.72: Executing BruteForceAttack.exe

Notice the username and password in each call. The connection attempt is made using a different username and password.

Double-click four or five times to run at least five instances of the **BruteForceAttack** application.

3.  Let's now check the Azure portal for alerts, if any, for the SQL injection and brute force attack simulations.

4. Log in to the **Azure portal** and open the **toystore** SQL database page. Search for and open the **Advanced Data Security** page:

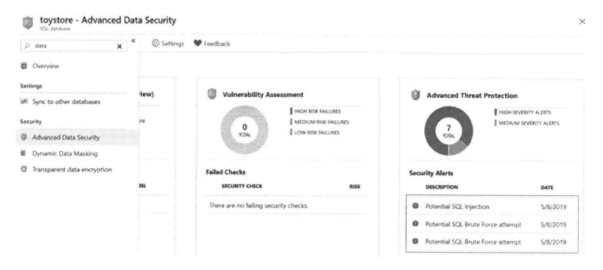

Figure 5.73: Advanced Data Security page

5. Notice that advanced threat protection lists the security alerts for the SQL injection and brute force attempt. Click on the **Potential SQL Injection** alert:

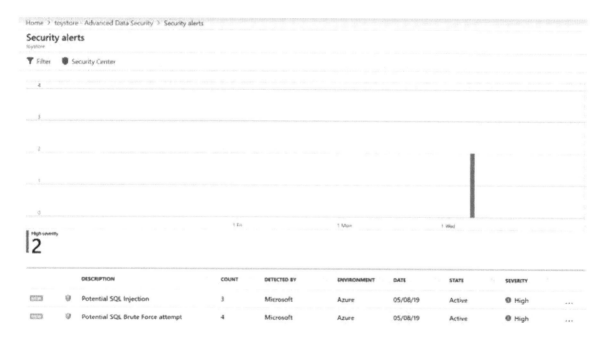

Figure 5.74: Potential SQL Injection alert

There are three SQL injection and four brute force attempt alerts from advanced threat protection.

6. Click on **Potential SQL Injection** to get its details:

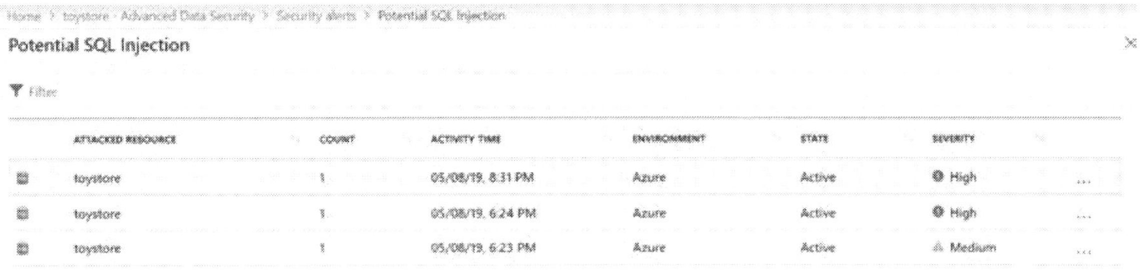

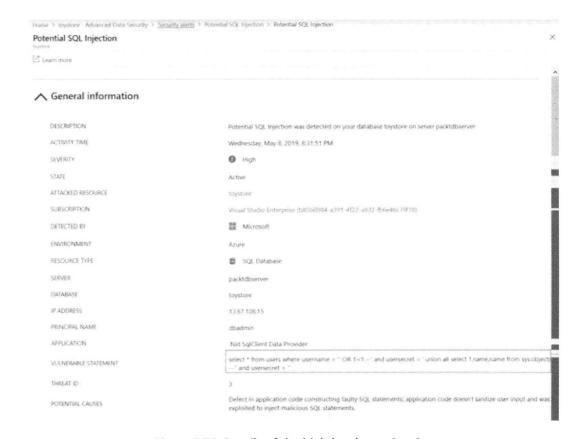

Figure 5.75: Potential SQL Injection details

The alert page gives details of the attached resource, count, time, environment, and severity.

7. Click on one of the **High** severity alerts to get its details:

Figure 5.76: Details of the high-level security alert

The alert details are quite comprehensive and even display the query used as part of the SQL injection attack.

As a database administrator, you can pass on the details to the development team and have them fix the query.

8. Close the SQL injection alert page. To find details on the brute force attempt alert, click on the **Potential SQL Brute Force attempt** alert on the **toystore – Advanced Data Security** > **Security alerts** page.

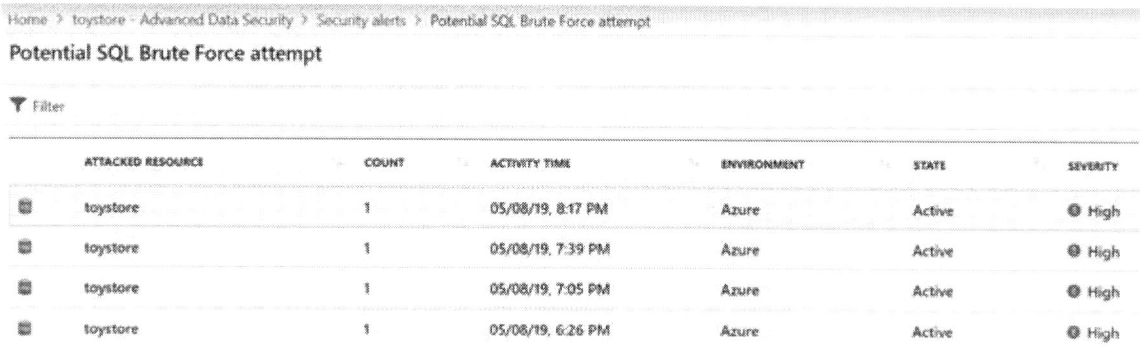

Home > toystore - Advanced Data Security > Security alerts > Potential SQL Brute Force attempt

**Potential SQL Brute Force attempt**

▼ Filter

| | ATTACKED RESOURCE | COUNT | ACTIVITY TIME | ENVIRONMENT | STATE | SEVERITY |
|---|---|---|---|---|---|---|
| | toystore | 1 | 05/08/19, 8:17 PM | Azure | Active | ⬤ High |
| | toystore | 1 | 05/08/19, 7:39 PM | Azure | Active | ⬤ High |
| | toystore | 1 | 05/08/19, 7:05 PM | Azure | Active | ⬤ High |
| | toystore | 1 | 05/08/19, 6:26 PM | Azure | Active | ⬤ High |

Figure 5.77: Potential SQL Brute Force attempt

There are four high-severity brute force attempt alerts. Click on any one of them to get its details:

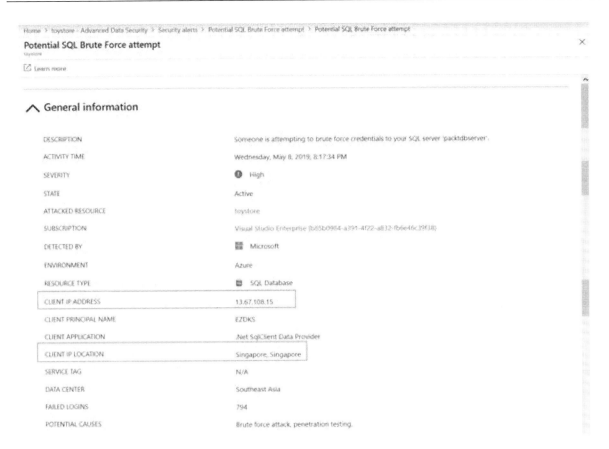

**Figure 5.78: Details of brute force alerts**

Notice that the details page has the client IP address used for the brute force attempt. To resolve the issue, make sure the mentioned IP address is blocked at the server firewall level.

## Summary

Security is one of the deciding factors for an organization when opting to put their data in the cloud. Microsoft provides the best security by not only securing Azure SQL Database, but by also securing data centers.

To connect to an Azure SQL database, the machine's IP address or the client IP address should exist in the firewall settings. If not, the connection request will be denied. Azure SQL Database allows SQL and Windows authentication as well. An organization can sync their domain with Azure, thereby allowing users to connect from domain accounts instead of SQL logins. Organizations can also create Active Directory groups and give access to a group instead of giving access to individual user domain accounts. In addition to this, you can use row-level security and dynamic data masking to further secure data by allowing users to only see the data they need in order to do their work. Azure SQL Database also provides proactive monitoring to detect threats such as SQL injection as and when they happen.

In the next lesson, we will learn about scaling out an Azure SQL database based on the needs of the application.

# Scaling out an Azure SQL Database

**Learning Objectives**

By the end of this lesson, you will be able to:

- Perform vertical and horizontal scaling

- Run cross-database elastic queries

- Create and maintain Azure SQL Database shards

This lesson covers how to vertically and horizontally scale your system to optimize the performance of your application.

## Introduction

You can easily scale up or scale down an Azure SQL database, either automatically or manually. There are two types of scaling: vertical and horizontal.

Vertical scaling refers to switching to a higher or lower service tier, or vertically partitioning the data, which is to store different schemas on different databases.

Horizontal scaling refers to dividing data from a single table into different individual databases.

This lesson will teach you how to autoscale Azure SQL databases and shard a database. The lesson also talks about how to run cross-database queries.

## Vertical Scaling

Vertical scaling can be of two types: scale-up or scale-down service tiers, or vertical partitions.

### Scale-up or Scale-down Service Tiers

Scaling up a service tier refers to switching to a higher service tier; for example, switching from Basic to Standard S0 or switching from Standard S0 to Standard S1.

Scaling down a service tier refers to switching to a lower service tier; for example, switching from Standard S1 to Standard S0, or switching from Standard S0 to Basic.

Scaling up a service tier allows you to maintain or improve database performance during peak business hours, and scaling down a service tier allows you to save costs during off-peak business hours.

Service tiers can be changed on the fly with zero downtime. When a service tier change request is sent to Azure SQL Database, it first creates a copy of the database in the requested service tier and switches to the database in the new service tier once the copy is ready.

You are charged for the new service tier once the service tier is changed, and not from the time the service tier change request is received.

The Azure SQL Database service tier can be changed from the Azure portal, using QL script, Azure PowerShell, or by putting the database in an elastic pool. Except for the Azure portal, these methods allow you to automatically change the service tier.

> **Note**
>
> An elastic pool is a group or pool of more than one Azure SQL database with varying usage. This is covered in detail in *Lesson 7, Azure SQL Database Elastic Pools*.

One of the most common vertical scaling use cases is to automatically scale up or scale down a service tier based on the DTU (Database Throughput Unit) usage:

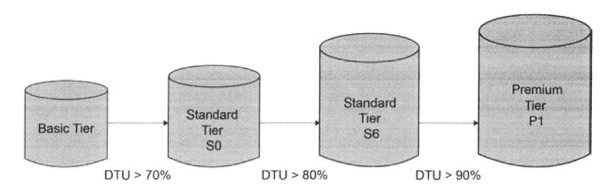

Figure 6.1: DTU of service tiers

For example, you can put a script in place that will automatically scale to a higher database service tier if DTU usage increases past a specified threshold, such as switching to Standard S0 if DTU usage is greater than 70%, and scale to a lower service tier if the DTU usage percentage is lower than the specified threshold, such as switching to the Basic service tier if DTU usage is less than 30%.

Another use case is to schedule scaling up and scaling down based on peak and off-peak business hours. For example, if a business expects higher traffic between 1:00 P.M. and 3:00 P.M., it could scale up to the Premium service tier during that time and scale down to the Standard service tier for the rest of the day.

## Using T-SQL to Change the Service Tier

Let's consider a scenario where Mike faces higher traffic than usual between 1:00 P.M. and 3:00 P.M. on the **toystore** database; he can use T-SQL to change the service tier as follows:

> **Note**
>
> Refer to **C:\Code\Lesson6\ChangeDBServiceTier-TSQL.sql** for the queries provided in the section.

1. Open SQL Server Management Studio on your local machine and connect to the **toystore** Azure SQL database.

> **Note**
>
> You can refer to *Lesson 1, Microsoft Azure SQL Database Primer*, for detailed steps.

2. Copy and paste the following query to get the current service tier of the **toystore** database:

```
-- Get the current database service tier
-- Run this in the toystore or your database context (and not master
database context)

SELECT * FROM sys.database_service_objectives
```

You should get the following output from this query:

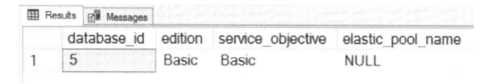

| | database_id | edition | service_objective | elastic_pool_name |
|---|---|---|---|---|
| 1 | 5 | Basic | Basic | NULL |

Figure 6.2: Current service tier of the toystore database

The **sys.database_service_objectives** DMV returns the current Azure SQL Database edition and the service objective or the performance level.

3.  Copy and paste the following query into a new query window. Set the database context to master:

```
SELECT *
    FROM sys.dm_operation_status WHERE resource_type_desc='database' AND
major_resource_id='toystore'
```

This query returns the details of any operation carried out on an Azure SQL database. You will use this query to monitor the progress of the **ALTER DATABASE** operation.

4.  Copy and paste the following code snippet in a new query window in SSMS:

```
-- Run Query 1,2 & 3 at once in a single T-SQL Batch.
-- Query 1: Change the databaseEdition or Service tier to Standard S0

ALTER DATABASE ToyStore MODIFY (Edition='Standard', Service_
objective='S0')
GO
-- Query 2: Get the current service objective

SELECT * FROM sys.database_service_objectives
GO


-- Query 3: Wait for the changes to be applied

Waitfor Delay '00:01:00'
GO


-- Don't run it along with Query 1, 2 & 3
-- Query 4: Get the current service objective
SELECT * FROM sys.database_service_objectives
```

The preceding T-SQL snippet consists of four queries:

**Query 1**: This runs an **ALTER DATABASE** command to change the SQL Database service tier to Standard and the service objective to S0.

**Query 2**: This gets the database edition and service objective for the **toystore** database.

**Query 3**: This adds a delay of 1 minute.

**Query 4**: This is the same as **Query 2**. It gets the current database edition and service objective.

Select **Query 1**, **Query 2**, and **Query 3**, and press F5 to execute them. You should get the following output:

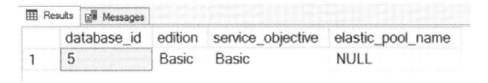

| | database_id | edition | service_objective | elastic_pool_name |
|---|---|---|---|---|
| 1 | 5 | Basic | Basic | NULL |

Figure 6.3: Output of the queries

5. While the queries are executing, quickly switch to the second query window, which has the query from *step* 3, and press F5 to execute the query. You should see the following output:

| | resource_type_desc | major_resource_id | operation | state_desc | percent_complete |
|---|---|---|---|---|---|
| 1 | Database | ToyStore | ALTER DATABASE | IN_PROGRESS | 0 |
| 2 | Database | ToyStore | ALTER DATABASE | COMPLETED | 100 |
| 3 | Database | ToyStore | ALTER DATABASE | COMPLETED | 100 |

Figure 6.4: Output of the select query

Notice that the **ALTER DATABASE** operation for the **toystore** database is in progress. Wait for the **ALTER DATABASE** query in the first query window to complete.

Once it is complete, rerun the query in the second query window. Notice that the value in the **state_desc** column changed to **COMPLETED** from **IN_ PROGRESS**.

Switch to the first query window (if you aren't already in it), select **Query 4**, and press F5 to execute it. Notice that the service tier has been changed to Standard S0.

The connection in the first query window will be disconnected when the switch from the Basic to the Standard service tier is made. You'll receive an error message, as shown here:

```
Msg 0, Level 11, State 0, Line 11
A severe error occurred on the current command. The results, if any,
should be discarded:
Msg 0, Level 20, State 0, Line 11
```

A severe error occurred on the current command. The results, if any, should be discarded:

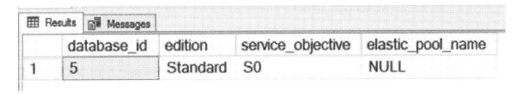

Figure 6.5: Standard S0 service tier

6. Press *Ctrl* + N to open a new query window in SSMS. Change the query context to the master database. Copy and paste the following query in the query window:

```
--Query 5: Automate the process
-- Execute in Master database
PRINT 'database update in progress...'
DECLARE
@databaseName sysname='ToyStore',
@databaseEdition varchar(100)='Basic',
@PerformanceTier varchar(10)='Basic'

Declare @dsql Varchar(MAX) =
    'ALTER DATABASE [' + @databaseName + '] MODIFY (Edition=''' + @
databaseEdition + ''', Service_objective=''' + @PerformanceTier + ''')';
SET @dsql = @dsql + '
WHILE(
exists (SELECT TOP 1 * FROM sys.dm_operation_status WHERE resource_type_
desc=''database'' AND major_resource_id=''' +
@databaseName + ''' AND STATE=1 ORDER BY start_time DESC))
    BEGIN
    WAITFOR DELAY ''00:00:05'' END'
EXEC(@dsql)
```

The query automates the process of switching between service tiers. It takes three parameters:

**databaseName**: The name of the database whose service tier is to be changed

**databaseEdition**: The new service tier name: Basic, Standard, Premium, or PremiumRS

**PerformanceTier**: The service objective, such as S0, S1, or S2

The **ALTER DATABASE** command is used to change the service tier as specified by the parameters.

The query then checks whether or not the service tier has been changed using the **sys.dm_operation_stats** DMV. If the database operation is in progress, it waits for 5 seconds and then checks the progress again.

7. Press F5 to execute the query. Once the query completes, the database service will be changed to Basic.

## Vertical Partitioning

In vertical partitioning, the data is partitioned in such a way that different sets of tables reside in different individual databases:

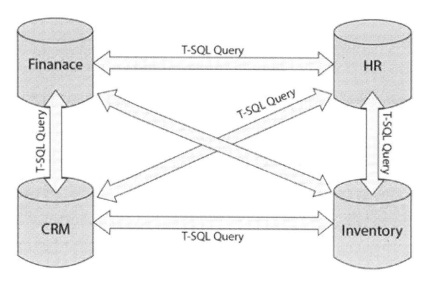

Figure 6.6: Vertical partitioning

For example, if there are four different schemas in a database, say Finance, HR, CRM, and Inventory, then each one of these is stored in one independent database, as shown in the previous diagram.

Vertical partitioning requires cross-database queries in order to generate reports, which require data from different tables in different databases.

Azure SQL Database doesn't currently support three- or four-part object names, such as `databaseName.SchemaName.TableName` (excluding `tempdb`). Therefore, cross-database queries are made using elastic queries.

## Horizontal Scaling

Horizontal scaling, or sharding, refers to partitioning the data from one single big table in a database across multiple independent databases based on a sharding or partitioning key. For example, a customer table is partitioned across multiple independent databases on `CustomerID`. Each independent database stores data for one or more customers.

Horizontal scaling can be helpful in the following situations:

- The data is too big to fit into one single database.

- The data is to be distributed to different locations for improved performance or for compliance. For example, European customers will get improved performance if their data is in a European data center rather than an Asian data center.

- Isolating tenants or customers to a database of their own for better management and performance. If all of the customer data is in a single database and there is blocking in the database because of a transaction made for a customer, say X, then all of the other customer queries will have to wait for the blocking to get resolved, causing a bad performance experience for the rest of the customers.

- A single database requires a Premium service tier to manage one big table. Dividing customer data across multiple independent Standard service tier databases will reduce the cost.

- All (or most) of the queries are made to the database filter on the sharding key.

Sharding is supported natively in Azure SQL Database, so we don't have to implement the sharding mechanism from scratch. However, we do need to create and manage shards. This can be done easily using Elastic Database Tools.

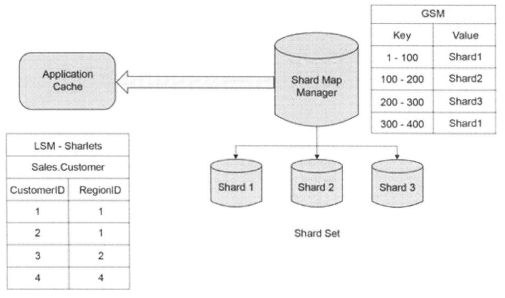

Figure 6.7: Horizontal partitioning

This diagram represents a generic sharded environment. The customer table is horizontally partitioned across three shards: Shard 1, Shard 2, and Shard 3. Let's examine each of these components in detail:

- **Shard**: A shard is an individual database that stores a subset of rows of a sharded table. Shard 1, Shard 2, and Shard 3 are the shards, each storing different rows of the customer table as defined by the mappings.

- **Shard set**: A group of shards that contains data for one single partitioned table is called a shard set. Shard 1, Shard 2, and Shard 3 together are called a shard set.

- **Sharding key**: A sharding key is the column name based on which the data is partitioned between the shards. In our example, `CustomerID` is the sharding key. Each shard stores data for a different customer ID. You can also define a composite sharding key.

- **Shard map manager**: A special database that stores global mapping information about all available shards in a shard set. The application uses the mapping information to connect to the correct shard based on the sharding key.

- **Shard maps**: Shard maps define the data distribution between different shards based on the sharding key. There are two types of shard map:

**List shard map**: This is a key-value pair with a one-to-one mapping between the sharding key and the shard. The key is the sharding key and the value is the shard (SQL database). This list shard map defines that Shard 1 will store the data for CustomerID 1 and CustomerID 4, Shard 2 will store the data for CustomerID 2, and Shard 3 will store the data for CustomerID 3:

| Key (Sharding Key - CustomerID) | Value (Shard/database) |
|:---:|:---:|
| 1 | Shard 1 |
| 2 | Shard 2 |
| 3 | Shard 3 |
| 4 | Shard 1 |

Figure 6.8: Key-value pairs between key and shard

**Range shard map**: This is a key-value pair where the key (a sharding key) is a range of values defined as (low value - high value).

| Key range (sharding key – CustomerID) | Value (shard/database) |
|:---:|:---:|
| 1 - 100 | Shard 1 |
| 100 - 200 | Shard 2 |
| 200 - 300 | Shard 3 |
| 300 - 400 | Shard 1 |

Figure 6.9: Range shard map

This range shard map defines that Shard 1 will store the data for CustomerIDs 1-99 and 300-399. Shard 2 will store the data for CustomerIDs 100-199, and Shard 3 will store the data for CustomerIDs 200-299.

- **Global Shard Maps (GSMs)**: GSMs are stored in a shard map manager database and record all the shard maps globally. This information is stored and managed by special tables and stored procedures created automatically under the _ShardManagement schema in the shard map manager database.

- **Local Shard Maps (LSMs)**: Also referred to as **shardlets**, these are the shard maps that track the local shard data within individual shards. The local shard maps or the shardlets are stored in individual shards and not in the shard map manager database. This information is stored and managed by special tables and stored procedures created automatically under the **_ShardManagement** schema.

- **Reference tables**: These are tables that aren't sharded and are available in all shards. These can also be stored in another database, say, a reference database, instead of storing the same data in individual shards; for example, a table with a list of countries or cities that contains master data common to all shards.

- **Application Cache**: Applications accessing the shard map manager cache the mappings in a local in-memory application cache. Applications use the cached mappings to route requests to the correct shards, instead of accessing the shard map manager for every request.

## Shard Map Manager

As discussed earlier, a shard map manager is a special database that maintains the global mapping information of a shard set. The mappings are maintained in tables that are automatically created under the **_ShardManagement** schema:

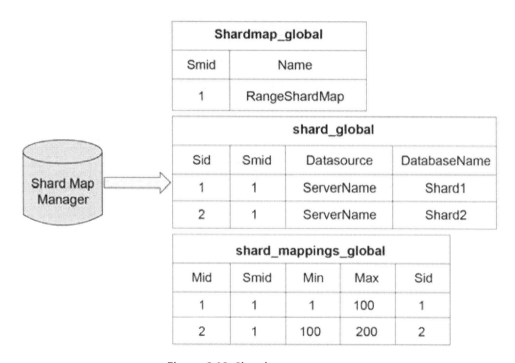

Figure 6.10: Shard map manager

The global shard maps are maintained in three tables, as shown in the preceding diagram:

- **shardmaps_global**: This table stores the type of shard map, which could be ListShardMap or RangeShardMap. In our example, we have RangeShardMap.

- **shards_global**: This table maps the shards (SQL databases) to the shard maps defined in the Shardmaps_global table. In our example, RangeShardMap has two shards, Shard 1 and Shard 2. The table also stores the server name the shard belongs to. This information is used when connecting to the shards.

- **shard_mappings_global**: This is the global shared map that stores the sharding key to shard mapping. In our example, customer IDs 1-99 are mapped to Shard 1 and 100-199 are mapped to Shard 2.

The information in the shard map manager is used by the client application to redirect requests to the correct SQL database based on the sharding key.

### Data-Dependent Routing

Data-dependent routing refers to routing a query to the correct database (shard) based on the sharding key specified in the query. This is the fundamental way of querying a sharded environment. The application doesn't maintain connection strings to the different shards. The application doesn't even implement the logic of selecting the shards based on the sharding key. This is done natively by using the functions provided in the Elastic Database client library.

The application defines a single connection using the **OpenConnectionForKey** method defined in the Elastic Database client library. The syntax for **OpenConnectionForKey** is given in the following snippet:

```
public SqlConnection OpenConnectionForKey<TKey>(

TKey key,

string connectionString,

ConnectionOptions options

)
```

It accepts three parameters, which are as follows:

- **TKey**: This is the sharding key used to determine which shard or SQL database in a shard set the query is to be made on.

- **connectionString**: The connection string only contains the credentials. The database and the server name are taken from the shard map manager system tables, based on the sharding key.

- **ConnectionOptions**: A connection option can be either **none** or **validate**. When it's set to **validate**, it queries the local shard map or the shardlet to validate that the shard key exists in the databases specified in the cached maps (in the application). This is important in an environment where shard maps change frequently. If the validation fails, then the shard map manager queries the global shard maps for the correct values and updates the application cache.

If the parameters specified are correct, **OpenConnectionForKey** returns a database connection that can be used to query the correct shard.

**Multi-Tenant Data Models**

Multi-tenant data models refer to how the tenants are placed in a sharded environment. There are two distinct models for placing tenants: database-per-tenant (single-tenant model) and a shared database – sharded (multi-tenant model):

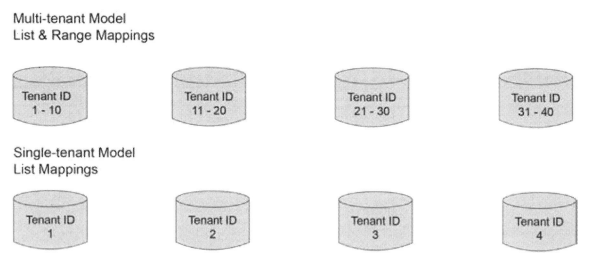

Figure 6.11: Multi-tenant and single-tenant data models

## Single-Tenant (Database-Per-Tenant)

As the name suggests, each tenant gets its own database. The tenant-specific data is limited to the tenant's database and isolated from other tenants and their data.

## Shared Database – Sharded

As the name suggests, a single shard or database is shared among multiple tenants. The tenants can either be mapped to shards or databases by using either range or list mappings, as discussed earlier.

Choosing between the two models depends on the following factors:

- **Isolation**: The single-tenant, or database-per tenant, model offers a higher degree of isolation than the shared database – sharded model.

- **Maintenance**: The single-tenant model will have as many databases as the tenants, which could be customers or employees. For example, 100 customers would mean 100 databases in the single-tenancy model, but in the shared database – sharded model, you can have 5 databases with 20 tenants each. Maintaining 5 databases would be easier than maintaining 100 databases.

- **Cost**: The cost depends on the amount of resource sharing between tenants. The more resource sharing (resource here refers to a shard, an SQL database), the lower the cost. The single-tenant model is good if all tenants have predictable workloads. This allows you to select an appropriate service tier for each tenant or shard. However, if the workload isn't predictable, which is often the case, databases can be either oversized or undersized. On the other hand, the shared database – sharded model with a higher degree of resource sharing offers a more cost-effective solution.

- **DevOps**: DevOps refers to the deployment of new changes to databases to resolve issues or when new features are added to an application. With the single-tenant model, it costs more to deploy and maintain an application, as each change has to be applied to all of the single-tenant databases. For example, if an application adds a new feature that allows customers to generate sales reports, and there are 100 customers, then this change has to be deployed on 100 databases. However, it'll take less time and cost to roll out the same feature in the shared databases – sharded model because of the smaller number of databases.

- **Business model**: An application's business model is an important factor when choosing between the two multi-tenant models. If application per- tenant revenue is small, then the shared databases – sharded model makes sense. A shared database model will offer less isolation, but it'll have lower deployment and resource costs. On the other hand, if per-tenant revenue is high, then it'll make sense to use the single-tenant model.

## Activity: Creating Alerts

In this section, you'll learn how to create an Azure SQL Database alert. Consider the following scenario, involving ToyStore Ltd. Mike has an Azure SQL database on the Basic service tier and has been asked to configure autoscaling to change the service tier to Standard S0 when the DTU is greater than 70%. For this purpose, he needs to first create an Azure SQL Database alert, which is triggered when the DTU is greater than 70%. Let's see how this can be done.

### Create an Azure Automation Account and Configure a Runbook

Azure Automation is an Azure service that allows you to automate Azure management tasks through runbooks.

A runbook is a job that accepts PowerShell or Python code and executes it as and when scheduled, or when invoked from an external program through a webhook:

1.  Open the Azure portal, https://portal.azure.com, and log in with your Azure credentials.

2.  In the left-hand navigation menu, select **All** services. In the **More services** pane's search box, type `Automation`. Select the **Automation Accounts** option that appears as a search result:

Figure 6.12: Searching for Automation Accounts

3.  In the **Automation Accounts** pane, click **Create Automation Accounts**:

No Automation Accounts to display

Try changing your filters if you don't see what you're looking for.

Create Automation Accounts

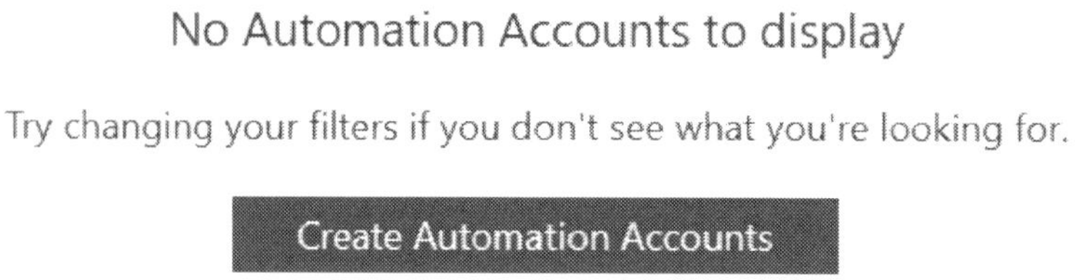

Figure 6.13: Automation Accounts pane

4.  In the **Add Automation Account** pane, provide the following values:

    Set the name of the automation account as **toystorejobs**.

    Select your Azure subscription type.

    Set **Resource group** as **toystore**.

    Set **Location** as **East US 2**.

    Set **Create Azure Run As account** to **Yes** (the default value).

    Click **Create** to provision the automation account:

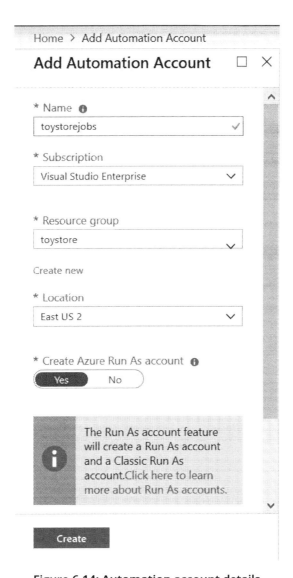

Figure 6.14: Automation account details

5.  Navigate to the **Overview** pane of the newly created `toystorejobs` Automation
    Account. Locate and select **Runbooks** in the **Process Automation** section:

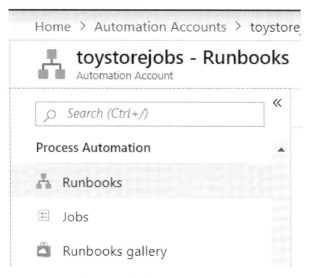

Figure 6.15: Runbooks pane

6.  In the **Runbooks** pane, select **Import a runbook** from the top menu:

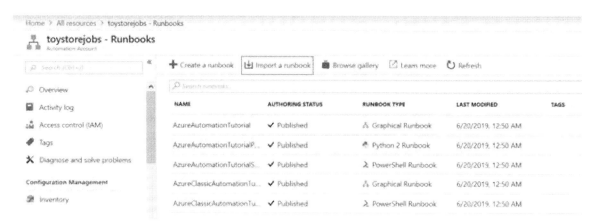

Figure 6.16: The Runbooks pane displaying the available runbooks
and different options to manage runbooks

7. In the **Import a runbook** pane, under **Runbook file**, navigate to `C:\Code\Lesson6\VerticalScaling` and select the `Set-AzureSqldatabaseEdition.ps1` file. Provide a **Description** (this is optional). Click **Create** to import the PowerShell runbook:

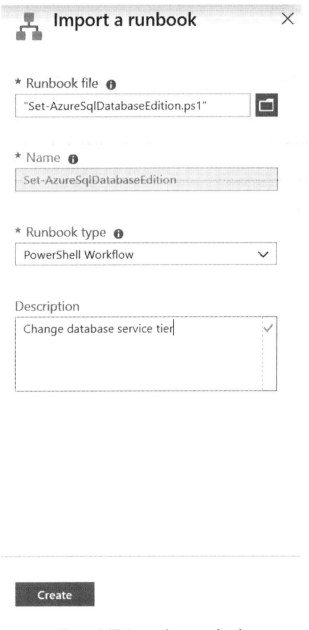

Figure 6.17: Importing a runbook

Once the runbook is imported, the **Edit PowerShell Workflow Runbook** pane will be opened for the `Set-AzureSqlDatabaseEdition` runbook:

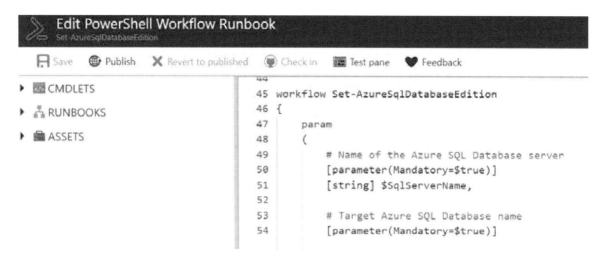

Figure 6.18: The Edit PowerShell Workflow Runbook page

This pane has the option to further modify the workflow if required. The PowerShell script is wrapped in a workflow tag specifying that it's a PowerShell Runbook workflow. The left-hand side of the window has three options:

**CMDLETS** has all the PowerShell commands you can use to write a PowerShell runbook workflow.

**RUNBOOKS** lists all existing PowerShell runbooks.

**ASSETS** are the variables, connections, credentials, and certificates that are required by a runbook to run.

The PowerShell script is self-explanatory. It takes five parameters:

**SqlServerName**: This is the logical Azure SQL server that hosts the Azure SQL database.

**databaseName**: This is the Azure SQL database name whose service tier is to be modified.

**Edition**: This is the desired Azure SQL database edition. The Azure SQL database will be on this edition after script execution.

**PerfLevel**: This is the desired service objective (S0, S1, and so on).

**Credential**: This is the name of the runbook credential asset that contains the username and password to connect to the Azure SQL database.

The PowerShell script connects to the given Azure SQL database and uses the `Set-AzureSqldatabase` command to change the database edition.

Once you are familiar with the script, select **Publish** in the top menu to publish the runbook.

8.  The next step is to create the credential asset to be used by the script to connect to the Azure SQL database. Close the `Set-AzureSqldatabaseEdition` runbook pane. Navigate to the **toystorejobs - Runbooks** pane and find and select **Credentials** in the **Shared Resources** section:

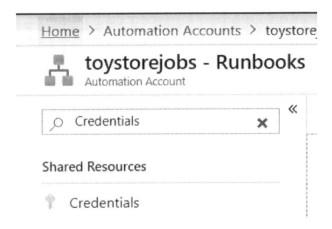

Figure 6.19: Shared Resources section in the Runbooks pane

Select **Add a credential** from the top menu:

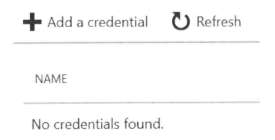

Figure 6.20: Adding a credential

9. In the **New Credential** pane, provide the following:

The credential name in the **Name** section

A description in the **Description** section – this is optional

Your Azure SQL Server username

Your Azure SQL Server password

Click **Create** to create the credential:

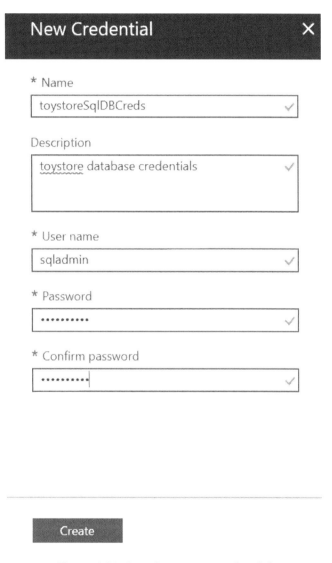

Figure 6.21: Creating a new credential

Credentials are shared assets and can be used in multiple runbooks.

10. The next step is to create the webhook for this runbook. On the **toystorejobs – Runbooks** page, select the **Set-AzureSqldatabaseEdition** runbook:

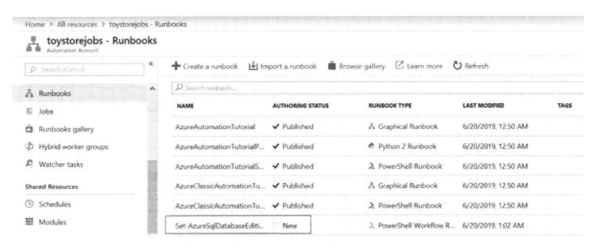

Figure 6.22: toystorejobs - Runbooks page

Click on the **Set-AzureSqlDatabaseEdition** runbook to open it.

11. On the **Set-AzureSqlDatabaseEdition** runbook page, click **Add webhook**. This will open the **Add webhook** page:

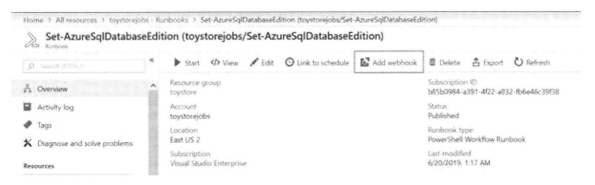

Figure 6.23: Adding a webhook

12. In the **Add Webhook** pane, select **Create new webhook**:

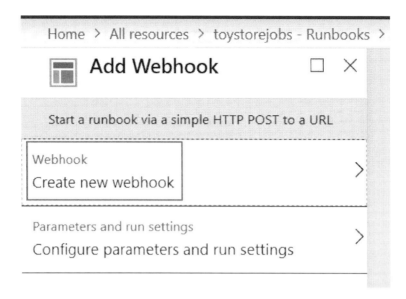

Figure 6.24: Creating a new webhook

In the **Create a new webhook** pane, enter the webhook name. The **Enabled** toggle is set to **Yes** by default – leave it as it is. The **Expires** data is set to one year – leave it as it is. Copy the webhook URL by clicking on the copy icon next to the **URL** textbox. It's important to copy and paste the URL before you click **OK** as the URL is inaccessible once the webhook has been created. Click **OK** to create the webhook:

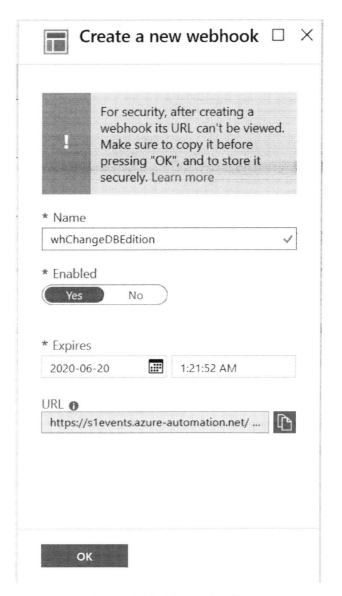

Figure 6.25: Adding details

The webhook will be created. The next step is to provide the PowerShell runbook parameters to the webhook. These parameters will be used to run the `Set-AzureSqldatabaseEdition` PowerShell runbook.

> **Note**
>
> The parameters mentioned here are the ones defined in the PowerShell script discussed in *Step 7*.

13. In the **Add Webhook** pane, select **Configure parameters and run settings**. In the **Parameters** pane, provide the **SQLSERVERNAME**, **DATABASENAME**, **EDITION**, **PERFLEVEL**, and **CREDENTIAL**. The credential used here is the one created in *Step 8*:

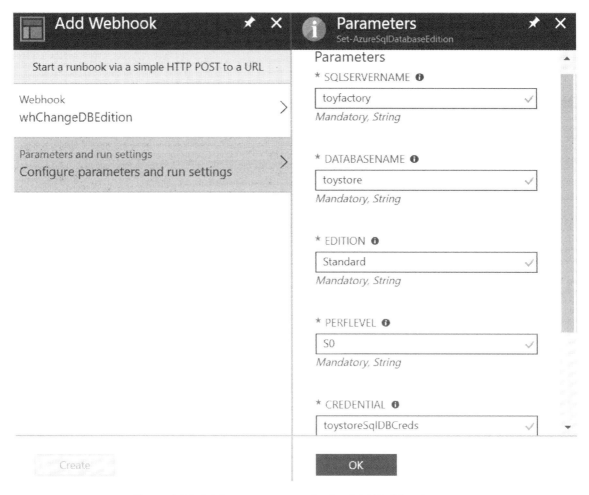

Figure 6.26: Adding parameters in the Add Webhook pane

14. Click **OK** to continue. In the **Add Webhook** pane, select **Create** to create the webhook and set the parameter values:

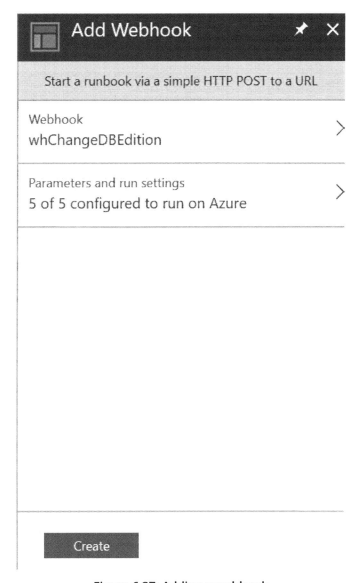

Figure 6.27: Adding a webhook

Now you have created and configured a PowerShell runbook, which runs a PowerShell command when triggered by a webhook.

The next step is to create an Azure SQL Database alert that is triggered when the DTU percentage is greater than 70%. The alert, when triggered, will call the webhook we just created.

15. On the Azure portal, navigate to the **toystore** Azure SQL database. In the **Overview** pane, find and click on **Alerts**, then select **New alert rule**:

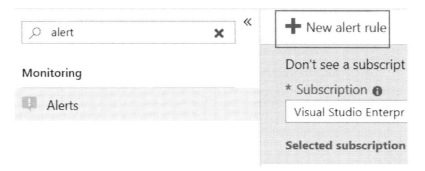

Figure 6.28: Adding a new alert rule

This opens the **Create rule** page. The **Create rule** page has three sections: **RESOURCE**, **CONDITION**, and **ACTIONS**. The **RESOURCE** is the Azure resource on which the rule is to be created. This is automatically set to the **toystore** database. The **CONDITION** is the alert condition that defines the metrics on which the alert is to be configured and the trigger logic. The **ACTIONS** define the actions to be taken when an alert is triggered:

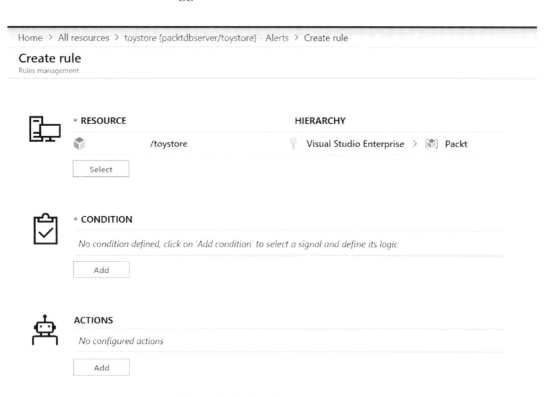

Figure 6.29: The Create rule page

16. Click **Add** under the **CONDITION** heading to add an alert condition. There can be more than one alert condition. On the **Configure signal logic** page, select **DTU percentage**:

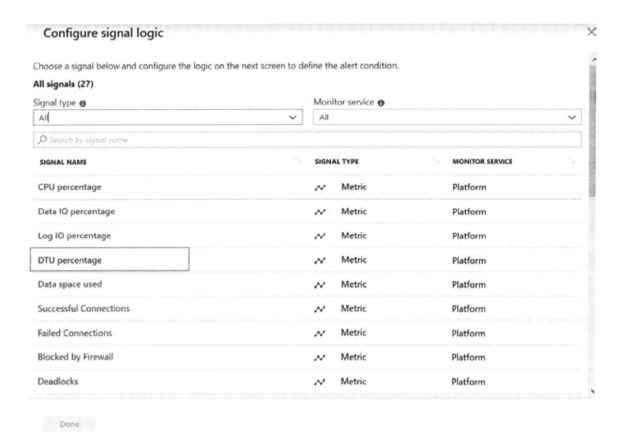

Figure 6.30: The Configure signal logic page

This opens the page to configure the alert's logic. Scroll down to locate the **Alert logic** section.

17. Select the **Static** threshold, set **Operator** to **Greater than**, set **Aggregation type** to **Maximum**, and set the **Threshold value** to **70**. Leave the rest of the values as the defaults:

Figure 6.31: Selecting the Threshold value

Click **Done** to save the configuration. The next step is to define the action.

18. On the **Create rule** page, click the **Add** button under **ACTIONS**:

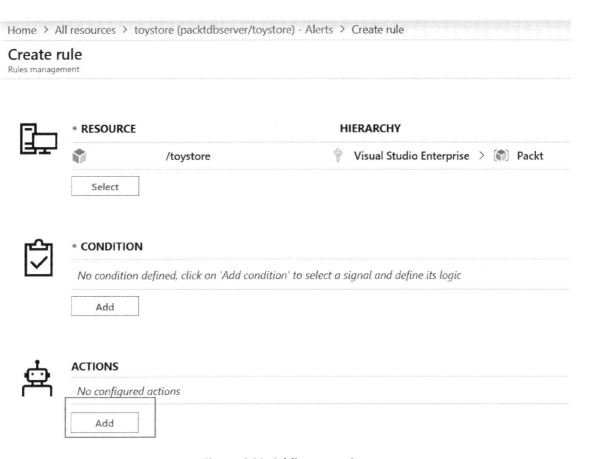

Home > All resources > toystore (packtdbserver/toystore) - Alerts > Create rule

## Create rule
Rules management

**\* RESOURCE**

**HIERARCHY**

/toystore

Visual Studio Enterprise > Packt

Select

**\* CONDITION**

*No condition defined, click on 'Add condition' to select a signal and define its logic*

Add

**ACTIONS**

*No configured actions*

Add

Figure 6.32: Adding an action

19. On the **Configured actions** page, select **Create action rule**:

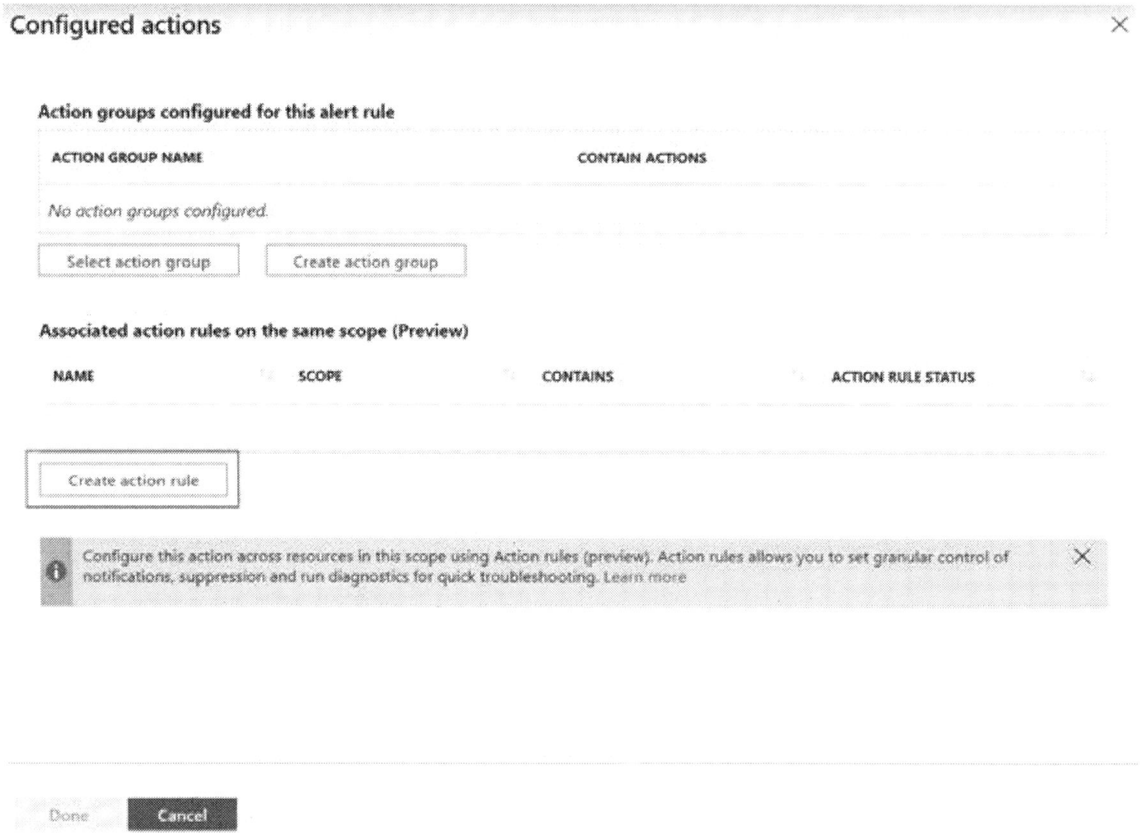

Figure 6.33: Creating an action rule

20. On the **New Action Rule** page, under the **DEFINE ON THIS SCOPE** dropdown, select **Action groups** and then click on **Create action group**:

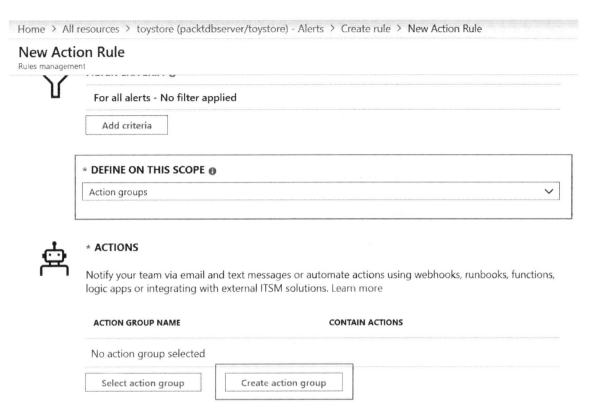

Figure 6.34: Creating an action group

21. On the **Add action group** page, set **Action group name** to **High DTU Action Group**, set **Short name** to **highdtu**, and set **Resource group** to **toystore**:

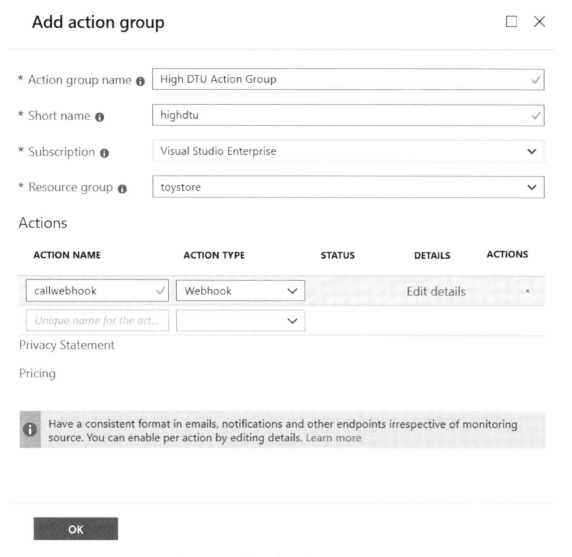

Figure 6.35: The Add action group page

22. In the **Actions** section, specify the **ACTION NAME**. Set **Action Type** to **Webhook**. This opens the **Webhook** page. Provide the webhook URI, which was copied previously:

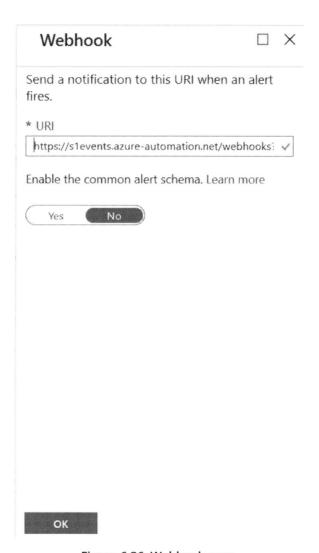

Figure 6.36: Webhook page

Click **OK** to return to the **Add action group** window. Click **OK** to create the action group. When the action group has been created, you'll be taken back to the **Configured actions** page.

23. On the **Configured actions** page, click **Select action group** and then select **High DTU Action Group** on the **Select an action group to attach to this alert rule** page. Click **Select** to continue:

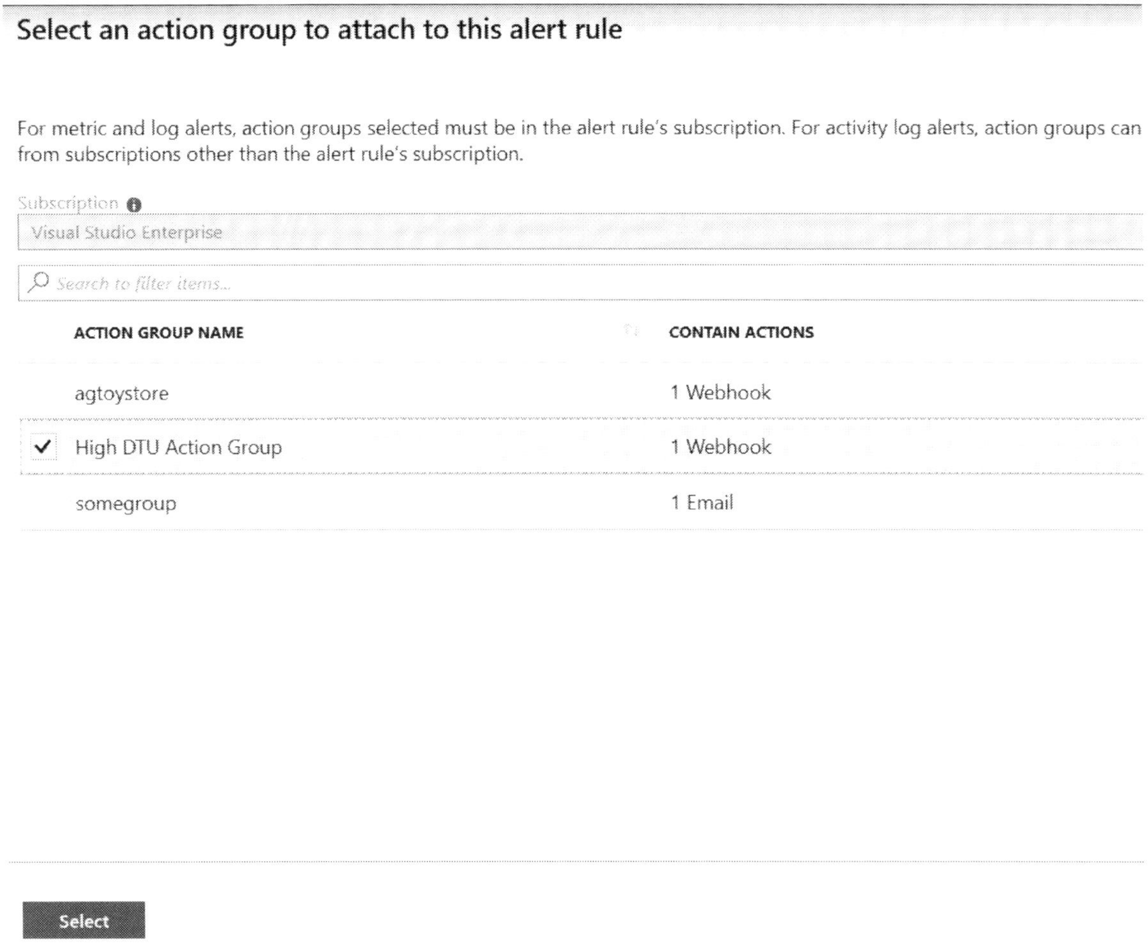

## Select an action group to attach to this alert rule

For metric and log alerts, action groups selected must be in the alert rule's subscription. For activity log alerts, action groups can from subscriptions other than the alert rule's subscription.

Subscription ⓘ

Visual Studio Enterprise

🔎 Search to filter items...

| | ACTION GROUP NAME | CONTAIN ACTIONS |
|---|---|---|
| | agtoystore | 1 Webhook |
| ✓ | High DTU Action Group | 1 Webhook |
| | somegroup | 1 Email |

Select

Figure 6.37: The Select an action group to attach to this alert rule page

24. You'll be taken back to the **Configured actions** page, where you can see that the action group and alert rule are listed as selected. Click **Done** to save the settings:

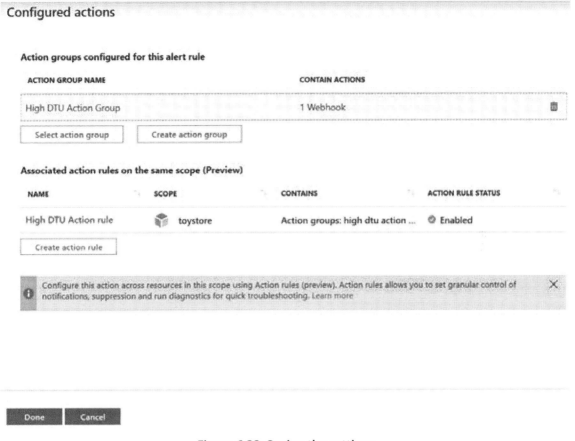

Figure 6.38: Saving the settings

25. You'll then be taken to the **Create rule** page. Scroll to the **ALERT DETAILS** section. Set the alert rule name to **High DTU Alert** and set the severity to **sev 1**. Click **Create alert rule** to create the rule.

> **Note**
>
> As the new alert feature is in preview, you may not see the rule listed on the Alerts page. To modify existing alerts, click on **Manager alert rules**.

This completes the autoscale setup. The next step is to run the workload and see autoscaling in action.

26. Open a new PowerShell window and change the directory to **~\Lesson06\ VerticalScaling**. Execute the following PowerShell command to start the workload:

```
.\Start-Workload.ps1 -sqlserver toyfactory -database toystore -sqluser
sqladmin -sqlpassword Packt@Pub2 -ostresspath "C:\Program Files\Microsoft
Corporation\RMLUtils\ostress.exe" -workloadsql .\workload.sql
```

The script parameters are as follows:

**Sqlserver**: The logical Azure SQL server name

**database**: The Azure SQL database name for which you created an alert earlier in this activity

**Sqluser**: The Azure SQL Server admin username

**Sqlpassword**: The Azure SQL Server admin password

> **Note**
>
> The script parameter values may be different in your case.

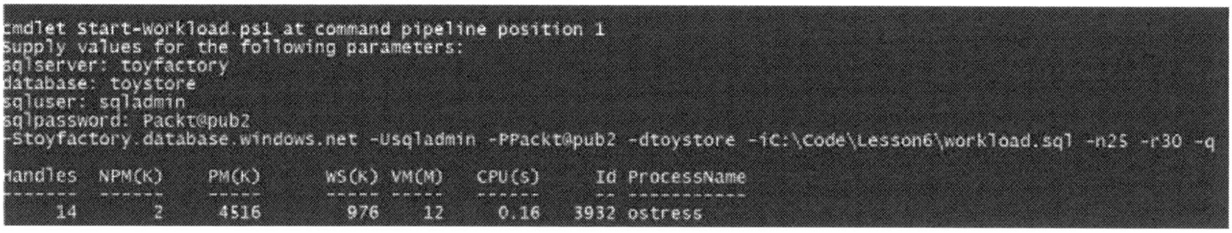

Figure 6.39: Starting the workload

The scripts start an instance of the **ostress** utility. The **ostress** utility runs 25 threads in parallel, executing the **workload.sql** file 30 times in each thread.

27. While the workload is running, monitor the DTU usage percentage on the **toystore** overview page in the Azure portal:

Figure 6.40: Monitoring the DTU percentage

28. To monitor the alert status, navigate to the **Alerts** section of the `toystore` database. We can see that one alert has been triggered:

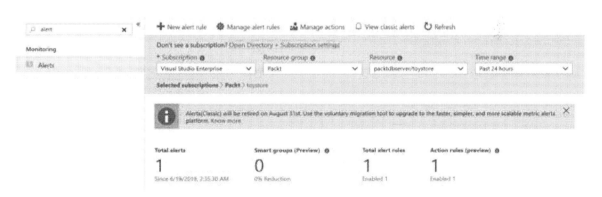

Figure 6.41: Triggered alerts in the Alerts section

29. Click on the **Total alerts** tile:

Figure 6.42: Total alerts tile

We can see that **High DTU Alert** has been triggered.

> **Note**
>
> It's advisable to open the **toystore** database's **Overview** pane in one browser tab and the `Set-AzureSqldatabaseEdition` runbook pane in another tab for easy monitoring.

30. Once the alert is active, navigate to the **Set-AzureSqldatabaseEdition** runbook pane on the Azure portal. Select **Jobs** in the **Resources** section. You should see the job status, as shown here:

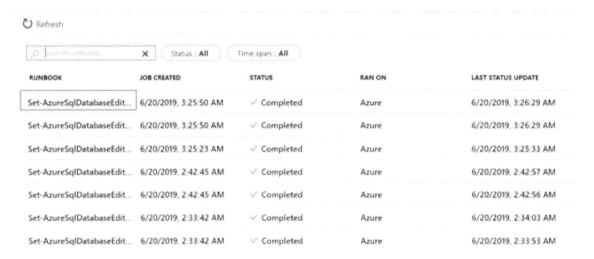

Figure 6.43: Job statuses in the runbook pane

Click **Completed** to check the job status:

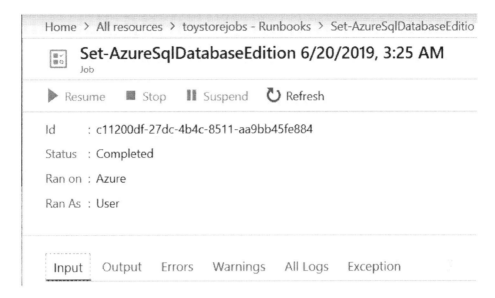

Figure 6.44: Checking job status details

You can verify the parameters passed to the job by clicking on **Input** and review the output from the PowerShell script by clicking on **Output**. The status indicates that the job has run successfully.

Switch to the **toystore** database's **Overview** page and notice that the database edition is now Standard (S0). This completes the activity.

## Activity: Creating Shards

In this activity, we'll discuss how to shard our **toystore** database. Consider the following scenario: Mike has been asked to implement sharding to improve the application performance of the **toystore** database. For this purpose, he can shard the **Sales. Customers** and **Sales.Orders** tables into two shards, **toystore_1_100** (with values of **customerid** from 1-100) and **toystore_200** (with values from 100-200). The following steps describe how this can be done:

> **Note**
>
> The **Application.Countries** table will be the reference, or the common table present in all shards. You can, however, extend the scripts used in this activity to shard other tables.

1. Download the Elastic Database Tool scripts.

2. Provision the **toystore_SMM** shard map manager database.

3. Rename **toystore database** as **toystore_shard_1_100**.

4. Provision the **toystore_shard_200** Azure SQL database.

5. Promote **toystore_SMM** to the shard map manager. This will create the shard management tables and procedures in the **toystore_SMM** database.

6. Create the range shard map in the shard map manager database.

7. Add shards to the shard map.

8. Add the sharded table and reference table schema to the shard map manager database.

9. Verify sharding by reviewing the shard map manager tables.

**Elastic Database Tool scripts**

The Elastic Database Tool scripts are a set of PowerShell modules and scripts provided by Microsoft to easily create and manage Azure SQL Database shards. They use the functions exposed by the Elastic Database client library to provide helper PowerShell cmdlets to easily create and manage shards.

> **Note**
>
> The Elastic Database Tool scripts are available at **C:\Code\Lesson06\Elastic DB tool scripts**. You can download the latest version from here:
>
> https://gallery.technet.microsoft.com/scriptcenter/Azure-SQL-DB-Elastic-731883db

Navigate to `C:\Code\Lesson06\Elastic DB tool scripts\ShardManagement` and open the `ShardManagement.psm1` script. `ShardManagement.psm1` contains functions such as `New-ShardMapManager`, `Get- ShardMapManager`, `New-RangeShardMap`, and **Add-Shard**. Each function has a synopsis section, which briefly describes the function's purpose.

> **Note**
>
> We won't use all of the functions listed in **ShardManagement.psm1**. However, you are free to explore them once you have completed the activity. When you first import the **ShardManagement** module, it checks for the Elastic Database client libraries' DLLs (in the folder from where the PowerShell script is executed), and downloads and registers them if not found.

## Saving Azure profile details to a file

Saving your Azure profile details to a file enables you to log in to your Azure account from PowerShell using the saved profile information. Otherwise, you would have to provide your Azure credentials in the **Authentication** dialog box every time you run an Azure command from PowerShell.

To save Azure profile details to a file, follow these steps:

> **Note**
>
> This isn't part of sharding; however, it'll save you time by not having to type your Azure credentials into PowerShell every time you run an Azure command in PowerShell.

1. Press *Windows* + *R* to open the **Run** command window. In the **Run** command window, type **powershell** and hit *Enter*. This will open a new PowerShell console window:

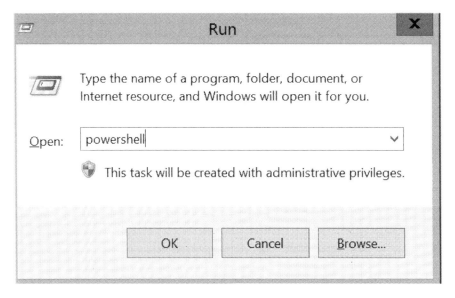

Figure 6.45: Opening a PowerShell console window

2. In the PowerShell console, execute the following command:

```
Add-AzureRmAccount
```

You'll have to enter your Azure credentials in the pop-up dialog box. After a successful login, control will return to the PowerShell window.

Run the following command to save the profile details to a file:

```
Save-AzureRmProfile -Path C:\code\MyAzureProfile.json
```

3. The Azure subscription details will be saved in the **MyAzureProfile.json** file in JSON format. If you wish to explore the **profile.json** file, you can open it in any editor to review its contents:

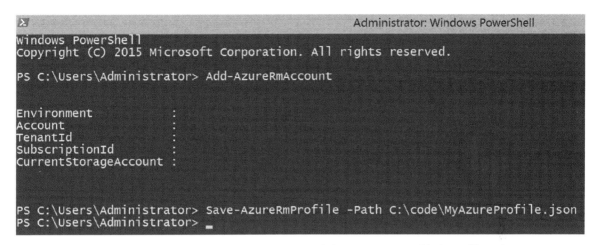

```
Windows PowerShell
Copyright (C) 2015 Microsoft Corporation. All rights reserved.

PS C:\Users\Administrator> Add-AzureRmAccount


Environment           :
Account               :
TenantId              :
SubscriptionId        :
CurrentStorageAccount :


PS C:\Users\Administrator> Save-AzureRmProfile -Path C:\code\MyAzureProfile.json
PS C:\Users\Administrator> _
```

Figure 6.46: Opening the contents of the MyAzureProfile.json file

> **Note**
>
> The **C:\Code** path is where all of the book lessons' code is kept.
>
> The PowerShell scripts later in the book use relative paths. If you have extracted the code to some other directory, say **E:\Code**, then save the **profile.json** file in **E:\Code** to avoid invalid path errors.

## Sharding the toystore database

We'll now learn how to write PowerShell commands using the Elastic Database Tool scripts to shard the existing *toystore* database.

> **Note**
>
> If you are short of time, you can execute the **C:\Code\Lesson06\Sharding\ Sharding.ps1** file, providing appropriate parameters.

1. Press *Window* + R to open the **Run** command window. Type `PowerShell_ ISE.exe` in the **Run** command window and hit *Enter*. This will open a new PowerShell ISE editor window. This is where you'll write the PowerShell commands:

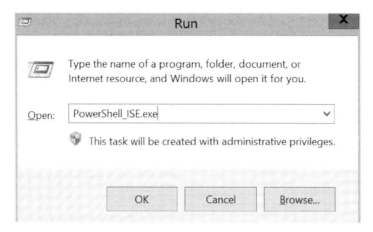

Figure 6.47: Opening the PowerShell ISE editor window

In the PowerShell ISE, select **File** from the top menu and click **Save**. Alternatively, you can press *Ctrl* + S to save the file. In the **Save As** dialog box, browse to the `C:\Code\Lesson06\Sharding` directory. In the **File name** textbox, type `Shard-toystore.ps1` and click on **Save** to save the file:

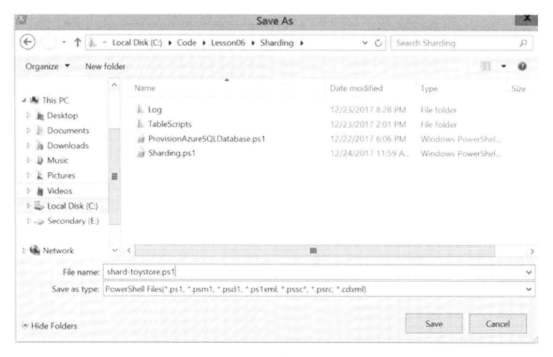

Figure 6.48: Saving the PowerShell file

2. Copy and paste the following code into the **shard-toystore.ps1** file to implement sharding. The code explanation, wherever required, is given in the following code snippet and in the comments within the code snippet.

3. Copy and paste the following code to define the script parameters:

```
param
(
    [parameter(Mandatory=$true)]
    [String] $ResourceGroup,
    [parameter(Mandatory=$true)]
    [String] $SqlServer,
    [parameter(Mandatory=$true)]
    [String] $UserName,
    [parameter(Mandatory=$true)]
    [String] $Password,
    [parameter(Mandatory=$true)]
    [String] $ShardMapManagerdatabase,
    [parameter(Mandatory=$true)]
    [String] $databaseToShard,
    [parameter(Mandatory=$false)]
    [String] $AzureProfileFilePath
)
```

The script accepts seven parameters:

**ResourceGroup**: This is the Azure resource group that contains the Azure SQL server and the database. This should be the same as the one you provided when creating the **toystore** database in *Lesson 1, Microsoft Azure SQL Database Primer*.

**SqlServer**: This is the logical Azure SQL Server name that hosts the **toystore** database.

**UserName** and **Password**: This is the Azure SQL Server admin username and password.

**ShardMapManagerdatabase**: This is the name of the shard map manager database. Prefix **_SMM** to the **toystore** database name to name the shard map manager database.

**databaseToShard**: The database you wish to shard, *toystore* in our case.

**AzureProfileFilePath**: The path of the JSON file that contains your Azure profile details. If it's not yet created, follow the steps in the *Save Azure profile details to a file* section to create one.

4. Copy and paste the following code to set the Azure context to your Azure profile:

```
# log the execution of the script
Start-Transcript -Path ".\Log\Shard-toystore.txt" -Append
...

...
}

#Login to Azure Account
if((Test-Path -Path $AzureProfileFilePath))
{
    $profile = Select-AzureRmProfile -Path $AzureProfileFilePath
    $SubscriptionID = $profile.Context.Subscription.SubscriptionId
...

    Provide your Azure Credentials in the login dialog box
    $profile = Login-AzureRmAccount
    $SubscriptionID =    $profile.Context.Subscription.
SubscriptionId
...

...
#Set the Azure Context
Set-AzureRmContext -SubscriptionId $SubscriptionID | Out-Null
```

This script does the following things:

Logs the script execution in the **Sharding.txt** file in the **C:\Code\Lesson06\ Sharding\Log** folder.

Sets the **AzureProfileFilePath** parameter to the Azure profile JSON file if the path isn't provided as the parameter.

Logs into the Azure account using the Azure profile JSON file. If the JSON path provided isn't valid, then it uses the **Login-AzureRmAccount** command. In this case, you will have to provide your Azure subscription username and password in the pop-up windows.

Sets the default Azure profile to your profile using **Set- AzureRmContext cmdlet**. This tells PowerShell to create and manage objects in your Azure profile.

Press *Ctrl* + S to save your work before moving on.

5. Copy and paste the following code to import the **shardmanagement** module. This will allow us to use the functions in **shardmanagement.psm1** in our PowerShell script:

```
# Import the ShardManagement module
Import-Module '..\Elastic DB tool scripts\ShardManagement\
ShardManagement.psm1'
```

Notice the **shardmanagement.psm1** file path. It is relative to the directory from where you are executing the **shard-toystore.ps1** script. Therefore, you will need to make sure that the Elastic Database Tool scripts folder is available in the ~\**Lesson06\ Sharding** folder.

6. Copy and paste the following script to set the **SQLServerFQDN** variable:

```
$SQLServerFQDN = "$SqlServer.database.windows.net"
```

The **SQLServerFQDN** variable has a fully qualified logical Azure SQL server name. This is required later in the script.

7. Copy and paste the following code to provision a new Azure SQL database to act as the shard map manager:

```
# Provision a new Azure SQL database
# call ProvisionAzureSQLdatabase.ps1 created in lesson 1 to create a new
Azure SQL database to act as Shard Map Manager

$command = "..\..\Lesson01\ProvisionAzureSQLdatabase. ps1 -ResourceGroup
$ResourceGroup -SQLServer $SqlServer
-UserName $UserName -Password $Password -SQLdatabase
$ShardMapManagerdatabase -Edition Standard"
Invoke-Expression -Command $command
```

The **command** variable specifies the **ProvisionAzureSQLdatabase.ps1** file and the required parameters. You can check *Lesson 1, Microsoft Azure SQL Database Primer*, to find out how to run the **ProvisionAzureSQLdatabase.ps1** PowerShell script.

Notice the relative path of **ProvisionAzureSQLdatabase.ps1**. You will have to change the path if **Lesson01** and **Lesson06** are not in the same parent directory.

The **Invoke-Expression** cmdlet runs the command specified in the **command** variable.

8. Copy and paste the following code to set up the individual shards:

```
# Setup the shards
# Rename existing toystore database to toystore_shard1
$Shard1 = $databaseToShard + "_Shard_1_100"
$Shard2 = $databaseToShard + "_Shard_200"

# Establish credentials for Azure SQL database server
$SqlServercredential = new-object System.Management.Automation.
PSCredential($UserName, ($Password | ConvertTo-SecureString
-asPlainText -Force))
...

...
# Create tables to be sharded in Shard2
$files = Get-ChildItem -Path ".\TableScripts\" ForEach($file in $files)
{
    Write-Host "Creating table $file in $shard2" -ForegroundColor Green
    Invoke-Sqlcmd -ServerInstance $SQLServerFQDN -Username
$UserName -Password $Password -database $shard2 -InputFile $file. FullName
| out-null
}
```

The preceding code does the following things:

Declares two variables, **Shard1** and **Shard2**. If the value of the **databaseToShard** variable is **toystore**, then **Shard1** = **toystore_ Shard_1_100** and **Shard2** = **toystore_ Shard_200**.

Renames the existing **toystore** database to **Shard1**; that is, **toystore_Shard_1_100**. The **Set-AzureSqldatabase** cmdlet is used to rename the database.

Provisions the Shard2 database, **toystore_Shard_200**. It uses **ProvisionAzureSQLdatabase.ps1** as described previously to provision a new database.

Creates the required tables, **Sales.Customer**, **Sales.Orders**, and **Application. Countries**, in the newly provisioned **shard2** database.

The create scripts for the tables are kept in **C:\Code\Lesson06\Sharding\ TableScripts**. **Get-ChildItem cmdlet** gets all of the files present in the **TableScripts** directory.

The **Invoke-Sqlcmd cmdlet** executes the scripts file on the **Shard2** database.

9. Copy and paste the following code to register the database created in the previous step as the shard map manager:

```
# Register the database created previously as the Shard Map Manager

Write-host "Configuring database $ShardMapManagerdatabase as Shard Map
Manager" -ForegroundColor Green
$ShardMapManager = New-ShardMapManager -UserName $UserName
-Password $Password -SqlServerName $SQLServerFQDN
-SqldatabaseName $ShardMapManagerdatabase    -ReplaceExisting $true
```

This code uses the **New-ShardMapManager** cmdlet from the **ShardManagement.psm1** module to register the newly created database in the previous steps as the shard map manager.

This creates the database objects required for shard management in the shard map manager database under the **ShardManagement** schema.

10. Copy and paste the following code to create a new shard map in the shard map manager database:

```
# Create Shard Map for Range Mapping
$ShardMapName = "toystorerangemap"
$ShardMap = New-RangeShardMap -KeyType $([int]) -ShardMapManager
$ShardMapManager -RangeShardMapName $ShardMapName
```

This code uses the **New-RangeShardMap** function from the **ShardManagement** module to create a new range shard map in the shard map manager database.

The **keytype** parameter defines the data type of the **sharding** key. In our case, the **sharding** key is **customerid**, which is of the integer data type.

**ShardMapManager** is the shard map manager object assigned to the **$ShardMapManager** variable in step 10. This tells the function to create the shard map in this particular shard map manager.

The **RangeShardMapName** variable is the name of the shard map, **toystorerangemap**.

11. Copy and paste the following code to add the shards to the shard map created previously:

```
# Add shards (databases) to shard maps
Write-host "Adding $Shard1 and $Shard2 to the Shard Map
$ShardMapName" -ForegroundColor Green
```

```
$Shards = "$Shard1","$shard2" foreach ($Shard in $Shards)
{
Add-Shard -ShardMap $ShardMap -SqlServerName $SQLServerFQDN
-SqldatabaseName $Shard
}
```

This code uses the **Add-Shard** function from the **ShardManagement** module and adds the individual shards, Shard1 (**toystore_Shard_1_100**) and Shard2 (**toystore_Shard_200**), to the **toystorerangemap** created previously.

**ShardMap** is the shard map object assigned to the **$ShardMap** variable in the previous steps. This tells the function the shard map to which the shards are to be added.

**SqlServerName** and **SqldatabaseName** are the logical server name and the database name of the shards to be added to the shard map.

This step will create the local shard management objects in the individual shards under the **ShardManagement** database.

12. Copy and paste the following code to add the low and high range key mappings on Shard1 (**toystore_Shard_1_100**):

```
# Add Range Key Mapping on the first Shard
# Mapping is only required on the first shard; currently it has all the
data.

$LowKey = 0
$HighKey = 200
Write-host "Add range keys to $Shard1 (Shard1)" -ForegroundColor

Green
Add-RangeMapping -KeyType $([int]) -RangeShardMap $ShardMap
-RangeLow $LowKey -RangeHigh $HighKey -SqlServerName
$SQLServerFQDN -SqldatabaseName $Shard1
```

This code uses the **Add-RangeMapping** function from the **ShardManagement** module to specify the key range for the first shard only. It takes the following parameters:

**Keytype**: The data type of the sharding key column. It is an integer in our case.

**RangeShardMap**: The range shard map object. This is assigned to the **$ShardMap** variable created previously.

**RangeLow**: The lower boundary of the range mapping, which is 0 in our case.

**RangeHigh**: The higher boundary of the range mapping, which is 200 in our case.

**SqlServerName**: The logical Azure SQL server name that hosts the shards.

**SqldatabaseName**: The name of the shard.

Mappings are added only to the first shard because it has all of the customer records (200 customers) at the moment.

In the next activity, you'll split the records between the shards using the split-merge utility.

13. Copy and paste the following code to add the sharded and reference table schemas to the shard map manager database:

```
# Add Schema Mappings to the $shardMap
# This is where you define the sharded and the reference tables Write-
host "Adding schema mappings to the Shard Map Manager database"
-ForegroundColor Green
$ShardingKey = "Customerid"
$ShardedTableName = "Customers","Orders"
$ReferenceTableName = "Countries"
...
...
# Get the schema info collection for the shard map manager
$SchemaInfoCollection = $ShardMapManager GetSchemaInfoCollection()

# Add the SchemaInfo for this Shard Map to the Schema Info Collection
if ($($SchemaInfoCollection | Where Key -eq $ShardMapName) -eq $null)
{
    $SchemaInfoCollection.Add($ShardMapName, $SchemaInfo)
}
else
{
    $SchemaInfoCollection.Replace($ShardMapName, $SchemaInfo)
}

Write-host "$databaseToShard is now Sharded." -ForegroundColor Green
```

This code adds the schema information of the sharded and reference table to the shard map manager database. The schema information includes the schema name, table name, and key column. This is done by initializing a schema info object of the `Microsoft.Azure.Sqldatabase.ElasticScale.ShardManagement.Schema.SchemaInfo` type, and then adding the table details to this object using the **Add** function. The `Schemainfo.Add` function takes three arguments: schema name, table name, and key column name. The `SchemaInfoCollection` variable gets the shard map manager schema info collection object. The schema is then added to the shard map manager by a `SchemaInfoCollection.Add` function call that takes two arguments: the shard map to add the schema details to and the schema details as defined in the schema info object.

14. This completes the script. Press *Ctrl + S* to save the script. Before you run the script, make sure you have configured the file paths correctly wherever required.

    If you don't have a ready **toystore** database, you can restore it using the **bacpac** file provided with the code files, `C:\Code\0_databaseBackup\toystore.bacpac`.

## Executing the PowerShell script

To execute the **shard-toystore.ps1** script, follow these steps:

1. Press *Window + R* to open the **Run** command window. Type PowerShell and hit *Enter* to open a new PowerShell console window.

2. Change the directory to the folder that has the **shard-toystore.ps1** script. For example, if the script is in the `C:\Code\Lesson06\Sharding` directory, then run the following command to switch to this directory:

   ```
   cd C:\Code\Lesson06\Sharding
   ```

3. In the following command, change the parameter values as per your environment. You can also copy the command from the **C:\Code\Lesson06\Executions.txt** file:

```
.\shard-toystore.ps1 -ResourceGroup toystore -SqlServer toyfactory
-UserName sqladmin -Password Packt@pub2
-ShardMapManagerdatabase toystore_SMM -databaseToShard toystore
-AzureProfileFilePath C:\Code\MyAzureProfile.json
```

> **Note**
>
> You may get the following warning during script execution. Ignore such warnings:
>
> WARNING: Could not obtain SQL Server Service information. An attempt to connect to WMI on '**Microsoft.WindowsAzure.Commands.Sqldatabase.dll**' failed with the following error: The RPC server is unavailable. (Exception from HRESULT: 0x800706BA)

4. Refer to the *Sharding the toystore database* section for parameter details.

Once you have changed the parameter values, hit *Enter* to run the command. This command will do the following:

Create a **Shard-toystore.txt** file in the **Log** folder and use this file for troubleshooting script errors.

Create a shard map manager database, **toystore_SMM**.

Rename **toystore database** as **toystore_Shard_1_100 (shard1)**.

Create a new database, **toystore_Shard_200 (shard2)**.

Create shard management objects in the **toystore_SMM** database under the **ShardManagement** schema.

Create a new range shard map, **toystorerangemap**.

Add **toystore_Shard_1_100 (shard1)** and **toystore_Shard_200 (shard2)** to the range shard map.

Add the key range mappings in **toystore_Shard_1_100 (shard1)**.

Add the table schema for **Sales.Customers**, **Sales.Orders**, and **Application. Countries** in the shard map manager database.

You should get the following output after successful execution of the script:

```
Configuring database toystore_SMM as Shard Map Manager
Adding toystore_Shard_1_100 to the Shard Map toystorerangemap Adding
toystore_Shard_200 to the Shard Map toystorerangemap Add range keys to
toystore_Shard_1_100 (Shard1)
Adding schema mappings to the Shard Map Manager database
toystore is now Sharded.
```

**Reviewing the shard configuration**

You'll now review the shard configuration the PowerShell script created:

1.  Open SQL Server Management Studio on your local machine and connect to the **toyfactory** Azure SQL server.

2.  Connect to Object Explorer (if Object Explorer isn't open, press F8 to connect to it). You should see the following databases:

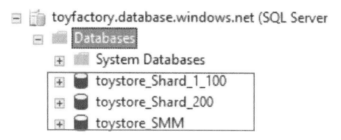

Figure 6.49: Connecting to the toystore server

**toystore_Shard_1_100** is the renamed **toystore** database. **toystore_Shard_200** is the new Shard 2 database. **toystore_SMM** is the shard map manager database.

3.  In **Object Explorer**, right-click **toystore_SMM** and select **New Query** from the **context** menu.

4. Execute the following query in a new query window:

```
SELECT
st.Name As ShardTables
FROM sys.tables st JOIN sys.schemas ss on st.schema_id=ss.schema_id
WHERE ss.Name=' ShardManagement'
```

You should get the following output:

| | ShardTables |
|---|---|
| 1 | ShardMapsGlobal |
| 2 | ShardsGlobal |
| 3 | ShardMappingsGlobal |
| 4 | OperationsLogGlobal |
| 5 | ShardedDatabaseSchemaInfosGlobal |
| 6 | ShardMapManagerGlobal |

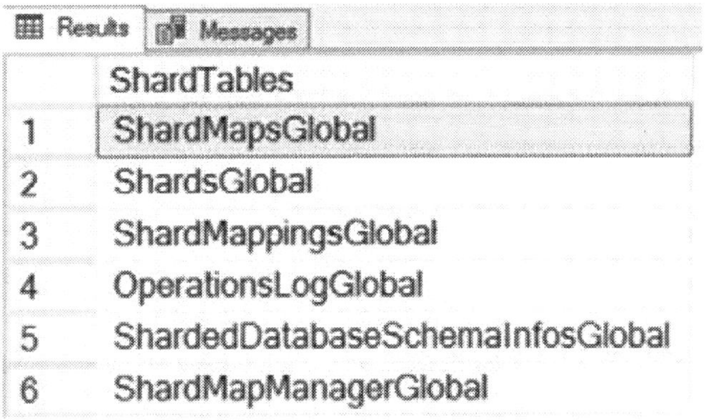

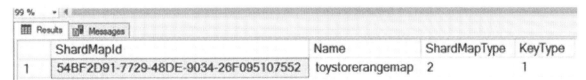

Figure 6.50: Selecting ShardTables

5. Six tables have been added to the **toystore_SMM** database.

6. Execute the following query to view the data for the **ShardMapsGlobal** table:

```
SELECT * FROM ShardManagement.ShardMapsGlobal
```

You should see the following output:

| | ShardMapId | Name | ShardMapType | KeyType |
|---|---|---|---|---|
| 1 | 54BF2D91-7729-48DE-9034-26F095107552 | toystorerangemap | 2 | 1 |

Figure 6.51: ShardMapsGlobal table

The **ShardMapsGlobal** table will have one row for each shard map you created. Notice that it contains **toystorerangemap**, which was created by the **Shard-toystore.ps1** script. Each shard map is assigned a unique **ShardMapId**.

7. Execute the following query to view the data for the **ShardsGlobal** table:

```
SELECT ShardId,ShardMapId,ServerName,databaseName FROM ShardManagement.
ShardsGlobal
```

You should get the following output:

| | ShardId | ShardMapId | ServerName | DatabaseName |
|---|---|---|---|---|
| 1 | 328A2192-2F62-4540-A943-79B8C08A878B | 54BF2D91-7729-48DE-9034-26F095107552 | toyfactory.database.windows.net | toystore_Shard_1_100 |
| 2 | CD40196A-3539-49E1-B230-CA3F74311FA6 | 54BF2D91-7729-48DE-9034-26F095107552 | toyfactory.database.windows.net | toystore_Shard_200 |

Figure 6.52: ShardsGlobal table

The **ShardsGlobal** table contains one row for each shard in the sharded environment. It has two rows, one for each shard, **toystore_ shard_1_100** and **toystore_Shard_200**.

The **ShardMapId** column is used to map a shard with its corresponding shard map in the **ShardsMapGlobal** table.

The table also stores the **ServerName** for each of the shards (databases). This table is used to route the requests to the correct shard based on the sharding key when a request is received from an application.

8. Execute the following query to view data for the **ShardMappingsGlobal** table:

```
SELECT MappingId,ShardId,ShardMapId,MinValue,MaxValue FROM
ShardManagement.ShardMappingsGlobal
```

You should get the following output:

| | MappingId | ShardId | ShardMapId | MinValue | MaxVal |
|---|---|---|---|---|---|
| 1 | 87B3C177-6A52-4FD8-9542-C850B7BA068D | 328A2192-2F62-4540-A943-79B8C08A878B | 54BF2D91-7729-48DE-9034-26F095107552 | 0x80000000 | 0x800C |

Figure 6.53: ShardMappingsGlobal table

**ShardMappingsGlobal** stores the low and high key-value mapping for each shard in the **ShardsGlobal** table.

The **ShardId** and **ShardMapId** columns map the rows with their corresponding shards and shard map in the **ShardsGlobal** and **ShardMapsGlobal** tables respectively.

9. Execute the following query to view the data for the **ShardeddatabaseSchemaInfosGlobal** table:

```
select * from ShardManagement.ShardeddatabaseSchemaInfosGlobal
```

You should get the following output:

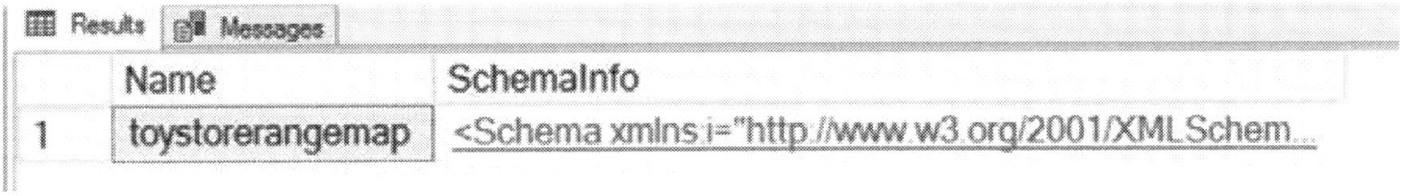

Figure 6.54: SharddatabaseSchemaInfosGlobal table

The **SharddatabaseSchemaInfosGlobal** table stores the schema info for each shard map defined in the **ShardsMapGlobal** table.

These are the same schema details as were provided in the **Sharding toystore database** section in the **shard-toystore.ps1** script.

In the results pane in SSMS, click the XML under the **Schemainfo** column. You should see the following XML:

```
<Schema xmlns:i="http://www.w3.org/2001/XMLSchema-instance">
    <ReferenceTableSet i:type="ArrayOfReferenceTableInfo">
      <ReferenceTableInfo>
        <SchemaName>Application</SchemaName>
        <TableName>Countries</TableName>
      </ReferenceTableInfo>
    </ReferenceTableSet>
    <ShardedTableSet i:type="ArrayOfShardedTableInfo">
      <ShardedTableInfo>
        <SchemaName>Sales</SchemaName>
        <TableName>Customers</TableName>
        <KeyColumnName>Customerid</KeyColumnName>
      </ShardedTableInfo>
      <ShardedTableInfo>
        <SchemaName>Sales</SchemaName>
        <TableName>Orders</TableName>
        <KeyColumnName>Customerid</KeyColumnName>
      </ShardedTableInfo>
```

Observe that it contains the schema, table, and sharding key column values for the **Sales.Customer**, **Sales.Orders**, and **Application.Countries** tables.

10. In **Object Explorer**, expand **toystore_Shard_1_100** and then expand **Tables**:

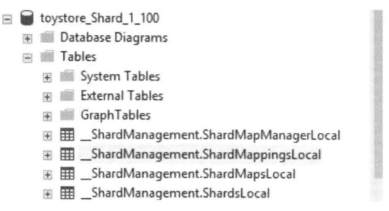

Figure 6.55: Tables in the toystore_Shard_1_100 database

We can see that, since **toystore_SMM** has global shard management tables, **toystore_Shard_1_100** has local shard map management tables. **toystore_shard_200** will also have local shard management tables.

The local shard management tables store shard metadata specific to the particular shard. You can query the tables to review the data if you want to know more.

This completes the activity.

## Activity: Splitting Data Between Shards

In the previous activity, Mike created two shards, **toystore_Shard_1_100** and **toystore_Shard_200**. However, all of the data is available in the **toystore_ Shard_1_100** database, and he has been requested to split the data between **toystore_Shard_1_100** and **toystore_Shard_200**. Therefore, he can use the split-merge service to split the data.

In this activity, you'll use the split-merge service to split the data between **toystore_Shard_1_100** and **toystore_Shard_200**.

The split-merge tool is an Azure web service deployed to your Azure environment. Once deployed, you can either invoke the web service from the web service URL or from PowerShell.

> **Note**
>
> A web service is any service that is available over the internet or intranet. It has a certain set of functions that can be either invoked from the web service's web interface, or using any of the programming languages supporting web service calls.

To deploy the split-merge cloud service in your Azure environment and then call the cloud service function to split the data, first follow these steps to deploy the split-merge cloud service:

1.  Open a browser and navigate to the following URL: https://docs.microsoft.com/en-us/azure/sql-database/sql-database-elastic-scale-configure-deploy-split-and-merge.

    Follow the instructions listed at this URL to deploy the split-merge service.

    In addition to the steps mentioned at the URL, make the following additional changes before deploying the web service. In the **ServiceConfiguration.cscfg** file, set the value of the following settings to **false**:

    ```
    <Setting name="SetupWebAppForClientCertificates" value="false" />
    <Setting name="SetupWebserverForClientCertificates" value="false"
    />
    ```

    Deploy the cloud service in a production environment, not staging, as mentioned at the URL.

2.  If you get an error when deploying the web service, refer to the **C:\Code\Lesson06\Splitting** folder for the sample files:

    **Serviceconfigurtion.cscfg: C:\Code\Lesson06\Splitting\SplitMergeLibraries\Microsoft.Azure.Sqldatabase.ElasticScale.Service.SplitMerge.1.2.0\content\splitmerge\service**

    **SplitMergeService.cspkg: C:\Code\Lesson06\Splitting\SplitMergeLibraries\Microsoft.Azure.Sqldatabase.ElasticScale.Service.SplitMerge.1.2.0\content\splitmerge\service**

    Self-signed certificates: **C:\Code\Lesson06\Splitting\Certificate**

Right-click on **toyfactory.cer** and select **Install** to install the certificate on your local machine. Upload the `toyfactory.pfx` file to Azure Cloud as per the instructions at the URL given previously. Make sure you have enabled the `toyfactory` Azure SQL Server firewall to allow connections from services within Azure. You can do this by switching the **Allow access to Azure services** toggle button to **ON** in the **Firewall** section of the `toyfactory` server:

Figure 6.56: The Firewall section of the toyfactory server

Once your web service is deployed, you should see this output in the Azure portal **Cloud service Overview** section:

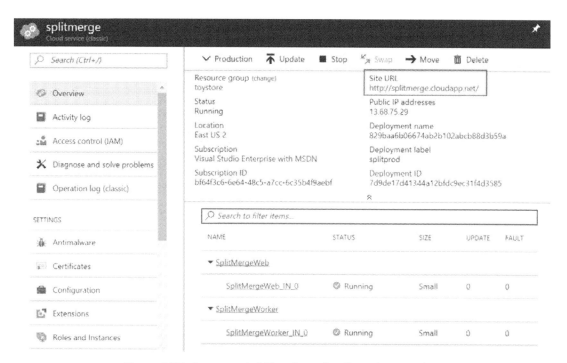

Figure 6.57: Azure portal Cloud service Overview section

3. Copy the web service URL, **http://splitmerge.cloudapp.net**, change **http** to **https**, and open the URL in a browser. If the web service is deployed successfully, you should see the following page:

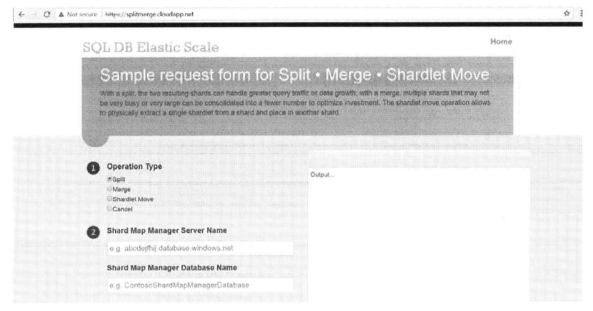

Figure 6.58: Successful deployment of the web service

You can split the data by either filling out the web form or by calling the web service using PowerShell.

Follow these steps to call the split-merge cloud service using PowerShell:

> **Note**
>
> If you are short of time, you can execute the **C:\Code\Lesson06\Splitting\ SplitToyStoreShard.ps1** file, providing appropriate parameters.

4. Press *Window* + *R* to open the **Run** command window. Type `PowerShell_ ISE.exe` in the **Run** command window and hit *Enter*. This will open a new PowerShell ISE editor window. This is where you'll write the PowerShell commands:

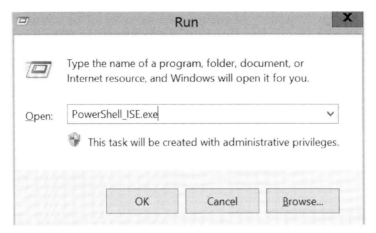

Figure 6.59: Opening a PowerShell editor window

In the PowerShell ISE, select **File** from the top menu and click **Save**. Alternatively, you can press *Ctrl* + *S* to save the file. In the **Save As** dialog box, browse to the `C:\Code\Lesson06\Splitting` directory. In the **File name** textbox, type `Split-toystore-shard.ps1` and click **Save** to save the file:

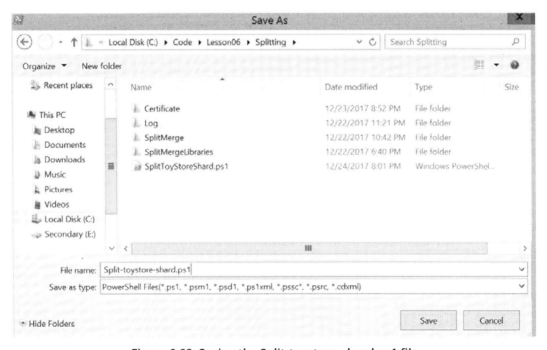

Figure 6.60: Saving the Split-toystore-shard.ps1 file

5. Copy and paste the following code into the **Split-toystore-shard.ps1** file to implement the split operation. The code explanation, wherever required, is given in the following code snippet and in the comments within the code snippet.

6. Copy and paste the following code to define the parameters:

```
param
(
        [parameter(Mandatory=$true)]
    [String] $ResourceGroup,
        [parameter(Mandatory=$true)]
    [String] $SqlServer,
        [parameter(Mandatory=$true)]
    [String] $UserName,
        [parameter(Mandatory=$true)]
    [String] $Password,
        [parameter(Mandatory=$true)]
    [String] $SplitMergeDatabase,
        [String] $AzureProfileFilePath,
        [parameter(Mandatory=$true)]
    [String] $SplitMergeServiceEndpoint,
        [parameter(Mandatory=$true)]
        [String] $ShardMapManagerDatabaseName,
        [parameter(Mandatory=$true)]
        [String] $Shard2,
        [parameter(Mandatory=$true)]
        [String] $ShardMapName,
        [parameter(Mandatory=$true)]
        [String] $SplitRangeLow,
        [parameter(Mandatory=$true)]
        [String] $SplitRangeHigh,
        [parameter(Mandatory=$true)]
        [String] $SplitValue,
        [bool] $CreateSplitMergeDatabase = $false

)
```

Most of the parameters were described in the previous activity. Here are the descriptions of the additional parameters:

**SplitMergedatabase**: This is the split-merge database we created as part of the split-merge cloud service deployment.

**SplitMergeServiceEndpoint**: This is the split-merge cloud service URL copied in the previous section.

**ShardMapManagerdatabaseName**: This is the shard map manager database we created in the *Activity: Creating Alerts* section.

**Shard2**: This is the shard2 database (**toystore_Shard_200**) we created in the *Activity: Creating Alerts* section.

**ShardMapName**: This is the shard map name (**toystorerangemap**) we created in the *Activity: Creating Alerts* section.

**SplitRangeLow**: This is the lower value for the range mapping. This is 0 in our case.

**SplitRangeHigh**: This is the higher value for the range mapping. This is 200 in our case.

**SplitValue**: This is the value at which the split will take place. This is 100 in our case.

**CreateSplitMergedatabase**: This is a Boolean value that, when set to true, will provision a new database to be used as the split-merge database. You can use this to provision the database if you haven't created it yet.

7. Copy and paste the following code to set the login to the Azure subscription:

```
Start-Transcript -Path "$ScriptPath\Log\SplitToyStoreShard.txt" -Append
$CertificateThumbprint = $null
# Get the parent directory of the script.
$ScriptPath = split-path -parent $MyInvocation.MyCommand.
Definition
# set the AzureProfileFilePath
$AzureProfileFilePath = "..\..\MyAzureProfile.json"
#Login to Azure Account
if((Test-Path -Path $AzureProfileFilePath))
{
    $profile = Select-AzureRmProfile -Path $AzureProfileFilePath
    $SubscriptionID = $profile.Context.Subscription.SubscriptionId
}
#Set the Azure Context
Set-AzureRmContext -SubscriptionId $SubscriptionID | Out-Null

# create the split-merge database.
# if you have already deployed the web service this step isn't required.

if($CreateSplitMergeDatabase)
```

```
{
#Create a database to store split merge status
$command = "..\..\Lesson01\ProvisionAzureSQLdatabase.ps1
-ResourceGroup $ResourceGroup -SQLServer $SqlServer -UserName
$UserName -Password $Password -SQLdatabase $SplitMergedatabase
-Edition Basic"
Invoke-Expression -Command $command Exit;


}
```

This code calls the **ProvisionAzureSQLdatabase.ps1** PowerShell script to create a new Azure SQL database to store the split-merge cloud service status. The database is created only if **CreateSplitMergedatabase** is set to true.

8. Copy and paste the following code to import the split-merge PowerShell module:

```
# Import SplitMerge module
$ScriptDir = Split-Path -parent $MyInvocation.MyCommand.Path Import-Module
$ScriptDir\SplitMerge -Force
```

The split-merge PowerShell module has helper functions to call the split-merge cloud service.

9. Copy and paste the following code to submit a split request:

```
Write-Output 'Sending split request'
$splitOperationId = Submit-SplitRequest '
    -SplitMergeServiceEndpoint $SplitMergeServiceEndpoint '
    -ShardMapManagerServerName "$SqlServer.database.windows.net" '
    -ShardMapManagerdatabaseName $ShardMapManagerdatabaseName '
    -TargetServerName "$SqlServer.database.windows.net" '
    -TargetdatabaseName $Shard2 '
    -UserName $UserName '
    -Password $Password '
    -ShardMapName $ShardMapName '
    -ShardKeyType 'Int32' '
    -SplitRangeLowKey $SplitRangeLow '
    -SplitValue $SplitValue '
    -SplitRangeHighKey $SplitRangeHigh '
    -CertificateThumbprint $CertificateThumbprint
```

This code calls the **Submit-SplitRequest** function defined in the **SplitMerge** module. The **Submit-SplitRequest** function submits the split request by specifying the different parameter values.

The **SplitMerge** module contains helper functions for merge requests as well. The merge operation refers to merging two range mappings into a single shard.

**Submit-SplitRequest** returns the operation ID value. The operation ID is assigned to the **$splitOperationId** variable and is used to get the split request status.

10. Copy and paste the following code to wait on the split request until it completes:

```
# Get split request output
Wait-SplitMergeRequest -SplitMergeServiceEndpoint
$SplitMergeServiceEndpoint -OperationId $splitOperationId
-CertificateThumbprint $CertificateThumbprint
```

This code calls the **Wait-SplitMergeRequest** helper function defined in the Split-Merge PowerShell module. The function checks for the split operation status of **$splitOperationId** and writes the status to the console.

Follow these steps to execute the PowerShell script:

1. Press *Window* + R to open the **Run** command window. Type **PowerShell** and hit *Enter* to open a new PowerShell console window.

2. Change directory to the folder that has the **shard-toystore.ps1** script. For example, if the script is in the **C:\Code\Lesson06\Sharding** directory, then run the following command to switch to this directory:

```
cd C:\Code\Lesson06\Splitting
```

3. In the following command, change the parameter values as per your environment. You can also copy the command from the **C:\Code\Lesson06\Executions.txt** file:

```
.\Split-toystore-shard.ps1 -ResourceGroup toystore
-SqlServer toyfactory -UserName sqladmin -Password Packt@pub2
-SplitMergedatabase toystore_splitmerge -SplitMergeServiceEndpoint
"https://splitmerge.cloudapp.net/" -ShardMapManagerdatabaseName
toystore_SMM -Shard2 toystore_Shard_200 -ShardMapName toystorerangemap
-SplitRangeLow 0 -SplitRangeHigh 200 -SplitValue
100 -AzureProfileFilePath C:\Code\MyAzureProfile.json
```

Once you have changed the parameter values, copy and paste the command in the PowerShell console window opened in *step 1* and hit *Enter*.

If the script executes successfully, you should get the following output:

```
Sending split request
Polling request status. Press Ctrl-C to end
Progress: 0% | Status: Queued | Details: [Informational] Operation has
been queued.
Progress: 5% | Status: Starting | Details: [Informational] Starting Split-
Merge state machine for request.
Progress: 5% | Status: Starting | Details: [Informational] Performing data
consistency checks on target shards.
Progress: 20% | Status: CopyingReferenceTables | Details: [Informational]
Successfully copied reference table [Applicati on].[Countries].
…

…
Progress: 80% | Status: CopyingShardedTables | Details: [Informational]
Successfully copied key range [190:200) for shar ded table [Sales].
[Orders].

Progress: 90% | Status: Completing | Details: [Informational]
Deleting any temp tables that were created while processing the request.
Progress: 100% | Status: Succeeded | Details: [Informational] Successfully
processed request.
```

4.  If you get an error in this command and your split-merge service is deployed correctly, then you can troubleshoot it by checking the **RequestStatus** table in the split-merge database.

    The **RequestStatus** table has one row for each split-merge request. The **Details** column contains the XML with the error details if the request fails.

### Verifying the split operation

Follow these steps to review that the split request has correctly moved the data:

1.  Open SQL Server Management Studio on your local machine and connect to the **toyfactory** Azure SQL server.

2.  In **Object Explorer**, right-click on the **toystore_Shard_1_100** database and select **New Query** from the context menu.

3.  In the **New Query** window, execute the following query:

    SELECT DB_NAME() AS databaseName, COUNT(*) AS TotalRows FROM Sales.
    Customers

    You should get the following output:

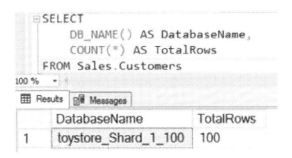

Figure 6.61: Output of the select query

4.  In **Object Explorer**, right-click on the **toystore_Shard_200** database and select **New Query** from the context menu.

5.  In the **New Query** window, execute the following query:

    SELECT DB_NAME() AS databaseName, COUNT(*) AS TotalRows FROM Sales.
    Customers

    You should get the following output:

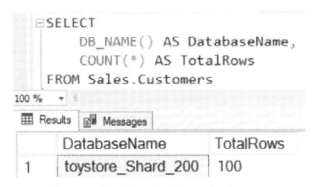

Figure 6.62: Output of the select query

This validates that the split-merge operation has successfully split 200 rows between the two shards, **toystore_Shard_1_100 (100 rows)** and **toystore_Shard_200 (100 rows)**.

6. In **Object Explorer**, right-click on the **toystore_SMM** database and select **New Query** from the context menu. Execute the following query in the new query window:

```
SELECT
sg.databaseName AS ShardName
,sg.ServerName AS ServerName
,smg.Name AS ShardMapName
,smg.KeyType
,CAST(MinValue AS SMALLINT) AS RangeLowKey
,CAST(MaxValue AS SMALLINT) AS RangeHighKey FROM [ ShardManagement].
[ShardMapsGlobal] smg
JOIN [ ShardManagement].[ShardsGlobal] sg ON sg.ShardMapID = smg.
ShardMapId
JOIN [ ShardManagement].[ShardMappingsGlobal] smng ON smg.
ShardMapID=smng.ShardMapID
AND sg.ShardId=smng.ShardId
```

You should get the following output:

Figure 6.63: Output of the select query

The **MinValue** and **MaxValue** columns are **varbinary** columns and are therefore converted to **SmallInt**.

If you remember the first activity in this lesson, the **ShardMappingsGlobal** table had only one mapping, which was added as part of the sharding configuration.

However, it now has two rows, and the second row for the **toystore_ Shard_200** shard is added as part of the split operation.

This completes the activity.

## Activity: Using Elastic Queries

In this activity, we will use elastic, or cross-database, queries to query the sharded tables (created in previous activities) across the shards as a single table.

To query multiple shards as a single table using elastic queries, follow these steps:

1.  Open SQL Server Management Studio on your local machine and connect to the **toyfactory** Azure SQL server.

2.  In **Object Explorer**, right-click on the **Master** database and select **New Query** from the context menu. In the new query window, execute the following query to create the **toystorereporting** database:

    ```
    CREATE DATABASE toystorereporting;
    GO
    ```

3.  Once the database is provisioned, navigate to **Object Explorer**, right-click on the **toystorereporting** database, and select **New Query** from the context menu.

    > **Note**
    >
    > You can also refer to the `C:\Code\Lesson06\ElasticQueries.sql` file for the queries in this activity.

4.  Execute the following query to create a master key:

    ```
    CREATE MASTER KEY ENCRYPTION BY PASSWORD = 'Packt@pub2';
    GO
    ```

    You may get the following error if a master key already exists in the database:

    ```
    Msg 15578, Level 16, State 1, Line 3
    There is already a master key in the database. Please drop it before
    performing this statement.
    ```

    Ignore the error and proceed to the next step.

5.  Execute the following query to create a database-scoped credential:

    ```
    CREATE DATABASE SCOPED CREDENTIAL toystore_creds WITH IDENTITY =
    'sqladmin', SECRET = 'Packt@pub2'
    GO
    ```

    The identity and secret should be the same as your Azure SQL Server administrator username and password.

6. Execute the following query to create the external data source. The external data source is essentially the connection details or the connection string of the external data source. In our case, the external data source is the shard map manager database:

```
CREATE EXTERNAL DATA SOURCE toystore_dsrc WITH
( TYPE=SHARD_MAP_MANAGER,
LOCATION='toyfactory.database.windows.net', DATABASE_NAME='toystore_SMM',
CREDENTIAL= toystore_creds, SHARD_MAP_NAME='toystorerangemap'
);
```

This query creates an external data source **toystore_dsrc** of type **Shard_Map_Manager**, which connects to the shard map manager database **toystore_SMM** using the **toystore_creds** database scoped credentials created in the previous step.

The shard map name in the external data source will help resolve the individual shards to get the data from.

We didn't specify individual shards as the external data source, **database_Name**, because it'll return the data of individual shards. However, our goal is to get data for the table from all shards.

> **Note**
>
> The external data source type can be Hadoop, RDBMS, or Blob Storage. For more details on external data sources, refer to this link: https://docs.microsoft.com/en-us/sql/t-sql/statements/create-external-data-source-transact-sql?view=sql-server-2017.

7. Execute the following query to create the **customers** table in the **toystorereporting** database. The table is created with the **EXTERNAL** keyword and on the external data source, **toystore_dsrc**, created in *step 6*:

```
CREATE EXTERNAL TABLE [dbo].[Customers](
  [CustomerID] [int] NOT NULL,
  [CustomerName] [nvarchar](100) NOT NULL,
  [BillToCustomerID] [int] NOT NULL,
  [CustomerCategoryID] [int] NOT NULL,
  [BuyingGroupID] [int] NULL,
  [PrimaryContactPersonID] [int] NOT NULL,
  [AlternateContactPersonID] [int] NULL,
  [DeliveryMethodID] [int] NOT NULL,
  [DeliveryCityID] [int] NOT NULL,
```

```
    [PostalCityID] [int] NOT NULL,
    [CreditLimit] [decimal](18, 2) NULL,
    [AccountOpenedDate] [date] NOT NULL,
    [StandardDiscountPercentage] [decimal](18, 3) NOT NULL,
    [IsStatementSent] [bit] NOT NULL,
    [IsOnCreditHold] [bit] NOT NULL,
    [PaymentDays] [int] NOT NULL,
    [PhoneNumber] [nvarchar](20) NOT NULL,
    [FaxNumber] [nvarchar](20) NOT NULL,
    [DeliveryRun] [nvarchar](5) NULL,
    [RunPosition] [nvarchar](5) NULL,
    [WebsiteURL] [nvarchar](256) NOT NULL,
    [DeliveryAddressLine1] [nvarchar](60) NOT NULL,
    [DeliveryAddressLine2] [nvarchar](60) NULL,
    [DeliveryPostalCode] [nvarchar](10) NOT NULL,
    [DeliveryLocation] [varchar](1) NOT NULL,
    [PostalAddressLine1] [nvarchar](60) NOT NULL,
    [PostalAddressLine2] [nvarchar](60) NULL,
    [PostalPostalCode] [nvarchar](10) NOT NULL,
    [LastEditedBy] [int] NOT NULL,
    [ValidFrom] [datetime2](7) NOT NULL,
    [ValidTo] [datetime2](7) NOT NULL
) WITH
(
DATA_SOURCE = toystore_dsrc,
SCHEMA_NAME = 'Sales',
OBJECT_NAME = 'Customers',
DISTRIBUTION=SHARDED(customerid)
);
```

dbo.Customers is an external table that gets its data from the toystore_dsrc external data source, the Sales.Customers table.

The distribution parameter specifies how the data is distributed for this table. In our case, the table is horizontally partitioned, hence the distribution used is sharded with customerid (the sharding key). The other available distributions are as follows:

**Replicated**: This means that each database has identical copies of the table.

**Round-robin**: This means that the table is horizontally partitioned, with partition logic specified in the application tier and the sharding method we discussed.

8.  Execute the following query to return all the rows from the customer table:

    ```
    SELECT * FROM dbo.Customers
    ```

    You should get all 200 rows.

    The database engine uses the information specified in the **toystore_dsrc** external data source to connect to and return data from all the shards.

9.  Execute the following queries to get the existing external data source and external tables:

    ```
    -- Get Existing External Data sources SELECT * FROM sys.external_data_
    sources;
    -- Get Existing External Tables SELECT * FROM sys.external_tables
    ```

    This completes the activity.

## Summary

In this lesson, we've seen how easy it is to scale up or scale down an Azure SQL database both automatically and manually. We've looked at both vertical and horizontal scaling. We've also learned how to autoscale Azure SQL databases and shard a database, as well as how to create and maintain Azure SQL Database shards. In the next lesson, we will learn how to scale databases using elastic pools.

# Azure SQL Database Elastic Pools

## Learning Objectives

By the end of this lesson, you will be able to:

- Explain the purpose of elastic pools
- Identify when to use elastic pools
- Select the size of an elastic pool
- Configure Elastic Database Jobs

This lesson teaches you to save costs and manage and scale multiple SQL databases by using elastic pools. You'll also learn how to implement Elastic Database Jobs to manage and maintain databases in an elastic pool.

## Introducing Elastic Pools

Azure SQL Database Elastic Pool is a cost-effective solution for managing and scaling a group or a pool of Azure SQL databases, with a utilization pattern characterized by low average utilization and infrequent spikes.

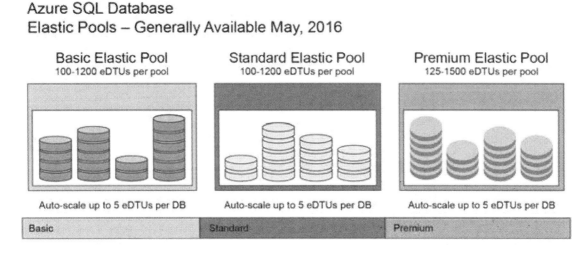

Figure 7.1: Elastic pools

All databases in an elastic pool:

- Belong to one Azure SQL server

- Share a set number of eDTUs

- Share a set amount of elastic pool storage

- Are priced for eDTUs and not individual databases like DTUs

- Can scale up to the given maximum amount of eDTUs

- Have a guaranteed minimum number of eDTUs

## When Should You Consider Elastic Pools?

In *Lesson 6, Scaling Out an Azure SQL Database*, we worked on sharding the **toystore** database into four individual shards. Each shard had 50 pieces of a customer's/tenant's data. Let's say that each individual database is sized to a Standard S3 service tier, for example, 100 DTUs, and has the DTU utilization levels shown in the following graph:

DTU Utilization by Time and Database

Figure 7.2: DTU Utilization by Time and Database of toystore_shard1

The preceding graph shows the DTU utilization by time for the **toystore_shard1** database. It is evident from the graph that **toystore_shard1** has an average DTU utilization of around 30 DTUs and a spike of 80 DTUs around 11:00 AM. Let's say that the other three shards have similar graphs; however, they peak at different times, as shown in the following graph:

DTU Utilization by Time and Database

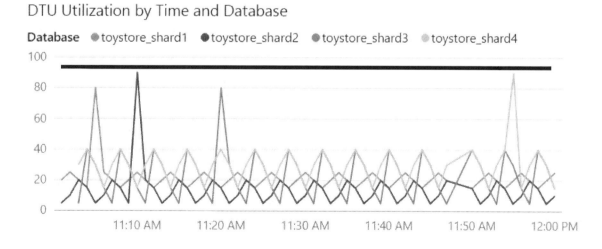

Figure 7.3: DTU utilization graph of multiple shards

The preceding graph shows the four shards in a combined graph. The average utilization is under 40 DTUs and the peak utilization is 90 DTUs. The database peaks at different points in time.

At this point, you might argue that you should use the Standard S2 service tier, which offers 50 DTUs and costs less than S3. This would suffice for most of the database's workload, which is below 50 DTUs. However, this would result in performance degradation for peak hours when the utilization is 90 DTUs, which is much greater than 50 DTUs.

You have two options here:

- Over-provision (Standard S3) to provide optimum performance for peak hours at a higher cost

- Under-provision (Standard S2) to save costs at the expense of lower performance and bad customer experience during peak hours

Elastic pools provide you with a third option, which provides the optimum performance at a lower cost.

The four shards are grouped together in an elastic pool with an eDTU of 100, as shown in the following diagram:

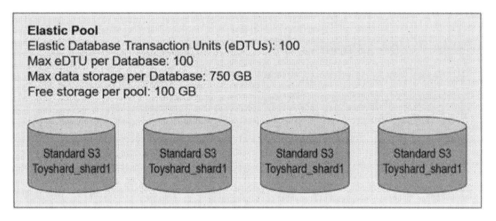

Figure 7.4: Grouping of shards in an elastic pool

This means that a database:

- In peak hours can consume a maximum of 100 eDTUs to meet the performance demand

- In off-peak hours (under light loads) can consume fewer eDTUs

- Under no load consumes 0 (zero) eDTUs

This not only solves the problem of over- and under-provisioning, but also saves costs, as you only have to pay for eDTUs and not the individual databases' DTUs.

A Standard S3 service tier that has a DTU provision of 100 is priced at $147/month. Four such databases will cost $588/month.

An elastic pool that has an eDTU provision of 100 is priced at $221/month, which means that you save $367/month (62% cost reduction) if you have the database in an elastic pool.

Let's say that as the number of customers increases, you plan to further shard the databases into eight shards. This means that you would have eight databases in an elastic pool. This would result in an 85% monthly cost reduction.

This is where elastic pools are very beneficial.

## Sizing an Elastic Pool

Elastic pools have great benefits, but only if they are sized properly. Otherwise, you might end up spending a lot more than expected on elastic pools.

Azure SQL databases automatically analyze historical database utilization numbers and provide elastic pool configuration recommendations on the Azure portal. They also provide eDTU estimates for a custom group of databases on a server. You can add or remove databases from the custom group to get the eDTU recommendations. Once you are satisfied with the pool's configuration, you can create the pool.

If you have to manually estimate whether or not an elastic pool would be more cost-effective than having individual databases, follow these steps:

1. Find the estimated eDTU provision using the following formula:

   MAX(<Total number of DBs X Average DTU utilization per DB>, Number of concurrently peaking DBs X Peak DTU utilization per DB)

2. Find the estimated pool storage provision by adding the individual database storage. Find the eDTU that provides the estimated necessary storage using this link: https://azure.microsoft.com/en-us/pricing/details/sql-database/managed/.

3. Using the link given in step 2, find the smallest eDTU that is greater than the largest eDTU from steps 1 and 2.

4. Compare the costs of the pool and the individual databases to evaluate the pricing benefits.

Let's apply the preceding method to our toystore example:

1. Estimated eDTU as per *step* 1:

```
Total Number of DBs= 4
Average DTU utilization per DB = 30 Number of concurrently peaking DBs = 1
Peak utilization per DB = 90
Estimated eDTUs as per Step 1 = MAX (4 * 30,1*90) => MAX (120, 90) =120
```

The estimated eDTU as per *step* 1 is 120.

2. Estimate eDTU as per *step* 2:

Let's say that each shard has a maximum storage of 100 GB. This means that the maximum storage for all four shards would be 4 * 100 = 400 GB.

As per the pricing details link, the 100 eDTUs per pool satisfies the preceding storage need:

Standard

| eDTUs PER POOL | INCLUDED STORAGE PER POOL | MAX STORAGE PER POOL ¹² | MAX NUMBER DATABASES PER POOL | MAX eDTUs PER DATABASE ³ | PRICE FOR eDTUs AND INCLUDED STORAGE ⁴ |
|---|---|---|---|---|---|
| 50 | 50 GB | 500 GB | 100 | 50 | ~$110.57/month |
| 100 | 100 GB | 750 GB | 200 | 100 | ~$221.13/month |
| 200 | 200 GB | 1 TB | 500 | 200 | ~$442.25/month |

Figure 7.5: Elastic pool pricing for the Standard service tier

Therefore, the estimated eDTU as per *step* 2 is 100.

3. Estimated eDTU as per *Step* 3:

The smallest eDTU that is greater than the largest eDTU as per *Step* 1 (120 eDTUs) and *Step* 2 (100 eDTUs) is 200. However, let's consider that the 100 eDTUs as 120 eDTUs is closer to 100 than 200.

## Comparing the Pricing

In this lesson, we calculated and compared that the 100 eDTU pool saves 62% on cost compared to having four individual Azure SQL databases.

## Sizing Best Practices

The following best practices will help you correctly size an elastic pool.

## Minimum Number of Databases

The minimum number of databases required for a pool to be cost-effective is driven by the following formula:

*Sum of individual database DTUs > 1.5 X eDTUs*

For example, for the **toystore** pool to be more cost-effective, the minimum number of databases in a pool can be calculated as:

*Sum of Individual database DTUs > 150 (1.5 X 100)*

This means that you need:

- At least two Azure SQL databases of the Standard S3 tier for the pool to be cost-effective

- At least four Azure SQL databases of the Standard S2 tier for the pool to be cost-effective

- At least eight Azure SQL databases of the Standard S1 tier for the pool to be cost-effective

## Maximum Number of Concurrently Peaking Databases

An elastic pool allows an Azure SQL database to peak to the maximum eDTUs available for that particular pool. However, not all databases can peak to the maximum eDTUs at the same time.

The maximum number of concurrently peaking databases shouldn't be greater than 2/3 or 67% of the total number of databases in the pool.

For example, the toystore pool has four databases, which means that for the pool to be effective, you only need 67% of the four databases in the pool, which means you only need two databases. If more than two databases concurrently peak, then the pool has to be sized by more than 100 eDTUs. If the pool is resized to more than 100 eDTUs, then more S3 databases need to be added to keep the pool cost-effective.

> **Note**
>
> If all of the databases in a pool have some utilization at any given point in time, then 67% of the databases can peak simultaneously.

### DTU Utilization per Database

The ideal utilization pattern of a database to be considered for an elastic pool should be low average utilization and short, infrequent high utilization. This utilization pattern is best for sharing eDTUs. If a database has a high average utilization, then it would take most of the eDTUs. This means that the other databases wouldn't get the required eDTUs and would have a lower performance.

A database with a peak utilization that is 1.5 times greater than its average utilization is a good candidate for a pool.

## Create an Elastic Pool and Add Toystore Shards to the Elastic Pool

In this section, we will learn how to create an elastic pool and add shards to it. Let's go back to our example of ToyStore Ltd. Mike analyzes the report of eDTUs and thinks of switching to Standard service tier 3. However, this would involve higher costs, so he plans to save on costs without damaging customer experience during peak hours. He creates an elastic pool and adds **toystore store** shards to it through the following steps:

1.  Open a browser and log in to the Azure portal (https://portal.azure.com/) using your Microsoft Azure credentials.

2.  From the left-hand navigation menu, select **All resources**. Under **All Resources**, click the **toyfactory** Azure SQL server to open the **toyfactory** overview blade.

3.  In the **toyfactory** overview blade, select **New pool** from the top menu:

Figure 7.6: New pool in toyfactory overview blade

4.  In the **Elastic pool** blade, provide the elastic pool name in the **Name** section and set the pricing tier as **Standard**:

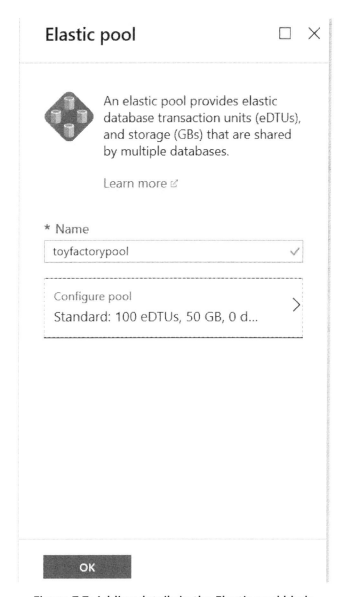

**Figure 7.7: Adding details in the Elastic pool blade**

Click **OK** to create the pool. It'll take 2-5 minutes for the elastic pool to be provisioned.

5. When the pool is provisioned, navigate to the **All resources** page in the Azure portal and type **toyfactorypool** in the search box. Click **toyfactorypool** to configure it:

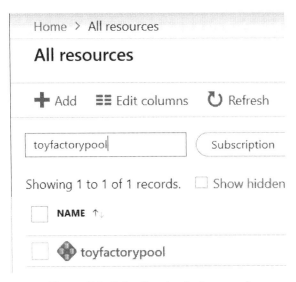

Figure 7.8: Selecting toyfactorypool

6. On the **toyfactorypool** page, select **Configure**:

Figure 7.9: Configuring toyfactorypool

The **Configure pool** page allows you to configure pool settings, add or remove databases, and configure per-database settings.

7. To add databases to **toyfactorypool**, select the **Databases** tab on the **Configure** page.

On the **Databases** tab, click **Add databases**:

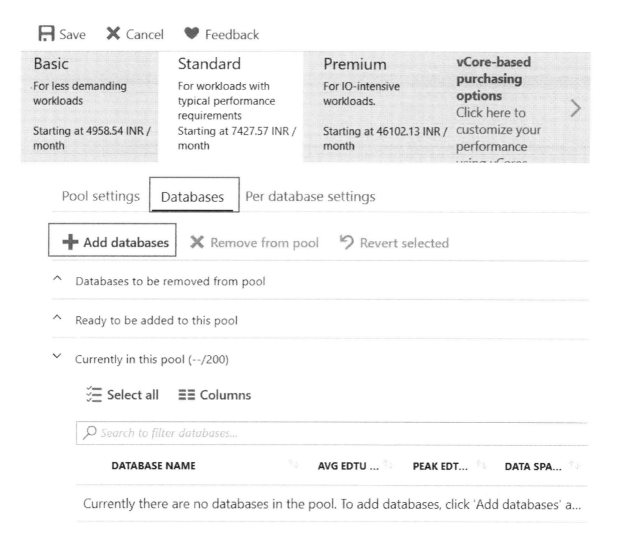

Figure 7.10: Databases tab in the Configure page

8. On the **Add databases** page, select **toystore_shard_1_50**, **toystore_50_100**, **toystore_100_150**, and **toystore_150_200**:

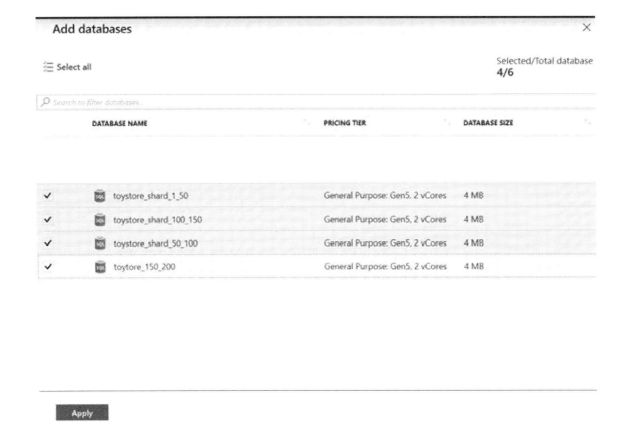

Figure 7.11: Adding databases

Click **Apply** to select the databases and go back to the **Configure** tab.

9. On the **Configure** tab, click **Save** to add the databases:

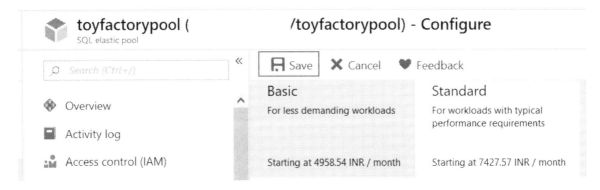

Figure 7.12: Saving the databases

# Elastic Database Jobs

Elastic Database Jobs or Azure-hosted Elastic Database Jobs can be used to schedule a T-SQL task such as index maintenance against an Azure SQL database, a group of SQL database elastic pools, or an Azure SQL database shard.

An Elastic Database Job can span multiple databases in the same subscription or in different subscriptions.

> **Note**
>
> Customer-hosted Elastic Database Jobs are deprecated. To find out more about migrating existing customer-hosted database jobs to Elastic Database Jobs (Azure hosted), refer to the following link: https://docs.microsoft.com/en-us/azure/sql-database/elastic-jobs-migrate.

The following diagram illustrates the different components of an Elastic Database Job:

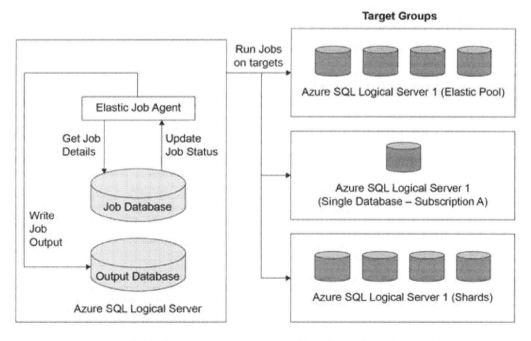

Figure 7.13: Different components of an Elastic Database Job

## Elastic Job Agent

An Elastic job agent is an Azure resource that's responsible for creating, executing, and managing jobs.

## Job Database

An existing clean (blank) Azure SQL database of the Standard (S0) or a higher-performance tier is used to store the job definitions, job status, Elastic Job agent metadata, and stored procedures to create and manage Elastic Database Jobs using T-SQL.

The database job performance tier can be increased based on the number of jobs scheduled and the frequency of the job scheduler; however, a minimum of the S0 tier is required.

## Target Group

A target group defines one or more SQL databases that a job is executed on. A target group can be:

- A single SQL database.
- An Azure SQL logical server. All databases in the server at the time of job creation are considered for job execution.
- An elastic pool. All databases in an elastic pool at the time of job creation are considered for job execution.
- A shardmap, all databases in a shardmap.

> **Note**
>
> Particular databases can be included or excluded individually when defining an Azure SQL Logical Server or an elastic pool as the target group.

## Job

A job is a task that can be either scheduled or executed on demand against a target group. A job can have one or more job steps. A job step requires a T-SQL script to be executed and the credentials to connect to the database(s) defined by the target group. The job output can be stored in a specified output database (SQL database) in detail.

The job database stores the job execution history in detail. The job history is purged every 45 days by a system clean-up job. The job history can be manually purged using the `sp_purge_history` stored procedure against the job database. The Elastic Database Jobs preview is limited to 100 concurrent jobs at any given time.

## Use Cases

Elastic Database Jobs are commonly used for:

- **Database Management and Maintenance**: Elastic Database Jobs can be used for deploying schema changes across; running database maintenance jobs, such as index rebuild; collecting database performance data; and updating reference data in a shard set.

- **Reporting**: Elastic Database Jobs can be used to aggregate data from a shard set and into a single reporting table. The reporting table can then be fed to Power BI, SSRS, or any of the reporting or visualization tools for creating reports. Normally, you would have to connect to each shard in a shard set to run the report query and insert the data into a single reporting table. Elastic Database Jobs make it easier to do this, wherein you only have to schedule the T-SQL and it is automatically executed on the shards.

## Exercise: Configuring an Elastic Database Job Using T-SQL

In this exercise, we'll talk about configuring an Elastic Database Job using T-SQL. An Elastic Database Job can also be configured using PowerShell. When configuring Elastic Database Jobs using T-SQL, the Elastic Database Job agent needs to be provisioned either using PowerShell or the Azure portal.

Follow these steps to create an Elastic Database Job:

1. Provision a blank SQL database to be used as the job database by executing the following script in a PowerShell console window:

```
C:\Code\Lesson01> .\ProvisionAzureSQLDatabase.ps1 -ResourceGroup Packt
-Location "East US 2" -SQLServer packtdbserver
 -SQLDatabase jobdatabase -Edition Standard -UserName dbadmin -Password
Awesome@1234 -ServiceObjective S0
```

The preceding command creates a Standard S0 blank SQL database, **jobdatabase**, to be used for the Elastic Database Job.

You may have to change the database name as you may get an error if **jobdatabase** already exists in Microsoft Azure.

2.  We now need to create an Elastic Database Job agent.

Log in to the Azure portal and search for **Elastic job agent**:

Figure 7.14: Elastic job agent

On the **Elastic Job agents** page, click **Add**:

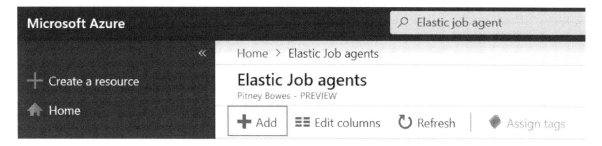

Figure 7.15: Adding new Elastic Job agents

In the **Elastic Job agent** window, provide the Elastic Job agent name, accept the preview terms, and select the **jobdatabase** instance provisioned in *step 1* as the Elastic Job agent database.

Click the **Create** button to provision the Elastic Job agent:

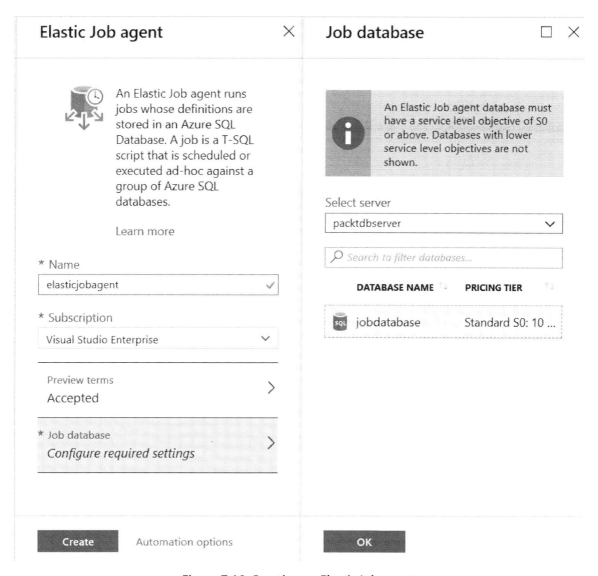

Figure 7.16: Creating an Elastic Job agent

Once an Elastic Job agent is provisioned, it'll be listed on the **Elastic Job agents** page:

Figure 7.17: The Elastic Job agents page

> **Note**
>
> As the feature is still in preview, you may not see the Elastic Job agent listed here. For details, please visit https://social.msdn.microsoft.com/Forums/en-US/69043053-5de3-40da-8e81-cbfa0ac8363a/elastic-job-agent-exists-but-not-showing-in-azure-portal?forum=ssdsgetstarted.

3. The next step is to create the credentials for the job to connect to the target database and execute the T-SQL queries as specified in the job step. You can create the queries in the following way:

Create a database-scoped credential for **jobdatabase** to connect to the target master database:

```
CREATE MASTER KEY ENCRYPTION BY PASSWORD = 'Very$trongpass123';
GO
CREATE DATABASE SCOPED CREDENTIAL jobmastercred
        WITH IDENTITY = 'masteruser' , SECRET = 'myPassword@123'
```

> **Note**
>
> The preceding query is to be executed against the **jobdatabase** instance created earlier in the exercise.

Create master key

Create a database-scoped credential for **jobdatabase** to connect to the individual target database in a given target group:

```
CREATE DATABASE SCOPED CREDENTIAL jobusercred
    WITH IDENTITY = 'jobuser', SECRET = 'myPassword@123'
```

Create a login in the target master database with the same identity and password as that of the **jobmastercred** credential in the job database:

```
CREATE LOGIN masteruser WITH PASSWORD='myPassword@123'
```

Create a user in the target master database for the **masteruser** login created previously:

```
CREATE USER masteruser FROM LOGIN masteruser
```

Create a login in the target master database with the same identity as the **jobusercred** credentials in the job database:

```
CREATE LOGIN jobuser WITH PASSWORD='myPassword@123'
```

Create a user in the target user database for the **jobcred** login. Grant the user relevant permission to run the T-SQL script, which is to be run as part of the Elastic Database Job:

> **Note**
>
> The following scripts are to be executed against **toystore** or any other user database.

```
CREATE USER jobuser FROM LOGIN jobuser
GO
GRANT ALTER ON SCHEMA::dbo to jobuser
GO
GRANT CREATE TABLE TO jobuser
```

The preceding scripts create a **jobuser** user for the **jobuser** login and grant the user permission to create tables against the **toystore** database.

4.  The next step is to add the target group. To add an Azure SQL Logical server as a target group, execute the following scripts in **jobdatabase** (the Elastic Job agent database).

    Add a target group:

    ```
    EXEC jobs.sp_add_target_group 'packtdbserver'
    GO
    ```

    Add a server target member:

    ```
    EXEC jobs.sp_add_target_group_member 'packtdbserver'
            ,@target_type = 'SqlServer'
            ,@refresh_credential_name = 'jobmastercred'
            ,@server_name = 'packtdbserver.database.windows.net'
    ```

    **referesh_credential_name** is the name of the credential created in **jobdatabase** to connect to the target group master database to refresh the list of databases in the target group Azure SQL Logical server.

    **packtdbserver** also contains **jobdatabase**. However, we would not like the job to run against **jobdatabase**. To exclude **jobdatabase** from the target group, execute the following:

    ```
    EXEC [jobs].sp_add_target_group_member @target_group_name =
    N'packtdbserver'
            ,@membership_type = N'Exclude'
          ,@target_type = N'SqlDatabase'
            ,@server_name = N'packtdbserver.database.windows.net'
            ,@database_name = N'jobdatabase'
    GO
    ```

    The **membership_type** value **Exclude** tells the job that the given database is to be excluded from the job execution.

    To see the existing target group and target group members, run the following query:

    ```
    SELECT *
    FROM jobs.target_groups
    WHERE target_group_name = 'packtdbserver';


    SELECT target_group_name,membership_type,target_type,refresh_credential_
    name,server_name,database_name
    FROM jobs.target_group_members
    WHERE target_group_name = 'packtdbserver';
    ```

You should get an output similar to this:

| target_group_name | target_group_id |
|---|---|
| 1 | packtdbserver | 390CD584-7B32-4B8B-81C9-0B3B5E1477D3 |

| | target_group_name | membership_type | target_type | refresh_credential_name | server_name | database_name |
|---|---|---|---|---|---|---|
| 1 | packtdbserver | Exclude | SqlDatabase | NULL | packtdbserver database windows net | jobdatabase |
| 2 | packtdbserver | Include | SqlServer | jobmastercred | packtdbserver database windows net | NULL |

Figure 7.18: Existing target group and target group members

The **jobdatabase** SQL database is excluded from the target group members.

5. The next step is to create an Elastic Database Job. We'll create a database job to create a customer table on the target members.

To create a job, execute the following:

```
EXEC jobs.sp_add_job @job_name = 'CreateCustomerTable'
      ,@description = 'Create new customer table'
```

The query creates a job name, CreateCustomerTable. Let's now add a job step to create the customer table.

```
EXEC jobs.sp_add_jobstep @job_name = 'CreateCustomerTable'
      ,@step_name = 'CreateTable'
      ,@command = N'IF OBJECT_ID(''Customer'') IS NULL
CREATE TABLE [dbo].[Customer] (ID int identity(1,1),FirstName
NVARCHAR(100),LastName NVARCHAR(100))'
      ,@credential_name = 'jobusercred'
      ,@target_group_name = 'packtdbserver'
```

The query adds a **CreateTable** job step to the **CreateCustomerTable** job. The command parameter specifies the T-SQL to create the customer table. The T-SQL first checks that a customer table exists; if not, it creates a new one. The T-SQL will therefore not error out if a customer table already exists in any of the user databases in the target group.

Observe that the **jobusercred** credential, mapped to **jobuser**, is used to run the job.

6. The next step is to execute and schedule the job. Run the following query to execute the job on demand:

```
DECLARE @jeid UNIQUEIDENTIFIER
       ,@lifecycle VARCHAR(100) = 'Created'
-- start job execution
EXEC jobs.sp_start_job 'CreateCustomerTable'
       ,@job_execution_id = @jeid OUTPUT

SELECT @jeid
```

7. Get the job execution status:

```
SELECT *
FROM jobs.job_executions
WHERE job_execution_id = @jeid

/*
Make sure Allow access to Azure services firewall rule is On
*/
WHILE (@lifecycle != 'Succeeded')
BEGIN
       SELECT *
       FROM jobs.job_executions
       WHERE job_execution_id = @jeid
       -- check job status until it succeeds
       SELECT @lifecycle = lifecycle
       FROM jobs.job_executions
       WHERE job_execution_id = @jeid
       ORDER BY start_time DESC

       WAITFOR DELAY '00:00:02'
END
```

The **jobs.sp_start_job** procedure is used to start an ad hoc run of a job. When a job starts, a unique job execution ID is assigned for that particular job run.

The job status is saved in the **jobs.job_execution** table.

The **while** loop gets the job status until it succeeds. You should get the following output:

Figure 7.19: Job execution status

The preceding screenshot shows the job status at different stages of the job execution. The next step is to schedule the job.

8. Schedule the job by executing the following query:

```
EXEC jobs.sp_update_job @job_name = 'CreateCustomerTable'
    ,@enabled = 1
    ,@schedule_interval_type = 'Minutes'
    ,@schedule_interval_count = 15
```

The query uses the **sp_update_job** stored procedure to schedule the job to run every 15 minutes. To get the job details, execute the following queries.

Get the job and job step details:

```
SELECT job_name,enabled,schedule_interval_type,schedule_interval_count
FROM jobs.jobs
WHERE job_name = 'CreateCustomerTable';
GO
```

```
SELECT js.job_name,js.step_name,js.command_type,js.command,js.credential_
name,js.target_group_name
FROM jobs.jobsteps js
JOIN jobs.jobs j ON j.job_id = js.job_id
        AND j.job_version = js.job_version
GO
```

Figure 7.20: Job and job step details

You can also monitor the jobs from the Azure portal. Log in to the portal and open the **elasticjobagent** page:

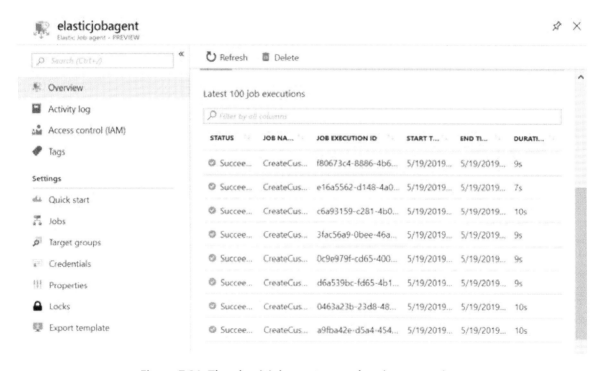

Figure 7.21: The elasticjobagent page showing executions

The **Overview** section lists the last 100 job executions. You can also check the **Credentials**, **Target groups**, and **Jobs** sections. However, the Azure portal doesn't allow the editing of any of the job objects.

Elastic Database Jobs provide similar functionality for Azure SQL Database as SQL Server Agent does for the on-premises SQL Server.

Elastic Database Jobs are optimized and designed for Azure SQL databases. Elastic databases, therefore, support the running of T-SQL queries against databases in the specified target group.

The other job types supported by SQL Server Agent, such as PowerShell, WMI, batch file, Integration Services, and Analysis Services, are not supported by Elastic Database Jobs. This goes along with the PaaS model of Azure SQL Database, wherein the customers don't manage the underlying infrastructure.

SQL Server Agent, on the contrary, is designed to run on premises and can therefore be used for job types other than T-SQL. An example is to schedule a PowerShell script to automate database backups of the on-premises databases. This, however, isn't required in Azure SQL Database as the backups are automated.

SQL Server Agent doesn't support a target group. A SQL Server Agent job step can be run against only one database. The T-SQL script scheduled can, however, access other databases in the instance.

Elastic Database Jobs make it easy to schedule jobs such as schema deployment or database maintenance. For example, to run index maintenance on two or more databases, schedule an Elastic Database Job with the index maintenance T-SQL script to run against the target group. The Elastic Database Job runs the job asynchronously against the specified target databases. However, when scheduling the index maintenance job with SQL Server Agent, the database iteration logic is to be written as part of the script itself. SQL Server Agent doesn't support the target group concept.

## Activity: Exploring Elastic Pools

Let's go back to our example of ToyStore Ltd. Mike finds out that the **toystore** sharded databases can be put into an elastic pool to save costs and get the benefits of vertical stability. In order to do a proof of concept, he uses PowerShell to create an elastic pool and add databases to that elastic pool. He also writes down PowerShell script to delete the elastic pool after he is done with the proof of concept. In this activity, we will create a new elastic pool, add databases to the elastic pool, and delete the elastic pool using PowerShell using the following steps:

> **Note**
>
> If you are short of time, you can execute the **C:\Code\Lesson07\ElasticPool\ Manage-ElasticPool.ps1** file, providing the appropriate parameters.

1. Press *Window* + R to open the **Run** command window. Type **PowerShell_ ISE.exe** in the run command window and hit *Enter*. This will open a new PowerShell ISE editor window. This is where you'll write the PowerShell commands:

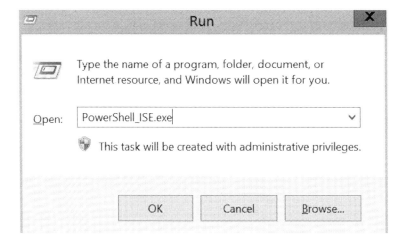

Figure 7.22: Running PowerShell_ ISE.exe

In the PowerShell ISE, select **File** from the top menu and click **Save**. Alternatively, you can press *Ctrl* + S to save the file. In the **Save As** dialog box, browse to the **C:\ Code\Lesson07\** directory. In the **File name** textbox, type **Manage-ElasticPool** and click **Save** to save the file:

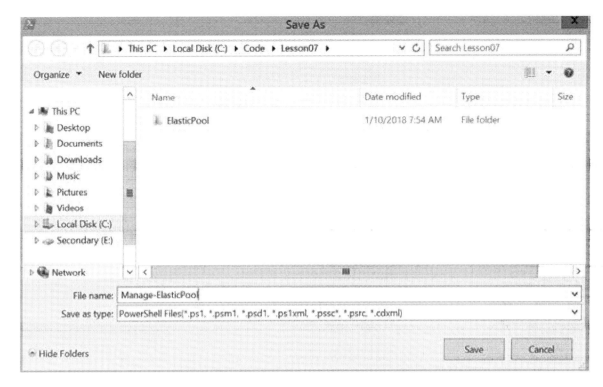

Figure 7.23: Saving the PowerShell file

2.  Copy and paste the following code snippets into the **Manage-ElasticPool.ps1** file, one after another. The code's explanation, wherever required, is given in the following code snippet and in the comments within the code snippet.

3.  Copy and paste the following code to define the script parameters:

```
param
      (
          [parameter(Mandatory=$true)]
            [String] $ResourceGroup,
          [parameter(Mandatory=$true)]
             [String] $SqlServer,
          [parameter(Mandatory=$true)]
              [String] $UserName,
          [parameter(Mandatory=$true)]
             [String] $Password,
          [parameter(Mandatory=$true)]
            [String] $ElasticPoolName,
          [parameter(Mandatory=$false)]
             [String] $ElasticPoolEdition,
          [parameter(Mandatory=$false)]
```

```
            [int] $eDTU,
        [parameter(Mandatory=$false)]
            [int] $MaxeDTU,
        [parameter(Mandatory=$false)]
            [int] $MineDTU=0,
        [parameter(Mandatory=$false)]
            [String] $AzureProfileFilePath,
        [parameter(Mandatory=$false)]
        # Create/Remove an elastic Pool
            [String] $Operation = "Create",
        # Comma delimited list of databases to be added to the pool
        [parameter(Mandatory=$false)]
            [String] $DatabasesToAdd




            )
```

The parameter descriptions are as follows:

**ResourceGroup**: The name of the resource group in which the elastic pool will be created. It should be the same as that of the Azure SQL server.

**SqlServer**: The Azure SQL server name in which the elastic pool has to be created.

**UserName**: The Azure SQL Server database admin username.

**Password**: The Azure SQL Server database admin password.

**ElasticPoolName**: The name of the elastic pool to be created or deleted.

**eDTU**: The elastic pool eDTU.

**MaxeDTU**: The maximum eDTUs available per database in the pool.

**MineDTU**: The minimum eDTUs available per database in the pool.

**AzureProfileFilePath**: The full path of the JSON file that has your Azure profile information.

**Operation**: The operation to be performed. Accepts two values: **Create** and **Remove**.

**DatabasesToAdd**: A comma-delimited list of the databases to be added to the elastic pool.

4. Copy and paste the following code to log in to Microsoft Azure and set the Azure context to your subscription:

```
# log the execution of the script
Start-Transcript -Path ".\Log\Manage-ElasticPool.txt" -Append

# Set AzureProfileFilePath relative to the script directory if it's not
provided as parameter

if([string]::IsNullOrEmpty($AzureProfileFilePath))
{
$AzureProfileFilePath="..\..\MyAzureProfile.json"
}

#Login to Azure Account

if((Test-Path -Path $AzureProfileFilePath))
        {
            $profile = Select-AzureRmProfile -Path $AzureProfileFilePath
            $SubscriptionID = $profile.Context.Subscription.SubscriptionId
        }
        else
        {
            Write-Host "File Not Found $AzureProfileFilePath"
-ForegroundColor Red
            # Provide your Azure Credentials in the login dialog box
            $profile = Login-AzureRmAccount
            $SubscriptionID =  $profile.Context.Subscription.SubscriptionId
        }

#Set the Azure Context
Set-AzureRmContext -SubscriptionId $SubscriptionID | Out-Null
```

The preceding code starts by logging into the **Manage-ElasticPool.txt** file created in the **Log** directory within the parent directory of the **Manage-ElasticPool.ps1** script.

It then checks for the profile information in the **json** file provided by the **AzureProfileFilePath** variable. If found, then it sets the PowerShell context to the subscription ID, as specified in the profile file. Otherwise it asks to manually log in to the Azure account to set the context.

5. Copy and paste the following code to create the elastic pool, if it doesn't already exist:

```
#Check if the pool exists
Get-AzureRmSqlElasticPool -ElasticPoolName $ElasticPoolName
-ServerName $SqlServer -ResourceGroupName $ResourceGroup
-ErrorVariable notexists -ErrorAction SilentlyContinue

if($Operation -eq "Create")
{
if([string]::IsNullOrEmpty($ElasticPoolEdition))
{
                 Write-Host "Please provide a valid value for Elastic
Pool Edition (Basic/Standard/Premium)" -ForegroundColor yellow
              Write-Host "Exiting...." -ForegroundColor Yellow
              break;
            }


       Write-Host "Creating elastic pool $ElasticPoolName "
-ForegroundColor Green
       # Create elastic pool if it doesn't exists
       if($notexists)
       {
 $CreateElasticPool = @{
ElasticPoolName = $ElasticPoolName; Edition = $ElasticPoolEdition;
Dtu = $eDTU; DatabaseDtuMin = $MineDTU; DatabaseDtuMax = $MaxeDTU;
ServerName = $SqlServer;
ResourceGroupName = $ResourceGroup;
};
New-AzureRmSqlElasticPool @CreateElasticPool;

}
else
{
Write-Host "Elastic pool $ElasticPoolName already exists!!!"
-ForegroundColor Green
}
if([string]::IsNullOrEmpty($DatabasesToAdd) -and $Operation -eq "Create")
            {
                 Write-Host "Please provide a valid value for
DatabasesToAdd parameter" -ForegroundColor yellow
```

```
                  Write-Host "Exiting...." -ForegroundColor Yellow
                  break;
              }
```

The preceding code uses the **Get-AzureRmSqlElasticPool** cmdlet to get the details of the given elastic pool name. If the elastic pool with the specified name is found in the given resource group, it succeeds; otherwise, it returns an error: **"Get-AzureRmSqlElasticPool ResourceNotFound: The Resource 'Microsoft.Sql/ servers/ toyfactory/elasticpools/adasdas' under resource group 'toystore' was not found"**.

The error is recorded in the **notexists** variable specified in the **ErrorVariable** parameter.

The code then uses **New-AzureRmSqlElasticPool** to create the elastic pool if the specified operation is **create** (the **$operation** parameter) and the **$notexists** variable isn't empty.

6. Copy and paste the following code to add the databases to the pool:

```
# Add databases to the pool if([string]::IsNullOrEmpty($DatabasesToAdd)
-and $Operation -eq "Create")
{
Write-Host "Please provide a valid value for DatabasesToAdd parameter"
-ForegroundColor yellow
Write-Host "Exiting...." -ForegroundColor Yellow break;
}
$Databases = $DatabasesToAdd.Split(','); foreach($db in $Databases)
{
Write-Host "Adding database $db to elastic pool $ElasticPoolName "
-ForegroundColor Green
Set-AzureRmSqlDatabase -ResourceGroupName $ResourceGroup
-ServerName $SqlServer -DatabaseName $db -ElasticPoolName
$ElasticPoolName
}
}
```

The preceding code splits the comma-delimited values, as specified in **$DatabasesToAdd**. It adds a variable into an array variable database. It then iterates through each of the databases in the array and sets the elastic pool using the **Set-AzureRmSqlDatabase** cmdlet.

7. Copy and paste the following code to remove or delete an existing elastic pool:

```
#remove an elastic pool

if($Operation -eq "Remove")
{
#Get all databases in the elastic pool
$epdbs = Get-AzureRmSqlElasticPoolDatabase -ElasticPoolName
$ElasticPoolName -ServerName $SqlServer -ResourceGroupName
$ResourceGroup

# iterate through the databases and take them out of the pool.
foreach($item in $epdbs)
{
$db = $item.DatabaseName;

#Take database out of pool
Write-Host "Taking database $db out of elastic pool $ElasticPoolName "
-ForegroundColor Green
        $RemoveDbsFromPool = @{
        ResourceGroupName = $ResourceGroup;
        ServerName = $SqlServer;
        DatabaseName = $db;
        Edition = 'Basic';
        RequestedServiceObjectiveName = 'Basic';
        };
        Set-AzureRmSqlDatabase @RemoveDbsFromPool;
        }

#Remove elastic pool
Write-Host "Removing Elastic Pool $ElasticPoolName "
-ForegroundColor Green
$RemovePool = @{
ResourceGroupName = $ResourceGroup; ServerName = $SqlServer;
ElasticPoolName = $ElasticPoolName;
};

Remove-AzureRmSqlElasticPool @RemovePool -Force;

}
```

The preceding code only works when the **$operation** parameter is set to **Remove**. An elastic pool can't be removed or deleted if it has databases assigned to it. First, the code gets all the databases in an elastic pool using the **Get-AzureRmSqlElasticPoolDatabase** cmdlet.

It then iterates through each database and takes them out of the pool using **Set-AzureRmSqlDatabase**.

It then removes the elastic pool using the **Remove- AzureRmSqlElasticPool** cmdlet.

This completes the script. Click **Save** from the **File** menu or press *Ctrl* + S to save the script. We'll now look at executing the PowerShell script:

1. Press the *Windows* + R keys to open the **Run** command window. Type **PowerShell** and hit *Enter* to open a new PowerShell console window.

2. Change the directory to the folder that has the **Manage-ElasticPool.ps1** script in it. For example, if the script is at the **C:\Code\Lesson07\** directory, then run the following command to switch to this directory:

   ```
   cd C:\Code\Lesson07
   ```

3. To delete an existing pool, execute the following command. You will have to change the parameter values as per your environment.

   > **Note**
   >
   > If you created **toyfactorypool** earlier in the lesson, then run this command to delete the pool. If you don't have an existing pool, then proceed to the next step, which is creating a pool. If you have an existing pool and you don't want to remove it, then you will have to create a pool and a separate set of databases for it:

   ```
   .\Manage-ElasticPool.ps1 –ResourceGroup toystore


   -SqlServer toyfactory –UserName sqladmin –Password Packt@
   pub2 –ElasticPoolName toyfactorypool –Operation Remove
   –AzureProfileFilePath C:\Code\MyAzureProfile. Json
   ```

4. To create a new pool and add databases to it, execute the following command. You will have to change the parameter values as per your environment:

```
.\Manage-ElasticPool.ps1 -ResourceGroup toystore -SqlServer toyfactory
-UserName sqladmin -Password Packt@pub2
-ElasticPoolName toyfactorypool -ElasticPoolEdition Standard
-eDTU 100 -MaxeDTU 100 -MineDTU 10 -AzureProfileFilePath C:\Code\
MyAzureProfile.json -Operation Create -DatabasesToAdd "toystore_
Shard_1_50,toystore_Shard_50_100,toystore_Shard_100_150,toystore_
Shard_150_200"
```

The preceding command will create **toyfactoryelasticpool** with 100 eDTUs and the databases specified by the **DatabasesToAdd** parameter.

## Summary

In this lesson, we've learned a simple and cost-effective way of managing multiple Azure SQL databases using an elastic pool. We've learned when and how to use an elastic pool effectively to be cost-effective without affecting database performance.

We've also learned how to use Elastic Database Jobs to manage and maintain the databases in an elastic pool. In the next lesson, you will learn how to implement standard and active geo-recovery for disaster recovery solutions.

# 8

# High Availability and Disaster Recovery

**Learning Objectives**

By the end of this lesson, you will be able to do the following:

- Describe built-in high-availability features in SQL Database

- Implement standard and active geo-recovery for Disaster Recovery (DR) solutions

- Implement standard and active geo-replication

- Implement the Accelerated Database Recovery feature

This lesson will teach you about the built-in high availability in Azure SQL Database. It'll also teach you how to implement a DR solution using standard and active geo-replication.

## High Availability

High availability refers to providing business continuity when the physical server hosting Azure SQL Database fails.

As discussed in *Lesson 1, Microsoft Azure SQL Database Primer*, Azure SQL Database is hosted on three servers – one primary server and two secondary servers:

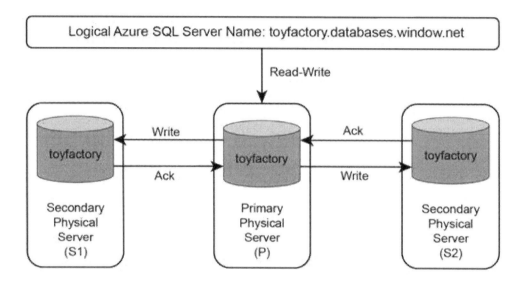

Figure 8.1: Azure SQL Database is hosted on three servers

The **toyfactory** database consists of three servers: one primary server and at least two secondary servers. The Azure SQL Server is just a logical server name used for connections. When an application sends a connection request, the gateway finds the current primary server and routes the request to it.

The primary and secondary servers are within the same data center and together form a quorum set.

All reads and writes are made to the primary server. Azure SQL Database uses a quorum-based commit method that makes sure that the data is hardened at the primary server and replicated to at least one secondary server before the transaction commits.

Although the chances of physical machine failure are very low, in a Microsoft Azure infrastructure with so many systems, machines may fail:

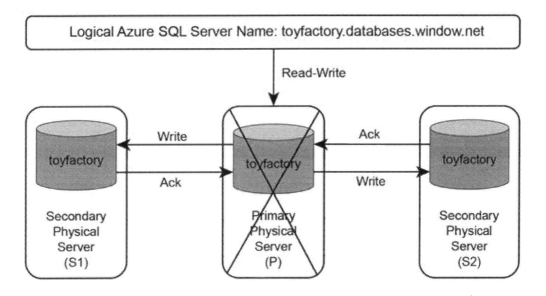

Figure 8.2: A machine failure in an Azure infrastructure

Let's say that the primary server fails because of a hardware failure. The system automatically detects the failure and performs an automatic failover to one of the secondary servers. The process of detecting a failure and failover to the secondary server takes no longer than 30 seconds. However, during the failover time, the database is unavailable for new connections and on-the-fly connections are terminated.

It is therefore important to implement retry logic in applications:

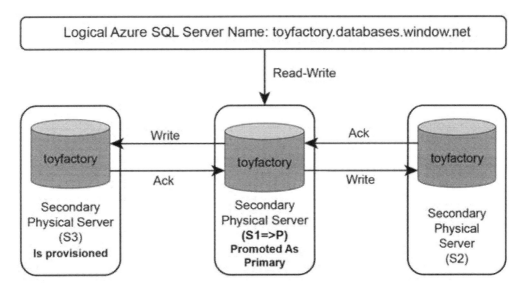

Figure 8.3: The creation of a secondary server

Once the failover is done, the system automatically creates a new secondary server and adds it to the quorum set.

As shown in the preceding diagram, the secondary server (S1) is promoted to the primary server as the primary server (P) failed, and a new secondary server (S3) is provisioned and made part of the quorum set.

This is how high availability is built into Azure SQL databases, and it is completely transparent to users.

This high availability is based on the popular Always On technology, which is also available in on-premises SQL servers. However, you would have to configure, manage, and maintain Always On in an on-premises environment. In Azure SQL Database, it's configured, managed, and maintained by Microsoft.

## Accelerated Database Recovery (ADR)

Accelerated Database Recovery, or ADR, is a new database recovery option that greatly increases the availability and decreases the time in scenarios such as crash recovery (database recovery in the event of a server/database crash), Always On availability group failover, and long-running transaction rollback (for example, a large bulk insert or an index rebuild rollback).

A SQL database consists of data and a transaction log file. A data file contains the table data. A transaction log file keeps track of all the changes made to the data and the schema; for example, if there is an insert in a table, the transaction log file contains the `insert` statement and whether the insert statement was committed or not.

To better understand ADR, let's first get an understanding of the current database recovery process.

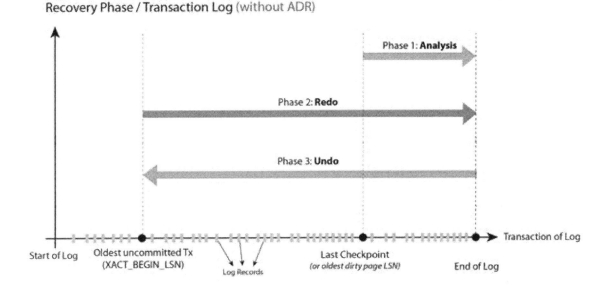

Figure 8.4: The recovery phase without ADR

> **Note**
>
> Image taken from https://docs.microsoft.com/en-us/azure/sql-database/sql-database-accelerated-database-recovery.

As shown in the preceding image, the current recovery process consists of three phases: **Analysis**, **Redo**, and **Undo**.

### Analysis

In the analysis phase, a forward scan of the transaction log is performed from the last checkpoint or the older dirty page LSN (log sequence number).

> **Note**
>
> A dirty page is a page in memory with data modifications. A checkpoint is the process of writing dirty pages from the memory to the physical disk. A checkpoint is therefore a point at which a database is in a consistent state.
>
> An LSN is a number assigned to each entry made on the transaction log.

The output of the analysis phase is a list of transactions:

- These are written to the log and committed but are not written to the physical database file.

- They are in the log file, but they don't have a commit or rollback or are already in the rollback state (active transactions).

> **Note**
>
> The transaction log is scanned from the last successful checkpoint, because all the dirty pages before the checkpoint will have already been written to the physical data file.

**Redo**

In this phase, the log is read forward from the oldest uncommitted transactions, and the transactions that were committed to the log but not to the database are redone. In other words, flush or harden all the dirty pages to disk, from the oldest uncommitted transaction to the end of the log, to restore the system to the state it was in at the time of the crash.

**Undo**

In this phase, the log is read backward from the end of the log to the oldest uncommitted transaction and all the active transactions at the time of the crash are rolled back or undone.

This process is good for recovering a database to a consistent state after a crash; however, it takes a long time and is proportional to the longest-running transaction.

The older the longest uncommitted transaction, the more log records there are to be scanned, thereby increasing the recovery time.

Moreover, the recovery time also depends on the amount of work the longest running transaction has performed. The more work it performs, the more time it takes to roll back and recover the database.

ADR addresses problems with the current database recovery process and provides faster database recovery.

ADR has the following new components, which are used to redesign the current recovery process.

**Persistent Version Store (PVS)**

Whenever a data row is modified, the previous version of the row is kept in PVS.

PVS is similar to the version store used in the Snapshot and Read committed isolation levels; however, PVS is stored in the user database instead of `tempdb`.

**Logical revert**

Logical revert is a process to perform undo/rollback operations using PVS.

In the current database recovery process, if a transaction aborts or rolls back, all other transactions have to wait for the first transaction to roll back to access the rows. However, in ADR, logical revert allows the other transaction to access the previous version of the rows from PVS instead of waiting for the first transaction to roll back.

**sLog**

sLog is a low-volume, in-memory log stream to store log records for non-versioned operations such as lock acquisitions and **Data Definition Language (DDL)** commands.

In other words, it stores the operations that don't go into PVS.

sLog is written to disk during the checkpoint operation and is kept low-volume by periodically removing entries for committed transactions.

**Cleaner**

This is an asynchronous process to clean obsolete row versions from PVS. The cleaner process runs every minute and can also be run manually using the `sys.sp_persistent_version_cleanup` system stored procedure.

The database recovery process with ADR is shown in the following diagram:

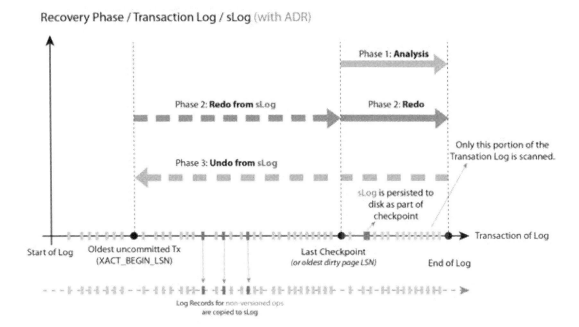

Figure 8.5: The recovery phase with ADR

> **Note**
>
> Image taken from https://docs.microsoft.com/en-us/azure/sql-database/sql-database-accelerated-database-recovery.

The ADR process consists of the same three phases as the current recovery process; however, the work performed by each phase differs from the current recovery process.

**Analysis**

The log is read forward from the last checkpoint to the end of the log.

sLog is rebuilt (read from disk into memory) and the log records for non-versioned operations are written into sLog from the transaction log.

### Redo

The redo is done in two phases:

- **Phase 1**: The sLog is read from the oldest uncommitted transaction to the last checkpoint and non-versioned log records are redone.

- **Phase 2**: The transaction is redone in the transaction log from the last checkpoint to the end of the log.

### Undo

The undo phase consists of the following:

- Undoing all of the non-versioned operations from sLog by reading it backward from the end of the log to the oldest uncommitted transaction.

- Using logical revert to perform a row-level, version-based undo, as explained earlier, in the *Logical Revert* section.

ADR is fast as it doesn't depend on the work or the duration of the oldest active transaction. The transaction log is scanned only from the last checkpoint to the end of the log.

Active transactions at the time of the crash are marked as aborted and the row versions for aborted transactions are ignored during the recovery process.

Other than fast database recovery, with ADR, the transaction log can be truncated aggressively during checkpoint and backup. This is because the log records for the oldest uncommitted transactions are not required for the database recovery.

ADR should be considered for long-running transaction workloads and scenarios where the transaction log size is high because of active transactions.

## Zone Redundant Configuration

The zone redundant configuration refers to having an Azure SQL Database replica in different Availability Zones. Azure Availability Zones are different data centers within the same region. Availability Zones provide additional availability in the event of power failure or network failure in a particular zone or data center.

Zone redundant databases are only supported in the Premium service tier for databases within 1 TB in size.

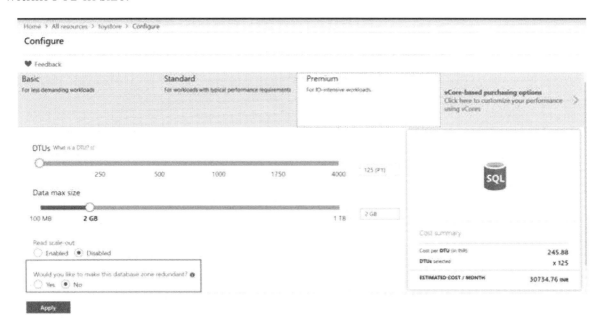

**Figure 8.6: The Configure pane**

Zone redundant configuration may impact the performance of some **online transaction processing (OLTP)** workloads. This is because the zone-redundant replica is in a different zone (data center) and the network latency between the two zones may affect performance.

Therefore, it's recommended to first test the zone-redundant configuration for the performance impact.

However, if there's a performance impact, the zone-redundant configuration can be easily turned off, as shown in the preceding image.

## Disaster Recovery

DR refers to having business continuity in the event of a natural disaster or hacking that terminates an entire Azure region.

There are two ways to implement DR: standard geo-replication and active geo-replication.

### Standard Geo-Replication

Standard geo-replication asynchronously replicates committed transactions from an online primary to an offline secondary in a predefined Azure region:

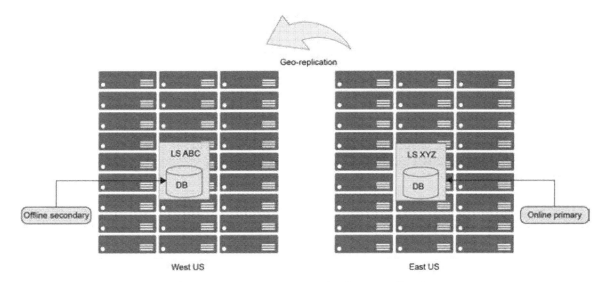

Figure 8.7: Figure 8.7: Standard geo-replication

In standard geo-replication:

Only one secondary is allowed in a DR paired region.

Each region has a DR pair that can only host the secondary database. The secondary database is offline and is unreadable. However, it is visible in the master database. The secondary database is readable when failover is done.

> **Note**
>
> The entire list of DR paired regions can be found here: https://docs.microsoft.com/en-us/azure/best-practices-availability-paired-regions.

- The secondary database is priced at discounted rates as it's unreadable.

- The secondary replica is supported across all service tiers.

Standard geo-replication is designed for environments where the only purpose of having geo-replication is to implement DR and not to offload reads to readable secondaries.

If an Azure region fails, you will get an alert on the Azure portal about the region failure. The state of the Azure SQL server on that region is set to degraded. You have two options from here:

- **Immediately perform a manual failover to the secondary database**

  Standard geo-replication has a **Recovery Point Objective (RPO)** of less than 5 seconds. An RPO is the maximum duration for which data might be lost from an outage. Therefore, if your application can survive a data loss of less than 5 seconds or you have a way of managing data loss in the application code, then it's advised to fail over to the secondary. Once the failover is done, you will have to ensure that the application is correctly configured to connect to the new primary. You will also have to protect the new primary by geo-replicating it to a different Azure DR pair.

- **Wait for the Azure region to recover**

  If your application is sensitive to data loss and there isn't any logic at the application end to control the data loss, you should opt to wait for the region to recover. However, if the outage is for more than 24 hours and Microsoft finds out, then it will take a long time to recover the region. Microsoft will force the failover of the primary database to the secondary databases. Therefore, if you decide to wait for the region to recover and Microsoft decides to force the failover after 24 hours, then you'll have data loss and 24 hours of availability loss:

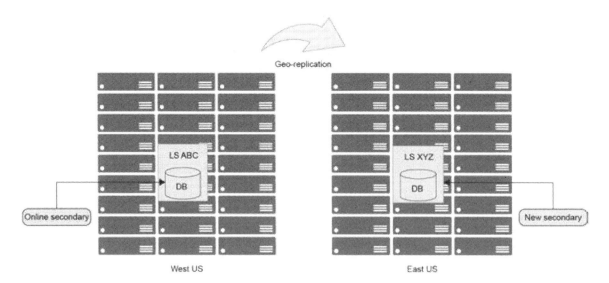

Figure 8.8: Database failover

Let's say that the East US region fails, and after the failover in the environment, it will be like what is shown in the preceding diagram. The West US region will act as the primary, with the East US acting as the new secondary once the region comes back online. However, you can use a different region other than East US to create a secondary database instead of waiting for the East US region to come back online.

## Active Geo-Replication

Active geo-replication uses Always On technology to asynchronously replicate data to a maximum of four readable secondaries in the same or any other Azure region. Active geo-replication is available across all performance tiers. A typical active geo-replication environment is shown in the following diagram:

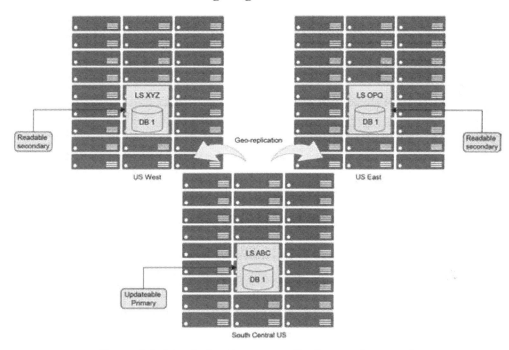

Figure 8.9: A typical active geo-replication environment

The **DB1** database is primarily stored in the South Central US region, with two readable secondaries in the US West and US East regions.

Manual failover is similar to what was explained in the *Standard geo-replication* section. However, when you fail over to the secondary database, the endpoint or the connection string is changed and you will have to make changes to the application so that you can connect to the new primary.

Once the failover is complete, all secondary databases will automatically point to the new primary. In addition to manual failover, active geo-replication also supports automatic failover using auto failover groups.

## Synchronous Replication

The default replication type in active geo-replication is asynchronous. However, if the application needs to have synchronous replication, then you can do so by calling `sp_wait_for_database_copy_sync` immediately after committing a transaction. This will block the calling thread until all of the committed transactions have been replicated to the secondary.

The procedure can add significant delay to the calling thread if the size of the transaction log is being replicated. It's advised to use this procedure to prevent the loss of critical data only, not all data.

## Auto-Failover Groups

Auto-failover groups allow you to automatically recover one or more groups of SQL databases in the event of a region failure. All databases in an auto-failover group should belong to a single server, and they will fail over to a single server as well.

**Auto-failover group terms**

- Failover group: A group of databases between the primary server and the secondary server, which are to be recovered as a unit if there is an outage in the primary region.

> **Note**
>
> The primary server is the one that hosts the primary database. The application can read and write on the primary database. The secondary server is the one that hosts the secondary database. The application can only read from the secondary databases. The data is asynchronously replicated from the primary database to the secondary databases. Primary and secondary servers can't be in the same region.

- Adding databases to a failover group: When a database within a server or an elastic pool is added to the failover group, a secondary database with a performance level similar to that of the primary database is automatically created on the secondary server. If the primary database is in an elastic pool, then an elastic pool with the same name is automatically created on the secondary server.

  When adding a database that already exists in the secondary database server, however, it's not part of the failover group, and so a new secondary database is created in the secondary server.

- Read-write listener: This is a DNS CNAME record that points to the primary server URL. It allows the application to transparently connect to the available primary server in the event of a failover. This is similar to an availability group listener in an on-premises Always On configuration. The application didn't connect to the primary or the secondary server URL. Instead, it connected to the read-write listener. In the event of a failover, the read-write listener will automatically point to the new primary (secondary) server. Therefore, unlike manual failover, the user doesn't have to change the application connection string in the event of a failover.

- Read-only listener: This is a DNS CNAME record that points to the secondary server. It allows the application to transparently connect to the secondary for read-only queries. If you want to offload the read workload to the secondary server automatically, you can do so by adding **ApplicationIntent=ReadOnly** in the application connection string. However, the read workload should be tolerant to a certain staleness of data. This is because the replication is asynchronous, and the secondary database will be some data behind the primary database.

- Failover policy: The default failover policy is set to automatic; however, this can be turned off if the failover process is controlled by the application.

  Manual failover is required if automatic failover is turned off and the failover process isn't controlled by the application.

  Manual failover can also be initiated at any time it is required, independent of the automatic failover policy. An example of manual failover is switching back to the primary region once the region recovers from the outage and is available to host resources.

- Grace period with data loss hours: This setting controls the duration the system fails for before initiating automatic failover. For example, if the grace period with data loss hours is set to 2 hours, then in the event of an outage in the primary region, failover will take place after 2 hours. However, if the outage is resolved before the grace period expires, failover isn't performed.

- Friendly failover: If there is an outage in the primary region that has not yet impacted on the databases (but may impact on the databases in the near future) and the databases are still online, friendly failover with full synchronization is immediately initiated, bypassing the grace period with the data loss hours value (there is no data loss involved in friendly failover – the grace period setting is only effective when friendly failover isn't possible).

- Upgrading the primary database service tier: The service tier and performance level of the primary database can be modified as and when required. The performance level within the same service tier can be modified without disconnecting the secondary database. In other words, you can upgrade the primary database from Standard S0 to Standard S1 without disconnecting the corresponding secondary database connection.

  However, if you are switching between service tiers, then it's recommended (and enforced) to first upgrade the secondary database and then the primary database to avoid the termination of the secondary database connection.

  If the secondary database is part of an auto-failover group, then it's advised not to downgrade the secondary database service tier. This is to avoid performance degradation in the event of a failover.

## Configuring Active Geo-Replication and Performing Manual Failover

Consider a scenario: Mike needs to ensure that the data of Toystore Ltd. is shielded from disaster or the failure of an entire region. To do this, Mike can configure active geo-replication using the Azure portal to recover data and maintain business continuity. He can also take precautions by performing manual failover from the primary server to the secondary server. This activity has the following aims:

- To configure active geo-replication using the Azure portal for the **toyfactory** database

- To perform manual failover from the primary server to the secondary server

The following section explains how to configure active geo-replication for a standalone Azure SQL database:

1. Open the Azure portal in a web browser ([https://portal.azure.com](https://portal.azure.com)) and navigate to the **toyfactory** database overview blade.

2. Under the **SETTINGS** menu, find and select the **Geo-Replication** option:

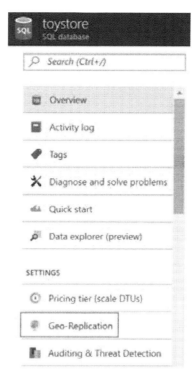

Figure 8.10: The Geo-Replication option in the SETTINGS menu

In the **Geo-Replication** blade, you will see a world map with **hexagons** denoting Azure regions:

Figure 8.11: The Geo-Replication blade displaying the Target Regions

The blue hexagon with a checkmark inside it is the region that currently has the primary database. The highlighted (in red) purple-outlined hexagon is the recommended Azure region for the secondary database. The green-outlined hexagons represent other Azure regions across the globe.

3.  Click the purple-outlined hexagon to open the **Create secondary** blade. It has the following pre-set options:

    **Region**: This shows you the region you selected to create the secondary server.

    **Database name**: The name of the database that is to be replicated.

    **Secondary type**: The type of the secondary database – readable or offline.

    **Elastic database pool**: The elastic pool the database is part of. It displays none if the database is not part of an elastic pool.

    **Pricing tier**: The secondary database pricing tier. This is inherited from the primary database.

    > **Note**
    >
    > The lock icon in front of an option indicates that the option is locked and can't be configured.

4.  Click the **Target server** option to create a new target server in the secondary region.

    In the **New server** blade, provide the **Server name**, **Server admin login**, and **Password**, as shown in the following screenshot:

    > **Note**
    >
    > The server admin name and password should be the same as those of the primary server. This is to avoid login issues resulting from orphaned users.

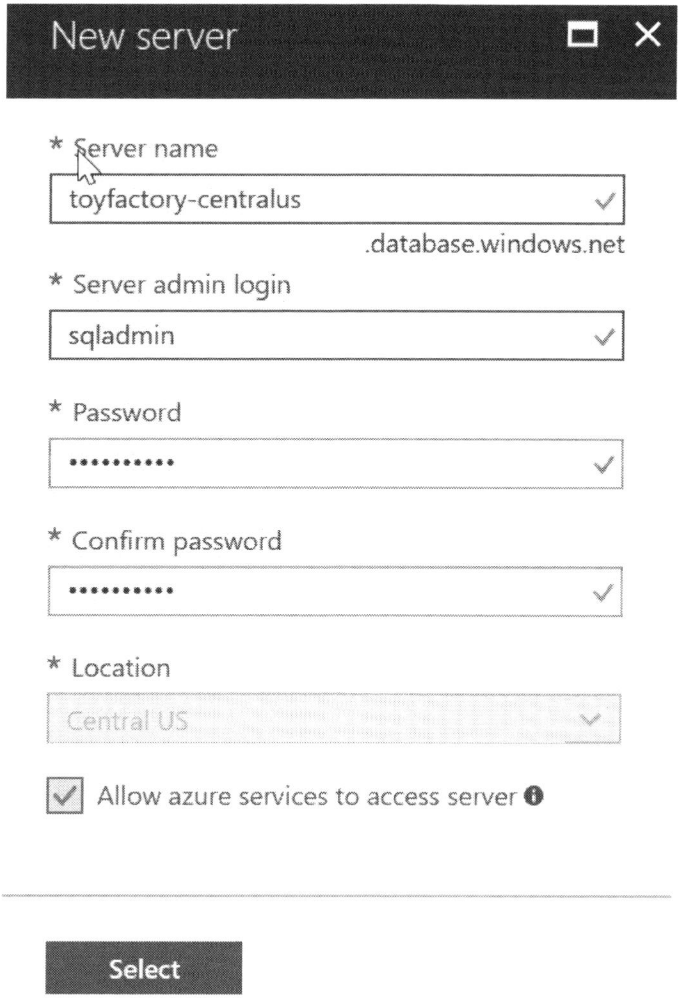

**New server** ☐ ✕

\* Server name

| toyfactory-centralus | ✓ |

.database.windows.net

\* Server admin login

| sqladmin | ✓ |

\* Password

| •••••••••• | ✓ |

\* Confirm password

| •••••••••• | ✓ |

\* Location

| Central US | ∨ |

☑ Allow azure services to access server ❶

**Select**

Figure 8.12: Creating a new target server

Click the **Select** button to continue.

5. You'll be taken back to the **Create secondary** blade:

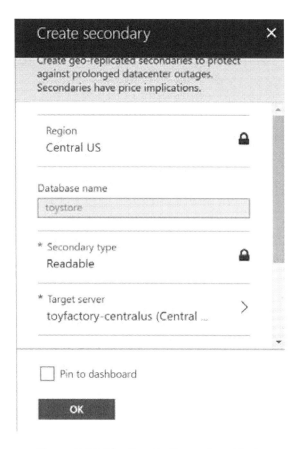

Figure 8.13: The Create Secondary blade

Click **OK** to create the secondary server and start the geo-replication.

As the geo-replication is being configured, you'll see an animated status on the **Geo-Replication** blade:

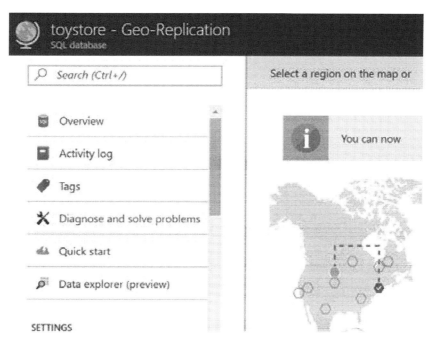

Figure 8.14: The Geo-Replication blade displaying the status of the replication

The dotted line between the regions indicates that the geo-replication setup is in progress.

Once the geo-replication is done, the dotted blue line will turn into a solid blue line, indicating that the active geo-replication is in place between the two regions:

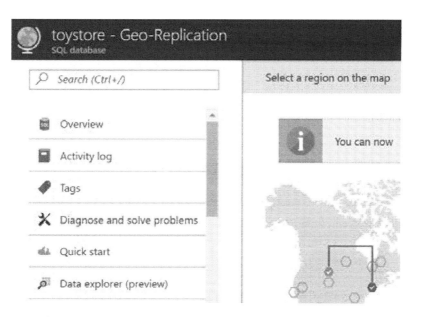

Figure 8.15: The Geo-Replication blade displaying the completion of the replication

6.  To verify this, open SQL Server Management Studio and sign into the new secondary server.

> **Note**
>
> When connecting to the secondary server, you'll have to add the firewall rule. It is therefore advised to use the database-level firewall on the primary server. This makes sure that the firewall rules are also copied to the secondary database during the active geo-replication setup so that you can log in easily.
>
> It's also advised to use contained users so that you don't have to move server logins to the secondary server.

7.  In the **Object Explorer** window, expand **Server**, and then expand **Databases**. You should see the **toystore** database. Expand the **toystore** database. You should see all the objects in the **toystore** database:

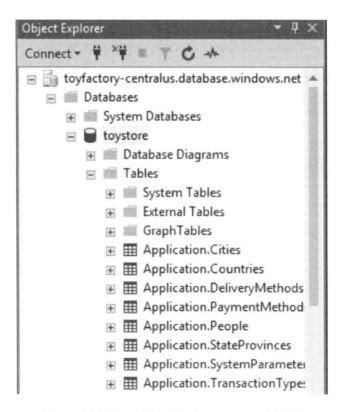

Figure 8.16: The Object Explorer pane of SSMS

8. Press *Ctrl* + N to open a new query window. Execute the following query in the new query window:

```
SELECT COUNT(*) FROM Sales.Customers GO
INSERT INTO Warehouse.Colors
VALUES(100,'Light Green',1,getdate(),getdate()+10);
```

The **select** query will return as a success; however, the **insert** query will fail with the following error:

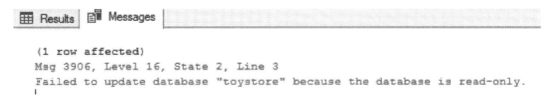

```
(1 row affected)
Msg 3906, Level 16, State 2, Line 3
Failed to update database "toystore" because the database is read-only.
```

Figure 8.17: The error displayed while inserting values

This is because the secondary database is read-only in an active geo-replication configuration.

9. In the same SSMS session, connect to the primary server and execute the following query against the **toystore** database in the primary server. Do not close the secondary server query window:

```
INSERT INTO Warehouse.Colors
VALUES(100,'Magenta',1,getdate(),getdate()+10);
```

One row will be inserted into the **Colors** table.

Switch over to the query window with the secondary database connection. Execute the following query to verify whether the newly inserted value has been properly replicated to the secondary database or not:

```
SELECT @@ServerName As SecondaryServerName,* FROM Warehouse.Colors
WHERE ColorName='Magenta'
```

You should get the following output:

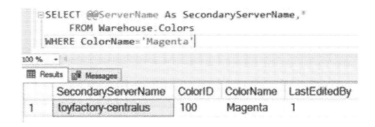

Figure 8.18: Confirming if the inserted data is replicated in the secondary database

The data has indeed been correctly replicated to the secondary database.

**Performing Manual Failover**

1.  In the **toystore geo-replication** blade, scroll down and locate the **PRIMARY** and **SECONDARIES** databases:

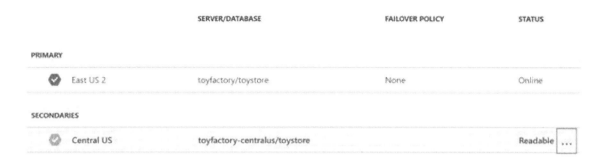

Figure 8.19: The toystore geo-replication blade denoting the primary and the secondary databases

2.  Select the three dots (highlighted in the red rectangle). In the context menu, select **Forced Failover**:

Figure 8.20: The Forced Failover option in the Contextual menu

3.  Click **Yes** on the **Failover** message pop-up window to start the failover:

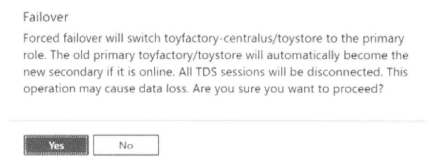

Figure 8.21: The Failover message pop-up window

The failover request will be submitted, and the failover will be initiated.

4.  To monitor the failover, scroll up to the top of the **Geo-Replication** blade. You'll see a dotted blue line animation denoting the failover:

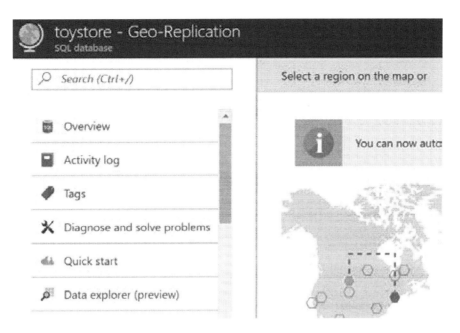

Figure 8.22: The Geo-Replication blade denoting failover in progress

Once the failover is complete, the dotted blue line will change to a solid blue line:

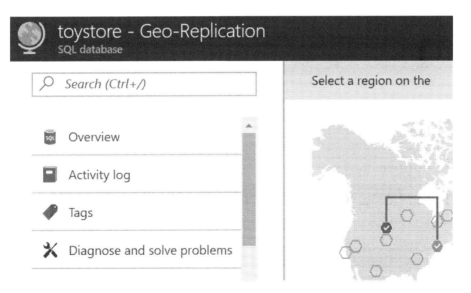

Figure 8.23: The Geo-Replication blade denoting failover is complete

Observe that the region color has also been reversed. The blue hexagon now denotes that the primary region is the Central US region, and the green hexagon denotes that the secondary region is now East US 2.

Additionally, you can perform *steps 5–8* to verify the failover.

## Configuring the Auto-Failover Group

This section covers the configuration of auto-failover groups for a standalone Azure SQL database. Consider the following scenario, again involving ToyStore Ltd.

Mike wants to ensure that whenever there is a disaster or an entire region fails, there is no effect on the business of ToyStore Ltd., so he configures auto-failover groups that allow him to automatically recover one or more groups of SQL databases. To configure an auto-failover group for a standalone Azure SQL database, the following steps need to be taken.

Adding databases to an existing failover group hasn't been supported in the Azure portal until now:

1. Log in to the Azure portal (https://portal.azure.com) and open the **toystore_Shard_1_50** database overview blade.

2. In the **Overview** blade, select **Geo-Replication** from the **Settings** section.

3. In the **toystore_Shard_1_50 Geo-Replication** blade, click the information icon above the world map:

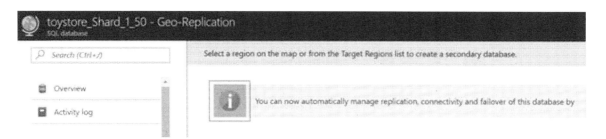

Figure 8.24: The toystore_Shard_1_50 Geo-Replication blade

4. In the **Failover group** blade, configure the following settings:

   **Secondary Server**: The Azure SQL server on another region that will host the secondary databases. You'll have to create a new server if you don't have one already.

   **Failover group name**: The name of the failover group.

**Read/Write failover policy**: The default value is **Automatic**. Leave it as it is.

**Read/Write grace period (hours)**: The default value is 1 hour. Leave it as it is:

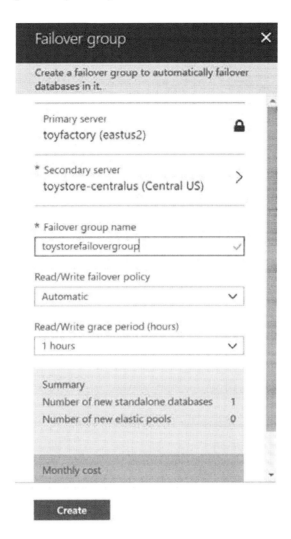

Figure 8.25: The Failover group blade

In the **Summary** section, observe that we only have one database in the failover group, which is **toystore_Shard_1_50**.

Click **Create** to provision the secondary server and the failover group.

Each failover group has a monthly cost associated with it. This cost is separate from the cost of the secondary database.

Once created, you can follow the steps from the previous section to fail over and verify the replication.

## Activity: Configuring Active Geo-Replication

Mike ensures that the data of the Toystore Ltd is shielded from the disaster. In case of a disaster or an entire region failure, he can recover or maintain his business continuity by configuring the Active Geo-replication **toystore** database using PowerShell.

To configure Active Geo-replication for the **toystore** database using PowerShell, perform the following steps:

> **Note**
>
> If you are short of time, you can execute the `C:\Code\Lesson08\`
> `ActiveGeoReplicatin\Manage-ActiveGeoReplication.ps1` file, providing the
> appropriate parameters.

1.  Press the *Window* + R keys to open the **Run** command window. Type `PowerShell_` `ISE.exe` in the **Run** command window and hit *Enter*. This will open a new PowerShell ISE editor window. This is where you'll write the PowerShell commands:

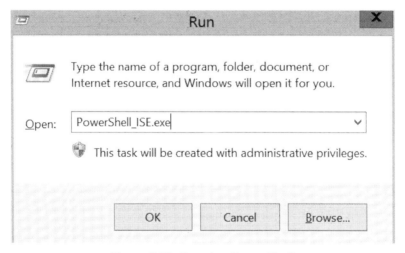

Figure 8.26: Opening PowerShell

In the PowerShell ISE, select **File** from the top menu and click **Save**. Alternatively, you can press *Ctrl* + S to save the file. In the **Save As** dialog box, browse to the `C:\Code\Lesson08\` directory. In the **File name** textbox, type `Manage-` `ActiveGeoReplication` and click **Save** to save the file:

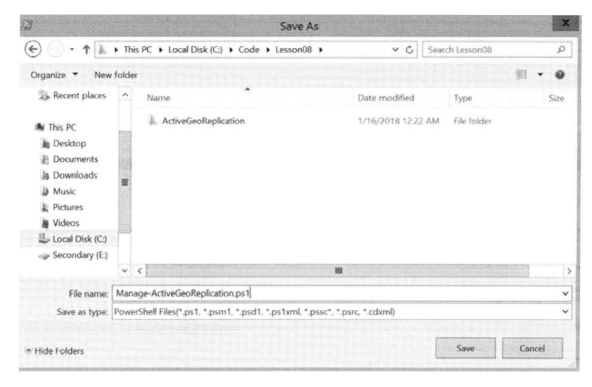

Figure 8.27: Creating the Manage-ElasticPool.ps1 file

2. Copy and paste the following code into **Manage-ElasticPool.ps1** to define script parameters:

```
param
    (
        [parameter(Mandatory=$true)]
        [String] $ResourceGroup,
        [parameter(Mandatory=$true)]
        [String] $PrimarySqlServer,
        [parameter(Mandatory=$true)]
        [String] $UserName,
        [parameter(Mandatory=$true)]
        [String] $Password,
        [parameter(Mandatory=$true)]
        [String] $SecondarySqlServer,
        [parameter(Mandatory=$true)]
        [String] $SecondaryServerLocation,
        [parameter(Mandatory=$false)]
        [bool] $Failover = $false,
        [parameter(Mandatory=$false)]
        [String] $DatabasesToReplicate,
```

```
        [parameter(Mandatory=$false)]
        # Add/Remove database to/from secondary server
        [String] $Operation = "none",
        [parameter(Mandatory=$false)]
        [String] $AzureProfileFilePath




    )
```

The parameter descriptions are as follows:

**ResourceGroup**: The resource group that hosts the primary Azure SQL server and databases.

**PrimarySqlServer**: The name of the primary Azure SQL server.

**UserName**: The primary and secondary Azure SQL server admin username.

**Password**: The primary and secondary Azure SQL server admin password.

**SecondarySqlServer**: The secondary Azure SQL server name.

**SecondaryServerLocation**: The secondary Azure SQL server location.

**Failover**: A Boolean value set to false by default. When true, the script does the failover from the primary Azure SQL server to the secondary SQL server.

**DatabasesToReplicate**: A comma-delimited list of Azure SQL databases to be replicated.

**Operation**: Accepts two values: **Add** and **Remove**. When set to **Add**, the active geo-replication link is established for the databases. When set to **Remove**, the active geo-replication link is removed for the databases.

**AzureProfileFilePath**: The full path of the Azure profile JSON file used for logging in to an Azure subscription.

3. Copy and paste the following code to log in to Microsoft Azure, and set the Azure context to your subscription:

```
# log the execution of the script
Start-Transcript -Path ".\Log\Manage-ElasticPool.txt" -Append

# Set AzureProfileFilePath relative to the script directory if it's not
provided as parameter

if([string]::IsNullOrEmpty($AzureProfileFilePath))
```

```
{
$AzureProfileFilePath="..\..\MyAzureProfile.json"
}

#Login to Azure Account

if((Test-Path -Path $AzureProfileFilePath))
    {
        $profile = Select-AzureRmProfile -Path $AzureProfileFilePath
        $SubscriptionID = $profile.Context.Subscription.SubscriptionId
    }
    else
    {
        Write-Host "File Not Found $AzureProfileFilePath" -ForegroundColor
Red


        # Provide your Azure Credentials in the login dialog box
        $profile = Login-AzureRmAccount
        $SubscriptionID =  $profile.Context.Subscription.SubscriptionId
    }

#Set the Azure Context
Set-AzureRmContext -SubscriptionId $SubscriptionID | Out-Null
```

The preceding code starts by logging into the **Manage-ElasticPool.txt** file created under the **Log** directory within the parent directory of the **Manage-ElasticPool.ps1** script.

It then checks for the profile information in the **JSON** file provided by the **AzureProfileFilePath** variable. If found, it then sets the PowerShell context to the subscription ID, as specified in the profile file; otherwise, it asks to manually log in to the Azure account to set the context.

4. Copy and paste the following code to provision the secondary Azure SQL server if it doesn't already exist:

```
if($Operation -eq "Add")
{
# Check if Azure SQL Server Exists
# An error is returned and stored in notexists variable if resource group
exists
Get-AzureRmSqlServer -ServerName $SecondarySqlServer
-ResourceGroupName $ResourceGroup -ErrorVariable notexists
```

```
-ErrorAction SilentlyContinue
# provision the secondary server if it doesn't exists if($notexists)
{
Write-Host "Provisioning Azure SQL Server
$SecondarySqlServer" -ForegroundColor Green
$credentials = New-Object -TypeName System.Management.
Automation.PSCredential -ArgumentList $UserName, $(ConvertTo- SecureString
-String $Password -AsPlainText -Force)
$_SecondarySqlServer = @{ ResourceGroupName = $ResourceGroup; ServerName =
$SecondarySqlServer; Location = $SecondaryServerLocation;
SqlAdministratorCredentials = $credentials; ServerVersion = '12.0';
}
                New-AzureRmSqlServer @_SecondarySqlServer;
        }
    }

    }
    else
    {
    Write-Host $notexits -ForegroundColor Yellow
    }
```

The preceding code will provision a new secondary Azure SQL server if the **$Operation** parameter is set to **Add**. The SQL server creation code is similar to what was used in *Lesson 1, Microsoft Azure SQL Database Primer*.

5. Copy and paste the following code to configure active geo-replication for the individual databases:

```
# Configure Active Geo-Replication for individual databases
if(![string]::IsNullOrEmpty($DatabasesToReplicate.Replace(',',''))
-and $Operation -eq "Add")
{
$dbname = $DatabasesToReplicate.Split(','); foreach($db in $dbname)
{
Write-Host "Replicating database $db to
$SecondarySqlServer " -ForegroundColor Green
#Get the database object for the given database name
$database = Get-AzureRmSqlDatabase -DatabaseName $db
-ResourceGroupName $ResourceGroup -ServerName $PrimarySqlServer #pipe the
database object to New-
AzureRmSqlDatabaseSecondary cmdlet
```

```
$database | New-AzureRmSqlDatabaseSecondary
-PartnerResourceGroupName $ResourceGroup -PartnerServerName
$SecondarySqlServer -AllowConnections "No"
}
}
```

The preceding code first checks whether the **$DatabaseToReplicate** parameter is empty. If it's not and the **$operation** parameter is set to **Add**, it splits the comma-delimited list of the databases and configures active geo-replication for each one of them using the **New-AzureRmSqlDatabaseSecondary** cmdlet.

**New-AzureRmSqlDatabaseSecondary** takes three parameters:

**PartnerResourceGroupName**: The resource group name that contains the secondary SQL Server. The primary and secondary resource groups are assumed to be the same in this script.

**PartnerServerName**: The name of the secondary Azure SQL server.

**Allowconnections**: This specifies the read intent of the secondary database. It's set to **All**.

6. Copy and paste the following code to remove active geo-replication for the individual Azure SQL databases:

```
if($Operation -eq "Remove")
{
$dbname = $DatabasesToReplicate.Split(','); foreach($db in $dbname)
{

Write-Host "Removing replication for database $db "
-ForegroundColor Green
$database = Get-AzureRmSqlDatabase -DatabaseName $db
-ResourceGroupName $ResourceGroup -ServerName $PrimarySqlServer
$database | Remove-AzureRmSqlDatabaseSecondary
-PartnerResourceGroupName $ResourceGroup -ServerName
$PrimarySqlServer -PartnerServerName $SecondarySqlServer
}
}
```

The preceding code runs when **$Operation** is set to **Remove**. It first splits the comma-separated database list in the **$DatabaseToReplicate** parameter. It then removes the replication link for each database using the **Remove-AzureRmSqlDatabaseSecondary** cmdlet.

**Remove-AzureRmSqlDatabaseSecondary** accepts three parameters:

**PartnerResourceGroupName**: The resource group of the secondary SQL server. The script assumes that it's the same as the primary SQL server.

**ServerName**: The primary SQL server's name.

**PartnerServerName**: The secondary SQL server's name.

This only stops the replication between the primary and the secondary databases; it doesn't delete the secondary databases. The database and server can be removed separately if required.

7. Copy and paste the following code to fail over individual databases to the secondary SQL server:

```
# failover individual databases from primary to secondary if($Failover -eq
$true)
{
$dbname = $DatabasesToReplicate.Split(','); foreach($db in $dbname)
{
Write-Host "Failover $db to $SecondarySqlServer..."
-ForegroundColor Green
$database = Get-AzureRmSqlDatabase -DatabaseName $db
-ResourceGroupName $ResourceGroup -ServerName $SecondarySqlServer
$database | Set-AzureRmSqlDatabaseSecondary
-PartnerResourceGroupName $ResourceGroup -Failover
}
}
```

The preceding code executes if the **$Failover** parameter is set to true. It first splits the comma-delimited list of the databases in **$DatabaseToReplicate** and then performs manual failover from the primary server to the secondary server using **Set- AzureRmSqlDatabaseSecondary**.

**Set-AzureRmSqlDatabaseSecondary** accepts two parameters:

**PartnerResourceGroupName**: The resource group of the secondary SQL server. The script assumes that it's the same as the primary SQL server.

**Failover**: Initiates the failover.

The database to fail over is piped to the **Set-AzureRmSqlDatabaseSecondary** cmdlet.

This completes the script. Press *Ctrl* + S to save the file.

**Executing the PowerShell script**

1. Press *Window* + R to open the **Run** command window. Type PowerShell and hit *Enter* to open a new PowerShell console window.

2. Change the directory to the folder that has the **Manage-ActiveGeoReplication.ps1** script inside of it. For example, if the script is in **C:\Code\Lesson08** directory, then run the following command to switch to that directory:

   ```
   cd C:\Code\Lesson08\ActiveGeoReplication
   ```

3. In the PowerShell console, execute the following command to establish active geo-replication for the **toystore_Shard_1_50** and **toystore_ Shard_50_100** databases:

   ```
   .\Manage-ActiveGeoReplication.ps1 -ResourceGroup toystore
   -PrimarySqlServer toyfactory -UserName sqladmin -Password Packt@pub2
   -SecondarySqlServer toyfactory-centralus
   -SecondaryServerLocation "Central US" -DatabasesToReplicate "toystore_
   Shard_1_50,toystore_Shard_50_100" -Operation "Add"
   -AzureProfileFilePath C:\Code\MyAzureProfile.json
   ```

   The preceding command will call **Manage-ActiveGeoReplication.ps1** to start active geo-replication for the **toystore_Shard_1_50** and **toystore_Shard_50_100** databases on **toyfactory** databases to the **toyfactory-centralus** secondary Azure SQL server.

4. You will have to modify the command to provide the relevant parameter values. In the PowerShell console window, run the following command to fail over the databases to the secondary SQL server:

   ```
   .\Manage-ActiveGeoReplication.ps1 -ResourceGroup toystore
   -PrimarySqlServer toyfactory -UserName sqladmin -Password Packt@pub2
   -SecondarySqlServer toyfactory-centralus
   -SecondaryServerLocation "Central US" -DatabasesToReplicate "toystore_
   Shard_1_50,toystore_Shard_50_100" -failover $true
   -AzureProfileFilePath C:\Code\MyAzureProfile.json
   ```

   The preceding command will fail over the databases from the primary server to the secondary server. In other words, the primary becomes secondary and vice versa.

5. In the PowerShell console window, execute the following command to remove active geo-replication:

   ```
   .\Manage-ActiveGeoReplication.ps1 -ResourceGroup toystore
   -PrimarySqlServer toyfactory -UserName sqladmin -Password Packt@pub2
   -SecondarySqlServer toyfactory-centralus
   ```

```
-SecondaryServerLocation "Central US" -DatabasesToReplicate "toystore_
Shard_1_50,toystore_Shard_50_100" -Operation "Remove"
-AzureProfileFilePath C:\Code\MyAzureProfile.json
```

The preceding command will remove the replication link between the primary and the secondary servers, though please note that the secondary server and the databases will not be removed.

## Activity: Configuring Auto-Failover Groups

In this activity, we will configure auto failover groups using PowerShell for ToyStore Ltd.

> **Note**
>
> If you are short of time, you can execute the **C:\Code\Lesson08\ ActiveGeoReplication\Manage-FailoverGroup.ps1** file, providing the appropriate parameters.

1. Press *Window* + R to open the **Run** command window. Type **PowerShell_ ISE.exe** in the **Run** command window and hit *Enter*. This will open a new PowerShell ISE editor window. This is where you'll write the PowerShell commands:

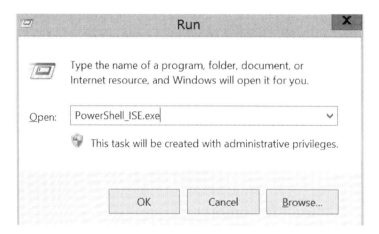

Figure 8.28: Opening PowerShell

In the PowerShell ISE, select **File** from the top menu and click **Save**. Alternatively, you can press *Ctrl* + S to save the file. In the **File Save** dialog box, browse to the **C:\ Code\Lesson08\** directory. In the **File name** textbox, type **Manage-FailoverGroup** and click **Save** to save the file:

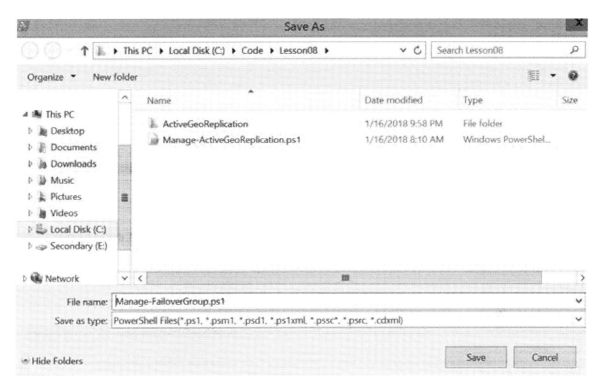

Figure 8.29: Creating a the Manage-FailoverGroup.ps1 file

2. In the **Manage-FailoverGroup.ps1** file, copy and paste the following code to define the script parameters:

```
param (
[parameter(Mandatory=$true)] [String] $ResourceGroup,
[parameter(Mandatory=$true)] [String] $PrimarySqlServer,
[parameter(Mandatory=$false)] [String] $UserName,
[parameter(Mandatory=$false)] [String] $Password,
[parameter(Mandatory=$true)] [String] $SecondarySqlServer,
[parameter(Mandatory=$false)]
[String] $SecondaryServerLocation, [parameter(Mandatory=$false)]
[bool] $Failover = $false, [parameter(Mandatory=$false)] [String]
$DatabasesToReplicate, [parameter(Mandatory=$true)] [String]
$FailoverGroupName, [parameter(Mandatory=$false)] [String] $Operation =
"none", [parameter(Mandatory=$false)] [String] $AzureProfileFilePath


)
```

Most of the parameters are similar to what was explained in the previous activity, except **FailoverGroupName**. This is the name of the failover group that is going to be created.

3. Copy and paste the following code to log into Microsoft Azure and set the Azure context to your subscription:

```
# log the execution of the script
Start-Transcript -Path ".\Log\Manage-ElasticPool.txt" -Append # Set
AzureProfileFilePath relative to the script directory if it's not provided
as parameter if([string]::IsNullOrEmpty($AzureProfileFilePath))
{
$AzureProfileFilePath="..\..\MyAzureProfile.json"
}

#Login to Azure Account #Login to Azure Account

if((Test-Path -Path $AzureProfileFilePath))
{
#$profile = Select-AzureRmProfile -Path $AzureProfileFilePath
$profile = Import-AzureRmContext -Path $AzureProfileFilePath
$SubscriptionID = $profile.Context.Subscription.SubscriptionId
}
    else
    {
        Write-Host "File Not Found $AzureProfileFilePath" -ForegroundColor
Red


        # Provide your Azure Credentials in the login dialog box
        $profile = Login-AzureRmAccount
        $SubscriptionID =  $profile.Context.Subscription.SubscriptionId
    }

#Set the Azure Context
Set-AzureRmContext -SubscriptionId $SubscriptionID | Out-Null
```

The preceding code starts by logging into the **Manage-ElasticPool.txt** file, created under the **Log** directory within the parent directory of the **Manage-ElasticPool.ps1** script.

It then checks for the profile information in the JSON file provided by the **AzureProfileFilePath** variable. If found, it then sets the PowerShell context to the subscription ID, as specified in the profile file; otherwise, it asks to manually log in to the Azure account to set the context.

4. Copy and paste the following code to provision a new secondary SQL server, if one doesn't already exist:

```
IF($Operation -eq "Create")
{
# An error is returned and stored in notexists variable if resource group
exists
Get-AzureRmSqlServer -ServerName $SecondarySqlServer
-ResourceGroupName $ResourceGroup -ErrorVariable notexists
-ErrorAction SilentlyContinue
# provision the secondary server if it doesn't exists
if($notexists)
    {
      Write-Host "Provisioning Azure SQL Server $SecondarySqlServer"
-ForegroundColor Green
      $credentials = New-Object -TypeName System.Management.Automation.
PSCredential -ArgumentList $UserName, $(ConvertTo-SecureString -String
$Password -AsPlainText -Force)
      $_SecondarySqlServer = @{
        ResourceGroupName = $ResourceGroup;
        ServerName = $SecondarySqlServer;
        Location = $SecondaryServerLocation;
        SqlAdministratorCredentials = $credentials;
        ServerVersion = '12.0';
          }
          New-AzureRmSqlServer @_SecondarySqlServer;
    }


else
{
Write-Host $notexits -ForegroundColor Yellow
}
```

The preceding code is the same as what was explained in *Lesson 1, Microsoft Azure SQL Database Primer*, to provision a new SQL server. The new server is provisioned only when **$Operation** is set to **Create**.

5. Copy and paste the following code to create the failover group:

```
# Create the failover group
Write-Host "Creating the failover group $FailoverGroupName "
-ForegroundColor Green
$failovergroup = New-AzureRMSqlDatabaseFailoverGroup '
```

```
-ResourceGroupName $ResourceGroup '
-ServerName $PrimarySqlServer '
-PartnerServerName $SecondarySqlServer      '
-FailoverGroupName $FailoverGroupName '
-FailoverPolicy Automatic '
-GracePeriodWithDataLossHours 1
}
```

The preceding code creates a new failover group if the **$Operation** parameter is set to **Create**. The **New-AzureRMSqlDatabaseFailoverGroup** cmdlet accepts the following parameters:

**ResourceGroupName**: The name of the resource group that contains the primary SQL server

**ServerName**: The primary SQL server name

**PartnerServerName**: The secondary SQL server name

**FailoverGroupName**: The name of the failover group to be created

**FailoverPolicy**: The failover policy, **Automatic** or **Manual**

**GracePeriodWithDataLossHours**: The value for the duration the automatic failover should wait after a region outage, in hours

The failover group is created at the primary server location.

6. Copy and paste the following code to add the databases to the failover group:

```
# Add databases to the failover group
if(![string]::IsNullOrEmpty($DatabasesToReplicate.Replace(',','')) 
-and $Failover -eq $false -and $Operation -eq "Create")
{
$dbname = $DatabasesToReplicate.Split(','); foreach($db in $dbname)
{
Write-Host "Adding database $db to failover group
$FailoverGroupName " -ForegroundColor Green
$database = Get-AzureRmSqlDatabase -DatabaseName $db
-ResourceGroupName $ResourceGroup -ServerName $PrimarySqlServer
Add-AzureRmSqlDatabaseToFailoverGroup -ResourceGroupName
$ResourceGroup -ServerName $PrimarySqlServer -FailoverGroupName
$FailoverGroupName -Database $database
}


}
```

The preceding code splits the comma-delimited database names in the **$DatabasesToReplicate** parameter and adds them to the group.

The **Add-AzureRmSqlDatabaseToFailoverGroup** cmdlet adds the databases to the group and accepts the following parameter values:

**ResourceGroupName**: The name of the primary SQL Server resource group.

**ServerName**: The primary SQL server's name.

**FailoverGroupName**: The name of the failover group the databases are to be added to.

**Database**: The database object of the database to be added. This is set by calling the **Get-AzureRMSqlDatabase** cmdlet.

The databases are added to the failover group and replication sync is started.

7. Copy and paste the following code to manually fail over all the failover groups to the secondary server:

```
# failover to secondary if($Failover)
{
Write-Host "Failover to secondary server $SecondarySqlServer "
-ForegroundColor Green
Switch-AzureRMSqlDatabaseFailoverGroup -ResourceGroupName
$ResourceGroup -ServerName $SecondarySqlServer -FailoverGroupName
$FailoverGroupName
}
```

The **Switch-AzureRMSqlDatabaseFailoverGroup** cmdlet does the manual failover. It accepts the following parameters:

**ResourceGroupName**: The failover group that includes the SQL Server resource group name

**ServerName**: The primary SQL server name

**FailoverGroupName**: The failover group name

8. Copy and paste the following code to remove the failover group and stop active geo-replication between the primary and secondary servers:

```
if($Operation -eq "Remove")
{
Write-Host "Deleting the failover group $FailoverGroupName "
-ForegroundColor Green
Remove-AzureRmSqlDatabaseFailoverGroup -ResourceGroupName
```

```
$ResourceGroup -ServerName $PrimarySqlServer -FailoverGroupName
$FailoverGroupName

# remove the replication link
$dbname = $DatabasesToReplicate.Split(','); foreach($db in $dbname)
{
Write-Host "Removing replication for database $db "
-ForegroundColor Green
$database = Get-AzureRmSqlDatabase -DatabaseName $db
-ResourceGroupName $ResourceGroup -ServerName $PrimarySqlServer
$database | Remove-AzureRmSqlDatabaseSecondary
-PartnerResourceGroupName $ResourceGroup -ServerName
$PrimarySqlServer -PartnerServerName $SecondarySqlServer
}
}
```

The preceding code is executed when the **$Operation** parameter is set to **Remove**. Now, **Remove-AzureRmSqlDatabaseFailoverGroup** deletes the failover group. It accepts the following parameters:

**ResourceGroupName**: The failover group resource group name

**ServerName**: The primary SQL server name

**FailoverGroupName**: The name of the failover group that is to be deleted

Removing the failover group doesn't stop replication sync.

The databases are still being replicated and are not part of a failover group. The databases can still fail to the secondary server individually, as shown in the previous activity.

**Remove-AzureRmSqlDatabaseSecondary** removes or stops the replication, as explained in the previous activity.

This completes the script. Press *Ctrl* + *S* to save the script.

## Executing the PowerShell script

1. Press *Window* + *R* to open the **Run** command window. Type **PowerShell** and hit *Enter* to open a new PowerShell console window.

2. Change the directory to the folder that has the **Manage- ActiveGeoReplication.ps1** script in it. For example, if the script is in the **C:\Code\Lesson08\** directory, run the following command to switch to that directory:

```
cd C:\Code\Lesson08
```

3. In the PowerShell console window, execute the following command to create a new failover group and add databases to it:

```
.\Manage-FailoverGroup.ps1 -ResourceGroup toystore
-PrimarySqlServer toyfactory -UserName sqladmin -Password Packt@pub2
-SecondarySqlServer toyfactory-centralus
-SecondaryServerLocation "Central US" -DatabasesToReplicate
"toystore_Shard_100_150,toystore_Shard_150_200" -Operation "Create"
-FailoverGroupName toyfactoryfailovergroup
-AzureProfileFilePath c:\Code\MyAzureProfile.json
```

The preceding command will create a new failover group, **toyfactoryfailovergroup**, and add the **toystore_Shard_100_150** and **toystore_150_200** databases to the newly created failover group.

The failover group name is the new endpoint to be used by the application to connect to the failover group. In other words, the application connects to **toyfactoryfailovergroup.database.windows.net** and not individual primary or secondary database endpoints.

This is similar to the AG listener in an Always ON configuration.

The Azure SQL server the failover group points to is transparent to the user. In case of a failover, the failover group endpoint points to the new primary. Therefore, unlike active geo-replication, you don't need to manage the database connection string (endpoint) within the application when the failover occurs.

4. In the PowerShell console window, execute the following code to perform the manual failover:

```
.\Manage-FailoverGroup.ps1 -ResourceGroup toystore
-SecondarySqlServer toyfactory-centralus -FailoverGroupName
toyfactoryfailovergroup -Failover $true -AzureProfileFilePath c:\ Code\
MyAzureProfile.json
```

The preceding command will fail over all the databases in the **toyfactoryfailovergroup** failover group to the secondary server and make it the new primary server.

You can verify this from the Azure portal.

5. Copy and paste the following command to remove the failover group and stop the replication between the primary and secondary servers:

```
# delete failover group and stop the replication
.\Manage-FailoverGroup.ps1 -ResourceGroup toystore
-PrimarySqlServer toyfactory-centralus -UserName sqladmin -Password Packt@
```

```
pub2 -SecondarySqlServer toyfactory -SecondaryServerLocation "Central US"
-DatabasesToReplicate "toystore_Shard_100_150,toystore_Shard_150_200"
-Operation "Remove" -FailoverGroupName toyfactoryfailovergroup
-AzureProfileFilePath c:\Code\MyAzureProfile.json
```

The preceding command will remove the **toyfactoryfailovergroup** failover group and break the replication link between the primary and secondary databases. However, the secondary server and the databases won't be deleted.

Notice that the **PrimarySqlServer** parameter value is **toyfactory-centralus** and that the **SecondarySqlServer** parameter value is **toyfactory**, which is the reverse of what we provided in step 1 when creating the failover group. This is because, when we did a manual failover, the primary and secondary server roles were reversed. As mentioned earlier, the failover group is maintained by the primary database, so, to delete the failover group, the primary is now the secondary and the secondary is the new primary.

## Activity: Evaluating Accelerated Database Recovery

In this activity, we'll evaluate the ADR performance of a transaction rollback.

ADR is enabled by default in an Azure SQL database. Therefore, it's advised to perform this activity on SQL Server 2019 Developer Edition.

> **Note**
>
> If you would like to perform the activity on Azure SQL Database, write an email to adr@microsoft.com to disable ADR on Azure SQL Server.

The **toystore_ADR** database used in the activity is similar to **toystore**, but with ADR off.

Perform the following steps to complete the activity:

1.  Connect to a database with SSMS and execute the following query to verify that ADR is off:

```
SELECT
    [Name],
    is_accelerated_database_recovery_on
FROM sys.databases
WHERE [Name]='toystore'
```

You should get an output similar to the following:

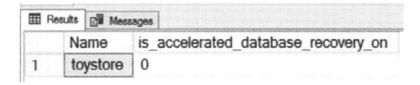

Figure 8.30: The result of the query denoting that ADR is turned off

> **Note**
>
> The database name may differ in your case.

The value **0** for **is_accelerated_database_recovery_on** confirms that ADR is turned off.

2.  Execute the following query to simulate a long-running transaction:

```
CREATE TABLE Orders
(
    OrderId INT IDENTITY,
    Quantity INT,
    Amount MONEY,
    OrderDate DATETIME2
)
GO
BEGIN TRANSACTION
DECLARE @i INT=1

WHILE (@i <= 10000000)
BEGIN
    INSERT INTO Orders VALUES(@i*2,@i*0.5,DATEADD(MINUTE,@i,getdate()))
    Set @i = @i + 1
END
```

The query creates an **Orders** table and inserts sample records into the **Orders** table in an explicit transaction. Observe that **BEGIN TRANSACTION** has no corresponding rollback or commit transaction.

Note the session ID of the query. The session ID of the query is in the bottom-right corner of the query window:

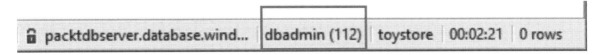

Figure 8.31: The session ID of the query

Let the query run for around five minutes or so.

3.  While the query is running, open a new query window and execute the following query to start the query rollback:

```
KILL 112
GO
KILL 112 with statusonly
GO
SELECT session_id,status from sys.dm_exec_requests where session_id=112
```

**Note**

The session ID will be different in your case.

In the **Results** tab, observe that the query status is **rollback**.

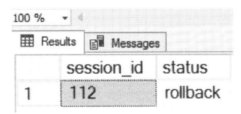

Figure 8.32: The Results tab denoting that the query status is set as rollback

In the **Messages** tab, observe that the estimated time remaining to roll back the transaction is **32 seconds**:

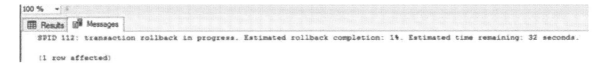

Figure 8.33: The Messages tab denoting the estimated time of the query

> **Note**
>
> The estimated time remaining may be different in your case.

Let's perform the preceding steps against a database with ADR turned on and measure the time taken for transaction rollback.

4. Open a new query window and connect to the **toystore_ADR** database:

> **Note**
>
> If you are performing the activity on SQL Server 2019, you can run the following command to enable ADR on an existing database.

```
ALTER DATABASE Toystore_ADR SET ACCELERATED_DATABASE_RECOVERY = ON;
```

5. Execute the following query to verify whether ADR is turned on or not:

```
SELECT
    [Name],
    is_accelerated_database_recovery_on
FROM sys.databases
WHERE [Name]='toystore_ADR'
```

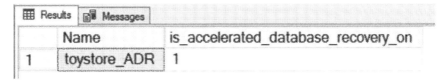

Figure 8.34: The result of the query denoting that ADR is turned on

The **is_accelerated_database_recovery_on** bit is **1**, which implies that ADR is turned on.

6.  Execute the following query to simulate a long-running transaction:

```
CREATE TABLE Orders
(
    OrderId INT IDENTITY,
    Quantity INT,
    Amount MONEY,
    OrderDate DATETIME2
)
GO
BEGIN TRANSACTION
DECLARE @i INT=1

WHILE (@i <= 10000000)
BEGIN
    INSERT INTO Orders VALUES(@i*2,@i*0.5,DATEADD(MINUTE,@i,getdate()))
    Set @i = @i + 1
END
```

The query creates an **Orders** table and inserts sample records into the **Orders** table in an explicit transaction. Observe that **BEGIN TRANSACTION** has no corresponding rollback or commit transaction.

Note the session ID of the query. The session ID of the query is in the bottom-right corner of the query window:

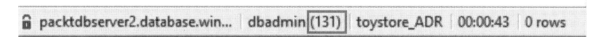

Figure 8.35: The session ID of the query is 131

The query session ID or the SPID is **131**.

Let the query run for around five minutes.

7.  While the query is running, open a new query window and execute the following query to start the query rollback:

```
KILL 131
GO
KILL 131 with statusonly
GO
SELECT session_id,status from sys.dm_exec_requests where session_id=131
```

In the **Results** tab, notice that the query status is **rollback**:

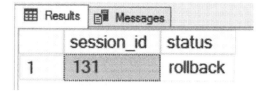

Figure 8.36: The Results tab denoting that the query status is set as rollback

In the **Messages** tab, notice that the estimated time remaining to roll back the transaction is **0 seconds**:

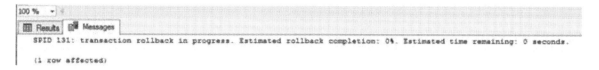

Figure 8.37: The Messages tab denoting the estimated time of the query (0 seconds)

ADR provides an instant **rollback**, compared to non-ADR, where the estimated time remaining to roll back was 30 seconds.

## Summary

In this lesson, you learned about high availability and DR features in Azure SQL Database. High availability is built into Azure SQL Database and is managed by Microsoft, whereas DR can be achieved by configuring active geo-replication as and when required. You also learned about ADR, a new feature introduced with Azure SQL Database and SQL Server 2019, which provides instant database recovery, transaction rollbacks, and aggressive log truncation. Furthermore, you saw how zone-redundant configuration provides additional high availability by having a copy of the database in multiple availability zones within the same region. In the next lesson, you will learn how to monitor an Azure SQL database using the Azure portal, dynamic management views, and extended events to help improve the performance of the application.

# Monitoring and Tuning Azure SQL Database

**Learning Objectives**

By the end of this lesson, you will be able to:

- Monitor and tune an Azure SQL database from the Azure portal

- Monitor an Azure SQL database using Dynamic Management Views

- Monitor an Azure SQL database using extended events

- Implement in-memory technologies to improve database performance

- Monitor an Azure SQL database using Azure SQL Analytics

This lesson teaches you different techniques to monitor and tune an Azure SQL database.

# Introduction

This lesson teaches you different techniques to monitor and tune an Azure SQL database. You will learn to monitor an Azure SQL database using the Azure portal, **Dynamic Management Views** (**DMVs**), and extended events. You will also learn how to tune an Azure SQL database using automatic tuning and Query Performance Insight. You will learn how to implement in-memory features to improve workload performance.

## Monitoring an Azure SQL Database Using the Azure Portal

The Azure portal provides multiple monitoring options, which are available in the **Monitoring** and **Intelligent Performance** sections of an Azure SQL database on the Azure portal.

The **Monitoring** section for an Azure SQL database on the Azure portal has the following options:

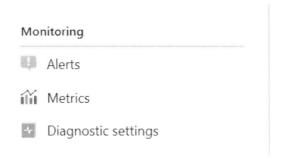

**Figure 9.1: The Monitoring section for an Azure SQL database**

The **Intelligent Performance** section for an Azure SQL database on the Azure portal has the following options:

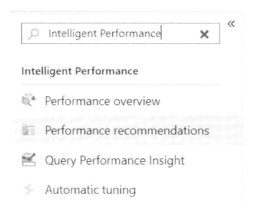

**Figure 9.2: Intelligent Performance section options**

Let's look at each of these options in detail.

## Monitoring Database Metrics

Database metrics such as CPU percentage, DTU percentage, and data I/O can be monitored in the overview section.

The overview section displays the **DTU percentage** for the past hour, the last 24 hours, or the last 7 days, in the form of a line chart:

Figure 9.3: The Overview section indicating the DTU percentage

You can even pin the chart to your Azure portal dashboard by clicking on the pin icon in the upper-right corner of the chart.

This way, you can monitor the DTU percentage as and when required.

> **Note**
>
> In order to see the graph working, a workload needs to be running. You can achieve this by executing the **Start-Workload.sql** file placed in the **C:\Code\ Lesson09** folder.

Open a new PowerShell command and run the following command:

```
.\Start-Workload.ps1 -sqlserver toyfactory -database toystore -sqluser
sqladmin -sqlpassword Packt@pub2 -workloadsql .\workload.sql
```

The preceding command will use the **ostress.exe** RML utility to execute the queries specified in the **workload.sql** file against the **toystore** database in the **toyfactory** Azure SQL Server.

For a more detailed analysis and to monitor other metrics, click the line chart:

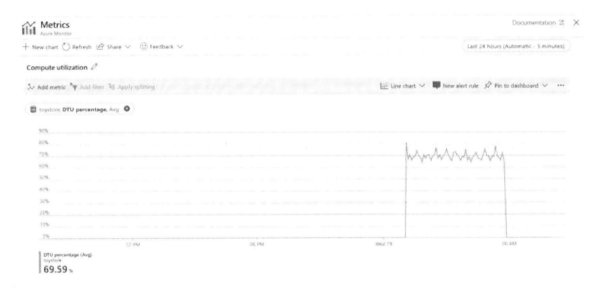

Figure 9.4: The Metrics blade showing the workload

The **Metrics** blade gives you further insight into the workload by allowing you to monitor other metrics, such as CPU percentage, data I/O percentage, and database size percentage. Hover the mouse over the line chart, and the metrics at that point in time will be displayed at the bottom.

The Metrics blade also allows you to view metrics in multiple ranges, such as the past hour, the past 24 hours, the past week, and even a custom time range.

Select the metrics you want to monitor together, name the chart, and pin it to the Azure portal dashboard for future monitoring.

> **Note**
>
> To name the chart, select the pen icon next to **Compute utilization**. The default chart name is Compute utilization.

You can select one or more metrics and analyze the type of workload. For example, in the preceding chart, the workload is CPU-intensive because the DTU percentage is equal to the CPU percentage, and because a data I/O percentage hasn't been recorded during the time period.

You can add an alert for proactive monitoring of a particular metric. For example, you can add an alert to send email notifications whenever the DTU percentage crosses a threshold, such as 80%, or if the database size gets bigger than 80%. In the next section, we'll talk about setting up alert rules.

You can even take preventative action automatically by using runbooks, similar to what was explained in *Lesson 6, Scaling Out an Azure SQL Database*.

## Alert Rules, Database Size, and Diagnostic Settings

In this section, we will discuss how to create alerts using the Azure portal, view the database size, and capture data using diagnostic settings.

**Alert Rules**

As stated earlier, you can create email alerts on metrics you wish to monitor.

To create an alert using the Azure portal, on the database **Overview** blade, select **Alerts** in the **Monitoring** section.

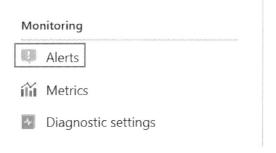

**Figure 9.5: The Monitoring section**

On the **Alerts** page, select **New alert rule** and fill out the alert details to create and set up the alert:

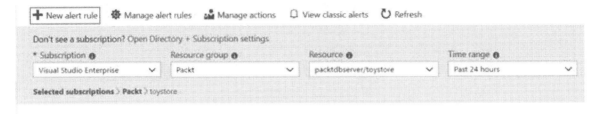

Figure 9.6: Monitoring alerts

On the **Create rule** page, you'll have to specify the alert **Condition** (when it is to be triggered) and the alert **Action** (what is to be done when the alert is triggered):

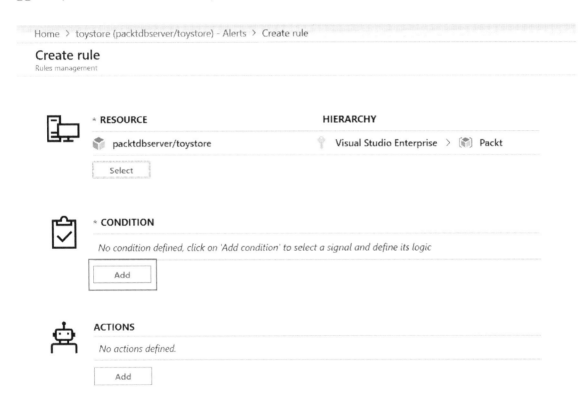

Figure 9.7: The Create rule page

To add a condition, click the **Add** button under the **CONDITION** heading.

On the **Configure signal logic** page, select **CPU Percentage** as the alert condition:

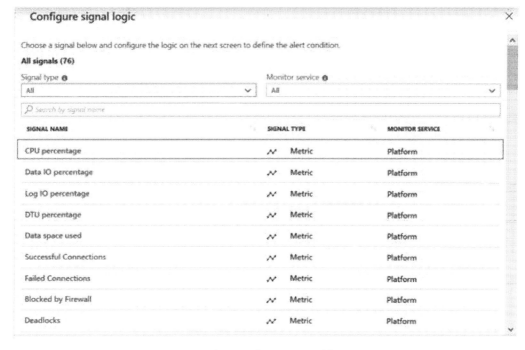

Figure 9.8: The Configure signal logic page

The new page displays a line chart for the last hour for the selected signal, **CPU percentage**. Scroll to the bottom and locate the **Alert logic** section.

The **Alert logic** section defines the threshold. There are two types of threshold, **Static** and **Dynamic**:

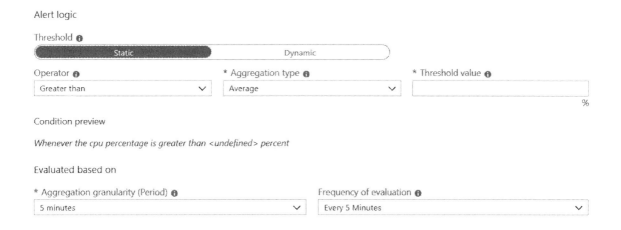

Figure 9.9: The Alert logic section (Static threshold)

A **Static** threshold defines a threshold value, say, 70%. Therefore, whenever, the average (as defined by the **Aggregation type**) CPU percentage is greater than (as defined by the **Operator**) 70%, the alert is triggered.

A **Dynamic** threshold uses advanced machine learning to automatically find out the threshold value using the metric's historical values:

Figure 9.10: The Alert logic section (Dynamic threshold)

The **Dynamic** threshold doesn't have a static threshold value. The **Threshold Sensitivity** defines the amount of deviation of the metric from the threshold to trigger an alert.

A high **Threshold Sensitivity** triggers an alert if there's the slightest deviation from the metric series pattern. A medium **Threshold Sensitivity** is less stringent and more balanced than a high threshold. A low **Threshold Sensitivity** triggers an alert when there's a large deviation from the metric series pattern. There are no defined values for deviation with high, medium, or low threshold sensitivities.

The **Dynamic** setting also allows us to configure the number of violations required during a certain time period to trigger an alert. This setting is found in the **Advanced** settings. The default is at least 4 violations in the last 20 minutes. This means that if, in the past 20 minutes, the CPU utilization has gone above the threshold of, say, 70% four times, then an alert is triggered.

The **Dynamic** threshold can also ignore data before a given time. When this is specified, the **Dynamic** threshold calculation is done after the date specified in the **Ignore data before** setting.

The **Dynamic** threshold setting helps us to configure alerts for different metrics when there are no defined alert threshold values.

Click **Done** to save the settings and return to the **Create rule** page.

On the **Create rule** page, we can see that the CPU percentage alert condition has been added.

The **ACTIONS** section defines the action or the steps to be performed when an alert is triggered. The action could be an email to the concerned person, or automated steps defined by webhooks, runbooks, or functions.

Scroll down to **ALERT DETAILS** and provide an **Alert rule name**, **Description** (optional), and **Severity**:

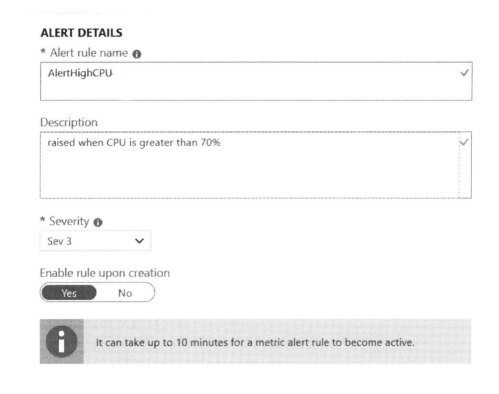

Figure 9.11: Actions section (ALERT DETAILS)

Click **Create alert rule** to create the alert.

You can also add a webhook to the alert to take preventative action automatically when the alert threshold is reached. For example, let's say you create an alert that sends out an email whenever the database size crosses the 80% threshold.

The administrator sees the email alert and increases the database size so that the customers aren't affected. However, you can automate this in the following ways:

- By creating an Azure Automation job that runs a PowerShell script to increase the database's size

- By creating a webhook for the Azure Automation job

- By specifying the webhook in the alert definition

The next time the database size percentage is greater than 80%, the alert will send out an email notification to the administrator and will trigger the webhook. This will start the Azure Automation job, and the database size will be increased.

## Database Data Storage

The **Database data storage** option in the database overview section provides a chart of the used, allocated, and maximum storage size:

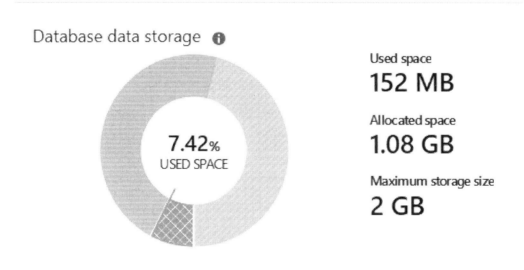

Figure 9.12: Chart of database storage

## Diagnostic Settings

**Diagnostic settings** allow you to collect data such as database wait statistics, timeouts, errors, and database blocks to troubleshoot performance issues or audit an Azure SQL database.

The following data can be captured using diagnostic settings:

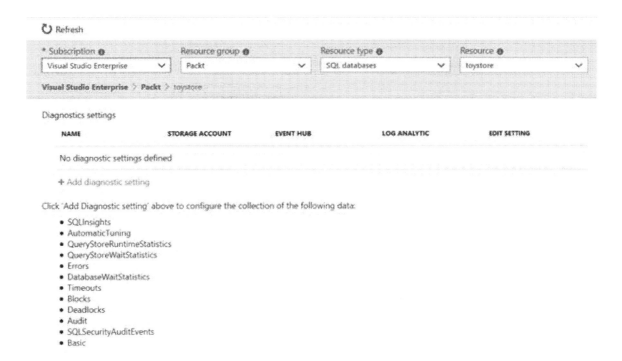

Figure 9.13: Data captured using diagnostic settings

To enable diagnostic settings, on the **toystore** database page, search for **diagnostic**, and click to open the **Diagnostic settings** page:

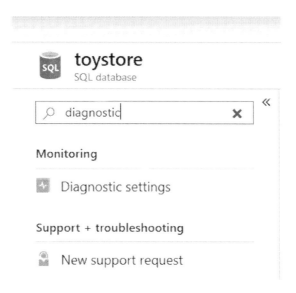

Figure 9.14: Diagnostic settings

On the **Diagnostics settings** blade, follow these steps:

1. Click **Add diagnostic setting** to add a new diagnostic setting.

2. Provide a name for this setting. For example, if you plan to collect wait stats, you can name it **toystore wait stats**.

3. Select **Archive** to a storage account and then select the storage account where the diagnostic data will be saved.

   You can also stream the data to an event hub for real-time monitoring or send it to Log Analytics.

4. Check **DatabaseWaitStatistics** and set the **Retention** to one day. The retention only applies to the **Archive to a storage account** option.

The **Archive to a storage account** option lets you save the diagnostic data to an Azure Storage container. The log files can therefore be used for troubleshooting as and when required:

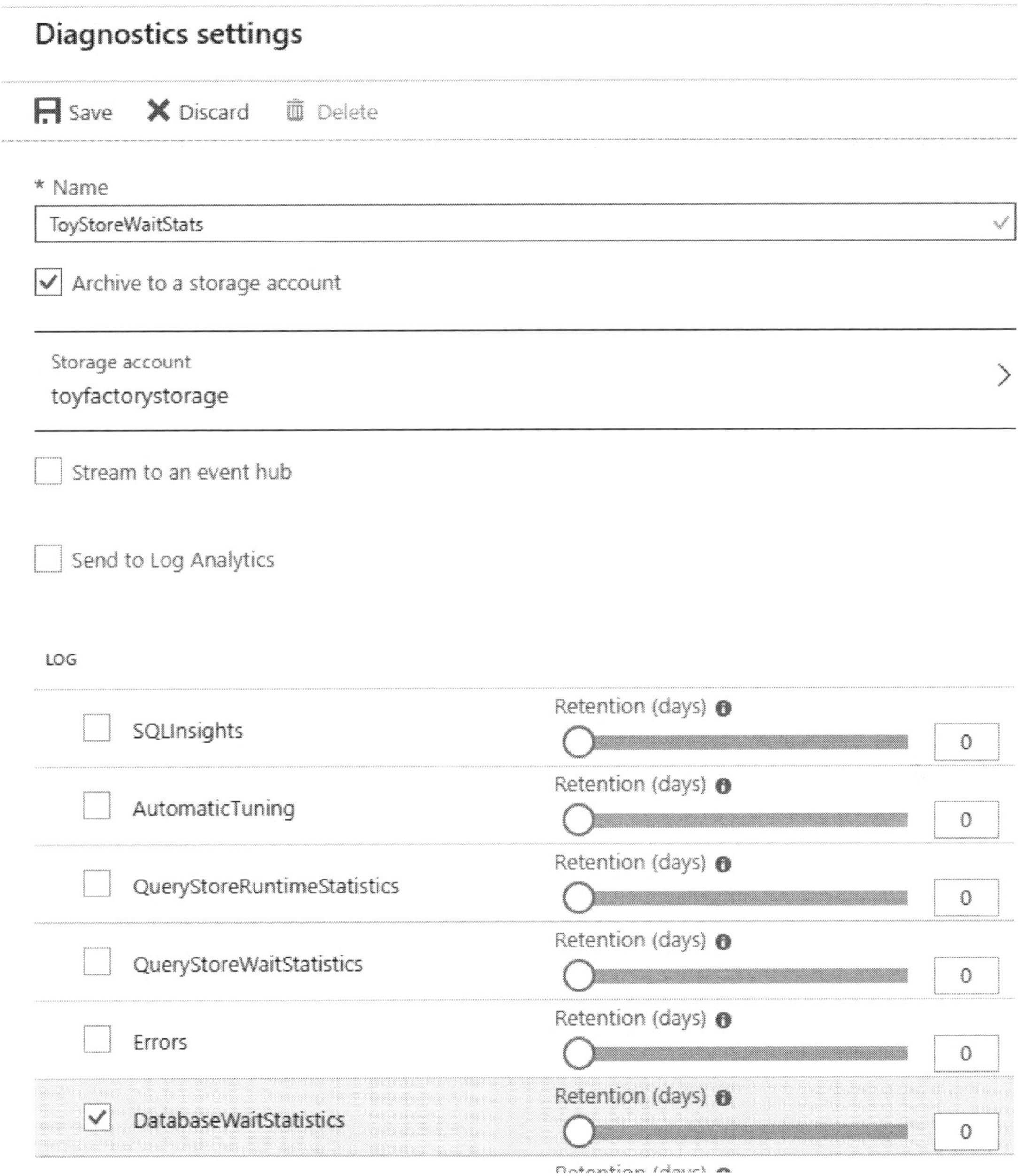

## Diagnostics settings

🖫 Save    ✕ Discard    🗑 Delete

\* Name

ToyStoreWaitStats    ✓

☑ Archive to a storage account

Storage account
**toyfactorystorage**    〉

☐ Stream to an event hub

☐ Send to Log Analytics

LOG

| | Retention (days) ❶ | |
|---|---|---|
| ☐ SQLInsights | ◯▬▬▬▬▬ | 0 |
| ☐ AutomaticTuning | ◯▬▬▬▬▬ | 0 |
| ☐ QueryStoreRuntimeStatistics | ◯▬▬▬▬▬ | 0 |
| ☐ QueryStoreWaitStatistics | ◯▬▬▬▬▬ | 0 |
| ☐ Errors | ◯▬▬▬▬▬ | 0 |
| ☑ DatabaseWaitStatistics | ◯▬▬▬▬▬ | 0 |

Retention (days) ❶

Figure 9.15: The Diagnostics settings blade

5. Click **Save** to start collecting data.

   The logs will be captured and archived to the given storage account:

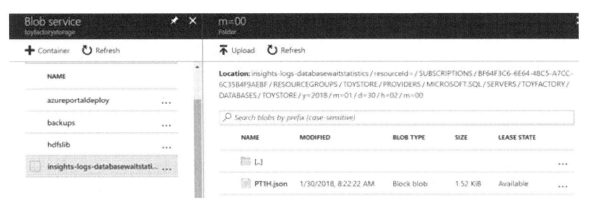

Figure 9.16: Logs captured to the storage account

The logs are saved in JSON format as shown in the following code:

```
{
"records": [

{
"LogicalServerName": "toyfactory", "SubscriptionId": "bf64f3c6-6e64-48c5-
a7cc-
6c35b4f9aebf",
"ResourceGroup": "toystore",
"time": "2018-01-30T02:42:27.2000000Z", "resourceId": "/SUBSCRIPTIONS/
BF64F3C6-6E64-48C5-
A7CC-6C35B4F9AEBF/RESOURCEGROUPS/TOYSTORE/PROVIDERS/MICROSOFT.SQL/
SERVERS/TOYFACTORY/DATABASES/TOYSTORE",
"category": "DatabaseWaitStatistics", "operationName":
"DatabaseWaitStatistcsEvent", "properties":
{"ElasticPoolName":"","DatabaseName":"t
oystore","start_utc_date":"2018-01-30T02:42:27.2000000Z","end_utc_
date":"2018-01-30T02:47:27.1530000Z","wait_type":"SOS_SCHEDULER_
YIELD","delta_max_wait_time_ms":0,"delta_signal_wait_time_
ms":3267,"delta_wait_time_ms":3266,"delta_waiting_tasks_count":51}
...
...
]
}
```

You can analyze the JSON in your favorite JSON editor, or in SQL Server 2016.

6. To delete the diagnostics setting, navigate to the diagnostics settings blade and click **Edit setting** next to the diagnostics setting you wish to delete:

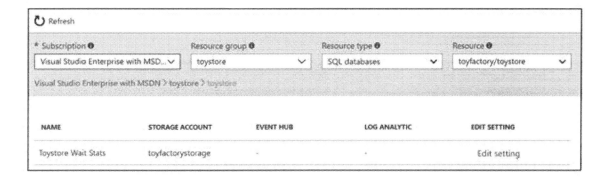

Figure 9.17: Editing a diagnostic setting

On the resulting blade, select **Delete** to delete the setting:

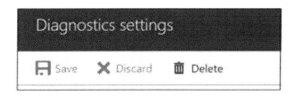

Figure 9.18: Deleting a diagnostic setting

## Query Performance Insight

Query Performance Insight works on top of the Query Store and requires that Query Store is enabled on the Azure SQL database.

Query Store, introduced in SQL Server 2016, records queries, plans, and runtime statistics for detailed query performance analysis.

In an on-premises SQL Server, Query Store provides a graphical interface, which lists queries by the time window. This helps with analyzing database usage patterns and query plan changes.

It provides an easy way to identify and force the best query plan out of multiple query plans for the same query.

> **Note**
>
> To read more about Query Store for on-premises SQL servers, visit https://docs.microsoft.com/en-us/sql/relational-databases/performance/monitoring-performance-by-using-the-query-store.

Query Performance Insights analyzes the data collected in the Query Store and does the following:

- Shows the percentage usage of CPU, data I/O, and log I/O database metrics, which constitute DTUs.

- Lists the top queries by CPU, data I/O, log I/O, duration, and execution count. It also provides further details on individual queries such as execution count, duration, CPU, data I/O, and log I/O percentage utilization.

- Lists performance recommendations for creating an index, dropping an index, fixing schema issues, and parameterized queries.

> **Note**
>
> Fix Schema Issue will be deprecated in the future. Use Intelligent Insights instead of Azure SQL Analytics.

Azure SQL Analytics (which is in preview at the time of writing this book) is a cloud monitoring solution that can be used to monitor one or more Azure SQL databases, managed instances, and elastic pools.

Azure SQL Analytics analyses diagnostic data that was logged by enabling the diagnostic settings (as discussed previously in the *Diagnostic settings* section) to provide insights such as blocks, resource limits, deadlocks, wait stats, and timeouts. Moreover, custom monitoring rules and alerts can also be set up to enhance existing monitoring capabilities.

Azure SQL Analytics uses the diagnostic logs for Azure SQL Database. Therefore, the first step is to enable diagnostic logs to send the logs to the Log Analytics workspace.

The Log Analytics workspace acts as a container for the Azure SQL Database diagnostic logs. The Log Analytics workspace is the input for Azure SQL Analytics.

To create a Log Analytics workspace, follow these steps:

1. In the Azure portal search box, type `Log Analytics Workspace` and select **Log Analytics workspaces** from the search result:

Figure 9.19: Searching on the Azure portal for Log Analytics

2. On the **Log Analytic workspaces** page, click **Add** to create a new Log Analytics workspace:

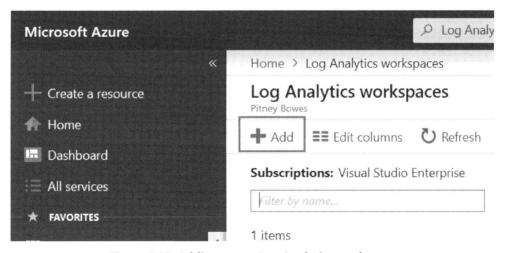

Figure 9.20: Adding a new Log Analytics workspace

3. On the **Log Analytics workspace** page, provide the values shown in the following screenshot:

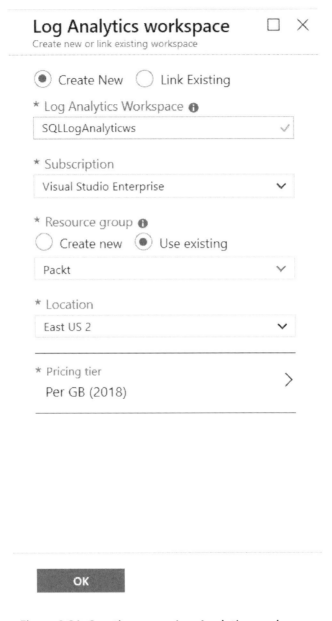

Figure 9.21: Creating a new Log Analytics workspace

> **Note**
>
> Choose a different name for your Log Analytics workspace.

4. Click **OK** to create the new Log Analytic workspace.

5. The next step is to send the diagnostic data to the Log Analytics workspace created in the previous steps. To do that, navigate to the **toystore** database page.

   In the search box, type `diagnostic`:

   > **Note**
   >
   > You can do it for all of the shards created in *Lesson 6, Scaling Out an Azure SQL Database.*

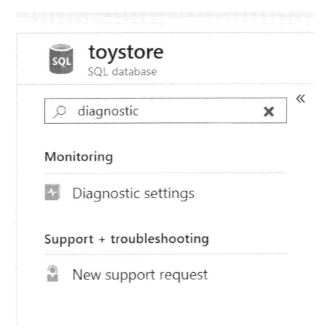

Figure 9.22: Diagnostic settings

6.  Select **Diagnostic settings** to open the **Diagnostic settings** page.

    If you already have a diagnostic setting, then click **Edit setting**; otherwise, select **Add diagnostic setting** to create a new one.

    As we already have an existing diagnostic setting from the previous exercise, we'll edit the existing one:

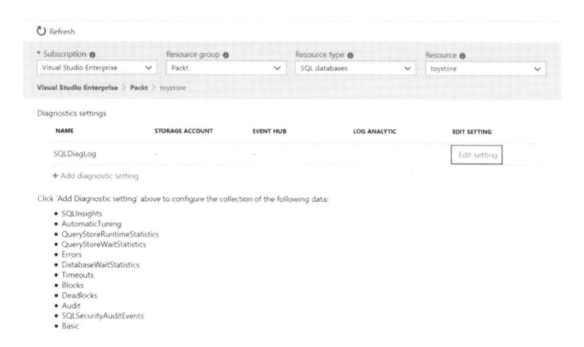

Figure 9.23: Editing an existing diagnostic setting

7.  On the **Diagnostic settings** page, check the **Send to Log Analytics** checkbox and then select the Log Analytics workspace created in the last step.

    Under the **Log** section, select all the values.

Click **Save** to save the settings:

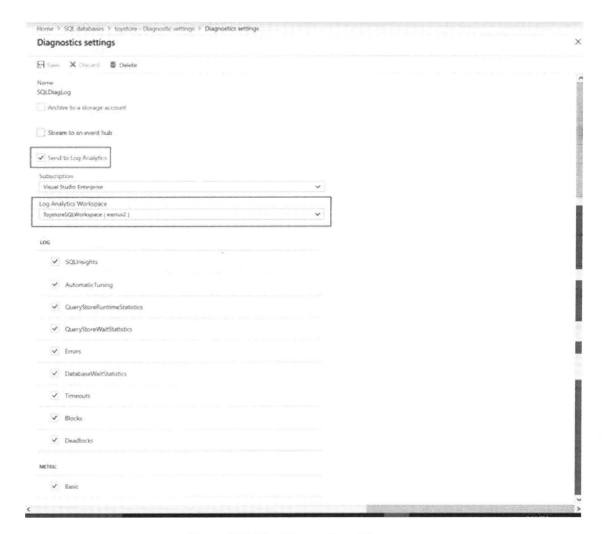

Figure 9.24: The Diagnostic settings page

We now have a Log Analytics workspace that's connected to the toystore diagnostic settings log. Do this for all the existing toystore shards.

The next step is to create an **Azure SQL Analytics** solution. Type `Azure SQL Analytic` in the search box and select **Azure SQL Analytics** from the search result:

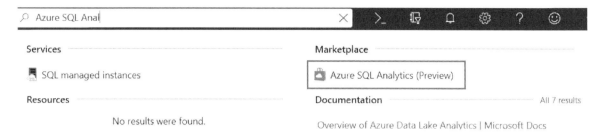

Figure 9.25: Azure SQL Analytics in the Marketplace

On the **Azure SQL Analytics** page, select the **Log Analytics workspace** created in the previous step, and click **Create** to create the Azure SQL Analytics solution:

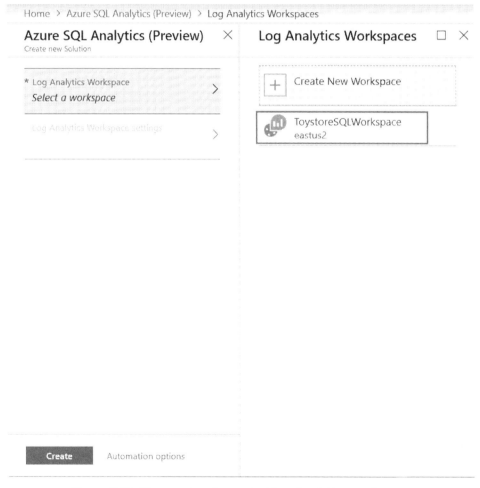

Figure 9.26: The previously created Log Analytics workspace

Once the Azure SQL Analytics solution is provisioned, it'll be available under **All resources** in the Azure portal, as shown here:

Figure 9.27: The All resources page in the Azure portal

As we don't have any workload or activity on the databases, we won't be able to see any analytics as such. Let's generate some activity and then review the insights from the Azure SQL Analytics solution.

To generate a workload, execute each of the following PowerShell scripts in its own PowerShell console window. There should be five different PowerShell console windows, one for each of the scripts.

> **Note**
>
> The PowerShell scripts are in the `~\IntelligentInsights\Lesson09` folder in the code bundle.

The `Blocking1.ps1`, `Blocking2.ps1`, and `Blocking3.ps1` scripts simulate a blocking scenario:

```
.\Blocking1.ps1 -server packtdbserver.database.windows.net -database
toystore -user dbadmin -password Awesome@1234
```

```
.\Blocking2.ps1 -server packtdbserver.database.windows.net -database
toystore -user dbadmin -password Awesome@1234
```

```
.\Blocking3.ps1 -server packtdbserver.database.windows.net -database
toystore -user dbadmin -password Awesome@1234
```

The `HighIO_Timeouts.ps1` script simulates a timeout scenario:

```
.\HighIO_Timeouts.ps1 -server packtdbserver.database.windows.net -database
toystore -user dbadmin -password Awesome@1234
```

The **HighIO1.ps1** script simulates a high log I/O scenario:

```
.\HighIO1.ps1 -server packtdbserver.database.windows.net -database toystore
-user dbadmin -password Awesome@1234
```

You will have to change the **server**, **database**, **user**, and **password** parameter values before you run the scripts.

Let the scripts run for an hour or so, and the analytics should show in another hour two. We can view the analytics by following these steps:

1.  To view the analytics, navigate to the **All resources** page on the Azure portal and locate and open the Azure SQL Analytics solution created in the previous section. If you are unable to locate this, go to **General**, and then **Workspace Summary**. In the **Azure SQL Analytics (Preview)** tile, click **View Summary**:

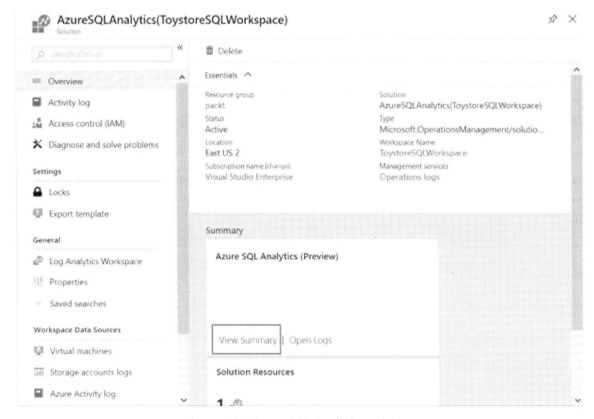

Figure 9.28: Azure SQL Analytics solution

2. The summary shows two Azure SQL databases for which Azure SQL Analytics was enabled. You can, however, monitor managed instances, managed instance databases, and elastic pools through one single monitoring interface:

Figure 9.29: Azure SQL Analytics – Summary

Click **Azure SQL Databases**. There's a lot of information being displayed. Let's look at the graphs one by one:

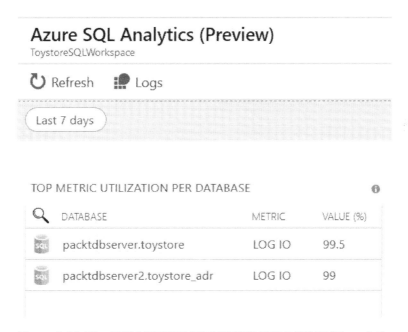

Figure 9.30: The TOP METRIC UTILIZATION PER DATABASE analytic

The **TOP METRIC UTILIZATION PER DATABASE** analytic displays the top basic metrics (CPU/I/O/memory) for each monitored database.

The top metric is **LOG IO**. This is because of the workload we ran in the previous step.

You can browse the Azure SQL Analytics for things such as blocks, wait statistics, and resource limits. However, let's see how Intelligent Insights helps to sum up the issues for a database.

3.  Click on the **packtdbserver.toystore** database in the preceding screenshot to open the insights for the database:

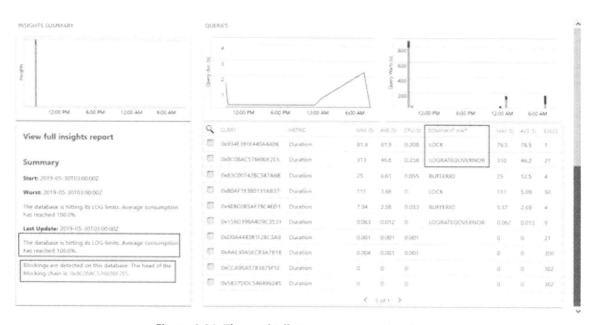

Figure 9.31: The packtdbserver.toystore database

We can see the two problems that we simulated with the workload we ran previously.

The **Insights** summary highlights the following:

- The database is hitting its LOG limits, and the average log consumption has reached 100%.

- The blocking provides the query hash for the head blocker. Clicking on the lead blocker query hash will give you the lead blocker query.

   Moreover, to get into details of the blocks, click on the blocking graph on the Azure SQL Analytics overview page.

The right side of the **Insights** page displays the top queries by duration. To get the details of a query, click the query row. For example, to find out the query text for the longest running query, sort the query by maximum duration (MAX (S)) and click on the top row:

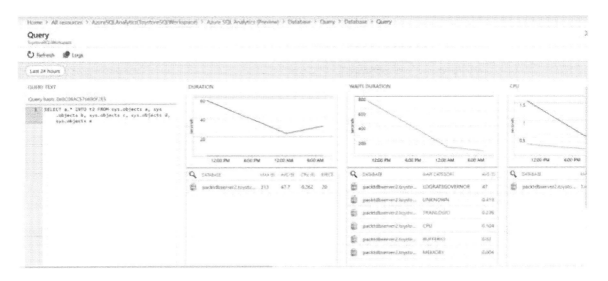

Figure 9.32: The Query page

Along with the query text, duration, waits duration, CPU, data I/O, log I/O, CPU, and a number of executions by time are also displayed.

> **Note**
>
> The preceding screenshot skips the rest of the metrics for the sake of brevity.

## Creating Alerts

Enabling diagnostic settings to send logs to the Log Analytics workspace allows us to create alerts for incidents such as blocking, resource limits, and deadlocks:

1. To create alerts, from the Azure portal, select the Log Analytics workspace created earlier:

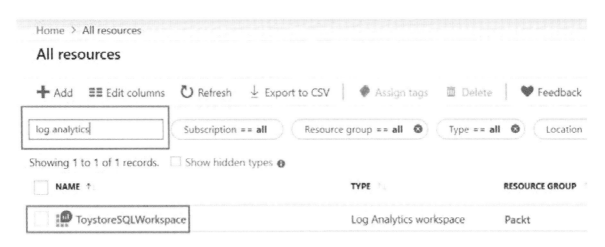

Figure 9.33: The previously created Log Analytics workspace

2. Click on the Log Analytics workspace, **ToystoreSQLWorkspace** (the name may be different in your case).

3. On the **Log Analytics workspace** page, search for **Alert** and click to open the **Alerts** page:

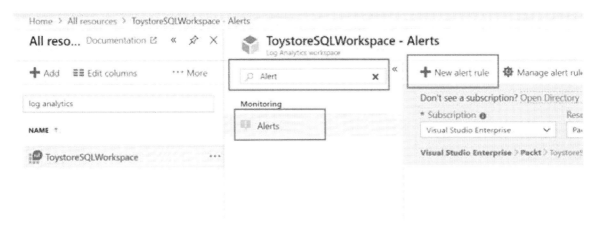

Figure 9.34: The Log Analytics workspace page

4.  Click **New alert rule** to define a new alert:

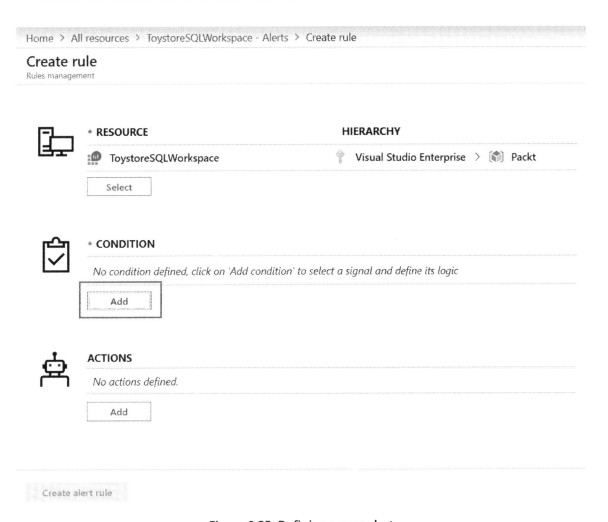

Figure 9.35: Defining a new alert

The **Create rule** page is where we define the alert condition and the action to be taken (if any) when the alert is raised:

1. Click the **Add** button under the **CONDITION** heading to define the alert condition.

2. On the **Configure signal logic** page, click on **Custom log search**. Signals are pre-saved queries that can be used to set up alerts. However, as we are defining a custom alert, we'll choose **Custom log search**:

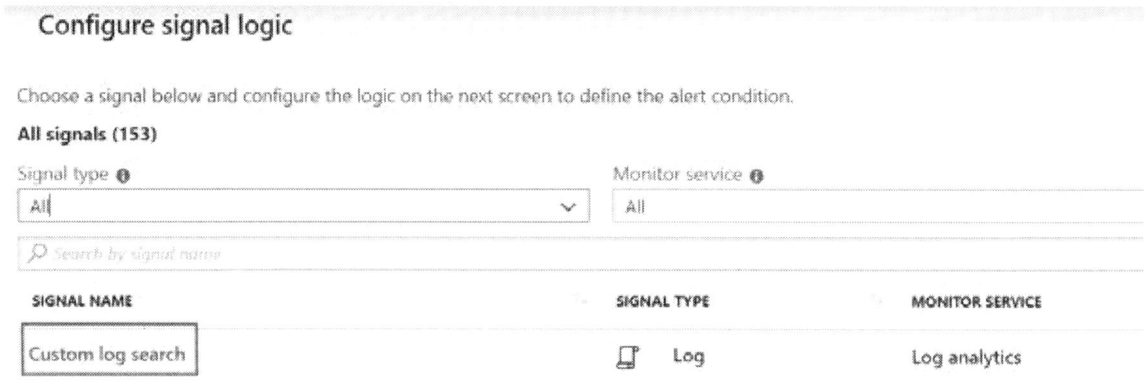

Figure 9.36: The Configure signal logic page

3. Custom log search sets up the alert on a user-defined log query. On the **Custom log search** page, copy and paste the following query in the **Search query** text box:

```
let time_range = 1h;
let block_threshold = 1;
AzureDiagnostics
| where ResourceProvider=="MICROSOFT.SQL"
| where ResourceId contains "/SERVERS/"
| where ResourceId contains "/DATABASES/"
| where (Category == "Blocks")
| summarize block_count = count() by DatabaseName_s, bin(TimeGenerated,
time_range)
| where block_count > block_threshold
```

This query returns the number of blocks grouped by databases in the past hour if the number of blocks is greater than 1:

1. In the **Alert logic** section, in the **Based on** drop-down menu, select **Number of results**, and in the **Operator** drop-down menu, select **Greater than**, and type in **0** as the threshold value.

   The alert is raised whenever there's been more than 1 blocking session in the past hour.

2. In the **Evaluated based on** section, set **Period** to **30** minutes and **Frequency** to **5** minutes.

   The query will run every 5 minutes on the data collected over the previous 30 minutes. If the blocking count is greater than 1 in any of the 5-minute runs, the alert will be raised:

Figure 9.37: Adding the time intervals for evaluation

3.  Click **Done** to save the alert configuration:

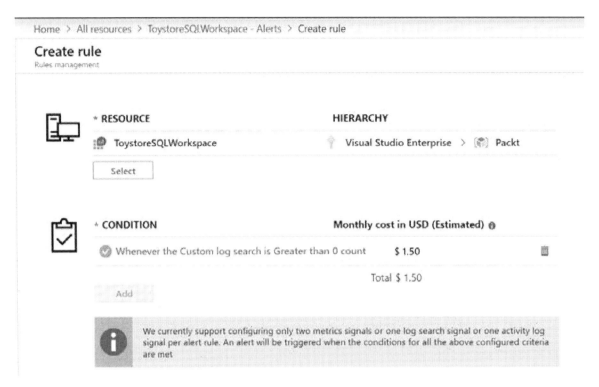

Figure 9.38: Saving the alert configuration

The alert condition has been added and will cost $1.50 per month.

4.  Scroll down to set the **Alert rule name** and **Severity**, and enable the rule upon creation:

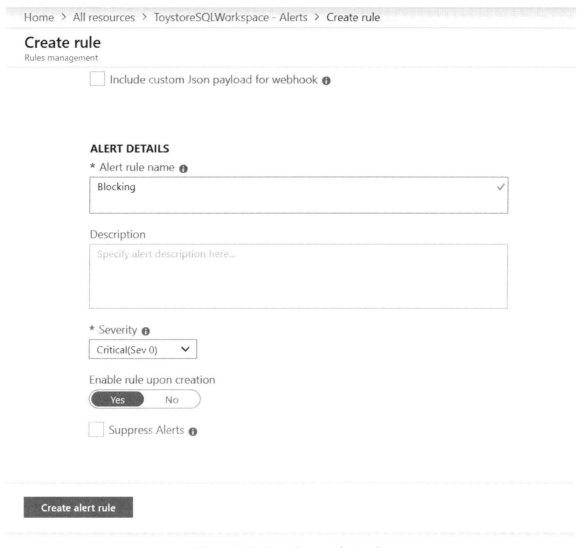

Figure 9.39: Creating an alert rule

5.  Click **Create alert rule** to create the new alert rule.

6. To test the alert, create a blocking scenario as explained in the previous steps. Navigate to the **Log Analytics workspace** page on the Azure portal, and we can see that the alert has been fired:

Figure 9.40: The Log Analytics workspace page

There are two new **Sev 0** errors. Click on **Sev 0** to view the alert details:

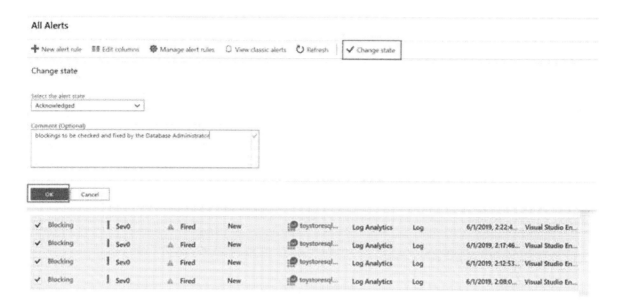

Figure 9.41: Changing the state of the alert to either Acknowledged or Closed

On the **All Alerts** page, we can change the state of the alert to either **Acknowledged** or **Closed**.

## Activity: Monitoring Azure SQL Database with Log Analytics and Power BI

In this activity, we'll learn how to import Log Analytics workspace data into Power BI, and we'll create a report in Power BI.

> **Note**
>
> The purpose of the activity is not to create a performance monitoring dashboard. The purpose is to explain how to get Log Analytics workspace data into Power BI, which can then be used to create a dashboard as and when required.

Follow these steps to complete the activity:

1.  Log in to the Azure portal. Search for and open the Log Analytics workspace:

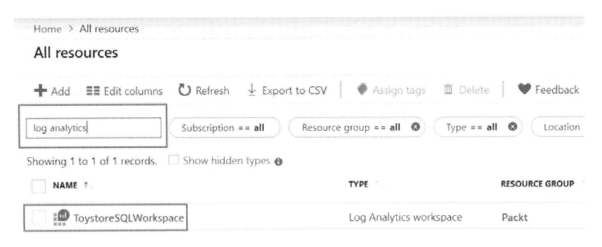

Figure 9.42: The Azure portal

2.  On the Log Analytics workspace page, find and open **Logs**:

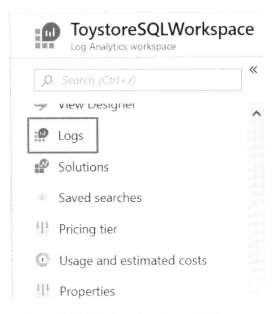

Figure 9.43: The Log Analytics Workspace

3.  On the **New Query 1** page, copy and paste the following query. Click **Run** to execute the query:

```
AzureMetrics
| where ResourceProvider=="MICROSOFT.SQL" | where ResourceId contains "/
SERVERS/"
| where ResourceId contains "/DATABASES/" and MetricName in ('cpu_
percent', 'physical_data_read_percent', 'log_write_percent', 'workers_
percent', 'sessions_percent')
```

The query gets the details for the **cpu_percent**, **physical_data_read_percent**, **log_write_percent**, **workers_percent**, and **sessions_percent** metrics.

4.  From the top-right menu, select **Export** and then select **Export to Power BI (M Query)**:

Figure 9.44: Exporting the query to Power BI (M Query)

In the resulting dialog box, choose to open the file with Notepad and click **OK**:

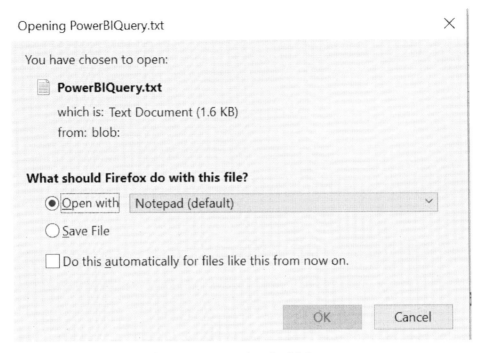

**Figure 9.45: Opening the M Query**

A new TXT file with the M Query will open. Save the query.

The next step is to use the M Query to create a Power BI report. To do this, open Power BI Desktop.

5.  In Power BI Desktop, on the **Home** tab, click **Get Data** and then click **Blank Query**:

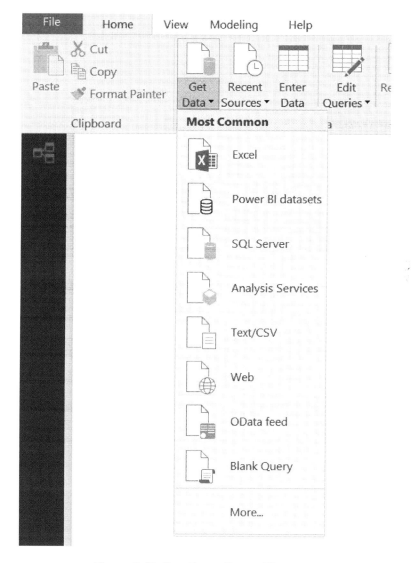

Figure 9.46: Creating a Power BI report

6. In the Power BI Query editor, right-click on **Query 1** and select **Advanced Editor** from the context menu:

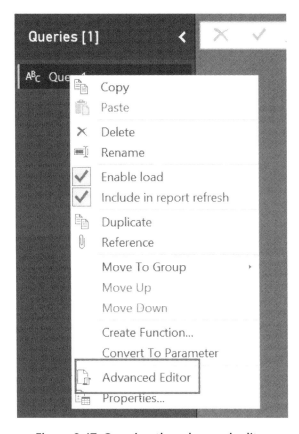

Figure 9.47: Opening the advanced editor

7. In the **Advanced Editor** for Query 1, copy and paste the M Query from *step* 4 and click **Done**:

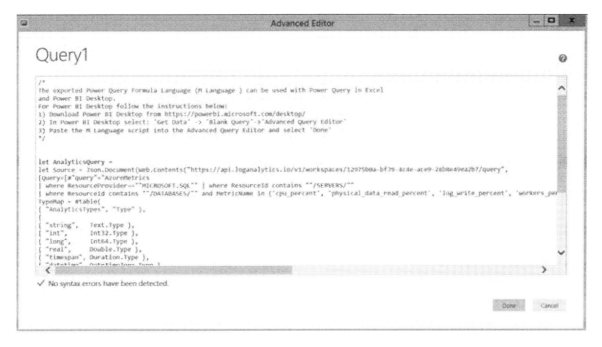

Figure 9.48: Copying and pasting the M Query into the advanced editor

8. The next step is to provide the credentials to Power BI to connect to the Log Analytics workspace. To do this, click on **Edit Credentials**:

Figure 9.49: Edit Credentials

9.  In the **Access Web content** window, select **Organizational account** and provide the username and password you use to log in to the Azure portal:

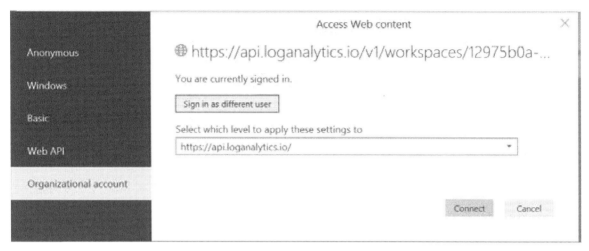

Figure 9.50: The Access Web content window

Click the **Connect** button to connect and fetch the query results from the Log Analytics workspace.

10. Power BI Query Editor will display a preview of the output from the query:

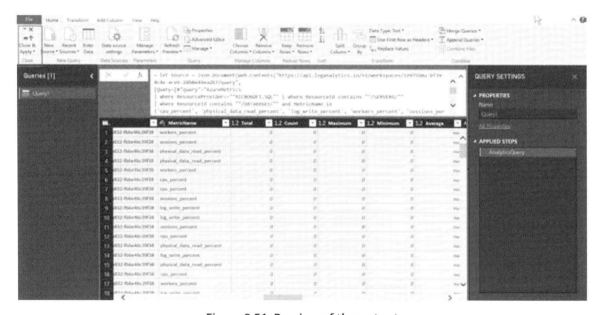

Figure 9.51: Preview of the output

11. In the data preview, right-click on the **ResourceId** column, select **Split column**, and then select **By Delimiter...**:

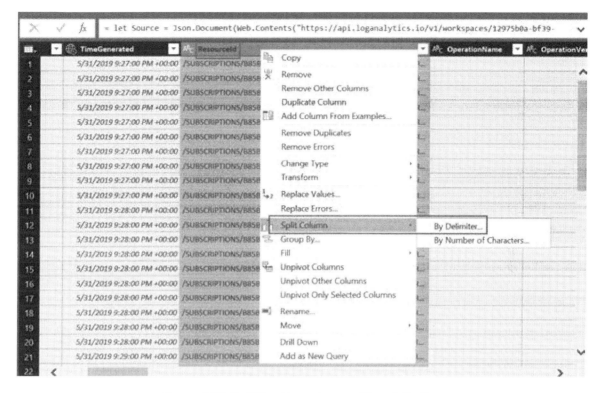

Figure 9.52: Splitting the column with a delimiter

12. In the **Split Column by Delimiter** window, choose **Right-most delimiter** and then click on **OK**:

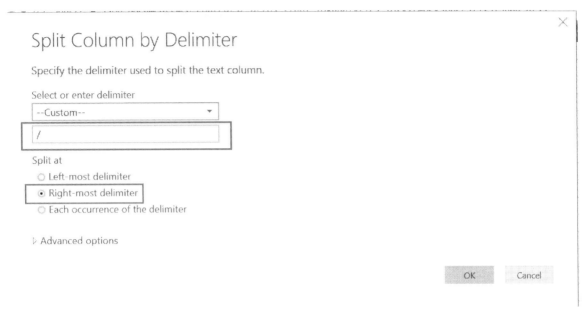

**Figure 9.53: The Split Column by Delimiter window**

This will create a new column called **ResourceId.2** with the database name by splitting the ResourceId column.

Double-click the new column and rename it **Database**:

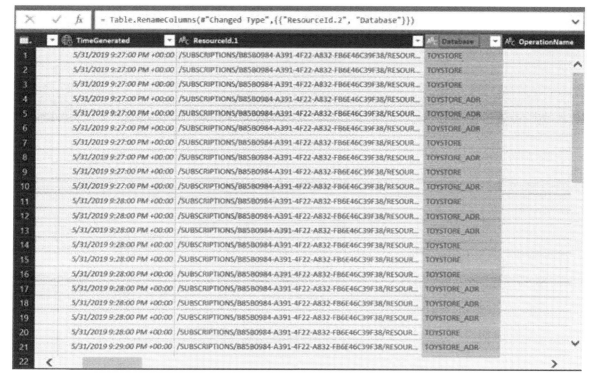

Figure 9.54: The new Database column

We are now ready to save the query and create a visualization on the imported data. To save the query, click on the **Close & Apply** button in the top left:

Figure 9.55: Saving the query

The next step is to create a line chart visualization to display the metrics' trends over time.

13. In the VISUALIZATIONS tab, select the line chart visualization:

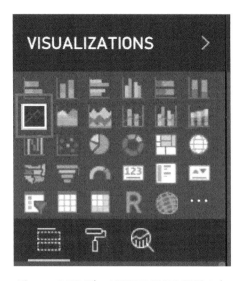

Figure 9.56: The VISUALIZATIONS tab

Click on the line chart to make it active.

14. From the Fields list, drag **TimeGenerated** to the Axis section of the visualization, Average to the values section of the visualization, **MetricName** to the **Legend** section of the visualization, and database to the **Visual Level Filters**, and select the toystore database.

    The **VISUALIZATIONS** section should be as shown in the following screenshot:

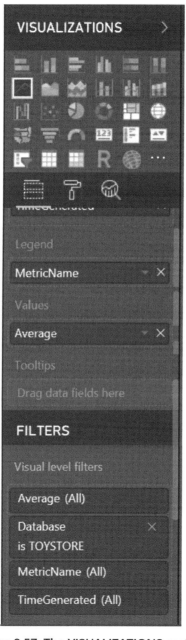

Figure 9.57: The VISUALIZATIONS section

You should now get a line chart, as shown in the following screenshot:

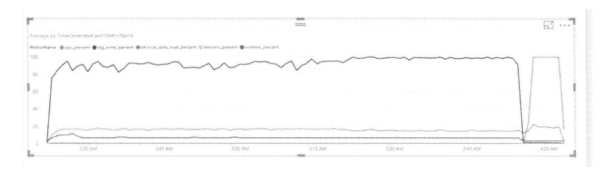

Figure 9.58: The output represented by a line chart

The line chart plots the different metric values (each metric is identified by a different color) against time for the toystore database.

This completes the activity.

## Monitoring Queries Using the Query Performance Insight Blade

In this section, we will learn how to monitor queries using the Query Performance Insight blade. Consider Mike, who plans to keep track of Query Performance Insight and to monitor queries of Toystore Ltd. He runs through a workload to generate some database activity and then observes the Query Performance Insight blade for the queries. Follow these steps in order to achieve this:

1. To start the workload, open a new PowerShell console window and execute the following command:

```
powershell.exe "C:\Code\Lesson09\Start-Workload.ps1 -sqlserver toyfactory
-database toystore -sqluser sqladmin -sqlpassword Packt@pub2 -workloadsql
"C:\Code\Lesson09\workload.sql"
-numberofexecutions 10"
```

> **Note**
>
> You may get the following warning. Ignore this.
>
> "WARNING: Could not obtain SQL Server Service information. An attempt to connect to WMI on 'Microsoft.WindowsAzure. Commands.SqlDatabase.Types. ps1xml' failed with the following error: The RPC server is unavailable. (Exception from HRESULT: 0x800706BA)"

The preceding command will execute the queries specified in the **workload.sql** file 10 times, as specified by the **numberofexecutions** variable. This will generate some database activity for you to analyze.

You will have to wait for another 5-10 minutes for the details to show on the Azure portal.

2. Navigate to the **toystore** database on the Azure portal (https://portal.azure.com). On the **Overview** blade, select **Query Performance Insight** in the **Support + Troubleshooting** section. You will then see the following:

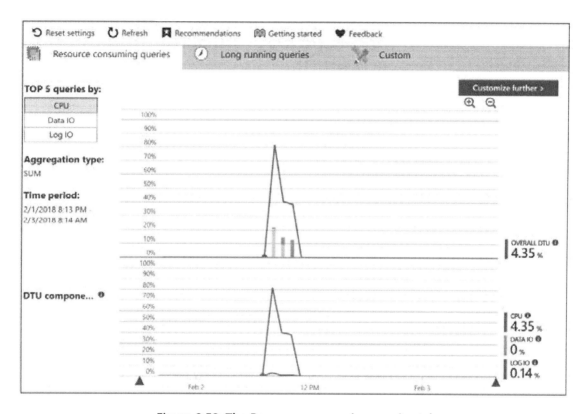

Figure 9.59: The Resource consuming queries tab

Click on a row below to get the details for the selected query. ⓘ

| QUERY ID | CPU[%] | DATA IO[%] | LOG IO[%] | DURATION[HH:MM:SS] | EXECUTIONS COUNT | # |
|---|---|---|---|---|---|---|
| 468 | 0.83 | 0 | 0.02 | 00:44:33.760 | 12 | ✓ |
| 492 | 0.47 | 0 | 0.01 | 00:27:01.780 | 5 | ✓ |
| 472 | 0.01 | 0 | 0 | 00:00:47.290 | 13 | ✓ |
| 480 | 0 | 0 | 0 | 00:00:00.360 | 262 | ✓ |
| 263 | 0 | 0 | 0 | 00:00:00.230 | 442 | ✓ |

Figure 9.60: Details of queries

Query Performance Insight displays a line chart showing CPU consumption of the past 24 hours by the top queries. CPU consumption is selected by default; however, you can all see five queries by **Data IO** and **Log IO** as well. The default aggregation applied is SUM, which is customizable, and the top five queries details include CPU%, Data IO%, Log IO%, duration, and execution count.

3. Click on **ID 472** to get the query's details. The query ID will be different in your case. The query details blade shows the following:

• Query text:

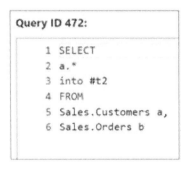

Figure 9.61: The query details blade showing the query text

- Overall CPU, Data IO, and Log IO
- CPU, Data IO, Log IO, Duration, and Execution count in a one-hour interval:

| INTERVAL | CPU[%] | DATA IO[%] | LOG IO[%] | DURATION[HH:MM:SS] | EXECUTIONS ... |
|---|---|---|---|---|---|
| 2/2: 9 AM - 10 | 0.22 | 0 | 0.01 | 00:00:27.000 | 8 |
| 2/2: 8 AM - 09 | 0.09 | 0 | 0 | 00:00:12.190 | 3 |
| 2/2: 10 AM - 11 | 0.06 | 0 | 0 | 00:00:08.100 | 2 |

Figure 9.62: The Query details blade showing the CPU, Data IO, Log IO, Duration, and Execution count in a one-hour interval

You can select an area or a portion on the timeline from the line chart to see insights for that time duration. To do that, click and hold the mouse at the starting point on the line chart and drag it to the time interval you wish to see the insight for:

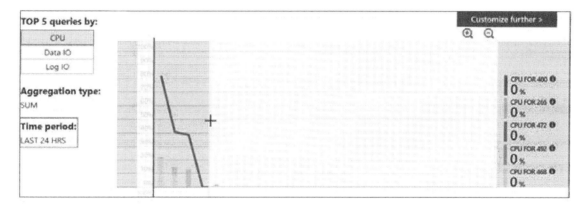

Figure 9.63: A line chart of the top 5 queries by CPU utilization

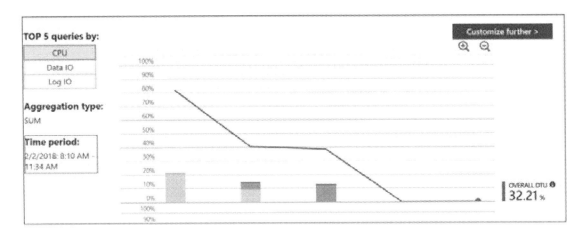

Figure 9.64: Graph showing the insights for the time period 8:10 AM to 11:34 AM instead of 24 hours

The second graph shows the insights for the time period from 8:10 AM to 11:34 AM instead of 24 hours, which is shown in the first screenshot.

You can also click on the zoom-in and zoom-out icons in the upper-right corner of the chart to change the time interval.

4. Close the query details blade to return to the **Query Performance Insight** blade. Select the **Long running queries** tab:

Figure 9.65: The Long running queries tab

| QUERY ID | CPU[%] | DATA IO[%] | LOG IO[%] | DURATION[HH:MM:SS] | EXECUTIONS COUNT | # |
|---|---|---|---|---|---|---|
| 468 | 1.23 | 0.01 | 0.02 | 00:44:33.760 | 12 | ☑ |
| 452 | 0.69 | 0 | 0.01 | 00:27:01.780 | 5 | ☑ |
| 472 | 0.02 | 0 | 0 | 00:00:47.290 | 13 | ☑ |
| 480 | 0 | 0 | 0 | 00:00:00.360 | 265 | ☑ |
| 265 | 0 | 0 | 0 | 00:00:00.240 | 303 | ☑ |

Figure 9.66: The top five long-running queries from the past 24 hours

The **Long running queries** tab displays the top five long-running queries from the past 24 hours.

The interval can be changed by clicking on either the **Custom** tab or the **Customize further** button. Click on a query to get the query details.

5. Select the **Custom** tab on the **Query Performance Insight** blade. The **Custom** tab provides options to further filter the insights on the **Time period**, **Number of queries**, **Metric type**, and **Aggregation type**:

Figure 9.67: The Custom tab on the Query Performance Insight blade

Change the **Metric type** to **Duration**, set the **Time period** to **Last 6 hrs**, and the **Aggregation type** to **max**. Then click **Go** to filter the insights:

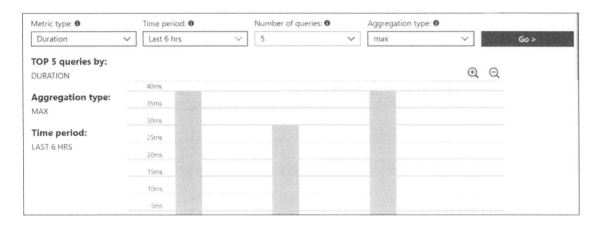

Figure 9.68: The top five queries with a maximum duration of six hours

This filters out the top five queries with a maximum duration of six hours. You can get further query details, as explained earlier in this section.

This completes the section.

# Monitoring an Azure SQL Database Using DMVs

DMVs return diagnostic data that can be used to monitor a database's health and performance.

## Monitoring Database Metrics

The metrics available on the Azure portal can also be monitored using the `sys.resource_stats` DMV. This DMV returns the historical analysis for all the databases in an Azure SQL server. The data is collected and aggregated every 5 minutes and is retained for 14 days.

The following query returns the resource utilization from the last six hours:

> **Note**
>
> You can also copy the queries from the **C:\Code\Lesson09\MonitoringDMVs.sql**
> file.
>
> The file location may change depending on where you have unzipped the code
> files.

```
-- Execute in master database
-- Get utilization in last 6 hours for the toystore database Declare
@StartTime DATETIME = DATEADD(HH,-3,GetUTCDate()),
@EndTime DATETIME = GetUTCDate() SELECT
database_name, start_time, end_time, avg_cpu_percent, avg_data_io_percent,
avg_log_write_percent, (
SELECT Max(v)
FROM (VALUES (avg_cpu_percent), (avg_data_io_percent), (avg_ log_write_
percent)) AS
value(v)) AS [avg_DTU_percent] FROM sys.resource_stats
WHERE database_name = 'toystore' AND start_time BETWEEN @StartTime AND @
EndTime ORDER BY avg_cpu_percent desc
```

The following query returns the average CPU utilization across databases. This helps us
find the most used databases:

```
SELECT
database_name,
AVG(avg_cpu_percent) AS avg_cpu_percent FROM sys.resource_stats
GROUP BY database_name
ORDER BY avg_cpu_percent DESC
```

You can further modify the preceding query to return databases exceeding a certain threshold value; say, databases with a CPU utilization greater than 80%.

The **sys.dm_db_resource_stats** DMV records data for individual Azure SQL databases every 15 seconds, and this is retained for an hour. This allows you to drill down for deeper insights into individual database utilization.

The following query returns the average CPU, data I/O, log IO, and memory utilization for the **toystore** database:

```
-- Get Average CPU, Data IO, Log IO and Memory utilization

-- Execute in toystore database SELECT

AVG(avg_cpu_percent) AS avg_cpu_percent, AVG(avg_data_io_percent) AS
avg_data_io_percent, AVG(avg_log_write_percent) AS avg_log_write_percent,
AVG(avg_memory_usage_percent) AS avg_memory_usage_percent

FROM sys.dm_db_resource_stats;
```

The following query returns the average DTU utilization for the **toystore** database over the past hour:

```
-- Get the Average DTU utilization for toystore database

-- Execute in toystore database SELECT

end_time, (SELECT Max(v)

FROM (VALUES (avg_cpu_percent), (avg_data_io_percent), (avg log_write_
percent)) AS

value(v)) AS [avg_DTU_percent] FROM sys.dm_db_resource_stats ORDER BY end_
time DESC
```

## Monitoring Connections

The DMVs used to monitor connections are the same as the ones used to monitor connections in an on-premises SQL Server, which are **sys.dm_exec_connections**, **sys.dm_exec_sessions**, and **sys.dm_exec_requests**.

The following query returns all sessions for the **sqladmin** login:

```
-- Get all sessions for user sqladmin SELECT
session_id,

program_name, status, reads, writes, logical_reads
from sys.dm_exec_sessions WHERE login_name='sqladmin'
```

> **Note**
>
> The login name may be different in your case.

The following query returns all requests for the **sqladmin** login:

```
-- Get all the requests for the login sqladmin SELECT
s.session_id,
s.status AS session_status, r.status AS request_status, r.cpu_time, r.total_
elapsed_time, r.writes,
r.logical_reads,
t.Text AS query_batch_text,
SUBSTRING(t.text, (r.statement_start_offset/2)+1, ((CASE r.statement_end_
offset
WHEN -1 THEN DATALENGTH(t.text)
ELSE r.statement_end_offset
END - r.statement_start_offset)/2) + 1) AS running_query_text FROM sys.dm_
exec_sessions s join  sys.dm_exec_requests r
ON r.session_id=s.session_id
CROSS APPLY sys.dm_exec_sql_text(r.sql_handle) AS t WHERE s.login_
name='sqladmin'
```

The **Dynamic Management Function (DMF)**, **sys.dm_exec_sql_text**, returns the query text for the given **sql_handle**.

The **query_batch_text** column returns all the queries being sent as a request in one batch. If you run the workload as mentioned earlier, you will realize that the **query_batch_text** column contains all the queries specified in the **workload.sql** file.

The **running_query_text** column returns the query that is currently being executed. It is calculated using the statement offset start and end values from the **sys.dm_exec_requests** DMV.

## Monitoring Query Performance

The following DMVs can be used to monitor query and procedure performance.

> **Note**
>
> The DMVs mentioned here are not specific to Azure SQL Database. They can be used on on-premises SQL servers as well. These are not the only DMVs used to monitor performance. You can get a complete list of DMVs for Azure SQL Database from https://docs.microsoft.com/en-us/sql/relational-databases/system-dynamic-management-views/system-dynamic-management-views?view=sql-server-2017.
>
> You can also refer to the following article for troubleshooting performance problems:
>
> http://download.microsoft.com/download/D/B/D/DBDE7972-1EB9-470A-BA18-58849DB3EB3B/TShootPerfProbs2008.docx
>
> This article is for Microsoft SQL Server 2008; however, it also applies to Azure SQL Database and other higher on-premises SQL Server versions.

The **sys.dm_exec_query_stats** DMV returns aggregated statistics such as execution count, reads, writes, and worker time for the cached query plans.

The following query returns the top five CPU-intensive queries:

```
SELECT
TOP 5
(total_worker_time/execution_count)/(1000*1000) AS [Avg CPU Time(Seconds)],
SUBSTRING(st.text, (qs.statement_start_offset/2)+1, ((CASE qs.statement_end_offset
WHEN -1 THEN DATALENGTH(st.text)
ELSE qs.statement_end_offset
END - qs.statement_start_offset)/2) + 1) AS statement_text, qs.execution_count, (qs.total_elapsed_time/execution_count)/(1000*1000) AS [Avg
```

```
Duration(Seconds)]

FROM sys.dm_exec_query_stats AS qs

CROSS APPLY sys.dm_exec_sql_text(qs.sql_handle) AS st ORDER BY total_worker_
time/execution_count DESC;
```

The following query returns the top five long-running queries:

```
SELECT

TOP 5

(total_worker_time/execution_count)/(1000*1000) AS [Avg CPU Time(Seconds)],

SUBSTRING(st.text, (qs.statement_start_offset/2)+1, ((CASE qs.statement_end_
offset

WHEN -1 THEN DATALENGTH(st.text)

ELSE qs.statement_end_offset

END - qs.statement_start_offset)/2) + 1) AS statement_text, qs.execution_
count, (qs.total_elapsed_time/execution_count)/(1000*1000) AS [Avg

Duration(Seconds)]

FROM sys.dm_exec_query_stats AS qs

CROSS APPLY sys.dm_exec_sql_text(qs.sql_handle) AS st ORDER BY (qs.total_
elapsed_time/execution_count) DESC;
```

You can order by the preceding query on the **total_logical_reads** column to get the top five I/O read-intensive queries.

## Monitoring Blocking

Blocking is a scenario where a query is waiting to acquire a lock on a resource that is already locked by another query. Blocking causes major performance problems and can bring a database to a halt.

The following query returns the blocking details:

```
-- Get blocked queries SELECT
w.session_id
,w.wait_duration_ms
,w.wait_type
,w.blocking_session_id
,w.resource_description
,t.text
```

```
FROM sys.dm_os_waiting_tasks w INNER JOIN sys.dm_exec_requests r ON
w.session_id = r.session_id
```

```
CROSS APPLY sys.dm_exec_sql_text (r.sql_handle) t WHERE w.blocking_session_
id>0
```

```
GO
```

In order to see the preceding query results, generate a blocking scenario by following these steps:

1. Open a new query window in SQL Server Management Studio and connect to the **toystore** database. Execute the following query:

```
Begin Tran
INSERT INTO [Warehouse].[Colors] (
ColorID, ColorName, LastEditedBy, ValidFrom, ValidTo
)
VALUES (
1001,
'Pulpy Orange', 1,
getdate(), getdate()
)
-- ROLLBACK
```

   The preceding query will open a new transaction to insert a new row in the **Colors** table. However, the transaction is left open and is not closed.

2. Open another query window in SSMS and connect to the **toystore** database. Execute the following query:

```
INSERT INTO [Warehouse].[Colors] (
ColorID, ColorName, LastEditedBy, ValidFrom, ValidTo
)
VALUES (
1001,
'Pulpy Green', 1,
getdate(), getdate()
)
```

   The preceding query tries to insert a row in the **Colors** table; however, it is blocked by the query in *step 1*.

3.  Run the following query to detect blocking:

```
-- Get blocked queries SELECT
w.session_id
,w.wait_duration_ms
,w.wait_type
,w.blocking_session_id
,w.resource_description
,t.text
FROM sys.dm_os_waiting_tasks w INNER JOIN sys.dm_exec_requests r ON
w.session_id = r.session_id
CROSS APPLY sys.dm_exec_sql_text (r.sql_handle) t WHERE w.blocking_
session_id>0
GO
```

You should get the following output. The **session_id** value may be different in your case:

Figure 9.69: Session ID 106 is blocked by session ID 130

Session ID 106 is requesting an exclusive lock on the **Colors** table; however, session ID 130 already has an exclusive lock on the **Colors** table. Therefore, session ID 106 is blocked by session ID 130.

To remove the block, uncomment and execute the **ROLLBACK** command in the first query.

## Extended Events

Extended events, introduced in SQL Server 2008, are lightweight methods used to capture diagnostic information in SQL Server.

Extended events are similar to SQL Trace; however, they're more lightweight and scalable than SQL Trace.

The following are the important components of an extended event:

- **Session**: An extended event session, when started, captures the specified data for one or more events.

- **Events**: Events are the activities or actions that the data is to be recorded for. For example, `sql_statement_starting` and `sql_statement_completed` are the events raised whenever a SQL statement is started or completed on the given database.

- **Event Fields**: Every event has a set of event fields or data points that are recorded whenever the event is triggered. For example, the `sql_statement_completed` event has a duration event field.

- **Global Fields**: These are the common data points to be recorded whenever the specified event occurs. Examples of global fields are `session_id`, `sql_text`, `database_name`, and `database_id`.

- **Target**: The target specifies the storage to be used for the data capture. The following targets are allowed in a SQL database:

- **Ring Buffer Target**: The data is stored in memory for a brief interval of time.

- **Event Counter**: Counts all events that occurred during a particular extended event session instead of capturing full event details. It can be used to characterize a workload to be CPU-intensive, I/O-intensive, or memory-intensive.

- **Event File Target**: Writes full event details to an Azure Storage Container. This allows you to do historical analysis on the saved data.

## Examining Queries

In this section, we'll examine queries made to the **toystore** database using extended events. Mike looks after the Query Performance Insight report of Toystore Ltd.

After generating the report, he plans to look at the extended events to track down the queries that are taking longer than 10 seconds to complete on the **toystore** database. We'll use extended events to capture such queries:

1.  Open a new query window in SQL Server Management Studio and connect to the **toystore** database.

    Execute the following query to create the extended event session:

    > **Note**
    >
    > You can copy the code from `C:\Code\Lesson09\CreateExtendedEvent.sql`.
    >
    > The file location may change depending on where you have unzipped the code files.

    ```
    CREATE EVENT SESSION [LongRunningQueries] ON DATABASE ADD EVENT sqlserver.
    sql_statement_completed
    ( ACTION
    (
    sqlserver.database_name, sqlserver.query_hash, sqlserver.query_plan_hash,
    sqlserver.sql_text, sqlserver.username
    )
    WHERE ([sqlserver].[database_name]=N'toystore' AND duration > 1000)
    )
    ADD TARGET package0.ring_buffer WITH (STARTUP_STATE=OFF)
    GO
    ```

    The preceding query creates an extended event session, **LongRunningQueries**, with event as **sql_statement_completed**, an action that specifies the global fields to capture, the target as ring buffer, and **Startup_State** set to **Off**, which means that the session will not automatically start when the SQL Server services are started.

Execute the following query to start the **LongRunningQueries** session:

```
-- Start the Event Session
ALTER EVENT SESSION [LongRunningQueries] ON DATABASE
STATE = START;
```

2. Execute the following PowerShell command to start the workload:

```
powershell.exe "C:\Code\Lesson09\Start-Workload.ps1 -sqlserver toyfactory
-database toystore -sqluser sqladmin -sqlpassword Packt@pub2 -workloadsql
"C:\Code\Lesson09\workload.sql"
-numberofexecutions 10"
```

Wait for at least one execution to complete.

3. Execute the following query to get the output from the extended event target:

> **Note**
>
> You can also copy the code from **C:\Code\Lesson09\ReadExtendedEventData.
> sql**.

```
            -- Get the target data into temporary table
SELECT
    se.name    AS [XEventSession],
    ev.event_name,
    ac.action_name,
    st.target_name,
    se.session_source,
    st.target_data,
    CAST(st.target_data AS XML)  AS [target_data_XML]
into #XEventData
FROM
                sys.dm_xe_database_session_event_actions  AS ac

    INNER JOIN sys.dm_xe_database_session_events          AS ev  ON
ev.event_name = ac.event_name
        AND CAST(ev.event_session_address AS BINARY(8)) = CAST(ac.event_
session_address AS BINARY(8))

    INNER JOIN sys.dm_xe_database_session_object_columns AS oc
        ON CAST(oc.event_session_address AS BINARY(8)) = CAST(ac.event_
session_address AS BINARY(8))
```

```
        INNER JOIN sys.dm_xe_database_session_targets        AS st
            ON CAST(st.event_session_address AS BINARY(8)) = CAST(ac.event_
session_address AS BINARY(8))

        INNER JOIN sys.dm_xe_database_sessions                AS se
            ON CAST(ac.event_session_address AS BINARY(8)) = CAST(se.address
AS BINARY(8))
WHERE
        oc.column_name = 'occurrence_number'
    AND
        se.name         = 'LongRunningQueries'
    AND
        ac.action_name = 'sql_text'
ORDER BY
    se.name,
    ev.event_name,
    ac.action_name,
    st.target_name,
    se.session_source
;
GO
-- Parse the target xml xevent into table
SELECT * FROM
(
SELECT
    xed.event_data.value('(data[@name="statement"]/value)[1]',
'nvarchar(max)') AS sqltext,
    xed.event_data.value('(data[@name="cpu_time"]/value)[1]', 'int') AS
cpu_time,
    xed.event_data.value('(data[@name="duration"]/value)[1]', 'int') AS
duration,
    xed.event_data.value('(data[@name="logical_reads"]/value)[1]', 'int')
AS logical_reads
FROM #XEventData
CROSS APPLY target_data_XML.nodes('//RingBufferTarget/event') AS xed
(event_data)
) As xevent
WHERE duration > = 10000000
GO
DROP TABLE #XEventData
```

The extended event data is stored in XML format. First, the query puts the target XML into a temporary table. The extended event target details are stored in a **sys. dm_xe_database_session_targets** DMV.

A sample target XML is shown in the following code:

```
<event name="sql_statement_completed" package="sqlserver" timestamp="2018-
02-03T16:19:28.708Z">
<data name="duration">
<type name="int64" package="package0"></type>
<value>1</value>
</data>
<data name="cpu_time">
<type name="uint64" package="package0"></type>
<value>0</value>
</data>
<data name="physical_reads">
<type name="uint64" package="package0"></type>
<value>0</value>
</data>
<data name="logical_reads">
<type name="uint64" package="package0"></type>
<value>0</value>
</data>
...

...
</data>
```

Each event has an XML element with event fields as the child elements. This makes it easy to parse the event data.

When parsing data, make sure that the event field data type is the same as what is mentioned in the XML. For example, for the statement field, the data type should be **nvarchar**, because in XML, the data type mentioned is the Unicode string.

Once you have at least one execution of the workload completed, you should get an output similar to the following:

| | sqltext | cpu_time | duration | logical_reads |
|---|---|---|---|---|
| 1 | SELECT a.* into #t1 FROM sys.objects a, sys.objects b, sys.objects c | 609000 | 381647796 | 90681 |

Figure 9.70: The result of the workload execution

The query returns all of the SQL statements that have durations greater than 10 seconds.

4. Run the following query to stop and drop the extended event session:

```
-- Stop the Event Session
ALTER EVENT SESSION [LongRunningQueries] ON DATABASE
STATE = STOP;
GO
-- Drop the Event Target
ALTER EVENT SESSION [LongRunningQueries] ON DATABASE
DROP TARGET package0.ring_buffer;
GO
-- Drop the Event Session
DROP EVENT SESSION [LongRunningQueries] ON DATABASE;
GO
```

> **Note**
>
> Here's some additional reading for extended events.
>
> More info on extended events DMVs can be found at https://docs.microsoft.com/en-us/sql/relational-databases/system-dynamic-management-views/extended-events-dynamic-management-views?view=sql-server-2017.
>
> More info on extended event lists can be found at https://docs.microsoft.com/en-us/sql/relational-databases/system-catalog-views/sys-server-event-sessions-transact-sql?view=sql-server-2017.

This completes the section.

# Tuning an Azure SQL Database

In this section, we'll look at the out-of-the-box performance tuning features provided by automatic tuning in an Azure SQL database.

## Automatic Tuning

Azure SQL Database automatic tuning utilizes artificial intelligence to continuously monitor and improve queries executed on an Azure SQL database.

Automatic tuning observes the workload and applies recommendations to speed up performance. The recommendations are applied when the database activity is low, so that there aren't any performance impacts when applying recommendations.

The following options are available for automatic tuning:

- **Create Index**: Automatically identifies and implements missing indexes to improve workload performance. It also verifies whether the indexes created have improved the performance.

- **Drop Indexes**: Automatically identifies and removes duplicate, redundant, and unused indexes.

- **Force Last Good Plan**: Using the execution plan, it automatically identifies the queries, that are slower than the previous good plan, and forces the use of the last known good plan to improve the query's performance.

  Automatic tuning has to be manually switched to **ON**, and is set to **OFF** by default. Also, it gives you an option to either automatically or manually apply the recommendations.

To enable automatic tuning, follow the following instructions:

1. Open a browser and log in to the Azure portal (https://portal.azure.com) with your Microsoft Azure credentials.

2. Open the **toystore** database and select the **Automatic Tuning** option from the **Support + Troubleshooting** section.

   On the **Automatic tuning** blade, under **Inherit from**, select **Don't inherit**. Under **Configure the automatic tuning option**, toggle **ON** for**FORCE PLAN** and the **CREATE INDEX** and **DROP INDEX** options. Click **Apply** to save the automatic tuning settings:

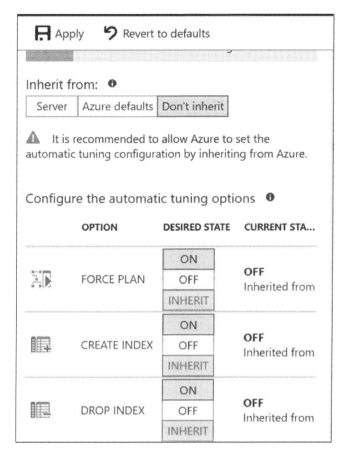

Figure 9.71: The Automatic tuning blade

Alternatively, you can also enable automatic tuning by executing the following query in the **toystore** database:

```
ALTER DATABASE current SET AUTOMATIC_TUNING = CUSTOM

ALTER DATABASE current SET AUTOMATIC_TUNING (FORCE_LAST_GOOD_PLAN
= ON, CREATE_INDEX = ON, DROP_INDEX = ON)
```

## In-Memory Technologies

In-memory technologies were first introduced in SQL Server 2012, and are built into the SQL Server database engine. They can improve performance significantly for workloads such as data ingestion, data load, and analytical queries.

In Azure SQL Database, in-memory technologies are only available in the Premium service tier.

Azure SQL Database has the following in-memory technologies: In-Memory OLTP and Columnstore Indexes. Let's talk about them briefly.

## In-Memory OLTP

As the name suggests, In-Memory OLTP improves performance for transaction processing scenarios where a major portion of the workload consists of inserts, updates, and deletes.

In-Memory OLTP is achieved by using one of the following objects:

### Memory-Optimized Tables

Memory-optimized tables are used to store data in memory. All of the data in a memory-optimized table resides in memory. Memory-optimized tables and disk-based tables can reside within the same database simultaneously.

A table is defined as being a memory-optimized table at the time of its creation. A memory-optimized table creation script is shown in the following code snippet:

```
CREATE TABLE dbo.Orders (

OrderId int not null IDENTITY PRIMARY KEY NONCLUSTERED,

CustomerId int not null, OrderDate datetime not null, Quantity int not null

)

WITH

(MEMORY_OPTIMIZED = ON, DURABILITY = SCHEMA_AND_DATA);
```

The **Memory_Optimized** keyword specifies whether the table is a memory-optimized table. The durability refers to retaining only schema, or schema and data, for the memory-optimized table. As the table is in memory, the data will go out of memory if the machine is restarted. However, if the durability is set to **SCHEMA_AND_DATA**, SQL Server makes sure that the data isn't lost.

There are two types of indexes allowed on an in-memory table, and these are hash and non-clustered indexes. The indexes don't contain data rows. Instead, they contain memory pointers to the data rows. The indexes are also in memory. Hash indexes are used to optimize point lookups and aren't suitable for range lookups. Non-clustered indexes are best suited for range lookups.

Memory-optimized tables can be accessed through the regular DDL and DML commands.

## Natively Compiled Procedures

A regular or InterOP stored procedure is compiled and the plan is cached within the SQL server. However, a natively compiled procedure is compiled into a DLL and is loaded in memory. This further improves DML command performance on memory-optimized tables.

> **Note**
>
> An InterOP stored procedure here refers to the regularly stored procedure, which is compiled, and the generated plan is cached into the SQL Server plan cache.
>
> This is unlike natively compiled procedures, where the procedure is compiled into DLL and loaded into memory.

A natively compiled procedure syntax is displayed in the following diagram:

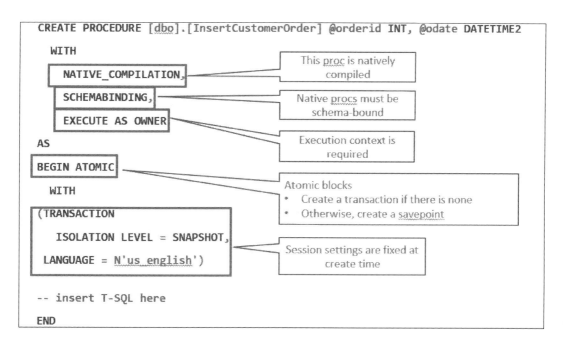

Figure 9.72: Syntax of a natively compiled procedure

A natively compiled procedure contains the regular T-SQL code as the **InterOP** or regular procedures; however, it's defined differently at the time of creation. The term **Native_Compilation** defines that the procedure is a natively compiled procedure and is to be compiled into DLL. A natively compiled procedure should be schema-bound and should have the execution context. A natively compiled procedure is always executed in a snapshot transaction isolation level. Memory-optimized tables and natively compiled procedures can be used together to speed up an OLTP workload and make it up to 20 times faster.

### Columnstore Indexes

Columnstore indexes, introduced in SQL Server 2012 (as non-clustered columnstore), use columnar storage instead of regular row-based storage to store data. A rowstore has rows with multiple columns arranged sequentially on a page; however, in a column store, values of a single column (from different rows) are stored contiguously.

> **Note**
>
> Clustered column store indexes were added in SQL Server 2014,    whereas non-clustered column store indexes were introduced in SQL Server 2012.

In a rowstore, this is how data is stored on disk:

```
Abel, Doctor, WA
Abha, Engineer, UT
Adrian, Doctor, HA
```

However, in a columnstore, the same information is stored as follows:

```
Abel, Abha, Adrian
Doctor, Engineer, Doctor
WA, UT, HA
```

This allows for faster response times and less storage for data warehouse scenarios.

Columnstore has better compression than rowstore, because values of the same data type compress better than the values of different data types (a rowstore contains columns with different data types, while a columnstore has values from the same column).

This improves query performance, as only those pages that contain the selected column values are scanned or fetched, thereby decreasing the reads.

For example, consider the following query:

```
SELECT Name, profession FROM Employees
```

The preceding query will only touch pages with the Name and Profession columns if run against a columnstore. However, against a rowstore, the query will run through all the pages. This significantly improves the performance in data warehouse scenarios with huge tables.

There are two types of columnstore indexes: clustered and non-clustered:

- **Clustered columnstore index**: Clustered columnstore indexes store the entire table data as columnstores. They reduce the storage footprint by up to 10 times its original size. They can be used on fact tables in a data warehouse to speed up queries and fit more data into the available storage.

  The syntax for creating a clustered column store index is as follows:

  ```
  CREATE CLUSTERED COLUMNSTORE INDEX CCS_Orders ON [Sales].[Orders]
  ```

- **Non-clustered columnstore index**: Non-clustered columnstore indexes are created on sets of tables columns and can co-exist. When introduced in SQL Server 2012, non-clustered column indexes weren't updatable; in other words, if you had a non-clustered column index on a table, you were not allowed to update the data in that table using the DML statements.

  However, starting from SQL Server 2016, they are now updatable and can be used to gain real-time operational insights into your transactional data. You can query the operational data directly instead of spending time doing ETL and loading the data into a data warehouse. You can do all of this without any impact on operations.

  The syntax for creating a non-clustered columnstore index is as follows:

  ```
  CREATE NONCLUSTERED COLUMNSTORE INDEX nccsix_CustomerID
  ON [Sales].[Orders] (CustomerID,ContactPersonID,OrderDate);
  ```

  > **Note**
  >
  > To learn more about columnstore indexes, refer to https://docs.microsoft.com/
  > en-us/sql/t-sql/statements/create-columnstore-index-transact-sql?view=sql-server-
  > 2017&viewFallbackFrom=sqlserver-2017.

  The preceding query creates a non-clustered column store index on **customerid**, **contactpersonid**, and **orderdate**. The columnstore structure is stored separately from the table structure.

Columnstore indexes have two types of data compression. The default columnstore compression is the **Columnstore_Archive** compression. A columnstore index is good at compression by design. A page in a columnstore index has data from one column, which is one data type. Therefore, compression is better when compressing data of a similar data type, instead of mixed data types, as is the case with row store.

The **columnstore_archive** compression further increases the compression rate. The compression is 37%-66% percent higher than the default columnstore compression. The archive compression can be used to compress infrequently used data to save disk space.

To enable **columnstore_archive** on an existing column store index, execute the following query:

```
ALTER INDEX nccsix_CustomerID ON [Sales].[Orders] REBUILD WITH (DATA_
COMPRESSION=COLUMNSTORE_ARCHIVE)
```

To disable **columnstore_archive** compression on an existing columnstore index, execute the following query:

```
ALTER INDEX nccsix_CustomerID ON [Sales].[Orders] REBUILD WITH (DATA_
COMPRESSION=COLUMNSTORE)
```

To create a new columnstore index with **columnstore_archive** compression, execute the following query:

```
CREATE NONCLUSTERED COLUMNSTORE INDEX nccsix_CustomerID_AC

ON [Sales].[Orders]

(

    CustomerID,

    ContactPersonID,

    OrderDate

) WITH(DATA_COMPRESSION=COLUMNSTORE_ARCHIVE)
```

> **Note**
>
> Starting from SQL Server 2019, you can use the **sp_estimate_data_compression_savings** DMV to compare the relative data compression benefits of columnstore indexes. However, this DMV isn't supported in Azure SQL Database.

## Activity: Exploring the In-Memory OLTP Feature

In this activity, we'll compare the performance of a disk-based table with a memory-optimized table for an OLTP workload for our **toystore** database. Let's consider a case where Mike wants to explore the new In-Memory OLTP feature using the memory-optimized tables. But before he does that, to check if it is truly profitable, he wants to compare the performance of disk-based tables and memory-optimized tables. This can be done via the following steps:

1. Run the following command in a PowerShell console to change the service tier of the **toystore** database to Premium tier. The in-memory technologies are only available in Premium service tiers:

   ```
   PowerShell.exe "C:\Code\Lesson02\ScaleUpAzureSQLDB.ps1" -resourcegroupname
   toystore -azuresqlservername
   toyfactory -databasename toystore -newservicetier Premium
   -servicetierperfomancelevel P1 -AzureProfileFilePath "C:\Code\
   MyAzureProfile.json"
   ```

2. Navigate to **C:\Code\Lesson09\InMemoryOLTP** and open the **CreateObjects.sql** file in a new SQL Server Management Studio. This query creates the following objects:

   **uspInsertOrders**: A traditional disk-based store procedure that inserts new orders, as specified by the **@numberoforderstoinsert** parameter. If **@numberoforderstoinsert** is set to 10, then it will insert 10 new orders into the **Sales.Orders** table.

   **Orders_Inmem**: The memory-optimized version of the **Sales.Orders** table. The schema is the same as that of the **Sales.Orders** table; however, it has **Memory_Optimized** set to **ON**.

   **Customers_Inmem**: The memory-optimized version of the **Sales.Customers** table. The schema is the same as that of the **Sales.Customers** table; however, it has **Memory_Optimized** set to **ON**. All of the existing customers in the **Sales.Customers** table are inserted into the **Sales.Customers_Inmem** table.

   **uspInsertOrders_Inmem**: This is a natively compiled version of the **uspInsertOrders** procedure. It inserts a number of orders, as specified by the **@numberoforderstoinsert** parameter, into the **Sales.Orders_Inmem** table.

   The query also runs the following query to automatically map all the lower isolation levels to the snapshot isolation level for memory-optimized tables:

   ```
   ALTER DATABASE CURRENT SET MEMORY_OPTIMIZED_ELEVATE_TO_SNAPSHOT = ON
   ```

   This changes the database context to **toystore**. Press F5 to execute the query.

3. Execute the following command in a PowerShell console. This will insert 10,000 orders into the **Sales.Orders** table using the **ostress** utility described at the beginning of the lesson:

```
PowerShell.exe "C:\Code\Lesson09\InMemoryOLTP\Start-Workload. ps1
-sqlserver toyfactory -database toystore -sqluser sqladmin
-sqlpassword Packt@pub2 -ostresspath '"C:\Program Files\Microsoft
Corporation\RMLUtils\ostress.exe"' -workloadtype disk"
```

The **workloadtype** parameter specifies which procedure is executed. If the value is **disk**, the **InterOP** procedure is executed (**uspInsertOrders**), which inserts a value into the **Sales.Orders** (disk-based) table.

Otherwise, if the **workloadtype** parameter is set to **inmem**, the natively compiled procedure is executed (**uspInsertOrders_Inmem**), which inserts a value into the **Sales.Orders_Inmem** (memory-optimized) table.

You should get the following output. The elapsed time might be different in your case:

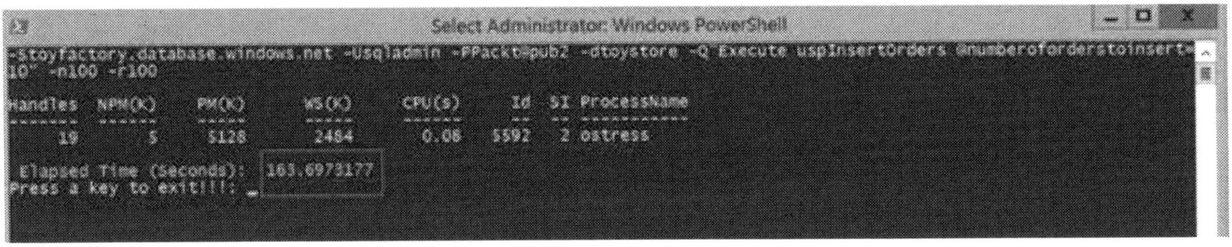

Figure 9.73: The elapsed time for the query execution

It took 163 seconds to insert 10,000 orders into the disk-based table. You can execute the following query to count the number of orders that have been inserted:

```
SELECT COUNT(*) FROM sales.orders WHERE orderdate=CONVERT(date, getdate())
Output of inserting orders into the Sales.Orders table
```

4. Execute the following command in a PowerShell console. This will insert 10,000 orders into the **Sales.Orders_Inmem** table using the **ostress** utility described at the beginning of the lesson:

```
PowerShell.exe "C:\Code\Lesson09\InMemoryOLTP\Start-Workload. ps1
-sqlserver toyfactory -database toystore -sqluser sqladmin-sqlpassword
Packt@pub2 -ostresspath '"C:\Program Files\Microsoft Corporation\RMLUtils\
ostress.exe"' -workloadtype inMem"
```

Figure 9.74: Output of inserting orders into the Sales.Orders_Inmem table

It took only 31 seconds to insert 10,000 records into the memory-optimized table using the natively compiled stored procedure.

You can execute the following query to count the number of orders inserted into the **Sales.Orders_Inmem** table:

```
SELECT COUNT(*) FROM sales.orders_Inmem WHERE orderdate=CONVERT(date,
getdate())
```

5. Navigate to **C:\Code\Lesson09\InMemoryOLTP** and open the **Cleanup.sql** file in SQL Server Management Studio:

```
-- Clean up
DROP PROCEDURE IF EXISTS uspInsertOrders_Inmem GO
DROP PROCEDURE IF EXISTS uspInsertOrders GO
DROP TABLE IF EXISTS [Sales].Orders_Inmem GO
DROP TABLE IF EXISTS [Sales].Customers_Inmem GO
-- delete inserted data from the orders table.
DELETE FROM sales.orders WHERE orderdate=CONVERT(date, getdate()) GO
-- Change the database edition to basic ALTER DATABASE toystore
MODIFY (EDITION = 'basic');
```

The script drops the memory-optimized objects, deletes the rows inserted into the **Sales.Order** table as a part of the activity, and changes the database edition to Basic from Premium. This completes the activity.

## Summary

In this lesson, we learned different ways of monitoring and tuning Azure SQL databases. We learned how to use performance metrics and Query Performance Insight to monitor database metrics and queries from the Azure portal. The lesson talked about using Azure SQL Analytics to monitor Azure SQL Database. Intelligent Insights, provided by the Azure SQL Analytics, can be used to set up alerts on different metrics such as CPU, log IO, blocks, and deadlocks. Intelligent Insights can also be used to fine-tune long-running or CPU-/IO-intensive queries to further optimize an Azure SQL database. We also learned how to set up alarms on database metrics, and proactively took action as and when alarms were raised. Finally, we learned about important DMVs and set up extended events to monitor an Azure SQL database. Following this, we learned how to set up automatic tuning to automatically tune an Azure SQL database, and we used in-memory OLTP to improve the performance of an OLTP workload. Performance tuning is a vast topic, and this book doesn't cover each and every aspect of this topic; however, it does give you an insight into the available options. You can explore these options in detail to optimize your environment.

In the next lesson, we will look into improving performance using in-memory technologies, online and resumable DDL operations, and SQL Graph queries and improvements.

# 10

# Database Features

## Learning Objectives

By the end of this lesson, you will be able to:

- Implement SQL Data Sync to sync an Azure SQL database with an on-premises database
- Use SQL graph queries create and query graph tables
- Implement SQL graph enhancements
- Create a model to predict future sales using the Azure Machine Learning service

This lesson talks about improving performance using in-memory technologies, online and resumable DDL operations and also talks about SQL Graph queries and improvements.

This lesson also covers the machine learning feature to execute in-database R scripts.

# Introduction

This lesson talks about the important database features available in an Azure SQL database. The lesson talks about **SQL Data Sync**, which is used to sync data between two or more Azure SQL databases or on-premises SQL servers, the SQL Graph capabilities and enhancements, and Machine Learning services available in an Azure SQL Database.

## Azure SQL Data Sync

As the name suggests, **Azure SQL Data Sync** allows bi-directional data sync between one or more Azure SQL databases and on-premises databases. The Azure SQL Data Sync service is free; however, there are charges for data movement into and out of Azure SQL Database.

The following diagram shows how data is typically synced between an Azure SQL database and an on-premises database:

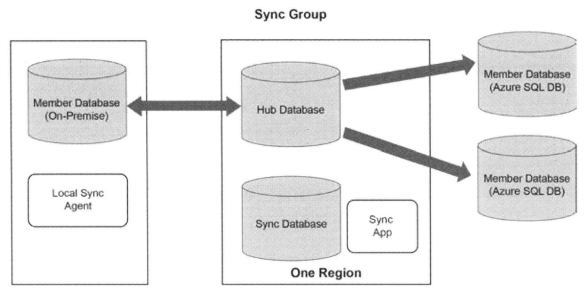

Figure 10.1: Syncing between an Azure SQL database and on-premises database

Azure SQL Data Sync consists of a sync group. A sync group has a hub database and one or more member databases. The data sync is always from hub to member, or from member to hub. There's no data sync between two member databases.

A sync group has the following components:

- **Hub database**: This should be an Azure SQL database. The data sync happens to or from the hub database.

- **Member database**: A member database is an Azure SQL database, an on-premises database, or a SQL server on an Azure VM.

- **Sync database**: This should be an Azure SQL database in the same region as the hub database. The sync database has the data sync metadata and log.

- **Sync schema**: This specifies the table and columns to be synced (not included in the diagram).

- **Sync direction**: The data sync direction can be from hub database to member database, from member database to hub database, or bi-directional.

- **Sync interval**: The frequency at which the data sync occurs.

- **Local sync agent**: The local sync agent or gateway is required for data sync from an on-premises database. The agent is installed on-premises and connects to the Azure SQL database for the data sync. To find out more about local sync agents, please visit https://docs.microsoft.com/en-us/azure/sql-database/sql-database-data-sync-agent.

Data Sync works by tracking data changes using insert, update, and delete triggers in a separate table in the user database. The sync app then takes care of merging the tracked data to the member database.

If there is a conflict, there are two potential solutions: either the hub wins, or the member wins. If the hub wins, changes in the hub database overwrite the changes in the member database. If the member wins, the changes to the member database overwrite the changes to the hub database.

Data Sync can be used for the following scenarios:

- Synchronizing on-premises data to Azure SQL Database when moving to the cloud. Consider a scenario where there's a database for multiple applications. The applications are to be moved to the cloud. Data for particular applications can be synced from on-premises to Azure SQL Database.

- To separate out the reporting workload from the transactional workload. The member database can be used for reporting, thereby offloading read workloads from the transactional database. The data sync is not real time, or as spontaneous as Always On or transactional replication. This should be considered when using Data Sync for such scenarios.

- Applications nowadays have users across the globe. Therefore, having a database closer to users speeds up the application's performance by reducing the network latency. Data Sync can be used to synchronize data between the databases in different regions.

Data Sync is not a recommended solution for disaster recovery, read-scale, and when migrating from an on-premise SQL server to an Azure SQL database.

Data Sync has the following limitations:

- Data Sync doesn't have transactional consistency; rather, it has eventual consistency. Data Sync guarantees that all changes will be synced eventually and that there will be no data loss. This implies that there can be a delay for the data to be synced between the target and member databases. Therefore, a member database can't be used for real-time reporting.

- Data Sync has a performance impact on the database as it uses triggers to track changes. It's therefore advised to assess data sync requirement before using it.

- The sync interval can't be less than 5 minutes. Data Sync, therefore, can't be used for scenarios where lower latency is required.

- Data Sync doesn't support Azure Active Directory authentication.

- A table participating in Data Sync can't have an identity column that's not the primary key.

- Data Sync doesn't support tables with the same name but different schema; for example, tables such as `Finance.Person` and `Sales.Person` aren't supported.

- Schema changes are not automatically synced. Workarounds are available.

- When using Always Encrypted, only the tables and columns that aren't encrypted can be synced.

- With encrypted columns, only columns up to 24 MB in size can be synced.

## Activity: Configuring Data Sync between Two Azure SQL Databases Using PowerShell

In this activity, we'll configure Data Sync between two Azure SQL databases using PowerShell. We'll configure Data Sync from the `toystore` database to the `toystore_report` database. The `toystore_rpt` database is a copy of the `toystore` database. We'll use the PowerShell script provided by Microsoft with a few modifications.

Before we configure the data sync, we'll restore a copy of the **toystore** database as **toystore_rpt** database. The **toystore_report** database will be the data sync member, and the **toystore** database will be the data sync hub.

To restore a copy of **toystore** as **toystore_rpt**, follow these steps:

1. Open a new PowerShell console window and change the directory to **Lesson04**.

2. Execute the following command to restore **toystore** as **toystore_rpt**:

   ```
   PS E:\Professional-Azure-SQL-Database-Administration-Second-Edition\
   Lesson04> .\PITRAzureSQLDB.ps1 -sqlserver toyfactorytem -database toystore
   -sqluser test -sqlpassword SuperSecret! -resourcegroupname toystore
   -newdatabasename toystore_rpt
   ```

   > **Note**
   >
   > You may have to change the file location, database user, and password.

3. You'll be prompted to provide the point in time to which to restore the database. Use the one mentioned in the prompt shown in the following screenshot:

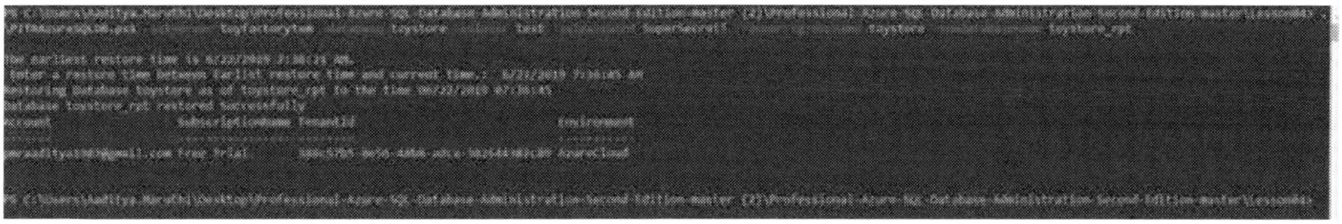

Figure 10.2: Specifying the point in time for restoration of the database

> **Note**
>
> The time highlighted in the preceding screenshot will be different in your case.

When the **restore** command completes successfully, the database will be created and will be available for use.

The next step is to configure Data Sync. The Data Sync PowerShell script is taken from the documentation (with some modifications), available at https://docs. microsoft.com/en-us/azure/sql-database/scripts/sql-database-sync-data-between-sql-databases.

The new version of the script is in the **Lesson10** directory in the code base for the book.

The script is explained with relevant comments, and it's recommended to go through the script before executing it.

The script creates the Data Sync metadata database, creates the Data Sync group, add the member database to the Data Sync group, updates the database schema from the hub database in the Data Sync metadata database, adds the specified tables and columns to be synced in the Data Sync metadata database, triggers a manual sync, verifies whether Data Sync is working properly, and updates the Data Sync schedule in order to run as specified by the **IntervalInSeconds** parameter.

The script expects the following parameters:

**SubscriptionID**: The subscription ID of the Azure subscription under which the objects will be created.

**ResourceGroupName**: The hub database server resource group name. As the Data Sync metadata is created under the same logical server as the hub database, the resource group for the hub and Data Sync metadata is the same.

**ServerName**: The Azure logical SQL Server name of the hub database.

**DatabaseName**: The hub database name.

**SyncDatabaseResourceGroupName**: The resource group of the sync database. This should be the same as **ResourceGroupName** parameter value.

**SyncDatabaseServerName**: The Azure logical SQL Server name for the Data Sync metadata database. This is the same as the logical server name for the hub database. This is not a pre-requisite. The logical server name for the Data Sync metadata database can be different; however, the location of the server should be the same as that of the hub server.

**SyncDatabaseName**: The Data Sync metadata database name.

**SyncGroupName**: The Data Sync group name.

**ConflictResolutionPolicy**: The Data Sync group conflict resolution policy.

**IntervalInSeconds**: The Data Sync frequency.

**SyncMemberName**: The name of the Data Sync member.

**MemberServerName**: The Azure logical SQL server name of the member database.

**MemberDatabaseName**: The member database name.

**MemberDatabaseType**: The member database type; either Azure SQL Database or an on-premises database.

**SyncDirection**: The data sync direction.

**TablesColumnsToSync**: A comma-separated list of the tables and columns to be synced.

**Hubdbuser**: The SQL user for the hub database. The script assumes that the user is the same for the hub database, Data Sync, and the member database.

**Hubdbpassword**: The password for the SQL user. The script assumes that the password is the same for the hub database, Data Sync, and the member database.

4. To execute the script, open a new PowerShell console window and change the directory to **Lesson10**.

5. Copy and paste the following command. You may have to change the parameter values to suit your environment:

```
.\ConfigureDataSync.ps1 -SubscriptionId "b85b0680-m764-9I88-x7893-
fb6e89c39f38" -ResourceGroupName Packt -ServerName packtdbserver
-DatabaseName toystore -SyncDatabaseResourceGroupName Packt
-SyncDatabaseServerName packtdbserver -SyncDatabaseName syncdb
-SyncGroupName toystoresyncdb -ConflictResolutionPolicy "HubWin"
-IntervalInSeconds 300 -SyncMemberName member1 -MemberServerName
packtdbserver -MemberDatabaseName toystore_rpt -MemberDatabaseType
"AzureSQLDatabase" -SyncDirection "Bidirectional" -TablesColumnsToSync
'[Sales].[Orders].[CustomerID]' -hubdbuser dbadmin -hubdbpassword
Awesome@1234
```

6. When the script completes successfully, navigate to the Azure portal to verify that the objects have been created.

7.  In the Azure portal, open the **toystore** database (the hub database) and select **Sync to other databases**:

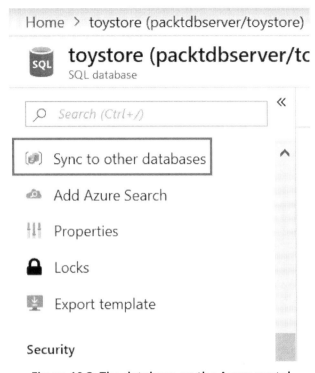

Figure 10.3: The database on the Azure portal

8.  Observe that the sync group, **toystoresyncdb**, is created as part of the execution of the preceding script:

Figure 10.4: Options on the Sync option

9.  Click the **Sync Group** name to open the **Database Sync Group** page:

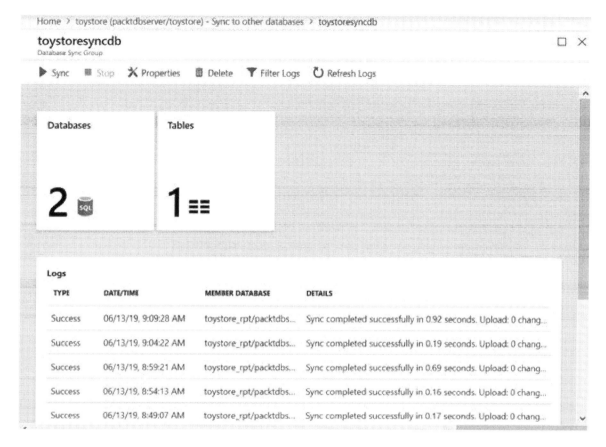

Figure 10.5: The Database Sync Group page

The **Database Sync Group** page lets you add or remove a data sync member and add tables and columns to sync.

10. Click the **Databases** tile to add/remove a data sync member:

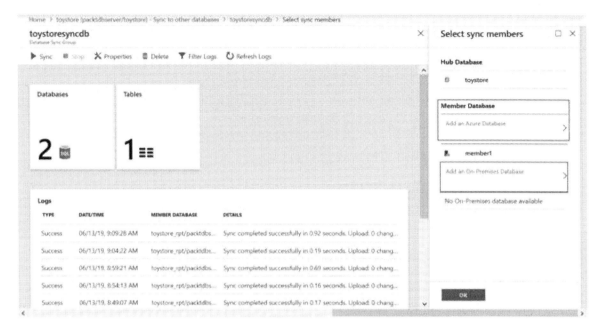

Figure 10.6: The Select sync members pane

11. Click the **Tables** tile to add/remove tables or columns to sync:

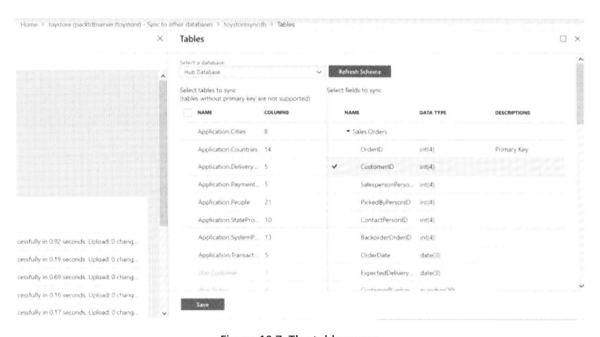

Figure 10.7: The tables pane

The existing tables or columns that are being synced are marked with a checkmark. To add tables and columns, check the one you want to add and click **Save**.

Let's now see Data Sync in action.

12. Connect to the **toystore** database in SSMS and execute the following query to update the **CustomerID** for a given **orderid**:

```
UPDATE Sales.Orders SET CustomerID=30 WHERE orderid=73096;
```

13. Switch to the **Azure portal Database Sync Group** window and click **Sync** to start the data sync:

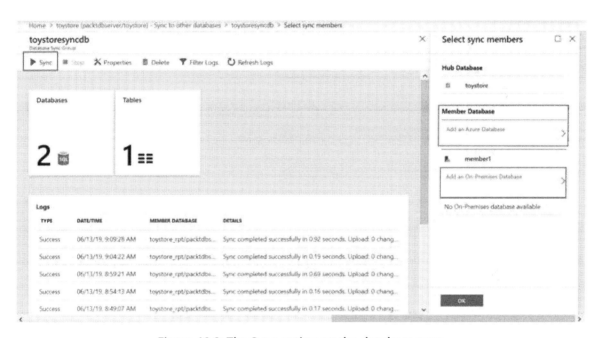

Figure 10.8: The Sync option on the database pane

14. In a new query window in SSMS, execute the following query against **toystore_rpt** (the member database) to verify that whether or not it has the updated **CustomerID** from **toystore** (the hub database):

```
SELECT * FROM Sales.Orders WHERE orderid=73096
```

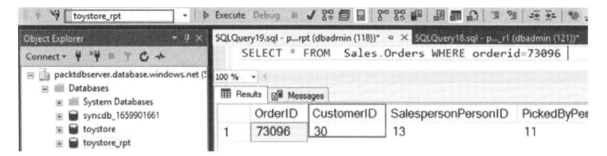

Figure 10.9: Query output on member database

The sync was successful, and the **CustomerID** column in both the hub and the member database has the same value for the **OrderID 73096**.

15. Once you are done, click **Delete** on the data sync group page to delete the sync group and the associated configuration:

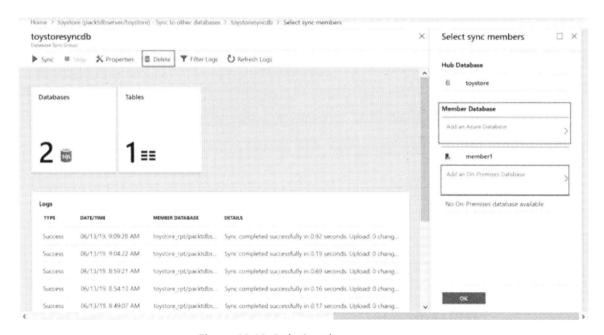

Figure 10.10: Deleting the sync group

This completes the activity. In this activity, we learned how to set up SQL Data Sync between two Azure SQL databases using PowerShell.

## Online and Resumable Data Definition Language (DDL) Operations

The online **CREATE INDEX** and **REBUILD INDEX** operations can now be paused and resumed as and when required, or when killed/failed.

The operation is marked as resumable by specifying **RESUMABLE=ON**. For example, the following **CREATE INDEX** operation is a resumable operation:

```
CREATE INDEX IX_Orders_CustomerID_Includes ON Sales.
Orders(CustomerID,Comments)

INCLUDE(DeliveryInstructions,InternalComments)

WITH(ONLINE=ON,MAXDOP=1,RESUMABLE=ON)

GO
```

To pause an ongoing online resumable **CREATE INDEX** operation, either kill the session or execute the **PAUSE** statement, as shown here:

```
ALTER INDEX IX_Orders_CustomerID_Includes on Sales.Orders PAUSE

GO
```

To resume a paused online resumable **CREATE INDEX** operation, either execute the **CREATE INDEX** query mentioned earlier or execute the following query:

```
ALTER INDEX IX_Orders_CustomerID_Includes on Sales.Orders RESUME
```

You can also specify the **MAX_DURATION** in minutes that the resumable operation should run before it's paused. For example, the following query runs for 1 minute. If the index isn't created in 1 minute, the operation is paused and can be resumed by using any of the methods specified earlier:

```
CREATE INDEX IX_Orders_CustomerID_Includes ON Sales.Orders(CustomerID)

INCLUDE(Comments,DeliveryInstructions,InternalComments)

WITH(ONLINE=ON,MAXDOP=1,RESUMABLE=ON,MAX_DURATION=1)

GO
```

The values for the **MAX_DURATION** must be between 1 and 10,080 minutes.

The following query returns all the ongoing resumable operations:

```
SELECT
        Object_Name(Object_id) AS TableName,
        [name] as IndexName,
        sql_text,
        last_max_dop_used,
        state_desc,
        percent_complete
FROM sys.index_resumable_operations;
```

Here's an example output from the preceding query when a resumable **CREATE INDEX** operation is running:

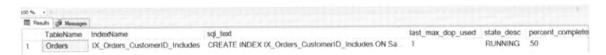

**Figure 10.11: Output for the CREATE INDEX operation**

The resumable operation has the following limitations:

- **SORT_IN_TEMPDB=ON** isn't supported.

- The resumable **CREATE INDEX/REBUILD INDEX** command can't be executed within an explicit transaction.

- Filtered index isn't supported with the resumable option.

- The **LOB**, **Computed**, and **Timestamp** columns can't be included.

## SQL Graph Queries and Improvements

A graph database consists of nodes and edges. The nodes are the vertices, and edges represent the relationship between the two nodes. The graph databases are optimized for implementing hierarchies and many-to-many relationships, and to analyze interconnected data and relationships. This is difficult to implement in a relational database.

The graph database functionalities were introduced in SQL Server 2017.

Let's look at modeling a very popular use case for a graph database: a social media application. A social media application allows users to follow, like, post, comment, and tag other users. Let's look at a simple model that allows users to do this:

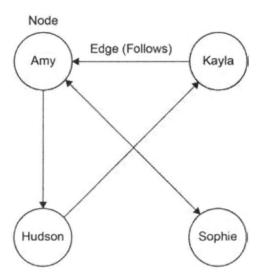

Figure 10.12: Social media model for following users

In the preceding diagram, the circles represent nodes and the lines represent edges or relationships. The relationship is "follows". The graph tells us that Amy follows Hudson, Hudson follows Kayla, Kayla follows Amy, Amy follows Sophie, and Sophie follows Amy.

In SQL Server, nodes and edges are represented as tables. Therefore, to model this example, we'll need two tables: a **Person** table, which is the node table, and a **follows** table which is the edge table.

The following query creates a node table called **Person**:

```
CREATE TABLE [Person] (
        Id int identity,
        FullName varchar(100),
        PhoneNumber varchar(25),
        EmailAddress varchar(100)
) AS NODE;
```

A node can have properties such as phone number and email address in the **Person** table.

Let's insert some sample records in the **Person** table:

```
Insert into Person Values ('Kayla Woodcock','(415) 555-0102','kaylaw@
wideworldimporters.com'),
```

```
('Hudson Onslow','(415) 555-0102','Hudson@wideworldimporters.com'), ('Sophia
Hinton','(415) 555-0102','Sophia@wideworldimporters.com'), ('Amy Trefl','(415)
555-0102','Amy@wideworldimporters.com');
```

The preceding query inserts people's details.

A select query executed on the **Person** table gives the following output:

| | $node_id_237716FDB2954B32847FA1EEAEF0069D | Id | FullName | PhoneNumber | EmailAddress |
|---|---|---|---|---|---|
| 1 | {"type":"node","schema":"dbo","table":"Person","id":0} | 1 | Kayla Woodcock | (415) 555-0102 | kaylaw@wideworldimporters.com |
| 2 | {"type":"node","schema":"dbo","table":"Person","id":1} | 2 | Hudson Onslow | (415) 555-0102 | Hudson@wideworldimporters.com |
| 3 | {"type":"node","schema":"dbo","table":"Person","id":2} | 3 | Sophia Hinton | (415) 555-0102 | Sophia@wideworldimporters.com |
| 4 | {"type":"node","schema":"dbo","table":"Person","id":3} | 4 | Amy Trefl | (415) 555-0102 | Amy@wideworldimporters.com |

Figure 10.13: The Person table output

Take a look at the **$node_id** column in the output. **$node_id** is a pseudo column that is a format node Id for each value in the node table. The **$node_id** column is used when inserting the relationships in the edge table.

Let's now create an edge table, as follows:

```
create table follows AS EDGE
```

```
GO
```

An edge table can also have properties; however, there's no property added in this example.

A **select** query on the **follows** table gives the following output:

Figure 10.14: Select operation on table

There are no records in the edge table. Take a look at the different columns in the edge table. **$edge_id** is a pseudo column that uniquely identifies an edge.

**$from_id** contains the **$node_id** of the node from where the edge originates.

The **$to_id** column contains the **$node_id** of the node at which the edge terminates.

Let's insert values into the follows table as per the following relationship:

*"Amy follows Hudson | Hudson follows Kayla | Kayla follows Amy | Amy follows Sophie | Sophie follows | Amy"*

```
insert into follows values

((select $node_id from Person where FullName='Kayla Woodcock'),(select
$node_id from Person where FullName='Amy Trefl')),

((select $node_id from Person where FullName='Amy Trefl'),(select $node_id
from Person where FullName='Sophia Hinton')),

((select $node_id from Person where FullName='Sophia Hinton'),(select $node_
id from Person where FullName='Amy Trefl')),

((select $node_id from Person where FullName='Amy Trefl'),(select $node_id
from Person where FullName='Hudson Onslow')),

((select $node_id from Person where FullName='Hudson Onslow'),(select $node_
id from Person where FullName='Kayla Woodcock'))

GO
```

A **select** query on the **follows** table gives the following result:

| | $edge_id_7A8EF8A74E1B4ABFA483EE84126278... | $from_id_ACB980579AF14A399178580C79ADE250 | $to_id_FB2CFFBF2C814CF4B6DC3FC69E5F5C43 |
|---|---|---|---|
| 1 | {"type":"edge","schema":"dbo","table":"follows","id":0} | {"type":"node","schema":"dbo","table":"Person","id":0} | {"type":"node","schema":"dbo","table":"Person","id":3} |
| 2 | {"type":"edge","schema":"dbo","table":"follows","id":1} | {"type":"node","schema":"dbo","table":"Person","id":3} | {"type":"node","schema":"dbo","table":"Person","id":2} |
| 3 | {"type":"edge","schema":"dbo","table":"follows","id":2} | {"type":"node","schema":"dbo","table":"Person","id":2} | {"type":"node","schema":"dbo","table":"Person","id":3} |
| 4 | {"type":"edge","schema":"dbo","table":"follows","id":3} | {"type":"node","schema":"dbo","table":"Person","id":3} | {"type":"node","schema":"dbo","table":"Person","id":1} |
| 5 | {"type":"edge","schema":"dbo","table":"follows","id":4} | {"type":"node","schema":"dbo","table":"Person","id":1} | {"type":"node","schema":"dbo","table":"Person","id":0} |

Figure 10.15: Output of the select query

The follows table correctly defines the relationship between each of the node IDs.

To query the relationships, a new **match** operator is used. The **match** operator is used in a **WHERE** clause. The following query lists all the people who are followed by Amy:

```
SELECT person1.Fullname ,person2.fullname

FROM person AS person1, person AS person2, follows

WHERE match(person1 - (follows) - > person2)

        AND person1.fullname = 'Amy Trefl'
```

Here's the output from the preceding query:

| | Fullname | fullname |
|---|---|---|
| 1 | Amy Trefl | Sophia Hinton |
| 2 | Amy Trefl | Hudson Onslow |

Figure 10.16: Output of the SELECT query

The syntax for the **Match** operator is defined as **(person1 - (follows) - > person2)**. The dash (-) refers to the **$from_id** field, and the **->** symbol refers the **$to_id** field of the edge.

This was a simple example of how a graph database can be implemented in SQL Server.

## Edge Constraints

Introduced in SQL Server 2019, edge constraints can restrict connections between nodes. To explain this, let's extend the preceding example with a new node that contains a list of the people with deactivated or inactive accounts. A deactivated account cannot follow any other person. Therefore, an active person (in the **Person** node) can follow an inactive person (in the **Blocked** node); however, an inactive person (in the **Blocked** node) can't follow an active person (in the **Person** node).

Execute the following query to create a **Blocked** node and mark **Hudson Onslow** as blocked or deactivated:

```
CREATE TABLE [Blocked] (
       Id int identity,
       FullName varchar(100),
       PhoneNumber varchar(25),
       EmailAddress varchar(100)
) AS NODE;
GO
Insert into Blocked Values ('Hudson Onslow','(415) 555-0102','Hudson@
wideworldimporters.com');
Let's drop and create the follows (edge) table with an edge constraint:
CREATE TABLE follows
(
```

```
CONSTRAINT ec_blocked Connection (Person To Blocked,Person To Person)
)
As Edge
```

The preceding query creates an edge table called **follows**, with an edge constraint called **ec_blocked**. The edge constraint only allows connections from the **Person** node to the **Blocked** node, and from the **Person** node to itself.

Execute the following query to insert relationships in the edge table. This is allowed as per the constraint definition:

```
insert into follows values

((select $node_id from Person where FullName='Kayla Woodcock'),(select
$node_id from Person where FullName='Amy Trefl')),

((select $node_id from Person where FullName='Amy Trefl'),(select $node_id
from Person where FullName='Sophia Hinton')),

((select $node_id from Person where FullName='Sophia Hinton'),(select $node_
id from Person where FullName='Amy Trefl')),

((select $node_id from Person where FullName='Amy Trefl'),(select $node_id
from Blocked where FullName='Hudson Onslow'));

GO
```

Let's now insert a connection from a **Blocked** node to a **Person** node, which isn't allowed as per the constraint's definition:

```
insert into follows values

((select $node_id from Blocked where FullName='Hudson Onslow'),(select
$node_id from Person where FullName='Kayla Woodcock'));

GO
```

The preceding query terminates with the following error:

```
Msg 547, Level 16, State 0, Line 58

The INSERT statement conflicted with the EDGE constraint "ec_blocked". The
conflict occurred in database "GraphDB", table "dbo.follows".
```

The statement has been terminated.

Other than the edge constraints, there are two more enhancements:

- The **MATCH** operator in the **WHERE** clause can use views. The view can be created by using **UNION ALL**, or using a **WHERE** clause to include a subset of nodes in a view.

- For example, the following two views can be used in a **MATCH** statement instead of the node tables:

```
CREATE VIEW AllPersons AS
SELECT *, 'follows' AS relation FROM Person
UNION ALL
SELECT *, 'blocked' FROM Blocked
GO

create view v1 as
select * from Person where fullname like 'Amy%'
```

- The **match** operator is supported with the **MERGE DML** statement. The **MERGE DML** statement allows you to run insert, update, and delete statements on a target table based on the values matched from the source table.

## Machine Learning Services

Machine Learning Services was first introduced in SQL Server 2016 (on-premises). Machine learning is now available in Azure SQL Database; it's in preview at the time of writing this book.

Machine Learning Services provides machine learning capabilities for Azure SQL Database and allows in-database R scripts to be run for high-performance predictive analytics. Running in-database R scripts uses the data in the SQL database instead of pulling the data over the network from a different source. In the absence of Machine Learning Services, you would have to set up R and get the data from a remote data source for the analysis.

Machine Learning Services makes it possible to run R scripts in stored procedures or T-SQL statements.

R is a programming language that's extensively used for data analysis, machine learning, and predictive analytics. R packages provide out-of-the-box methods to implement statistical and machine learning algorithms such as linear and non-linear regression, linear and non-linear classification, and linear and non-linear decision tree classification.

Common R packages such as Microsoft R Open, RevoScaleR, and MicrosoftML are preinstalled in Machine Learning Services and are available to use without any software or infrastructure setup. Machine Learning Services also supports installing additional R packages if required.

## Differences between Azure SQL Database Machine Learning Services and SQL Server Machine Learning Services

The SQL Database and SQL Server Machine Learning Services are quite similar; however, there are some important differences:

| Machine Learning Services | |
| --- | --- |
| **Azure SQL Database** | **SQL Server (on-premise)** |
| R is supported. R version is 3.4.4 | R & Python are supported |
| Yes. The ML services are availbale once you signup for the preview | No. Enabled by setting "external scripts enabled" using sp_configure |
| sqlmlutils or CREATE EXTERNAL LIBRARY can be used to install R packages | New package installation can be with sqlmlutils, CREATE EXTERNAL LIBRARY and using RGUi |
| Packages can't make outbound network calls | Packages can make outbound network calls |
| Not possible to limit R resources using Resouce Governor. In Preview, R resources can use maximum 20% of SQL Database resources | Can limit R resources using Resource Governor.[AD1] [ah2] |

Figure 10.17: Differences between SQL Database and SQL Server Machine Learning Services

The Azure Machine Learning Service public preview:

- Supports single and elastic pools.

- Supports vCore based purchasing model in the General Purpose and Business Critical service tiers. managed instance and Hyperscale aren't supported.

- Is available in West Europe, North Europe, West US 2, East US, South Central US, North Central US, Canada Central, Southeast Asia, India South, and Australia Southeast.

> **Note**
>
> To sign up for the preview, email Microsoft support at sqldbml@microsoft.com.

## Activity: Using Machine Learning Services in an Azure SQL Database to Forecast Monthly Sales for the toystore Database

In this activity, you'll use linear regression on the monthly sales data in the **toystore** Azure SQL database to forecast the sales for the coming months. You'll run R scripts in Azure SQL Database to train and save a model in a database table. You'll then use the saved model to forecast the sales in upcoming months.

> **Note**
>
> The Machine Learning Services public preview should be enabled on the Azure SQL database in order to perform the steps mentioned in the activity.

All the steps in this activity are on the **toystoreml** Azure SQL database with Machine Learning Services public preview enabled. You can use an existing or a new Azure SQL database; however, Machine Learning Services public preview should be enabled on the Azure SQL Database.

Follow these steps to complete the activity:

> **Note**
>
> The queries used in the activity can also be copied from the **~/Lesson10/ ActivityMachineLearning.sql** file in the code bundle.

1. We'll import the monthly sales data into the **MonthlySales** table in the **toystoreml** database. The **MonthlySales** table will be used to train the machine learning model.

   Execute the following query to create the **MonthlySales** table:

   ```
   CREATE TABLE [dbo].[MonthlySales](
           [year] [smallint] NULL,
           [month] [tinyint] NULL,
           [Amount] [money] NULL
   )
   ```

   Execute the following **bcp** command in a command-line console window. The **bcp** command inserts the data in the **~/Lesson10/MonthlySales.dat** file into the **MonthlySales** table:

   ```
   bcp MonthlySales in "E:\Professional-Azure-SQL-Database-Administration-
   Second-Edition\Lesson10\MachineLearning\monthlysales.dat" -c -t -S
   toyfactoryml.database.windows.net -d toystoreml -U dbadmin -P Awesome@1234
   ```

You'll have to change the server name, database name, user, and password as per your environment.

You should get the following output from the **bcp** command:

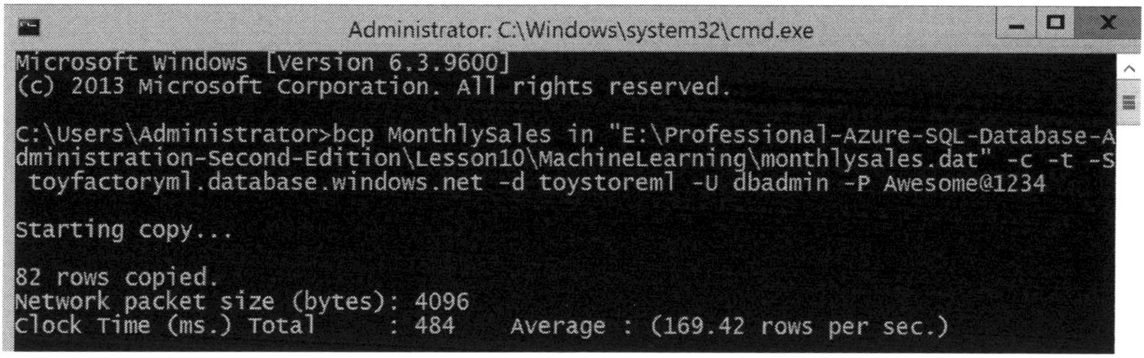

Figure 10.18: Output of the bcp command

Open a new query window in SSMS, connect to the **toystoreml** database, and query the **MonthlySales** table:

```
SELECT * FROM MonthlySales
```

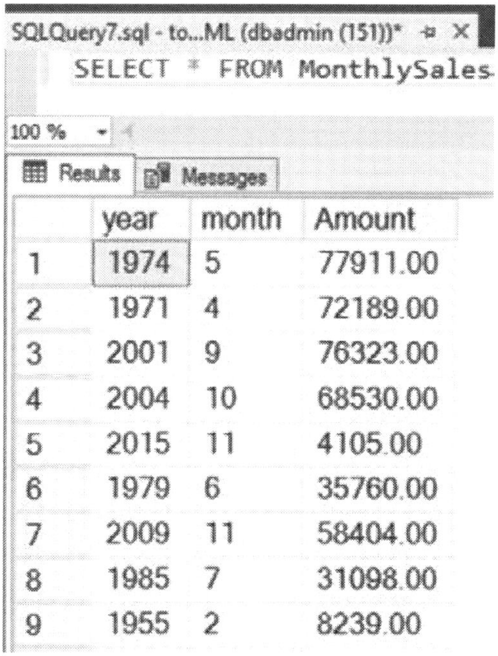

Figure 10.19: The MonthlySales table data

The **MonthlySales** table contains the monthly sales amount for each year. We'll use this data to predict the sales amount for the upcoming months.

2.  Before we start with creating the model, execute the following query in SSMS to verify whether the Machine Learning Services public preview is enabled on the database:

    ```
    EXECUTE sp_execute_external_script
    @language =N'R',
    @script=N'print("Hello World")';
    ```

    If you get an error instead of the following output, then Machine Learning Services isn't enabled on the Azure SQL database:

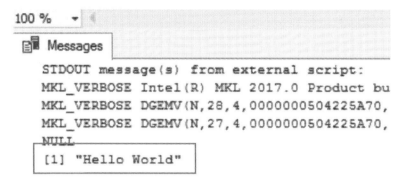

Figure 10.20: Output for Hello world

The **sp_execute_external_script** stored procedure executes a given R script on a given dataset. The dataset is a valid database query.

3.  The **MonthlySales** table has three columns: year, month, and amount. The amount column contains the sales amount for the given year and month.

    The linear regression model will describe the relationship between the sales amount (dependent variable) and the year and month (independent variables).

    A linear regression algorithm requires a formula to describe the relationship between the dependent variable (amount) and the independent variables (year and month), as well as input data, to train the model.

    The linear regression formula is defined in an R script, and the input data is provided from the **MonthlySales** table.

    Execute the following query to create a **generate_linear_model** procedure to create a linear regression model:

    ```
    DROP PROCEDURE IF EXISTS generate_linear_model;
    GO
    CREATE PROCEDURE generate_linear_model
    AS
    BEGIN
    ```

```
        EXECUTE sp_execute_external_script @language = N'R',
                                            @script = N'
lrmodel <- rxLinMod(formula = amount ~ (year+month), data = MonthlySales);
trained_model <- data.frame(payload = as.raw(serialize(lrmodel,
connection=NULL)));
'    ',
                                            @input_data_1 = N'SELECT
year,month,amount FROM MonthlySales',
                                            @input_data_1_name =
N'MonthlySales',
                                            @output_data_1_name = N'trained_
model'
    WITH RESULT SETS
    (
        (
            model VARBINARY(MAX)
        )
    );
END;
```

**sp_execute_external_script** executes the R script against the data from the **MonthlySales** table.

The **@script** variable has an R script that uses the **rxLinMod** function. The first argument to **rxLinMod** is the formula that defines the amount as dependent on the year and month. The second variable defines the dataset.

**@input_data_1** is the SQL query that sets the training data to train the model.

**@input_data_1_name** is the name given to the data return by the query in **@input_data_1**. The dataset's name is used as the second argument to the **rxLinMod** function.

**@output_data_1_name** is the name of the output dataset.

The procedure returns a model in the **varbinary** data type.

4. The next step is to execute the **generate_linear_model** procedure and store the data model in a table.

   Execute the following query to create a table and then execute the **generate_linear_model** procedure to store the model in the table:

```
DROP TABLE IF EXISTS dbo.monthly_sales_models
GO
CREATE TABLE dbo.monthly_sales_models
```

```
(
    model_name VARCHAR(30) NOT NULL
        DEFAULT ('default model') PRIMARY KEY,
    model VARBINARY(MAX) NOT NULL
);
GO
    INSERT INTO dbo.monthly_sales_models
(
    model
)
EXECUTE generate_linear_model;
GO
Query the monthly_sales_models table to verify the row inserted.
SELECT * FROM monthly_sales_models
```

You should get output similar to this:

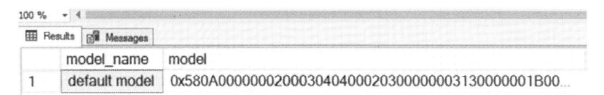

Figure 10.21: Output for the generate_linear_model function

5.  The next step is to insert the year and month in the **MonthlySales** table for which we need to predict the sales amount.

    Execute the following query to insert the values:

```
INSERT INTO dbo.MonthlySales
(
    year,
    month
)
VALUES
(2019, 7),
(2019, 8),
(2019, 9),
(2019, 10),
(2019, 11);
GO
```

6. The next step is to predict the sales amount for the year and month inserted in *step* 5. These year and month values were not in the **MonthlySales** table and the sales amount is not available for them.

   Execute the following query to predict the sales amount:

```
DECLARE @salesmodel VARBINARY(MAX) = (
                                      SELECT model FROM dbo.monthly_
sales_models
                                      WHERE model_name = 'default
model'
                               );

EXECUTE sp_execute_external_script @language = N'R',
                                   @script = N'
 current_model <- unserialize(as.raw(salesmodel));
 new <- data.frame(NewMonthlySalesData);
 predicted.amount <- rxPredict(current_model, new);
OutputDataSet <- cbind(new, ceiling(predicted.amount));
 ',
                                   @input_data_1 = N'SELECT [year],[month]
FROM [dbo].[MonthlySales] where amount is null',
                                   @input_data_1_name =
N'NewMonthlySalesData',
                                   @params = N'@salesmodel
varbinary(max)',
                                   @salesmodel = @salesmodel
WITH RESULT SETS
(
    (
            [year] INT,
        [month] INT,
        predicted_sales INT
    )
);
```

   The query passes the new year and month values and the saved model to the **rxPredict** function to generate the predictions for the sales amount.

   The **@salesmodel** variable contains the model created in *step* 4.

The **@script** parameter is the R script that generates predictions. The **rxPredict** function takes two arguments, the model and the new data. The first argument, **current_model**, is the unserialized form of the **@salesmodel**. The second argument, **new**, is the data from the T-SQL query as specified in the **@input_data_1** parameter.

The **@input_data_1** parameter specifies the data for the prediction. The query selects the year and month from the **MonthlySales** table where the amount is not available.

**@output_data_1_name** is the name given to the dataset returned by the query specified by the **@input_data_1_parameter** parameter.

**@params** defines the **@salesmodel** input parameter. **@salesmodel** contains the model created in *step 4*.

You should get an output similar to this:

| | year | month | predicted_sales |
|---|---|---|---|
| 1 | 2019 | 7 | 53488 |
| 2 | 2019 | 8 | 54847 |
| 3 | 2019 | 9 | 56206 |
| 4 | 2019 | 10 | 57565 |
| 5 | 2019 | 11 | 58924 |

Figure 10.22: Output for the predicted monthly sales data

Note that this is not a business-ready solution to forecast sales. It only illustrates the use and benefits of Machine Learning Services for analyzing the data in an Azure SQL database by running in-database R scripts.

# Summary

In this lesson, we learned about database features, Azure SQL Data Sync, online and resumable DDL operations, and SQL Graph.

Azure SQL Data Sync is an easy-to-set-up process of syncing data between two or more Azure SQL databases, or an Azure SQL database and an on-premise SQL server. Data Sync can be used to support cloud migration or to offload reporting workloads.

Resumable DDL operations allow **CREATE INDEX** and **REBUILD INDEX** tasks to be paused or resumed as and when required. This helps when we need to recover from problems wherein a long-running **CREATE INDEX** or **REBUILD INDEX** statement causes blocking and slows system performance.

SQL Graph Database capabilities provide a flexible and easy way to implement many-to-many relationships or hierarchies.

With this, we have learned how to successfully set up an Azure SQL database, migrate our data from an on-premises database to provisioned cloud databases, how to scale these databases as per our requirements, and how to manage the cost optimally. We also looked at how to secure these databases and the built-in high-availability features of Azure SQL Database. We also worked with some of the more advanced concepts of Azure SQL Database. We will now be able to work on applications that are built on the Azure SQL Database with ease.

# Index

## About

All major keywords used in this book are captured alphabetically in this section. Each one is accompanied by the page number of where they appear.

Printed in Great Britain
by Amazon

37668651R00319